# WHY MEN?

NANCY LINDISFARNE
JONATHAN NEALE

# Why Men?

*A Human History of Violence and Inequality*

HURST & COMPANY, LONDON

First published in the United Kingdom in 2023 by
C. Hurst & Co. (Publishers) Ltd.,
New Wing, Somerset House, Strand, London, WC2R 1LA
© Nancy Lindisfarne & Jonathan Neale, 2023
All rights reserved.

The right of Nancy Lindisfarne & Jonathan Neale to be identified as the authors of this publication is asserted by them in accordance with the Copyright, Designs and Patents Act, 1988.

Distributed in the United States, Canada and Latin America by
Oxford University Press, 198 Madison Avenue, New York, NY 10016, United States of America.

A Cataloguing-in-Publication data record for this book
is available from the British Library.

ISBN: 9781805260165

This book is printed using paper from registered sustainable and managed sources.

www.hurstpublishers.com

Printed in Great Britain by Bell and Bain Ltd, Glasgow

*For*
*Edward, Ruard and Siobhan*

# CONTENTS

| | |
|---|---|
| *Acknowledgements* | ix |
| Introduction: The Parable of the Australian Toilet Frog | 1 |

## PART ONE
## THE EVOLUTION OF HUMAN EQUALITY

| | |
|---|---|
| 1. Domination and Competition among Gibbons, Gorillas, Baboons ... | 19 |
| 2. ... Chimpanzees and Bonobos | 29 |
| 3. How Humans Became Equal by Sharing Meat ... | 45 |
| 4. ... by Sharing Childcare ... | 61 |
| 5. ... by Sharing Orgasms ... | 71 |
| 6. ... and Overthrowing the Dominance of Bullies | 87 |

## PART TWO
## THE INVENTION OF INEQUALITY

| | |
|---|---|
| 7. Agriculture, Predatory Elites and Class | 103 |
| 8. Naturalising Inequality | 123 |
| 9. Why Men? | 145 |
| 10. Salmon, Pigs and Rituals: Are We Wrong? | 163 |
| 11. Equality among Rebels in the Mountains and Forests | 195 |

## PART THREE
## HUNGER GAMES AND POPULAR RESISTANCE

| | |
|---|---|
| 12. Who Will Die with Him? | 221 |
| 13. Cahokia: Freedom and Equality after 'Collapse' | 231 |
| 14. The Courage and Clothing of Joan of Arc | 267 |
| 15. Mutiny in a Time of Revolution | 283 |
| 16. The Gendering of Torture at Abu Ghraib | 297 |

## PART FOUR
## APOLOGISTS FOR INEQUALITY

| | |
|---|---|
| 17. Darwin, Racism and Sexual Selection | 315 |
| 18. Engels, Graeber and Radical Confusions | 333 |
| 19. Chagnon, Pinker and War | 347 |
| Envoi | 365 |
| *Note on Methods* | 367 |
| *Notes* | 373 |
| *Bibliography* | 393 |
| *Index* | 419 |

# ACKNOWLEDGEMENTS

We have been working towards this book for a long time and we have met with such interest, insights and generosity on the way.

Our hearts are with our children, Edward, Ruard and Siobhan to whom we dedicate the book, and with Natalia Olmos-Serrano, Friedlind Riedel and our grandchildren, Ira, Corinna, Miguel, Athena, Ethan and Ilva.

We were blessed with loving parents—Margaret Self Ruschill and Jim Ruschill, Bobby and Terry Neale—no one of whom ever stopped travelling, reading, and questioning during the whole of their long lives. And we thank Bruce Self, Kate Channock and Peter Neale for forever.

We owe a special debt to the people who got us going. Nancy remembers with gratitude Grace Desmond, Yvonne Lanagan, Ronald Kurtz at Grinnell, Barbara Ward at the School of Oriental Studies, London, and the friends and colleagues from the London Women's Anthropology Group of the early 1970s.

Jonathan wants to thank his teachers—Halsey Tischenor, Steve Ludlam, Phil Thornhill and James Woodburn. And all his co-workers at the Pregnancy Advisory Service in London from 1980–90 for everything they taught me about feminism. And especially Martin Dockrell—his enormous wisdom which has informed this whole book. We also owe a very great deal to Pablo Mukerjee for encouraging us to begin and to Andrea Cornwall and Frank Karioris for friendship and the great pleasure of working together over the years.

For their kindness and support over the long haul, our thanks to the splendid people who have lived the book with us every step of the way—Selin Akyuz, Miriyam Aouragh, Heidi Armbruster, Brian Ashley, Tayfun and Mesude Atay, Stephen and Helen Barton, Chris Baugh, Janet Baum, Andrea and Philip Bird, João Camargo, Dixi Carrillo, Marty and Kit Carson, Vic Conran, Jeff and Janette Davies,

# ACKNOWLEDGEMENTS

Shaun Dey, Veronica Doubleday and John Bailey, Paul and Faith Dunn, Anna Eden, Mike Evans, Pim Fakkeldy, Panagotis Geros, Fatima Guray, Pearl and Doug Hill, Eliza Hilton, Bill Hoss, Gustaaf Houtmann, Chris Jones, Kalbir Kaur-Mann, Niki Khan, Stephanie Kitchen, Christiane Kramer-Hus-Hus, Helen Lackner, Cassandra Lorius, Thalia and Mayo Marriott, Sally Mitchison and John Charlton, Brendan Montague, Richard Moth, Galy Osorio-Rivera, Maia Pal, Jim and Karen Pratt, Fliss Premru, Parvathi Raman, Gabriella Rasuly-Palaczek, Nasreen Rehman, Sue and Sally Richardson, Carolyn Rozier, Dana Slaymaker, Mark Slobin, Lilijana Stepančič, Paulette and Joe Taykowski, John Treat, Lewis Turner, Sharon and Bob Utz, Alison Wade, Clare Walters and Sophie Williams, and Lale Yalçin and Friedrich Heckmann.

We owe many thanks to our careful readers of crucial chapters—Sayyid Habibullah Adil, Clare Davies, Helen Dixson, Katherine Harloe, Joe Haynes, Teresa Hayter, Nik Jeffs, Alexandra Maclean, Tim Marshall, Winthrop Munro, Amanda Padoan, David Radford and Richard Tapper.

And especially to Ruard Absaroka, Nick Evans, Star Livingstone and Betty Moxon, who read every word of the manuscript and gave us invaluable feedback.

The book has come together thanks to the wisdom, enthusiasm and care of Lara Weisweiller-Wu, our remarkable editor at Hurst. Old school. Being guided by Lara has been an education and a delight. And many thanks to Ross Jamieson, Daisy Leitch, Eliza Wright and all the team at Hurst for helping us get the book out and into the world.

And last but not least, we thank each other—it has been a terrific journey.

*Nancy Lindisfarne*
*Jonathan Neale*
*Oxford, 2023*

# INTRODUCTION

## THE PARABLE OF THE AUSTRALIAN TOILET FROG

This book is about how love endures. It is also about how our human capacity for kindness and empathy can imprison us in ruthless competition and violent hierarchies. Both ways of living with each other are rooted in our evolutionary past and this paradox is at the heart of our human nature. And this book is also about how, for centuries and today, a set of popular ideas and popular books by people from society's dominant elite have obscured this paradox, leaving many of us convinced that war, violence, oppression and inequality are the only natural order of things—and male.

The work of these famous authors of 'big boy' human history—men like Steven Pinker, Jared Diamond and Yuval Noah Harari—is clever and confusing. They deplore violence, but say it is now better controlled and managed than in earlier times. Yet, unfortunately, they say, competition, aggression, violence and warfare are an inevitable part of human nature. This is the law of evolution, they say, because men must fight each other to possess women sexually.

This is fantasy posing as science, and we have written this book to challenge it.

There is now a great deal of evidence from primatologists, archaeologists and anthropologists that we actually became equal as we became human. As human beings evolved, we developed a complex adaptation as ambush hunters of big game—deer, elk, antelope and much else. This was a challenging niche for puny creatures like ourselves, so how did we do it? By becoming cooperative, and living in groups organised by egalitarian principles, instead of the bullying and pecking orders characteristic of almost all our primate cousins.

In short, people shared meat, shared childcare, shared orgasms and resisted inequality. Preventing bullying fitted with hunting and gathering as a way of life and became part of who we are.

However, the tendency to create dominance hierarchies was also part of our primate inheritance. It did not disappear, but it was suppressed. Creating, and submitting to, hierarchy remained part of our human nature. Understanding this apparent contradiction—our simultaneous disposition both to equality and inequality—is basic to understanding ourselves as human beings.

We tell this human history as a drama in two parts. Our frame is ecological. Act One is the story how early humans built egalitarian societies in order to adapt and survive—societies not wholly unlike those of hunter-gatherers in recent times. Act Two is about the creation of class society, a decisive break with our long ancestral experience of sharing with equals. The invention of agriculture some 12,000 years ago was a revolution in slow motion. It brought with it new politics, new technologies and a new relationship to the wider world. Act Three has yet to be written. We can only guess at the adaptation that will come with climate change. But having a clear view of what has gone before has been another reason we have written this book.

We have long known about the agricultural revolution. But how this history—and 'human nature'—is to be understood has changed greatly. What is new is the overwhelming scientific evidence that inequality is not an inevitable aspect of 'human nature'. Rather, it has only ever been part of the story. Since the 1980s the science has been remarkable, and there has been an enormous flowering of research in the field of human evolution. There are now many amazing new studies of primate behaviour, new archaeology of early humans and new ethnographies of near contemporary hunter-gatherers. Thanks to chemical microanalyses, DNA sampling, radiocarbon dating and patient work of archaeologists in humble homes, we have learned a great deal about the people who lived in pre-class and then early class societies. What is now clear is that, for more than 200,000 years, human beings lived in egalitarian societies where men and women were also equal. This is a remarkable and precious insight that comes from the new science.

Seeing this history afresh, three things stand out. The first is that wherever class societies and socio-economic elites appeared, men and women became unequal too. So with class inequality came patriarchal domination, and cults of male violence. The consistency

# INTRODUCTION

of this association is extraordinary, the persistent links between economic and gender inequality; between sexism and other isms, and the exercise of class power. The central question then becomes 'Why men?', and the answers are to be found between our primate heritage and the character of class society.

The second thing we can learn from our new understanding of this history is that human beings have not forgotten that they are adapted to favour equality. As a result, hierarchies and the violent domination they produce have been challenged and subverted again and again.

The third revelation of 'human nature' is a consequence of the second. Over these past 12,000 years, elites have constantly had to reconfigure class relations—starting with gender inequality—in an effort to suppress dissent and secure their privilege. This, not some inescapable fact of evolutionary biology, is the root of human violence—and the root of the present tyranny of conservative ideas about human evolution.

*The Tyranny of Bad Science*

Such ideas have been with us since the invention of class society, but the contemporary version stems from the publication of *Sociobiology* by the Harvard biologist E.O. Wilson in 1975. His ideas fitted with the zeitgeist and the beginnings of neoliberalism, and they caught fire. Sociobiology was soon an academic field in its own right, now usually known as evolutionary psychology.[1]

The gist of the ideas about gender in sociobiology and evolutionary psychology is that men and women are 'naturally' different and unequal. This claim is made with certainty and backed by the assumed authority of Charles Darwin. It is a claim which presents itself as utterly scientific and completely up to date. It is also a claim which is hard to gainsay. Indeed, many people nowadays find the statement that men and women are naturally different and biologically unequal both accurate and obvious. And they would agree with what it entails: that men are obsessed with dominance—and sex. So men compete to use as many women as possible to pass on their genes.

By contrast, the argument goes, women can only have a limited number of children, so women concentrate on ensuring the survival of their children. To do this, women became part of nuclear families where the man brings home the bacon for the woman to cook for the family. There is a further spin: women take care to mate with men of 'superior genetic quality'. Incidentally, this logic would also suggest that the most powerful men in society are also genetically superior.

Given these strategies of reproduction, evolutionary psychologists consider men naturally violent and promiscuous, and women naturally caring and faithful. They argue that hunting was crucial to the human adaptation, and that the division between men who hunt big game and women who gather and cook is the source of gender inequality.

You know this argument. The familiarity of the paradigm is the measure of its power. Here we take on these conservative arguments about human nature.

Other people also find this argument ugly and unpalatable. Among them are many feminists and leftists who argue that no one should be trapped in a predetermined destiny as a member of a group or class with a 'natural' place in a pecking order. Rather, they believe, human beings should enjoy freedom and equal opportunities and equal outcomes. But there is a habit among feminists and leftists of taking these ideas a step too far, and insisting not only that there is no such thing as women's nature, or working-class nature, or Black nature, but more broadly that there is no such thing as human nature. But of course there is, and everyone knows it. Anyone who has lived closely with horses or dogs knows there are such things as horse nature or dog nature. We too are animals. There is such a thing as human nature. Part One of this book will be about what that nature is, and how it is rooted in our evolution.

Right from the get-go many people saw sociobiology as a sexist, classist palaeo-fantasy. The primatologist Sarah Blaffer Hrdy was at Harvard in the 1970s:

> The years between 1971 and 1975 were heady times for those of us then graduate students in the life sciences at Harvard. The discipline of sociobiology was born [there]. Yet it would be misleading to remember only the intellectual excitement of those years. Within the Harvard of that time there was no overlap at all between feminism and evolutionary biology, not even a common language.

# INTRODUCTION

> Feminists were outraged at what they took the sociobiologists to be saying, and the sociobiologists were mystified to discover that feminists were demonstrating at their lectures. As a woman in the midst of all this, I felt quite alone.[2]

Hrdy kept her nerve and became our leading feminist primatologist. However, the ideas of sociobiology, and then evolutionary psychology, held sway for the next thirty years. But Hrdy was not alone. The Dutch and American primatologist Frans de Waal says he felt like a toilet frog among biologists for the last three decades of the twentieth century. The toilet frog, a real Australian amphibian, sits in the toilet and holds onto the sides like grim death with its 'suction cup toes', no matter what. For all that time, de Waal says now, sociobiology kept falling on his head:

> The argument typically ran as follows: (1) natural selection is a selfish, nasty process, (2) this automatically produces selfish and nasty individuals, and (3) only romantics with flowers in their hair would think otherwise. Here is a characteristic statement [by the biologist Michael Ghiselin], cited over and over again in the literature:
>
> 'No hint of genuine charity ameliorates our vision of society, once sentimentalism has been laid aside. What passes for cooperation turns out to be a mixture of opportunism and exploitation … Given a full chance to act in his own best interest, nothing but expediency will restrain [a person] from brutalizing, from maiming, from murdering—his brother, his mate, his parent or his child. Scratch an "altruist" and watch a "hypocrite" bleed.'[3]

But then, says de Waal, after years of such viciousness, around about 2000, 'a curious thing happened: the theory vaporized'. By 2010 the field had turned 180 degrees, and everyone was agreed that humans were 'supercooperators':

> How radically attitudes have changed is clear every time I show audiences the notorious Ghiselin statement that had landed me in the toilet to begin with: 'Scratch an altruist and watch a hypocrite bleed.' Although I have featured this cynical line for decades in my lectures, it is only since about 2005 that audiences greet it with audible gasps and guffaws at something so outrageous, so out of touch with how they see themselves, that they can't believe it was

ever taken seriously. Had the author never had a friend? A loving wife? Or a dog, for that matter?[4]

What propelled the general change is clear. The wider political environment had altered. The anti-globalisation movement had arrived, and George Bush had gone to war. A new generation of college students were increasingly repelled by the masculine styles and catastrophic policies of the old elite.

From the turn of the twenty-first century the approach of primatologists to human evolution changed a great deal. But there were still problems. Sociobiology was becoming evolutionary psychology, and increasingly located in psychology departments. The primatologists were changing. But many evolutionary psychologists paid no attention, and even today still subscribe to the ideas of manhood red in tooth and claw. And it is the evolutionary psychologists, not primatologists, who continue to dominate the media and popular understanding. The origin myth of the alpha male remains useful and exciting to many who subscribe to neoliberal values, or who simply believe that our societies are meritocracies, where everyone has an equal chance, but not equal ability nor the same desire to succeed.

There is another problem. The standard response of outraged feminists has been to insist that gender inequality is 'socially constructed'. But this response simply cannot answer the question: why is gendered inequality constructed differently at different times?

What's worse, having arrived at this impasse, the social construction school have no alternative understanding of evolution and human gender. This leaves them vulnerable. Their arguments can look like little more than assertion, because they have no counter to right-wing ideologies of evolutionary psychology.

There can also be problems when feminists doubt themselves in their private lives. In times of personal distress, it is all too easy to fall back on the gender stereotypes we know so well. In the long dark teatime of the soul, all women may seem naturally caring, and all men bastards. The slippage occurs easily because the social construction school have a critique of evolutionary psychology, but no other scientific understanding to build on.

Here we want to make a scientific argument about difference and inequality in human evolution. The basic problem with evolutionary psychology is not that it is right-wing science, but that

# INTRODUCTION

it is bad science. There are three steps to explain why the method is unscientific.

The first step is to give full credit to the studies of animal behaviour used by evolutionary psychologists. These are good science. When sociobiologists write about fire ants or olive baboons, they pay careful attention to the sources in the literature. They do the reading.

The second step is when evolutionary psychologists compare animal societies to human societies. Then they start to write bad science, in part because they do not do the reading in social sciences. Worse, they assert things which are astonishingly ethnocentric but which they take as 'common sense'. The giveaway is the missing footnote. They do not cite sources for their assertions about humanity. This neglect is probably one reason that sociobiology has moved from sociology departments to psychology departments. Sociologists would not tolerate scholars who did not read sociology.

The third step, equally as unscientific, is that evolutionary psychologists compare primates and other animals to humans of their own class and culture. They also often compare primate behaviour to psychology experiments done on American college students at elite universities. These studies are then used to prove that humanity is cruel and selfish, rather than that students at Yale and Stanford are cruel and selfish.

They do not give explicit reasons for choosing these comparisons. But the implicit assumption is that men and women of their class and nationality are the benchmark for defining human normalcy. This ethnocentrism also seems to excuse them from having to do the reading.

These are basic problems of method in all sociobiology. It is not just reactionaries who do not do the reading and assume that Americans can be used as the standard against which to judge others. The very best of the feminist, liberal and socialist biologists, including ones we rely on heavily in writing this book, do the same thing. These have become ingrained mistakes in the discipline.

So, what should we think about human nature instead? What should we be basing that understanding on? In this book, the answer is twofold: first we need to look at the evidence—the real evidence—about early humans' relationship to equality; then, we need to consider human history, and how it has taken us down a different, violent path.

*Human Origins*

In Part One of this book, 'The Evolution of Equality', we consider what human nature is, and how it is rooted in our evolution. We draw on recent research—in primate behaviour, primate biology, archaeology and anthropology—to show how we evolved from our primate ancestors into egalitarian, non-sexist hunter-gatherers who dealt with bullies, and shared food, childcare and sexual joy. And along the way we say a lot about gibbons, baboons, gorillas, chimpanzees and bonobos.

The mechanisms and contexts of inequality among other primates matter because they are the baseline for humanity. Because evolutionary psychologists rely so heavily on analogies with primate behaviour, it is particularly important to present the primate evidence in the new ways primatologists now understand it. We look at this in Chapters 1 and 2, and what we learn from our primate cousins is that very small changes in bodies and livelihoods in very closely related species can create diametrically opposite constellations of individual relations and power in a group. Then there are the many physical and genetic differences between humans and other primates. These can tell us a great deal about the development of human society and sexuality. Here we are not talking about the fossil record. Rather, we are directly comparing us now with other primates now.

One example would be the size of male testicles. Chimpanzees have very big testicles, presumably because female chimps have sex with many different partners, and the male with more sperm has a better chance of getting to the egg first and passing on his genes. Great big gorilla males have very small testicles, presumably because the female gorillas usually mate only with the dominant male in their small band.

Human testicles are about midway between chimps and gorillas in size. This suggests that during our history as a species females have tended towards monogamous relationships, but they have also tended to have other sexual partners as well.

# INTRODUCTION

Here is another example. Kevin Hunt has compared the chimpanzee genome to the human genome. He noticed three kinds of genetic changes that were particularly marked in chimps and must have come after they split off from the joint ancestor of both chimps and humans. One kind made it possible for chimps to endure higher levels of pain. The second kind enabled the immune systems of chimps to repair inflammations and wounds more quickly. The third kind of genetic change enabled chimps to stay calm while enduring higher levels of stress.[5]

Kevin Hunt suggests that these changes are all related to the very high levels of fighting and competition that have been observed among male chimps in the wild. They would have helped male chimps to deal with the pain from the frequent wounds they sustain in fights, heal those wounds more quickly, and live with the anxiety of waiting to see if another fight was about to kick off.

This suggests that the joint ancestor of both chimps and humans had much less aggression between males than chimps display in the wild today.

Notice that we keep using the words 'presumably' and 'suggests'. They are important words because they point towards a crucial question of method. When you want to think about how we became human, and what it means to be human, no one piece of evidence will settle the argument. We must use all the sorts of evidence available to build a more or less convincing picture. The other kinds of evidence run through the rest of Part One, which deals with early humans.

First, there are the caves where early humans lived. We lived in other places too, it's just that the remains in caves are better preserved. Fossil teeth and bones are important here, but very rare. We have thousands of times more examples of the tools humans made. These teach us a great deal about how humans hunted and butchered. But they teach us much less about how they gathered, because we have stone axes, but almost no wooden digging sticks.

The most important evidence from caves is about the diets of different humans in different times and places. Scientists can now tell a good deal about this by examining the bones of prey animals, and by microscopic and chemical investigations of human teeth, bones, faeces and hearths.

# WHY MEN?

Then there is field research by anthropologists who lived with contemporary hunters and gatherers over the last century. We need to be clear, however, about what this evidence can and can't tell us.

There is one way of looking at the societies of hunters and gatherers which goes back to nineteenth-century thinkers like Charles Darwin, Henry Morgan and Friedrich Engels. These thinkers saw human evolution as a process of change from primate ancestors to ancient humans, to primitive hunter-gatherers, through savage herders and forest farmers to civilised modern humans. In this way of classifying humanity, contemporary hunters were closer to our primate ancestors in their intelligence and artistic lives than we are now. This was a racist view of society, deeply influenced by colonialism, that ranked all of humanity in a hierarchy with white Europeans at the top.

Some readers may find this a harsh description of Darwin and Engels. It is, but it is also accurate. We return to consider the work of both thinkers in Chapters 17 and 18.

In this book we are looking at accounts of hunter-gatherer societies over the last hundred years for a different reason. We do not think that their societies and brains were primitive. Moreover, all recent hunting societies had histories as long and complex as Chinese government officials today or truck drivers in Norway. What we think is something different, which is that all human societies adapt to their environment and the way they make a living. The ways that contemporary hunters have built their societies tell us about how people just like us live when they make a living that way. They are evidence not for how we are different from ancient hunters, but for how we might be the same.

There are flaws and gaps in all these kinds of evidence. To make sense of human evolution, we have to put all kinds of evidence together. Happily, a flowering of research and analyses of gender and evolution in the twenty-first century allows us to build a new synthesis. We rely particularly on the work of the anthropologist Richard Lee, the primatologists Sarah Hrdy and Frans de Waal, and Christopher Boehm, who is both an anthropologist and a primatologist. But we could not have gotten far without the work of the primatologists Jane Goodall, Alexander Harcourt, Takeshi Furuichi, Kelly Stewart and Shirley Strum; the anthropologists Jean Briggs, Loretta

# INTRODUCTION

Cormier, Nancy Howell, Laura Rival, Marshall Sahlins and James Woodburn; the archaeologists Martin Jones, Sharyn Jones and Mary Stiner; the writer Elizabeth Marshall Thomas and many others.

In Part One, some of what we say relies on the scientific consensus. In some controversial areas we follow one particular thinker or school. In a few places our analysis is, as far as we know, original. We try to keep our readers posted as to which is which.

*Human Society*

Part Two is 'The Invention of Inequality'. Here we turn from human evolution to human history: once our species invented agriculture, predatory elites could control food surpluses. They used force and introduced sexist ideologies to sustain class inequality. But weighing against this new ruthless exploitation of other people and the natural world was the persistence of love, hope and resistance. We have found five ideas very useful for explaining the tug of these two forces, which are ultimately two sides of human nature; these five ideas have guided our account in Part Two.

One: the rule of elites is arbitrary. Aristocrats do not have blue blood. Neither do kings and queens rule by divine right. Norman feudal lords in England were not better people than their Anglo-Saxon serfs. Nor is there any good reason why the white settlers should take the land of Native Americans or Aboriginal Australians. Nor were plantation owners in Jamaica more deserving human beings than those they enslaved.

Two: this meant that, from the beginning of class society, elites required two things to sustain their rule. One was violence, often performed and always lurking, a necessary part of any system of economic inequality. But violence alone is never enough to sustain domination. Ideas too are needed—ideas which can convince the oppressed that there is no alternative to their violently enforced oppression, because both violence and inequality are part of the human condition.

Three: this inequality started with gender. Love, sexual pleasure and a disposition to equality were fundamental to human evolution. We are social animals and have always needed love to survive as human beings. But in the class societies in which we started living

## WHY MEN?

12,000 years ago, our need for love makes us vulnerable. It is at the root of the intimate association between class inequality and gender inequality, and the contradictions that creates. We learn about gendered inequality before we can talk. We learn it from people who love us, and we learn it through their love for us and for each other. This makes gendered inequality a part of our very being.

Just think how domestic or workplace battles are infused with everyday sexism. Think how easy it is to blame each other, and in doing so, how we lose sight of the inequalities of class that shape our lives. And when inequality is naturalised so deeply through all our relationships, we become tangled in love knots, and it becomes nearly impossible to say, 'No, inequality is NOT natural, but benefits a few people and harms many others.'

Four: marking difference justifies and enforces inequality, and this is often necessitated by economic change. Important economic changes inevitably challenge elite privilege. New technologies appear—the wheel, gunpowder, steam power, the internet. New people grab control of raw materials—gold and silver, cotton and sugar, coal and oil and gas. Or new people take over established businesses or the banks. When change threatens ruling-class power, they respond as quickly and effectively as they can. This is not to say ruling classes are homogeneous, or that their interests are identical. Clearly, they are not. But they do share a commitment to inequality. To make the new forms of inequality seem natural, they work hard to reshape our ways of thinking: with the latest version of an unequal hierarchy, we get the latest set of ideas about difference. They change the rules about who we can marry. They impose austerity and squeeze education and social services, support police violence, crack down on immigrants, reopen debates about abortion, attack queer culture, revoke transgender rights, and perhaps above all, hide domestic abuse and sexual violence. And they find new ways of describing the perfect family and how we should live, what we should think and what we should wear. They decide who is 'us' and who is 'them'.

Five: elites not only impose ideas of difference but convince us that such difference is 'natural' and meaningful. Nowhere has this been more true than with gender, as a comparison with race shows us. We know that differences in skin colour are real, and biologi-

## INTRODUCTION

cal. But we also know that these differences are trivial compared with what all people have in common as human beings. Such differences can become enormously important when they are weaponised by elites to divide and rule. Over time, as elites adapt to resistance and social change, old forms of discrimination are reconfigured into new Others for new times—into new versions of caste, sectarian or cultural supremacy, or new versions of white power, antisemitism and Islamophobia. Still, most people are familiar with the argument that beneath such surface differences, we are all the same. That is a basic argument from people who believe in equality in every society.

However, sexism is so insidious that when we say that men and women are ultimately the same, many people find the idea unfamiliar and strange and often hold up biological differences as an explanation. Even today, and even in places where gay marriage is legal and gender fluidity is spreading, many people find the idea of sameness abhorrent.

Of course, our bodies differ, including our reproductive organs, genitals and a range of secondary sexual characteristics. But so what? Like skin colour, the differences lie on a continuum. Maleness and femaleness, our fertility, our experience of desire and sexual habits do not differ in kind, only in degree. And meanwhile we are the same in the ways our hearts and lungs and metabolism work, in the ways we perceive the world, and in our speech, our emotions and our needs as social animals.

The trick is to escape the prevailing assumptions about differences, whether these are racial, ethnic or whether they suggest that women and men are fundamentally different, with pink and blue brains.[6] This is not because there are not horrific histories which were perpetrated along these lines, nor because the legacy of those histories is not still with us. Of course they are. But to escape from being divided and ruled, we need to discover the strength of our sameness and our similarities to get the measure of our power. And humans have been doing this for as long as they have had to.

The last two chapters of Part Two do different jobs. For the sake of balance, in Chapter 10, we look at exceptions to our argument about the intimate relationship between class and gender inequality posed by complex hunter-gatherers of the Pacific northwest, slash-

# WHY MEN?

and-burn agriculturalists in Papua New Guinea and Indigenous Australians. In Chapter 11, we close Part Two with stories of four rebel societies in remote forests and mountains to show what equality between men and women can look like in practice today: the Lahu hill people in southern China, the Huaorani of Amazonian Ecuador, and the Piaroa and Pemon of Venezuela.

*Resistance to the Hunger Games*

Even with the violent imposition of created notions of inequality and difference, it took thousands of years to consolidate class rule. Many people rebelled, others fled to deep jungle, inaccessible swamps, or distant hills or deserts. In Part Three, we consider how centuries of class control, on the one hand, was met by resistance from below on the other.

The histories we tell in Part Three are gendered in an almost infinite variety of ways. We begin with the ritual sacrifice of a captive girl by Viking slavers. In our second example, we focus on Cahokia, a city-state in what is now Illinois, that flourished from 1050 to 1300. This story begins with the ritual killing of more than a hundred young women, but takes us to the eventual overthrow of the city-state and the rise of egalitarian societies that flourished for the next four centuries. The chapter finishes with a twist in which we see how colonial and contemporary racism and sexism have worked to hide the deaths of the young women in plain sight.

Our third example is the ritual execution of Joan of Arc in 1431, where we explain the relationship between her fight to wear the clothing of men and the class struggle between French peasants and English lords. Our fourth history is the story of two seamen in the British Royal Navy who, in 1797, were hung for making love to each other. Our last example is the court-martial of Sabrina Harman, who helped to expose the abuse of male detainees by American guards and interrogators at Abu Ghraib prison in Iraq in 2003.

Running through our species' history of resistance to inequality are the instincts that human nature can be, and has been, otherwise; but, in the age of modern science, the battle of ideas has become harder and harder to pin down. Part Four, 'Apologists for Inequality', looks at intellectuals who have justified inequality and violence as natural.

# INTRODUCTION

We begin with Charles Darwin's breakthrough in *On the Origin of Species*: the idea of 'natural selection', an idea we use throughout this book. When he came to write *The Descent of Man*, Darwin turned to another idea, 'sexual selection'. That led him to a framework that emphasised the genetic superiority of men, the white race and the upper classes. To round off our introduction to social evolutionary ideas, we turn to the very useful work of the radical biologist Joan Roughgarden.

The sexist and racist side of Darwin's work served elites at home and abroad. More surprising, however, is the way these ideas have been taken up by their political opponents. The most influential Marxist work on prehistory is Friedrich Engels' 1881 book, *The Origin of the Family, Private Property and the State*. Engels relied heavily on Darwin and other Victorian students of prehistory. The result is a book riddled with historical mistakes, and full of racism and sexism. And in this chapter we also look at the flawed recent work of David Graeber and David Wengrow.

In recent years two influential scholarly and popular writers have restated Darwin's argument for sexual selection. Napoleon Chagnon has argued from his ethnography of the Yanomamo in Venezuela that 'primitive' humans were fierce and warlike because men who killed were more likely to win women and father children. Steven Pinker has attempted an argument from archaeology and ethnography for the great antiquity of warfare. We take both scholars apart.

Our long human history has taught us to prize equality and fairness. The golden rule—to do unto others as we would have them do unto us—is perhaps the simplest and basic moral guide to understand. As witnesses to the violence done to others, we understand that there but for the grace of God go we.

So we do our best to subvert and mock elite power. And we experience compassion in the best of lovemaking, in our delight in the laughter of a small child, when we care for someone and someone cares for us, when we get lost in music and dance, worship or collective political action.

Class rule is never secure. People flee oppression, they revolt and topple tyrants. Look at the women and men who fought to end slavery and colonialism, and for the vote, and for pensions, healthcare and social security. And in moments of resistance, we share feelings and dreams far bigger than ourselves. We can forget, momentarily at least, the colour of our skin, our sex and gender identity. And when we do manage to put our commonality before our differences, our resistance explodes in power and joy.

We end with some thoughts on resistance, Me Too, Black Lives Matter and climate change, which calls upon our species to embark on a third great adaptation.

Knowing that everything is in the balance has given us the courage to write this alternative history of human nature.

# PART ONE

# THE EVOLUTION OF HUMAN EQUALITY

Part One tells the story of how we became human by becoming equal. It explains why the human adaptation required a shift from the dominance hierarchies of our primate ancestors to more egalitarian societies. And we explain why that went hand in hand with equality between women and men.

# 1

## DOMINATION AND COMPETITION AMONG GIBBONS, GORILLAS, BABOONS …

Primates include apes, monkeys, lemurs and a few other species of small furry animals. There are now many first-rate field studies of primates, and they reveal enormous variation in social organisation. In this chapter we focus on gibbons, gorillas and baboons. The next chapter is about chimpanzees and bonobos.

We look at the ways these five kinds of primates adapt to their environment. One reason is to understand where our ancestors were coming from. The more important reason, though, is to introduce the idea of looking at the evolution of a species in terms of the interplay between environment, getting food and social organisation. We want to explain how this interplay works because this is the framework we will use to see how gender changed in human evolution.

Later in the book, we will use the same framework to explain how gender changed after humans invented agriculture—from which flowed all the inequalities and hierarchies of human history, and the patriarchal violence holding them up. The same framework is essential now in the face of the climate change caused by the current economic and social adaptation of the human species. The threat of climate change means we now have to change our adaptation again.

The possibilities of adaptation for living species, the parameters and permutations, are endless. This is what evolution is all about. Adaptation is a way of talking about the relationship of a particular species to its total environment—the climate, geology, soils, plants and other animals. Each adaptation is a constellation of traits—

anatomy, physiology, sexual behaviour, feeding strategies, protection from predators, social organisation and ways of thinking.

The principles behind all adaptations are not hard to grasp: they are all about survival and reproduction. These two imperatives can encourage a community of primates to adapt to cooperate, share and be at peace with one another. Or they can foster competition within the group.

For example, primates need to protect themselves from predators. One obvious and popular defensive strategy is to live together in large groups. But large groups can come with enormously wearing pressures of competition over the other necessities of survival and reproduction: food and mates.

Primates have to eat. Competition is less fierce for primates like baboons and gorillas, who eat mainly grasses and leaves found everywhere. Competition is more ferocious among gibbons and chimps, who depend on rich but widely spaced supplies of fruit. Where competition over food is direct and face-to-face, the animal that gets more food is more likely to survive.

Third, the process of evolution depends on reproduction. Small changes—genetic mutations—create other differences between animals. If those changes help an animal survive and breed, the next generations will look, or act, a bit more like that animal.

Several different processes can influence which animals manage to reproduce. First, they have to survive. Then there can be female 'sexual selection'—she chooses males with certain characteristics. There can be sexual choice by males. There can be competition and fighting between males over access to breeding females. There can also be competition and fighting between females, males, couples or groups over safe, rich territories in which to raise their young.[1]

So for most primates there is a constant tension between such competition and the need to protect each other from predators. Different species solve this problem in different ways. Adaptation is the key to understanding these differences.

Treating adaptation in this comprehensive way has implications for how we compare primates with humans. It is a mistake to compare primates in terms of any single trait, or any bit of anatomy. These are simply the wrong units of comparison. It is misleading to compare female–female sex among bonobos with lesbian sex in

## GIBBONS, GORILLAS, BABOONS ...

California, or baboon male fights with New York office politics. Yet this kind of jump is all too familiar in the palaeo-fantasies of evolutionary psychology. Rather, the trick is to show how the enormous variety of changes associated with the evolution of humans fit together. Only then can we see how the human disposition to equality is part of that adaptation.

*The Song of the Gibbon*

Gibbons and siamangs (hereafter both simply gibbons) are eighteen species of closely related apes who live in the rainforests of Southeast Asia.[2] They are the smallest of the apes, which allows them to live high in the forest canopy. Gibbons swing from branch to branch in daring, rhythmic leaps that no other ape can match, and no predator except the occasional eagle can follow. This adaptation protects them but means the young cannot travel on their own—they must cling on to their mother as she travels from treetop to treetop.

Gibbons live mostly on edible forest fruits which are surprisingly dispersed and only available for short periods. So gibbons cannot live in large groups. They have adapted by living in pairs of one male and one female, with their infant and adolescent children. The paucity of resources is another reason gibbons are smaller than other apes.

Each pair of gibbons occupies a territory. On each side are the neighbouring territories of other pairs. There may be occasional fights at the borders. But every day each pair goes to the edges of their territory and sings to their neighbours and each other. Their neighbours sing back. When a couple are newly joined, their songs are awkward and choppy. It takes months and years to get it right. This is also true when a partner dies, and the survivor must find a new song mate.

These territories allow these small apes to space out in a forest even when the resources are not lush. The singing allows them to keep their neighbours at bay without the risks of fighting. The territorial system also limits the population. Those who cannot pair up and sing do not reproduce.

Like most mammals and birds who live in isolated pairs, male and female gibbons are the same size. Most researchers have reported that neither males nor females dominate. However, the Italian primatologist Claudia Barelli and her colleagues found it was more complicated than that among white-handed gibbons in Thailand. There the female was first in line when the pair went after food. The females seemed to be leading and deciding where to go. They reached the food first, and usually ate first as well. Barelli and her colleagues give an evolutionary explanation—the female needs more nourishment than the male because she spends much of her life pregnant or lactating.[3]

The male and female gibbons raise their young together, but the mother always carries the young. When the children reach adulthood, they are driven from the territory to make their own way elsewhere if they can. The parents have sex when the female is ovulating, but she does not ovulate when she is pregnant or nursing. So they have a few days of sex every few years.

Like other primates, gibbons compete over food and reproduction. But that competition is placed *outside* the small group of the pair and their young. The competition is between pairs, and the best singers win. In a later chapter we return to singing and harmony among humans, where music works differently.

*The Gentle Tyranny of Silverback Gorillas*

Among apes, gorillas are in many ways the opposite of gibbons: in diet, size, gender inequality and childcare. Gorillas live in forests in central Africa and protect themselves from predators by brute force. Gibbons live in Asian forests and protect themselves by fleeing through the trees.

Gorillas are big, which helps. Mature silverback male gorillas average 160 kilos, about twice the size of average human males. One silverback can, and does, protect a whole band of gorillas. Their size also allows gorillas to feed safely on the forest floor. This is a good thing, because their size also means that gorillas have trouble reaching fruit high in the branches. The silverbacks, indeed, spend most of their time on the ground.[4]

Gorillas eat fruits, like other apes. But their stomachs have also adapted to eat vast amounts of leaves and rough foliage. Unlike gibbons, they do not defend food sources. Their main food, foliage, is freely available to all. This feeding pattern allows them to live in

## GIBBONS, GORILLAS, BABOONS ...

larger groups than gibbons, but smaller groups than baboons. The median number is about eight, although some troops have twenty. The central animal in each group is an adult silverback, with one or more adult females and their young. Often there is an adolescent male or two, and very rarely another silverback.

Male dominance is very clear—the big guy is in charge. Infants and young gorillas stay close to him when the troop travels, and they play with him a lot. If a mother dies or leaves the troop, the silverback will often take over the care for her offspring, and welcome that juvenile into his nest. When the group moves, the silverback leads. Adult females too like to stay close to the silverback.

As they mature, females leave their natal troop to join another. Then, after a few years, the female often leaves the second group to join a third. Females seem indifferent to other females unless they are kin, in which case they get along well. If females are unrelated, the female pecking order is unclear, and when females fight each other, in almost all cases they leave wounds.

Gorillas are not territorial. They move slowly over large ranges, always as a group. They simply cannot do the kind of patrolling necessary to defend a territory. But when two groups of gorillas meet, the two silverbacks display at each other, beating their chests and roaring. It is at this moment that females, when they wish, silently switch from one group to another. Occasionally the two groups move together for a day or two, and sometimes the silverbacks fight.

When they are younger, males move in all-male groups, only to settle alone when they become silverbacks. Then they wait, and perhaps a female joins them. At that point, the silverback begins to build his own band, as the big guy. Within the band he dominates. But female choice is critical. Female choice started the band and every female who joins it chooses to do so. There are lessons for analysing human societies here—even where male domination appears absolute, pay careful attention to the consequences of female choices.

When an adult female leaves one troop for another, she will leave any young she has behind to be looked after by the silverback. She has good reason. Among gorillas, the dominant silverback in a band does not change all that often, but when a new silverback takes over, he is usually a newcomer to the group, and he usually kills all the infants he finds there. This is probably why gorilla mothers do not take their offspring with them when they slip away to join a new troop and a new silverback. But if a silverback is dangerous to the offspring of other fathers, this in no way contradicts the striking gentleness and toleration he shows for his own offspring. He cares for the orphans left behind by disappearing mothers for the same reason he has evolved to kill the infants who are not his. In both cases, the result of his actions is that there will be more gorillas like him: homicidal, gentle and caring.[5]

*Fighting and Friendship: The Exhausting Complexity of Baboon Politics*

Gibbons and gorillas are apes. We focus on them partly because we are closely related. But our next example, baboons, are monkeys, not apes. So they are more distantly related to us. But they provide an important comparison because like humans they have adapted to live on the ground in the African plains—the savannah. Most other monkeys and apes live in the forest on ripe fruits and leaves. On the savannah there is much less fruit, so baboons have adapted to digest a wide variety of other foods, including grasses, roots, insects and small animals. Here we look at three very similar subspecies in eastern and southern Africa: yellow, olive and chacma baboons.[6]

Baboons live in much larger groups than gorillas, and competition is *inside* the group. Life on the savannah exposes baboons to lions, hyenas and many other predators. Baboons cannot outrun these hunters, and there are few tall trees for refuge. Their adaptation is living in large 'troops' of fifty or more. Twenty or thirty adult baboons are a match for any predator.

But groups of that size present intellectual challenges for any primate. Primates are intensely social animals. It takes considerable intelligence to keep track of dominance hierarchies in a large group. What primatologists call 'dominance' is a central fact of life for many—but not all—primates. The word 'dominance' is misleading, because it carries a weight of extra meaning from English usage. Primate dominance is not the same as human class relations. It is not the power of one group over another. Rather, the notion of dominance among primates refers to a pecking order among individuals, like that among chickens. What 'primate dominance' means is that if two monkeys have a fight, the one that wins is dominant.

There are two pecking orders among baboons. One is a hierarchy among females of a troop, the other is a hierarchy among males.

Female baboons remain in the same troop all their lives, and adolescent males leave to join a new troop. That means the backbone of baboon society is a sisterhood. One mother and her daughters are dominant over every other 'matriline' in the troop. The number two mother and her daughters defer to the top mother and daughters, but they are dominant over all the other females. And so on, all the way down. The sisters of each matriline all back each other up in any fight, so they all maintain the same place in the hierarchy. The mother comes to the support of the youngest in any conflict within the family. So when they reach adulthood, the youngest adult daughter wins any fight against her sisters, and then the next youngest, and so on.

These simple processes produce a hierarchy in which everyone has a place. From time to time challenges rearrange the order, but a group of sisters often hold their place in the ranking order for years.

Females toward the bottom of the dominance hierarchy lead nervous, anxious lives, often literally looking over their shoulders, and listening for the barks of dominant females. They have fewer offspring, and their offspring are less likely to survive to adulthood.

The male rank order is much less stable. Remember, female baboons stay in the groups where they were born, but males change groups. So new young males are constantly entering a troop, making friends with high-ranking females and forming new alliances with other males. For males, rank order is a shifting and stressful kaleidoscope of interaction. This is because baboon males have evolved to compete hard for rank. The driving force of this evolution is that a high-ranking male has more sex and fathers many more offspring, which spreads his genes.

Remember, however, that the male baboon does not want to pass on his genes. He just wants to have sex. The evolutionary consequence is that he passes on his genes. This is why baboons have evolved to want a lot of sex.

Female baboons only have sex for a few days before and after their period of ovulation. During that period, they have swollen and colourful genitals and are sexually exciting to male baboons. At other times in the cycle, and while pregnant or nursing, they do not have swellings and they do not have sex.

So in a troop of fifty baboons, only one or two females are likely to be sexually active at any one time. They are most exciting to males right in the middle of ovulation when they are most likely to conceive. The highest-ranking male is most likely to father her child.

Individual ranking is not steady and any given pecking order changes over time. No one animal will be an 'alpha male' for more than a few months or years. So no single male is father to all the young in the troop. Typically, there are challenges for position at all levels every few weeks or months. The winner of those challenges is often not the strongest or the biggest baboon, but the animal who can mobilise the strongest allies in any fight.

This puts a strong premium on social intelligence. The larger the group of primates, the harder it is to keep track of all the alliances, friendships and kinship relations within the group. So there is a close association between brain size and group size in primates. In proportion to their body size, a baboon has as big a brain as a chimpanzee.

The need for alliances also means that baboons, like most primates, spend a good deal of time making friends. Friendships are maintained by 'grooming'—picking through the other animal's hair for insects and parasites. The animal being groomed experiences pleasure, and is often higher in the pecking order than the groomer. Because baboons live in large groups, they have to groom a lot.

In this system of breeding, males evolve to win fights. So an adult male is twice the size of an adult female, and all adult males are dominant over all adult females. But this does not produce an elite of 'alpha males'. A male baboon who lives for twenty years may only be an alpha for a few months or years, if at all.

Moreover, the 'alpha males' are not leaders. They make no decisions and offer no advice. When the troop moves, the oldest adult female is in front, for she has lived in the area all her life. When predators strike, the ones who fight back are adult females and the younger males around the edge of the troop. The alpha male may fight, or he may turn and run for the nearest tree. And in the end, the males are lonelier, and more stressed, than are the females with their steady rankings and their sisters nearby.

It is essential to the workings of this system that most females ovulate only a few times over their lives. If many females were ovulating, the sheer chaos and strain of competition in such large troops would wreck the lives of most males. They would not have time to eat, and baboons have to spend about half of each waking day eating and chewing.

In sum, the baboon adaptation to living on the open plains involves much social intelligence but considerable inequality among females, among males, and between males and females. Humans, as we shall see, also evolved on the African plains, but in the opposite direction, towards equality. As we will see, the key difference lay in what they ate.

2

## ... CHIMPANZEES AND BONOBOS

So far we have looked at three quite different kinds of primates—gibbons, baboons and gorillas. Now we narrow the focus to two very closely related species of ape. Chimpanzees and bonobos are physically very similar. They both belong to the genus *Pan*, named for the playful old Greek god of the forest. The two species are closely related enough that they have been able to mate and raise fertile young.

But it is now abundantly evident that the two species have radically different forms of social organisation. Chimpanzee males are violent bullies, and dominant over all females. And chimpanzee groups sometimes, though rarely, fight sustained wars with each other. Bonobos are peaceful. The number one animal in a bonobo group is female, and adult females have more sex with each other than they do with males. Indeed, bonobos use sex all the time to avoid conflict.

Much discussion of these two species is centred, implicitly or explicitly, around the question: are humans chimps or bonobos? We have some answers to this question. But our central interest in this chapter is different. We want to explore the way that slight changes in the environment and slight changes in the adaptation of a species can produce radical and totalising changes in social organisation and gender relations. This is an important point to keep in mind when we look at what happened to human evolution as we became ambush hunters and diggers of tubers. And it is equally important when we look at how the invention of agriculture led to the invention of class society.

Chimpanzees and bonobos are also our closest living relatives. One statistic often quoted is that we humans share 98% of our DNA

## WHY MEN?

with chimpanzees. That statistic is misleading, because the question of which genes to count is complicated. And to keep some perspective, by the same methods we share 60% of our DNA with bananas.

*Bands of Brothers and Sex in the Shrubbery: The World of Chimpanzees*

We start with chimpanzees. Chimps are bigger than gibbons, who are also apes. They are smaller than humans, and much smaller than gorillas. Male chimpanzees average about 45 kilos, and the females are about 15% smaller.[1]

Chimpanzees cannot digest all the vegetation gorillas do. Instead, they specialise in eating ripe fruits—more than three quarters of their diet by weight. Unlike the various species of monkeys which share their territory, chimps cannot digest unripe fruit. Despite their size, chimps are also able to reach many fruits that monkeys cannot. This is because the long grasping fingers and strong arms of chimps mean they can hang from a high branch and reach out to the fruit on branches too thin to carry the weight of their monkey neighbours.

This specialisation in ripe fruits has several consequences. Chimps are big animals, which enables them to see off the various species of monkeys which compete for fruit. But they need very large territories to roam in, to take advantage of widely spaced fruit trees as they ripen. They also need big brains, for they seem able to remember all the medium and large fruit trees in a wide area, and to keep track of when they might ripen. Their large size also means that a small party of chimps can deal with a leopard, the only predator besides humans which can threaten them.

Chimps live in communities, usually of 30 to 100 individuals, who share a territory. But the whole community rarely comes together. There is simply not enough fruit in any one place at any one time for them to be able to do that. Toshi Nishida and his colleagues observed one community of thirty individuals at Mahale in Tanzania who managed to forage all together for four or five months of the year. But the communities studied by Jane Goodall and her colleagues 170 kilometres to the north were never able to forage as a full group—there was simply not enough ripe fruit.

So chimps forage for food every day in smaller ad hoc groups, usually called 'parties'. These parties keep joining together, splitting up, and joining together, with different individuals coming and going. Primatologists call this 'fission and fusion' social organisation.

Some days a group of three makes sense, and some days ten. Sometimes there are parties of one female and her young, sometimes two females together, sometimes a few males travelling together, and sometimes mixed groups form. Chimps also seem to be doing constant calculations not just of which trees are about to ripen where, but of the likely amount of fruit, the necessary size of the party, and whether it makes sense to travel that far. Chimps also use 'pant-hoots' which carry great distances to alert other chimps to large treasure troves of fruit.

We saw that baboon females spend all their lives in the troop where they were born, and that adolescent males move away to other troops. Among chimpanzees it is the opposite. Females move to a new troop when they reach adolescence, and usually stay there. But most males spend all their lives together. One result of the chimpanzee pattern is that males are likely to be friendlier with other males than females are with other females. Bands of brothers and male cousins are the backbone of chimpanzee society. These males are lifelong friends, and they spend a great deal of time grooming each other, or just lying nearby, enjoying each other's company.

When females first join a community, they travel around a good deal with larger groups led by adult males. In a few years, once they know the ground, each female usually carves out their own core area where they will raise their children and do most of their feeding. There is a dominance hierarchy between the females. The dominant females have better territories, with better food, than the lower-ranking females. Because they are better fed, the higher-ranking females are more likely to survive, and more likely to see their offspring survive. So for female chimpanzees, rank in the female pecking order is a matter of life and death.[2]

Like baboons, female chimpanzees are sexually active in and around their period of ovulation. The area around their genitals swells, and males find that very attractive. As primatologists say, the females 'cycle'. For chimpanzees, though, the pecking order for mating works in a different way from both baboons and gorillas. Among chimps, all adult males are dominant over all adult females. But the number one male chimp cannot even try to control mating in the same way as the number one baboon. Baboons of a troop move and eat together. With some effort the alpha male of the moment can see everyone. Chimps are too dispersed, and other males, and females, are often out of sight of the alpha chimp.

When a female starts to cycle a lower-ranking male may try to lead her away from the usual haunts of the larger group, using a combination of kindness and violence. She usually tries to evade him. If she does, within a few days most or all of the adult males in the larger territorial group will gather around her. At this point the top-ranked male is likely to impregnate her. But because these animals are dispersed in trees and thick shrubbery, other males may also manage to sneak up and have sex with the cycling female, particularly if the two of them are friends.

In general, the dominant male usually has sex with a female at the peak of her ovulation, and he is the male most likely to have sex with her then. No wonder that DNA tests can now show that about half the infants born are offspring of the dominant male. But female chimps are attractive, and want sex, for long periods both before and after ovulation. These are the times when they mate with less dominant males. It seems likely that this works as a protection against infanticide, because none of the males she has mated with will kill her young.

This means that females have a lot of sex both before and after ovulation. They also have very quick sex. Male chimps have very sensitive spines on the tip of their penis, which enable them to climax very quickly. This helps less dominant males to have fast covert sex behind the shrubbery where the dominant male cannot see them. Because female chimpanzees have such long periods of oestrus, and because they have sex with so many males, even the average male has sex something like six times a day.

This is probably associated with the fierce conflicts over dominance ranking among males. The flexibility of chimp groups and the unpredictable movements of both males and females are probably also important. Chimpanzee politics are complicated, with a lot of manoeuvring for allies. As among baboons, the question is not who can beat up whom, but who can gather enough allies to win a fight. Challengers to a dominant male often recruit one ally but have been known to recruit as many as four. The alpha male will try to hold onto an ally as well. But there is a problem in holding onto allies whom you also dominate, so over time coalitions are unstable.

Chimpanzees are highly intelligent, and the males bring that intelligence to bear in their politics and coalitions. This jockeying for dominance can build toward a climactic fight, which often involves slashing with canines, beating, kicking and stomping.

But physical size is not important in chimpanzee dominance. The largest male is not usually the dominant male. The key fights which establish dominance sometimes happen between two males. More commonly, two to four males gang up against one. Perhaps two or three hold down the loser, while the dominant male attacks him.

Chimpanzee politics are also tricky because of the way parties combine and disperse. Baboons stay in one troop. Every male baboon has a pretty good picture of the current state of the hierarchy at any one time, because he has seen or heard the fights over the last month. But chimp males are not necessarily so well informed. They can, and do, walk into a group they have not seen for days only to discover that one of their allies has changed sides, or perhaps a new alpha has taken over. The returning chimp often has only seconds, at best, to survey the whole group before a sudden attack alerts him to the change. Life is particularly hectic for the alpha male, who has to keep track of complex and shifting politics he has not seen, and to do so in a very large group. It is no wonder chimps are smart.

The Demonic Male Controversy

Chimps also sometimes fight what look like wars. Each large community of chimpanzees has a home range that overlaps with the home ranges of other communities. And because chimps live mainly on fruits, they need to move quickly and widely to ensure they have enough to eat. This mobility also means they can defend large territories.

For years, communities will live at peace with their neighbours, and peace is more common than war. Jane Goodall, for example, saw no killing between groups during her first eight years of observation in the wild. But when conflict did break out at Gombe, the males of one group killed all the males in the other group, one by one, over four years.[3]

## WHY MEN?

This killing looked a lot like human warfare. All the adult males in the band and the only infertile adult female patrolled the border. They moved in absolute silence, communicating with gestures and facial expressions. When they found a lone male from another band, they would pounce and often kill him. If it was a lone female, they would herd and drag her to get her to come back with them. Sometimes she did, and sometimes she escaped back to her group.

Such sustained wars have since been found at many other field research sites. These are not battles. At Gombe, for example, the full community was never able to travel and forage together. But all the males were able to do so, not when foraging, but when patrolling. They were looking for lone males or young. The median number of attackers against a lone male, across all chimpanzee groups studied, is eight males against one.

Many chimpanzee researchers were impressed by the evidence for male conflict over dominance, and especially by the murderous warfare over territory. In their influential book of 1997, Richard Wrangham and Dale Peterson coined the phrase *Demonic Males*, and drew comparisons with human nature. Their main argument linked four things together—competition for dominance, warfare between groups, the fact that males were the aggressive sex, and the evolutionary closeness of humans and chimpanzees. We need to look at the ensuing controversy with some care.[4]

Wrangham is a distinguished scientist who has spent a lifetime studying chimpanzees, first at Jane Goodall's field site in Gombe, and then at the field site he has led for many years at Kibale in Uganda. He was also the first researcher at Gombe to cross an invisible wall and do field research at Nishida's 'Japanese' field site at Mahale, 110 miles away. And he has made important contributions in many areas. The most important of these are his ideas about the role of fire and cooking in human evolution, which we will come to in the next chapter. His co-author on *Demonic Males*, Dale Peterson, was not a knee-jerk militarist, and had been a conscientious objector in the US during the Vietnam War. Their work should be taken seriously.

The leading figure in opposition to Wrangham was R. Brian Ferguson, the doyen of anthropological studies of war. Ferguson accepts that some bands of chimps, sometimes, make war. And he accepts that other kinds of lethal violence are not uncommon inside bands of chimps. But he introduced two important caveats which point to a different interpretation.[5]

First, Ferguson said that this kind of 'warfare' had been seen in only two of the many populations of chimps that have been the subject of long-term field studies. In a total of 200 years of field observation across all the populations, there have been only eight years of warfare in the two populations at Gombe and Mahale. Killing within the group is much more common, particularly infanticide by males.

Ferguson argued that the wars at Gombe and Mahale had a great deal to do with human impact. At Gombe, the war began after Goodall and her team began 'provisioning' the local chimps, feeding them large amounts of bananas. Two communities came to the provisioning point, and one group was given many more bananas than the other. This was not done on purpose, but the war that followed was between these two groups. Provisioning later stopped, and there has been no war at Gombe since.

Mahale is only 60 miles as the crow flies from Gombe. Ferguson traced the conflict there to increasing pressure from local farmers which pushed two bands of chimpanzees into each other. In addition, the researchers at Mahale had hired local farmers to grow large amounts of bananas for the chimps there.

However, most field researchers on chimps did not accept Ferguson's argument that human actions caused these episodes of chimpanzee warfare. In 2014 *Nature* published a paper, 'Lethal aggression in *Pan*', organised by Wrangham and authored by thirty scientists from many different field sites. This paper showed that there had been deaths in 'warfare' in many other groups, not just at Gombe and Mahale. The authors argued that chimpanzees kill other chimps, and practise warfare, while closely related bonobos do neither of these things. So, they said, there is something biologically different about chimps.[6]

Wrangham won the argument, because other researchers on chimpanzees could see that he used real facts and realities as his evidence. There is an important lesson here. In science, truth is not always on the side of the good guys. It may be tempting to look at the politics of researchers, and the political implications of their arguments, and then choose your side. That's an easy way to make a mistake, or to make facts disappear. Don't do it.

But let's not go overboard either. Ferguson's work on human warfare is foundational, as we will see in later chapters. And there are some important qualifications to make to 'Lethal aggression in *Pan*'. The first qualification has to do with numbers.

'Lethal aggression' brought together data from 18 communities of chimpanzees, observed over 426 community-years. The headline figure was that over that time there had been 152 killings. Of these, 99 were 'confirmed' because researchers saw the killing, the body or the injuries. Another 53 were only 'suspected', where there was no direct evidence, but a fit younger male disappeared without explanation.

If we break down the evidence, we can see that more than half of the killings were infanticide and killings of youngsters under the age of five. These are the numbers:

Killing infants within the community (45)
    Confirmed 25
    Suspected 20

Killing infants from other communities (40)
    Confirmed 33
    Suspected 7

Killing adults within the community (18)
    Confirmed 12
    Suspected 6

Killing adults from other communities (49)
    Confirmed 29
    Suspected 20

That is a total of 99 confirmed kills:

58 kills of infants,
29 kills of adults from other communities,
12 kills of adults within the community.

Remember that these numbers come from 426 community-years of observation. So what was the danger to any one adult male in any given year?

These are communities of 30 to 100 individuals. Assume the average number of adult males in a group is 15. Almost all the adults killed within the group are males. So that means that on average the chance that any particular male chimp will be killed by another male from the same community is about once in every 355 years. For a male chimp who lives 30 years, including 15 years as an adult, that's a 4% chance of such a death over a lifetime. That's something a male has to watch out for, and a real worry, like leopards and snakes.

But it is uncommon. Pain, panic, humiliation and injury are far more common. Almost all, if not all, male and female chimpanzees have experienced these consequences of aggression many times. Killing is relatively unimportant, but beatings are an important part of life.

The second qualification we need to make to 'Lethal aggression' has to do with the effect of humans on chimpanzee warfare. Wilson, Wrangham and their colleagues establish that there is no statistical sign that chimpanzee deaths from warfare are a result of human pressure from encroaching farmers. What they did find, however, were clear signs that communities with more population densities were more likely to become involved in warfare. So were communities with many males. This makes sense and is in line with what we know about territorial competition in many other species.

But the phrase 'human pressure' is misleading. What other chimpanzee researchers had suspected is misleading. Remember, Ferguson suggested two possible kinds of human activity provoking chimp warfare. The 'encroaching farmer' theory was put to rest by 'Lethal aggression'. But the other idea was not. The suspicion was that the first reported chimp wars, at Gombe and Mahale, had happened because researchers were feeding the chimpanzees large amounts of bananas and other desirable food at one feeding site. Crucially, these bonanzas of food brought males from neighbouring communities into direct competition with each other over food, face to face, in a way that would never otherwise happen.

That the researchers did 'provision' the animals in this way was perfectly reasonable. It is what bird watchers like us do when we put out feeders. In a situation where it can take five years or more of steady trekking every day to get a community of chimps to the point where they can tolerate observers, this made sense. And when

Goodall at Gombe and Nishida at Mahale realised what might be happening, they stopped feeding the animals.

In fact, 20 of the 49 confirmed and suspected killings in warfare between 1970 and 2014 happened in Gombe and Mahale between 1970 and 1982, in the wars that may well have been stoked by feeding. We cannot be sure, but the connection looks reasonable.

However, the implications of this finding for whether war is a 'natural' chimp or human instinct are not what they seem. This feeding was the opposite of human pressure from farmers encroaching on chimpanzee territory. It was humans giving chimpanzees expanded food resources. This is a point to bear in mind when we come to human warfare. For as we will see, it was not usually population pressure that produced warfare among humans. Rather, it was the possibility of a large surplus in one place that was not found in others.

For example, warfare and class inequality were common among First Nations peoples living along what is now the west coast of Canada. But this was not because of population pressure. It was because the villages which occupied the rivers with fantastically rich salmon runs every year could enjoy a large surplus, and also decided not to share with their neighbours who lived in the far more barren interior. It is in general wealth, not poverty, that creates war among humans.

The Last Common Ancestor

There is another point to bear in mind. It has to do with evolution and genetics, and it's this. The human and chimpanzee line split about six or seven million years ago. Up to that time, we had what palaeontologists call the LCA—the Last Common Ancestor.

Keep in mind that people are not descended from a Common Ancestor who was like chimps. People and chimps are descended from a Common Ancestor who may have been more like us, more like chimps, or unlike both.

Most people have a deeply ingrained habit of seeing primate evolution as a ladder. As our ancestors climbed that ladder, we assume, they passed through many stages. Each stage was less primitive, more developed, better than the last. So things we regard as primitive and backward—male violence, female promiscuity, sex in public, picking your nose—are assumed to be part of the earlier stage. But that is not how evolution works. There is no hierarchy of development.

This is important because, as we said earlier, scientists have now decoded both human and chimpanzee genomes, and they can tell what genes changed after the diversion. The main changes they have found are in three areas. Chimpanzees have changed to recover better from wounds and inflammation, to endure pain better, and to cope more calmly with very high stress situations. All three sets of changes would fit an animal experiencing increased and violent competition over rank. And all three distinguish chimps on the one side, from humans and the Common Ancestor on the other.

Which brings us to bonobos, who are far more closely related to chimps than to humans, but have strikingly different social systems from chimps.

*The Joy of Sex: The Very Different World of Bonobos*

Bonobos and chimpanzees diverged from a common ancestor between one and two million years ago—so, much more recently than humans split from the common ancestor of chimps and bonobos. Two things changed, and these appear to have made a lot of difference. The first is that bonobos lived on one side of the Congo River, and chimps on the other. On the bonobo side of the river, the forest was richer, with more concentrations of fruit. That meant that bonobos could travel in larger groups. Their groups are still flexible, like those of chimps, but the whole group is together much more often. That made possible a change in the patterns of dominance.[7]

Secondly, there is a change in bodily sexuality and sexual behaviour. Both female and male bonobos have sex all the time, instead of just at the height of their cycle. And they have a lot of sex. Females have sex with males and females, and so do males. This does not mean some of them are personally 'gay'. Rather, all females and all males have sex with both sexes. Adults have a lot of sex with juveniles, and juveniles with each other. They fuck, they lick, they suck, stroke and tug in a wide variety of positions. Almost all the actual copulation between adult males and adult females comes at times when the females are displaying swellings. But there is more of this heterosex than among chimpanzees, because female swellings last more than half the total cycle.[8]

Females have more sex with other females than they do with males. And females seem to prefer sex facing each other and rubbing their vulvas together—what in people is called tribbing or the scissors position. This suggests that female bonobos want sex with their vaginas only during their periods of ovulation and swelling, but sex with their clitorises all the time.

Males have sex with each other less often than females do with each other. But they still have a lot of it, in many positions. 'Duelling penises' is popular. Another friendly coupling is where two males hang together by their feet from a branch, side by side, giving each other hand jobs.

Bonobo sex is obviously fun, and much of it is loving. It also transforms dominance. When a fight breaks out between two male bonobos, a female often intervenes to have sex with one of them. When things get tense between two bonobos of either sex, they are likely to move straight to sex. Bonobos use sex to avoid fights, to stop fights once they start and to console losers after fights. They use sex to change the subject.

This level of sexual activity means that no bonobo male could control everyone's sexual behaviour. He would get very hungry, and very stressed. The group travelling together, and the constant sexual activity, make possible another unusual feature in primate society—the dominant animal in the group is female. This does not mean that all females dominate all males. This is not a reverse image of chimpanzee society. Rather, the animals are all ranked in order, and different males fit in between females in the hierarchy. But the top animal is female.

The rank order between mothers produces the rank order between younger females. Sisters rush to each other's defence, just as we saw with baboons. So each 'matriline' stands in the dominance ranking in accord with the ranking of their mother. In the event of a fight between daughters, the mother always intervenes on the side of the younger. This produces a ranking among all females, with the youngest daughter of the alpha mother at the top and the oldest daughter of the weakest mother at the bottom. This ranking does change over lifetimes, as individuals grow, weaken and die, but it is far more stable than ranking among male chimps.

There is another striking fact about bonobo dominance rankings which observers in several different field sites did not notice for many different years, because it never occurred to them to look for it. All infant bonobos, up to the age of five, are dominant over all adult male bonobos. When an infant threatens an adult male, the adult runs screaming.

We have fallen, at times, into language that implies bonobos solve social problems consciously. In one way, that is true. It is clear enough that bonobos sometimes think along the lines of: 'sex would stop this fight'. But they can think this way easily because dispositions bonobos are born with allow them to do so. Their sexuality and sexual practices are an adaption which has enabled some bonobos to survive better than others, some bonobo groups to survive better than others, and allowed those bonobos to fill an ecological space better than another species.

De Waal's Question

But these adaptations are an evolutionary process. Frans de Waal is one of the leading contemporary authorities on bonobos, and has done important work on empathy, sympathy and moral sense among primates. He asks the question: how might an animal that was something like a chimp, and something like a bonobo, evolve into a bonobo?

De Waal has emphasised the way that many chimps, and many other primates, will comfort an animal who has lost a dominance fight. Indeed, among many species of primate, females often intervene to stop loud fights between males. Sometimes all the nearby females will intervene, shouting loudly and swinging around, to stop the fight. Some dominant males too—not all, but some—often intervene in fights, particularly fights between females.[9]

In years of experience watching both captive and wild chimpanzees, de Waal was at first sensitive to male dominance and male violence. His first book, *Chimpanzee Politics*, was about coalitions among aggressive males in a zoo in Arnhem, in the Netherlands.[10]

As a young man de Waal had been emotionally overwhelmed by a murder among chimps he was studying. He was very fond of them, the way all chimp researchers come to be. He watched a dominance confrontation build for months, with the alpha male under challenge from a coalition of two younger males. The chimps were enticed into indoor enclosures for the night. One evening the alpha male and his two challengers ended up in one cage by themselves, while the rest of the chimpanzee group fetched up in another cage. The keepers could not move the three males—no human can tangle with a grown chimpanzee. That night, in the dark, the two challengers beat the alpha male almost to death and ripped out his testicles. De Waal came in the morning, and looked into the eyes of the old alpha, whom he loved, and who died later that day. De Waal also looked into the eyes of the successful challenger and saw no remorse. He knew, he felt, what it was like to look into the eyes of a murderer.

De Waal has told this story many times since. His book about those chimps concentrated on male dominance and political alliances. But over the many years since, he watched first captive bonobos in San Diego and then captive chimpanzees near Atlanta, Georgia. And gradually he began to think differently about that night in Arnhem. More and more, he thought that it had happened because the three males were locked away from the females and the other adult males—a direct result of their captivity, not a reflection of how they live in nature. He remembered all the times he had seen a shrieking group of chimps surround a fight and break it up. De Waal took more seriously a point Shirley Strum had made long before. All primates spend far more time grooming each other than they do in confrontations. That keeps them free of pests and parasites, prolonging their lives and relieving itches, but it also builds friendships and alliances. Strum's estimate for famously confrontational and competitive baboons was that they spend a hundred times more minutes in their lives in grooming than they do in confrontation or conflict.[11]

There was also one chimp leader de Waal had known who seemed to constantly intervene to stop any fight and restore peace. Not all alpha male chimps are like that. It was clearly in part a matter of personality. But those personalities were there. De Waal observed one unusual peacemaker:

> In our group of chimpanzees, which lives under my office window at the Yerkes Primate Center near Atlanta, Georgia, we didn't

know for about one year after the death of the previous alpha female who was going to be the new one. Normally, it's one of the oldest females, so our bets were on three females ranging between 30 and 35 years of age. Unlike males, females rarely show open rivalry over the top spot, which is decided by a combination of age and personality, both of which are non-negotiable.

One day, I watched as a small scuffle grew into something that sounded extremely serious. The chimpanzees were screaming so loudly, and the males moving so fast, that I feared a bloody ending. Suddenly all commotion stopped. The males sat down, panting heavily, while several females hung around them. The atmosphere was extremely tense, and it was clear that nothing had been settled. Then I saw who was our alpha female.

Peony, who had been resting in a corner, got up and literally all eyes turned towards her. Some youngsters approached her, some adults grunted softly the way they do to alert others, while Peony slowly and deliberately walked towards the center of the scene followed by everyone who had remained on the fringes. It looked almost like a procession, as if the queen arrived to mingle with the commoners. All that Peony did was groom one of the two males who had been central to the fight, and soon other individuals followed her example, grooming each other. The second male joined the grooming clique as well. Calm returned. It was as if no one dared to start things up again after Peony had so gently put a period behind it.[12]

De Waal was thinking mainly about captive chimps. Unlike wild chimps, all adult males and adult females in Georgia lived together—like bonobos. That gave the females in Georgia, and the group, more opportunity to control dominant males than among chimps in the wild. De Waal began to think maybe the fact that bonobos were almost always together was one factor that had made female dominance possible. The constant, inventive and convivial sexuality was the other.

Indeed, when two groups of bonobos with neighbouring territories meet in the wild there is excitement, and then the females and males on each side cross the line. The two groups travel and eat together for several days, and males and females have sex outside their group. So do females and females, and sometimes males and males.

## WHY MEN?

Things can become tense. There is fighting between individual males from different groups. And there is increased aggression against males from within the groups. But males from different groups also groom each other.[13]

No one has yet seen one group of bonobos fight another. That does not mean it cannot happen—there is one suspected case, where a young male left his group for some time and returned with an injured foot.[14] And it took years of observing chimps before any human saw a chimp war.

Kevin Hunt, the author of the best book on the evolution of chimpanzees, tells a story from Nahoko Tokuyama's field research to illustrate just how different life is among bonobos:

> It was in the evening, past the time bonobos normally have settled into their sleeping nests for the night. A female was in estrus, her flamboyantly swollen estrus swelling stimulating an unrestrained sexual excitement among four males, including the community's alpha male... They noisily leapt from branch to branch around the female, displaying erections and disturbing what should have been a time of quiet repose for the group... Their overheated commotion went on and on, seemingly with no end in sight. At last, three high ranking females had had enough. Exploding from beneath, they attacked the four males, scattering them and then ignominiously three of the four into the night, each yelping in retreat. They surrounded the fourth, the alpha male, seized him, and, ignoring his screams of panic, bit him repeatedly—part of a toe was bitten off completely. As the attack wore on he was at last able to break free from the females and flee in the darkness. He failed to reappear the next day, and the day after that; then his absence extended for an entire week. In fact, he limped back into the group only three weeks later, short both a bit of dignity and a bit of a toe.[15]

As Hunt says, that is an unimaginable story among chimpanzees.

3

# HUMANS BECAME EQUAL BY SHARING MEAT

There is one more thing about chimpanzees (and not bonobos) that may seem relevant to human aggression. First Jane Goodall, and then other researchers, found a great deal of evidence for chimpanzee hunting. They hunt and kill birds, baboons, colobus and vervet monkeys, bush pig and other species. And male chimps do almost all the hunting.

Male chimps hunt in groups, surrounding and picking off their prey. This means most hunting happens when there is an abundance of ripe fruit, and several males can come together. They specialise in hunting monkeys, and particularly the young. The sight of an adult male grabbing a baby monkey from the arms of its terrified mother and beating its head against a tree is unnerving for some people. But it is not a sign of aggression, any more than in humans who go fishing.

But there are two big differences from human hunting. First, adult male and female chimps get about 10% of their nutrition from meat. Animal meat and fat were the source of about half or more of calories for ancestral humans.

Second, the chimpanzee hunter who catches the game eats the meat. What chimps catch, they control, wherever they come in the pecking order. This means that no more dominant chimp will grab meat from another. Nor will any successful hunter necessarily share the catch with others. Instead, other males and adult females will sit nearby, holding out an upturned palm to ask for some of the meat. A chimpish pecking order would not have worked once humans began to rely on meat for half their diet. With a pecking order, the less successful hunters and almost all the females would get little meat. The young would get almost none.

## WHY MEN?

Once humans began to specialise in hunting, they had to do something about the primate dominance hierarchy they inherited, or they would not have been able to eat, or to raise their young. The next four chapters explain what they—we—did.

Gibbons eat fruits, baboons eat grass and roots. Early humans learned to be ambush hunters, an adaptation that led to equality among males, among females, and between males and females. Until 12,000 years ago humans lived exclusively by such 'foraging'—hunting, fishing and gathering plants—without domestic animals or farming. The archaeology tells us this. But the archaeology on its own can't tell us that much about early human social organisation.

However, we have a wealth of accounts of such foragers from the nineteenth and twentieth centuries from Africa, North America, South America, Asia and Australia. It makes sense that people who have lived this way in recent times provide a window onto human evolution. Still, this contemporary material needs to be treated judiciously. As we said emphatically in Chapter 1, none of these accounts are about people without history, who have lived perfectly unchanging since the dawn of humanity.

Moreover, recent foragers were people living in the margins—in the northern Arctic, the deserts of Namibia, the badlands of Utah or the hills and the rainforests of Southeast Asia and South America. Most ancient hunter-gatherers certainly lived in environments with much more food and water. Almost all recent hunter-gatherers have been in contact with farmers for a long time and their societies have been anything but static. These are important points of difference and should be given proper weight. Three brief examples make clear why this is so.

The Aka pygmies in the Central African Republic live in the rainforest by hunting with nets. They are short people, and distinctive looking. They can be seen in paintings from ancient Egypt, and they were hunters back then too. But in the eighteenth century the neighbouring farmers fled into the forests to hide from slave traders and lived with the Aka for decades. After the slave trade ended, for several decades around 1900 the Aka mainly hunted elephants to sell their ivory into the global market. In the 1960s the Aka lived in villages alongside farmers for several months a year, and the farmers treated particular Aka families as their serfs. But for rather more months of the year, the Aka lived in the forest, where they were a free people.[1]

The anthropologist Peter Gardner offers another example of the marginal status of recent foragers, and their long history of contact. Gardner started fieldwork with the Paliyan in south India in 1962. They lived in the forests in the hills and avoided direct contact with local farmers. They left their forest products at the edge of the forest, and Tamil villagers left the Paliyan goods in return, but they never spoke to each other.

One day Gardner understood something:

> At the close of one hot, dry day, I sat with nomadic Paliyans in their encampment watching a train make its way across the cultivated plain below. It brought home the fact that Paliyans gather and hunt wild food on the very threshold of our modern world. Did this portend a period of rapid change? Still pondering the matter and turning away from the evening glare, I was jarred to see the sun's rays illuminating the towering gates of Minakshi Temple in Madurai, 45 kilometers away. This not so distant city—a perennial center of poetry, power and commerce—had been active in trade with First and Second Century Rome. Some Paliyan forage, then, in the immediate proximity of an ancient seat of civilization. It is comparable to subsisting on wild foods within sight of Notre Dame Cathedral or Big Ben. While the location and character of the Tamil/Paliyan frontier will have changed in diverse ways over the centuries, we need to recognize the likelihood that the Paliyan have been in contact with powerful neighbors for millennia and we must consider the possibility that their shy stance is an adaptation developed long ago.[2]

Indeed, the anthropologist Loretta Cormier thinks that the Guajá hunter-gatherers she studied in Brazilian Amazonia were originally refugees fleeing from Portuguese colonialism. She cannot be sure, but her guess is that the Guajá were originally farmers who were enslaved, then escaped and turned to hunting and gathering as a way to survive hidden in the forest.[3]

In fact none of these recent foraging peoples are living the pristine lives of our ancient human ancestors. Rather they have all been in contact with people from class societies, whether ancient

Egyptians, ancient Indians, or sixteenth-century Portuguese explorers. On the other hand, there is a staggering fact—all of these groups of hunter-gatherers live in similar kinds of societies that have similar forms of organisation and social structure.

The San groups in southern Africa, the various groups of pygmies in central Africa, the Hadza in Tanzania, various groups in the hills across India and in the forests of Southeast Asia, the indigenous people in Tierra del Fuego, the Australian and Tasmanian Aborigines, the hunting peoples of Canada, Alaska and Greenland, the Andaman Islanders in the Bay of Bengal, and many more groups, all lived into the twentieth century in societies without rich and poor, without chiefs, and without inequality between men and women.[4]

There is one possible exception to this generalisation. All accounts of Australian Aboriginal societies agree that they resembled other hunters in most respects. People were economically equal, they were obliged to share food and all other goods, and people could move easily from one group to another. But the evidence about gender equality is different. In parts of Australia, older men not only controlled the marriages of younger women, they also often married the girls themselves and sometimes had several wives. Many anthropologists therefore argue that Australians had economic equality but gendered inequality. Other anthropologists, including us, are less sure. But the evidence is complex, and we will return to it.

The similarity between all the other groups of hunters outside Australia, however, suggests what we might expect from either an ecological or a Marxist point of view. Hunter-gatherers live as they do, not because they have always lived that way, but because that way of life goes with that way of making a living. So it makes sense that people who had once been farmers and then went into the forest live that way too.

*Commonalities*

Let's look at what almost all these societies had in common. They lived by a combination of gathering plants, hunting and fishing. Men, women and children gathered fruit, vegetables and roots. Men, women and children also caught insects, birds, and small and medium size animals. In most of these societies, only men hunted the larger animals. But where they used nets or blowpipes, men and women often hunted together.

There was rarely enough food for people to remain permanently in one place. Small bands moved from camp to camp, often within a home territory. Individuals or small groups also moved regularly from one band to another. They did that to find new sources of food, for a change of scene, to visit relatives and, often, to avoid social tension.

People only owned as much as they could carry on their backs. People might carry a spear, a bow and some arrows or a blowpipe and some poison darts, perhaps a hand axe, a small musical instrument, an ostrich egg full of water, a pointed digging stick, a string or leather bag, a necklace, and a baby. Most people had only the one set of clothes they stood up in, and they built new shelters each time they moved.

This way of life made class society difficult. It is hard to exploit people who have no property and can leave whenever they want. Critically, these people had no stores of food that could last for months, or could be confiscated by raiders or bullies.

These hunters shared. Women, men and children ate a lot of the roots, fruits, seeds, small animals, fish and insects as they found them. But people always shared the meat of big animals with everyone in the camp. They did not have chiefs, leaders or dominant males. And they talked over decisions endlessly until they had something like consensus.

Given what we know about the dominance hierarchies in which most of our ape and monkey cousins live, this raises the question: how did we first become an ape that shared food and waited patiently for consensus?

Until recently our ancestors were spread very thinly upon the face of the earth, so we have a limited fossil record compared to pigs or horses. However, new advances in molecular archaeology and the study of DNA mean we now know a great deal about what early humans ate, how they butchered meat, how they ate together and about their fires, clothing, parasites, health and burial customs. We start with the changes in how they worked and ate.

# WHY MEN?

Beginnings

Ten million years ago the ancestors of gorillas split from those of chimps, bonobos and humans. Estimates vary, but about six or seven million years ago in Africa the ancestors of human beings split from the ancestors of contemporary chimps and bonobos, who would not diverge for several more million years. As humans were splitting off, the climate in Africa was becoming much drier. In many parts of the continent, grasslands with scattered trees and bushes replaced dense tropical forest. The ancestors of chimps and bonobos stayed in the forests and ate and slept in the trees. The line that eventually produced humans adapted to life on the open savannah over several million years.

The savannah lacked the forest fruits that chimps rely on. Instead, the early humans learned to make pointed digging sticks to find tubers and roots hidden well below the ground. This was a specialist adaptation few other animals larger than a rabbit, and no other primates, possessed. The tubers were a rich source of calories, more reliable than fruit and easier to digest than plants.

It is often said that women were the first tool users, because digging sticks are now mostly used by women. But in the early days it is entirely possible that both women and men used the sticks. We began not as hunters, or as gatherers, but as diggers.

Scholars of evolution have perhaps not paid as much attention as they might to digging. One reason we have already mentioned: stone tools for hunting have survived, and wooden digging sticks have not. Another reason is the influence of archaeological work with Stone Age humans in the far north, and during the European Ice Age, who for obvious reasons ate more protein than the more numerous humans in Africa. There may also be some residue of sexism, in overvaluing hunting. But it is striking that hardly anyone, for example, has explored the possible connection between bipedalism (walking on two legs) and the use of digging sticks.

Those early hominins also hunted, killing small animals as other primates did. But the most important change was when they started hunting big game, mostly ungulates—deer, horses, antelopes, cattle and the like.

These proto-humans of the savannah lived alongside other specialist hunting species like lions, cheetahs, leopards, wolves and hyenas. But they developed a hunting strategy that afforded them a specialist niche, and that helped protect them from other carnivores. Most of the other predators hunted at night, while humans hunted in the heat of day while the others slept.

Almost all the other predators pursued a strategy of cutting out the weaker animals in a herd—the old, the young and the sick—and running the animal down using explosive speed over short distances. Humans did things differently and became ambush hunters. They made hunting weapons—pointed spears, arrows, blowpipes and darts, throwing sticks and boomerangs. Working alone or in pairs, they also chose to target different animals in the herd from other predators. They were not concerned to select those that were vulnerable, because they had only one chance to bring an animal down. So ambush hunters chose to target a large, healthy animal which was perhaps easier to hit and would provide more meat.[5]

Humans sought to get as close as possible to their prey without attracting notice. Their aim was to wound an animal and then run it to the ground, perhaps over a great distance. These new humans had much weaker arms and legs than their ape ancestors, and their hands and legs took on a different shape, more adapted to tool-making and running. Their hands and fingers, wrists, elbows and shoulders were adapted to throwing. The combined joints multiplied the leverage that propelled the spear or arrow. Spear-throwers and slings increased the leverage and made the weapon go further and strike harder. At some point the new humans also learned how to put plant or insect poisons onto their arrows or darts to slow down a wounded animal.

Sharing Meat and Tubers

These hunting bands needed to share meat to survive. There were several reasons for this. One was that they could not store the meat. To get the maximum use of the food, many humans had to share it out over a few days. More fundamental, there had to be some social way of sharing meat with those too young to hunt.

Among recent hunting and gathering societies, most big-game hunters fail on any given day. The hunter does not get close enough, or misses, or the animal escapes. Another hunter may be lucky and succeed, so sharing is a kind of insurance. Other carnivores don't need that insurance. Although cheetahs or lions fail in most attempts, they make many attempts and are more likely than humans to succeed on any day.

Another way of sharing makes humans different from other carnivores. Predators like lions and wolves seem not to differ all that much in hunting ability, and they hunt together. People live and share food in camps, but they usually hunt alone or in pairs, and hand–eye coordination is not evenly distributed. Perhaps two or three out of ten hunters in a camp will bring home most of the meat. Fieldwork with contemporary hunter-gatherers has shown that it takes about twenty years to learn enough to reach peak ability as a hunter. Men in their forties and fifties seem to bring home more meat than younger men.[6]

Careful analysis of data collected among !Kung hunters in Botswana in the 1960s, for example, showed that men and women in their twenties and thirties—the parents of young children—brought home enough calories to feed themselves, but no more. The extra calories collected by older women and men were necessary to feed the children of the whole camp.[7]

Humans have never been simply hunters. Even after big-game hunting began, this did not replace all other hunting. The diet continued to feature smaller animals, fish, birds, reptiles and insects. And ambush hunting, whether your prey is big or small, is simply too unreliable to be the sole source of nutrition. Outside of the Far North and the Eurasian Ice Ages, almost all human hunters have relied on a steady supply of tubers, roots, nuts, fruit and vegetable matter for about half their calories. Critically, that supply also ensures that no one starves on the days or weeks when there is little or no meat in the camp. Humans had to find a way of sharing the meat of big game, but also a way of sharing other food with the hunters.

In order to share food humans had to change. Most primate societies—not all—have a rule that an animal can keep what food they find, once they hold it in their hand. As we have seen, chimpanzees allow any animal who participated in a hunt to take some of the meat. Other chimps then sit begging for a share, and may get some. But the young get little meat, and the successful male or female hunters get far more than any other animal. This works for occasional hunters like chimps. It is not a system that would work for human children for whom meat was half their diet.

Pecking orders are another problem for carnivores. Herbivorous zebras can graze and eat alongside each other, as can grazing baboons. Chimps can sit alongside each other, each picking and eating fruit. The pecking order may allow one chimp to reach for the biggest fruit first, but all animals eat, including the young. Carnivores, however, have to share the meat with the young after the adults catch it.

Different species of carnivore solve this problem in quite different ways. The solutions depend on three things—if they hunt alone or in packs, if they ambush, and how they manage the care of the young while the hunt is on. One solution among many hunting species is to form an isolated breeding pair, like eagles, who share their catch only with each other and their young. Another solution is for a mother to live alone with her young, as do leopards and cheetahs. But remember, big cats and most other predators are better than us at hunting, with a higher success rate. This could not have been a solution for human ambush hunters who worked alone or in pairs, and on most days failed to bring home big game. Moreover, a human mother and children who lived and hunted alone would have been eaten by leopards.

A different solution is found among lions. There are several female lionesses in a pride. They do most of the hunting, while the dominant male takes the first share of the food. Lionesses will leave the pride to have their cubs, often with another pregnant female, and occasionally a helpful adolescent. They do not reintroduce the cubs to the pride until they are two to three months old.

Yet other solutions are found among other pack hunters. Among wolves, for example, a pack—an extended family of several adults—forms around one breeding pair. Only that pair have offspring, and all the other adults hunt to feed that pair's pups. This limits the rate at which the group can reproduce. But every member of the pack is well-fed.

Hyenas hunt in packs, but each female takes meat back to her own young. No male would dare to take her kill, because female hyenas are bigger and dominant over males. Interestingly, female hyenas have large penises, and in one species give birth through their penis. Some biologists describe these penises as very large clitorises. In any case, this was not the road taken by human evolution. More's the pity.

Contemporary hunter-gatherers almost always bring back big game to a central camp to share. The remains of early human camps in caves also show a concentration of the bones of large game animals, often with marks on them of butchery and cooking.[8]

Ambush hunting with weapons, the human specialisation, required some system of sharing among all members of a band. Such a system requires justification and a set of rules. The logic of this is based on considerations of age, gender and the division of labour, though in detail these vary widely between different hunter-gatherers.

*Neanderthals*

The case of our ancestors' close relatives is relevant here: Neanderthal hunters. What can we learn about the how early humans survived and prospered from the less fortunate Neanderthals' way of organising their own hunting societies?

Neanderthals have long presented something of a problem for anthropologists. One reason is race. Anthropologists are agreed that among humans there are no such things as different races. But in the past, there were two groups of humans who were different from modern *Homo sapiens*, us, but not that different—Neanderthals and Denisovans.[9]

Ancestral humans, called *Homo erectus*, migrated into Europe and Asia more than a million years ago. Over the next 500,000 years they developed into two new groups, Neanderthals and Denisovans. For half a million years Neanderthals were the only group of humans in much of Europe and the Middle East. Because there have been more palaeontologists there, we know quite a lot about them. Denisovans were discovered much more recently in Siberia.

These new groups are often classified as separate species from *Homo sapiens*. However, it is clear from genetic evidence that our ancestors could, and did, have sex with both groups and produce fertile offspring. So maybe we were all one species and three subspecies, or maybe we were three closely related species, like zebras and horses. In any case, we are looking at something not entirely different from the old idea of race.

Perhaps for this reason, many anthropologists argued until recently that modern humans and Neanderthals could not have children together. This sometimes went with an assumption that modern humans had exterminated Neanderthals. Other scientists had assumed that modern humans wiped out Neanderthal men in warfare but may have taken Neanderthal women as mates. However, new ways of analysing the genome have shown that a Neanderthal father and a modern human mother was a more common pairing than a modern human father and a Neanderthal mother. It seems we got along.

What we do know, though, is that modern humans developed in Africa about 200,000 years ago. Then, about 80,000 years ago, modern humans began moving out of Africa and through the Middle East into Europe and Asia. They spread with astonishing speed and were in Australia within 20,000 years. They were also experiencing a population explosion, spreading across all of Europe, Asia and then into the Americas.

Along the way they mixed with both Neanderthals and Denisovans. Genetic analysis shows that people in Europe, Asia and Oceania have about 3% Neanderthal in their genes. That's an average, and in some people it's more and in some less. In most of Asia and Oceania, people have an average of 2% Neanderthal genes and 3% to 5% Denisovan genes. The highest percentages of Denisovan genes are in New Guinea and among indigenous Australians. People whose ancestors stayed in Africa have no Neanderthal or Denisovan genes.

This does not mean that Denisovans were living in Australia or that Neanderthals were living in the Americas. What it means is that modern humans mixed socially and sexually with both groups in their migrations out of Africa. Which suggests that we, and they, were all human. But it is also striking how low the share of Neanderthal and Denisovan ancestry is. This also points to a population explosion. There were simply many more modern humans coming out of Africa, and their numbers were expanding rapidly.

Conversely, within 50,000 years, by 30,000 years ago, there were no populations of Neanderthals and Denisovans left. What happened?[10]

Steven Kuhn and Mary Stiner have a reasonably convincing argument.[11] They point to evidence that Neanderthals, who lived mostly in very cold European climates, ate little vegetable material and depended mainly on large game. The prevalence and positions of old wounds on Neanderthal skeletons indicates that they were ambush hunters who stabbed their prey at close quarters, rather than using bows or other weapons to strike from a distance. There is almost no evidence that women were doing anything other than hunting, and young Neanderthals were fit and active. If that is so, Kuhn and Stiner ask, what were the women and the young people doing? Their answer is that they must have been hunting alongside the men.

The Neanderthal gendering of hunting, Kuhn and Stiner say, only allowed relatively small populations. This is true of all carnivores living as top-chain predators. Lions and tigers are examples. And top-chain predators not only have small populations, but their numbers are also very unstable.

By contrast, Kuhn and Stiner suggest, the new division of labour among modern humans, and their mixed diet, enabled them to spread swiftly, with a greater population density in each area.

We cannot know for certain, but Kuhn and Stiner are probably right. If so, there is an interesting implication. Many theories have assumed that men and women became unequal because there was a division of labour among hunters and gatherers. This theory suggests the opposite. Humans became successful as a species, and men and women became equal, partly as a consequence of the division of labour between them.

*Fire and Cooking*

Many animals can share between a mother and her young, or between a couple and their offspring. But a pecking order of dominance makes it difficult to share in this way in larger groups. The solution humans found to the problem of food sharing was to reorder gender relations and childcare in new ways.

These new gender relations, and the habit of ambush hunting itself, depended on fire. At a certain point, perhaps two million years ago, perhaps more recently, early humans discovered how to make fire. That had several different effects.

First, fire helped to keep predators at bay. All other apes make nests in trees for safety. The only exceptions are adult male gorillas, who are too big to sleep easily in the trees but are big enough to defend themselves on the ground. Early humans, however, were much smaller, and probably were ground-dwellers long before they discovered how to make fire. That also helped people stay warm, which meant they could move into colder parts of the world. Clothing made from hides and furs helped with that too. In many hunter-gatherer groups even today, people take informal turns so that someone is always awake tending a fire.

The main consequence of domesticating fire, though, was cooking. Cooking food had crucial knock-on consequences for human bodies and social organisation. Cooking softened up tubers, vegetable food, meat and fish. This meant that more calories could be digested from the same amount of food. That increased the chances of survival, because the human brain could grow bigger. Those brains now consume an enormous amount of calories, about 20% of our total intake, and put a considerable strain on the body.[12]

If we look at other primates, the best predictor of brain size is the size of the social group. Scientists think this is because the more animals you have to keep track of in a complex social system, the more intelligence you need. But that increase in brain size can only come about if some other part of the primate's body is using less energy. With humans, that part of the body is the digestive system. That's partly down to our diet. Chimps and bonobos—and gorillas even more so—eat a large variety of high-fibre fruits and vegetation that humans can no longer digest. This is partly because apes have large lower intestines where bacteria slowly digest the fibre—and the bacteria, not the apes, gain the energy. Humans have much smaller lower intestines, and a small digestive tract as a whole. It's also a direct result of using fire. In most primates, digestion uses about 25% of total calories they need to survive, in humans about 10%. For humans, cooking does a big part of the job of digestion.

Cooking and the change in diet also afforded us a lot of free time for hunting. Humans typically spend an hour or less a day chewing their food, while other apes chew six hours a day. A human that had to chew that much could not wound an animal, track it and then drag it home to share.

Cooking also fits with an altered division of labour between the sexes. The division of labour among recent hunter-gatherers is not that all men hunt and all women gather and cook. Rather, the work of finding food is parcelled out such that all women and all men gather on some days, that all women and all men hunt small animals as they find them, and that only men go on dedicated hunts for big game.

By the same token, all men and all women know how to cook, and sometimes do so, though most cooking is done by women. More important, this is not a division of labour where each man brings home the meat of big-game animals for his immediate family. Men who hunt big game bring meat back to share with all the households in the camp. In some of these societies, the cooking happens at the hearth of the hunter, and then the food is distributed. In others meat is first butchered and then distributed raw to all the households of the camp.

This point needs emphasising, because there is a recurrent tendency among some evolutionary biologists to assume that when humans began to hunt big game, males began to exchange meat with females in return for sex. What actually happens is that existing humans who hunt share meat with everyone in the band.

We would argue rather that there is an effective division of labour among hunters and gatherers, but the logic is perhaps not obvious. Men are not big-game hunters because they are stronger or more coordinated. The variation in athletic ability among humans means that a physically gifted woman is more athletic than the average man. Nor is it size. Again, there is a continuum of size among men and women.

Rather, the need for surprise is a good reason why nursing mothers of small children are not involved in ambush hunting, as anyone hoping for absolute quiet while holding a baby or toddler will recognise. And of course, carrying a smaller person while tracking a wounded animal is a problem. Moreover, ambush hunting is dangerous, and men are more easily disposable than women for the survival and reproduction of the species. But almost all women in recent hunting and gathering societies have hunted and caught smaller animals.

Where hunters use nets, as among some Ituri and Aka groups in central African forests, men and women hunt big game together. Where beaters drive the animals towards the bows of the hunters, as among some caribou hunters in the Far North, men and women

## HUMANS BECAME EQUAL BY SHARING MEAT

also hunt together. Men and women also share fishing and shellfish gathering in many places.

It would be perfectly possible for women without children to hunt, or women without very small children, or women with older children. But what we usually see in practice is pretty consistent—men hunt big game. There is no such pattern among other apes. Among bonobos, females do most of the hunting, and among chimps an infertile adult female may hunt with groups of males.[13]

Part of the difference is that humans ambush-hunt. The other part is that we have adapted to a balanced diet. The humans who go off to hunt need to be assured of a diet of vegetable matter every day so they do not go hungry, and big-game meat on some days so they can thrive. If someone gathers and hunts small animals, and someone else hunts big game, and they share at the end of the day, then everyone survives.

If you need a division of labour where some people hunt big game, and other people hunt small game and gather, and both groups are obliged to share, the division of labour by sex is a solution that works. In this system developed by our ancestors, difference is not the basis for hierarchy; it's a way of continuing to live equally and cooperatively.

# 4

# HUMANS BECAME EQUAL BY SHARING CHILDCARE

The division of labour went along with an important change in childcare. Infanticide by males is a problem for many primate mothers, and it slows population growth. But as we shall see, human evolution produced a different solution. Men, women and children all cared for children safely.

Among many species of mammals, adult males kill the young in the band who are not related to them. Among lions, for instance, when a new male takes over a pride, he kills all the cubs. Male baboons and chimpanzees do this too. Not every male does this, but it is common in all three species.

From the point of view of survival of the species, killing the young is insane—and a colossal waste of energy. Male infanticide is bad for the species, bad for the group and bad for the female. But it persists because it increases a particular male's chances of reproduction. This is not just because there are fewer offspring of other males. More important, when her infant is killed, the mother starts her ovulation cycle again and the new male breeds with her. So he sires several offspring quickly.

For this to happen, it is not necessary for the male to think, 'I will kill the other babies, so my offspring will be more likely to survive and my genetic material will be passed on.' Two much simpler dispositions are all that is necessary. One is 'kill the young'. The other is 'don't kill the young of any female I have mated with'. A male with these dispositions is more likely to have young survive, and those young are more likely to have his disposition to infanticide.

The importance of this for human evolution was first suggested by the primatologist Sarah Hrdy. One reason Hrdy could have this insight was that she was an American feminist of the women's liberation generation. The second reason was that her first field research was among langurs, long-tailed monkeys in an Indian city. Many primatologists, like anthropologists, are destined for life to see the world through the prism of their first field research.[1]

The feminism meant that Hrdy watched female langurs. She did not start with male dominance, but with females living in a hierarchical system. As Hrdy watched, she also tried to see the females as pursuing strategies of their own. This meant that she paid a lot of attention to sexual selection by females. She was interested in which males the female langurs were trying to have sex with, and how that helped pass on the females' genes. Hrdy also paid a lot of attention to infanticide by males, because it bulked so large in the lives of female langurs.

Hrdy has published several different accounts of watching one langur mother for weeks, as a new male stalked the infant clinging to her abdomen. The mother made sure to stay near other females who would defend her, and she stayed in the trees away from the male. But he kept following, and then sitting there, watching. Avoiding him made it hard to eat, and the mother grew exhausted. Eventually she dropped her guard. He grabbed the infant and killed it. Then the male mated with her, and she gave birth to an infant who carried on his genes.[2]

The experience of watching that female go through this ordeal, day after day, stayed with Sarah Hrdy. When she came to write about human evolution, she put considerable emphasis on the high rates of infanticide among chimpanzees and gorillas. For example, a team of researchers analysed forty-seven years of field data on chimpanzees at Gombe in Tanzania. They found that 25–30% of infant deaths were due to infanticide, mostly by males, but sometimes by females other than the mother. Percentages from other long-term field studies of chimpanzees vary widely, with most reporting less infanticide than at Gombe, but all reporting some.[3]

As Hrdy says:

> Given the company chimpanzees keep, it is understandable that a mother would be reluctant to allow even a well-intentioned older sibling to hold her baby. Caring and attentive as a sister would be, she

> might not be sufficiently experienced or imposing to ward off a more dominant adult... Ape mothers insist on carrying infants everywhere ... because the available alternatives are not safe enough.[4]

By keeping close hold of infants, ape mothers can protect their young. But this means births must be spaced widely so that the female can raise each offspring to independence.

Sarah Cheney and Robert Seyfarth studied chacma baboons in the Okavango Delta marshes in Botswana:

> Whatever the mood in the group at the time, the arrival of a new immigrant male disrupts everything. Youngsters run to inspect the newcomer, boldly racing up to him, staring, and then quickly whirling around to present their rumps as a sign of submission. Resident adult males are more seriously upset. They become vigilant and restless, warily tracking the new male's every move, but avoiding any direct confrontation... The most dramatic reactions to a new immigrant, however, come from lactating females, who raise their tails, grab their infants, and race away screaming whenever he begins to approach... Their anxiety is well founded, because most immigrant males who rise to the alpha position commit infanticide... At least 53% of all infants born during our study have died as a result of confirmed or suspected infanticide.[5]

Cheney and Seyfarth have a convincing explanation of why infanticide is so high among these particular chacma baboons. Conditions in the Okavango marshes are difficult, and during the annual floods many baboons are eaten by crocodiles. The average alpha male holds his position for only eight months. If he does not kill off some babies and impregnate new females swiftly, none of his genes will survive. This favours the evolution of infanticide among this particular subspecies in these particular marshes. Rates of infanticide among other groups of baboons are lower, though everywhere the behaviour is common.

Female baboons in turn have two evolutionary adaptations to cope with the threat of infanticide. One is what heteronormative primatologists call 'promiscuity'. At the high point of her cycle of ovulation, when she actually conceives, the female is likely to be mating with the dominant male. But in the days before and after this high point, she will mate with many males in the group. This helps her young to survive, because the other males will not attack her young either.

The other protection is friendship. Barbara Smuts studied a troop of olive baboons in Kenya. She found that most adult females had a special male friend. Smuts describes one such friendship: 'I had no trouble recognising Virgil and Pandora 100 m away, travelling slightly apart from the rest of the troop, wandering slowly toward me.'

It was late afternoon, and both baboons had eaten their fill. Virgil sat, leaned back and relaxed. He spotted Pandora, and flashed his eyelids, grunted and smacked his lips at her.

> Pandora, 5 m away, looked up and made a similar face back at Virgil and ... headed towards him with the ungainly trot of a baboon anxious to get somewhere fast, but too lazy to run. As she approached, Virgil lip-smacked and grunted with increasing intensity, as if encouraging her to make haste. When she arrived, she plopped herself down on her back next to him and, dangling one foot in the air, presented her flank in an invitation for grooming. Virgil responded promptly, gently parting the sparse hairs on her belly with his hands, every now and then lightly touching her skin with his lips to remove a bit of dead skin or dirt from her fur... After a few moments, they were joined by two of Pandora's offspring, Plutarch, a juvenile male, and Pyrrha, an infant female. Pyrrha was in a rambunctious mood, and she used Virgil's stomach as a trampoline, bouncing up and down with the voiceless chuckles that accompany baboon play. Every now and then Virgil opened his half-shut eyes, peered at Pyrrha, and gently touching her with his index finger he grunted, as if to reassure her that he did not mind the rhythmic impact of her slight body against his full stomach.
>
> [Then] Virgil moved away, slowly clambering up the cliff face where the troop would spend the night. He glanced back at every few steps at Pandora and her family, who followed right behind. Finding a good spot halfway up the cliff, Virgil made himself comfortable. Sitting upright, he leaned backwards against the rock face, and grasping his toes in his hands, let his head sink to his chest—a typical baboon sleeping posture. Pandora sat next to him, leaning

her body into his, one hand on his knee, her head against his shoulder. Her offspring squeezed in between Pandora and Virgil, and, in the dimming light, I could not tell where the body of one baboon began and the other left off. This is how they would remain for the rest of the night.[6]

The most common number of male friends for an adult female, Smuts found, was two. She argues, convincingly, that there were evolutionary advantages to any female in such friendships. Her male friends would defend her offspring from attack by other adults. The relationship was not sexual, though the friends might be among those mating with her during her rare cycles.

What the male gains is friendship, comfort and relaxation in the lonely and stressful life of a male savannah baboon. Indeed, one long-term study of baboons in Amboseli in Kenya found that baboons with close female friends lived longer than baboons without, and longer than successful alpha males.[7]

Infanticide, though, poses a problem for almost all primates. Competition between males created an evolutionary logic which reduced the ability of each female to reproduce herself, and also reduced the ability of the species as a whole to reproduce, slowing population growth.

*The Human Solution*

Human evolution produced a different solution. Sarah Hrdy has developed a theory to explain this. Her important insight was that the burden of childcare did not fall on the mother. All humans were disposed to nurture all children, not just their own. This was an enormous saving in energy and one of the processes that made men and women more equal.[8]

It is often said that because early humans had such big brains and narrow hips that our babies had to be born early in order to make it through the birth canal. So once outside the womb we were helpless for much longer than other primates and other carnivores. Evolutionary psychologists often say this is why women are so caring, and men are hunters and more aggressive. None of this is true.

There are important anatomical and social differences which mark off human childcare practices from those found among other primates. But they are not what the palaeo-fantasists suggest. What is striking is that human women have more babies, and raise them for shorter times than do gorillas, chimpanzees and bonobos, all great apes like us. On average, hunter-gatherers give birth every four years, and the other apes spend six to eight years on each offspring. This is despite the fact that our young grow more slowly and have a lot more to learn.

Three to four years is the average birth spacing in most known foraging societies. Among farmers, a recent development, women have usually given birth to more children—sometimes even ten or fifteen young in a lifetime.

This three- to four-year birth spacing among hunter-gatherers is in part because a woman is less likely to conceive while breastfeeding. There is a useful and not accidental hormonal feedback. It can also be due, in various places, to a taboo on sex while the baby is still breastfeeding. In such cases, the interval may be a result of the infant's parents trying to avoid ejaculation in the vagina during her fertile period.

Hrdy's idea was that humans are different, and that matters. A human mother, in all societies, can and does hand an infant to other women, men and children. More important, those other people care for the young. When the child is small, that caring means that some person is always responsible, and always keeps the child in sight, if not in their arms. When children grow older, they can play and move together, in groups. But every adult of the band or village will keep a casual eye on the children and respond to cries.

Each child will have several carers, of different importance. Usually the child's father is one of them. But in most hunter-gatherer societies we know about, and in most farming communities, the most common carers are older children, often siblings or cousins. In practice, the toddler is with an older child, but also with the other children in the group.

Often, too, the carer is a grandmother. This is connected to another physical difference between humans and other apes. Sometimes people say that humans are the only primate with the menopause. But this is not quite accurate. Among chimpanzees, bonobos and gorillas, females also use up all their eggs as they approach middle age. But the ape females then die at this point, as do most male apes of the same age. What happens with people is that both males and females live on into their forties, fifties and sixties.

At these ages, males can still reproduce. The question biologists ask is: why would a female animal live on past reproductive age? Of what use could that be, in passing on the genes of the female, or her group? One answer is that both grandmothers and grandfathers can mind the camp. Of course, most childcare is done by other children.

This is also true, incidentally, in most farming societies today. But almost everywhere hunter-gatherers are careful to leave at least one adult in charge of the camp during the day. This helps to protect the children from predators, while the children's mothers and fathers get on with the work of hunting and gathering. But just as no one child has one carer all the time, no one role—grandmother, big brother, father, or sister—makes a person the main carer. Mothers and bands fit the caring work to the people and the relationships available. If a mother, or any responsible adult, dies or leaves, the baby or the child can still survive. It also provides short-term insurance if the mother is injured or sick for a time.

Among !Kung hunters, for instance, women carry small babies when they gather or hunt small game, and nurse them as they go. But after the first year, it drains energy to carry a bigger child, and mothers leave them behind in camp. In camp someone will be mending weapons and bags, or just resting—and that person keeps an eye on all the children.

This shared caring provides humans with important evolutionary advantages. One is that it solves the problem of the helpless child who has to learn for so long. Shared caring allows infants the time to develop their big brains in safety, while allowing their parents to go on to reproduce again sooner. This means that in good times human populations can grow and spread out more quickly than those of other apes. This is to the advantage of the species, and it multiplies the genes of the parents too.

Shared caring also provides an insurance that the species can grow with less waste of energy. This may also help explain why human grandmothers and grandfathers both live long lives.

In the late 1960s Nancy Howell and Richard Lee counted the calories produced and consumed by different !Kung age groups.

They found that men and women in their forties and fifties were bringing in more calories than younger people. Men who hunted also took years to learn their craft. With older women, it was because they were less encumbered by babies, and they worked hard. Without this extra work by older people, the camp would not have been able to feed the young.[9]

Old-fashioned approaches to hunter-gatherers used to see motherhood as something that confined a mother to the home and the camp. The woman tended the cooking pot, it was thought, while the men went out to hunt. What we now understand is that sharing childcare and long-lived grandparents allowed women to leave home on many days to gather food on their own.

However, a word of caution is in order. Many primatologists and evolutionary psychologists have accepted Hrdy's theory but reduced it to what is called the 'grandmother hypothesis'. This leaves out the insight that everyone shares in childcare and that other children do more childcare than grandmothers. Moreover, at any one time the majority of women do not have a grandmother available.

We would suggest that the survival of both grandmothers and grandfathers had another major advantage—wisdom. The philosopher of science Kim Sterelny has argued convincingly for the centrality of learning through long apprenticeships in human evolution. Sterelny questions the model that assumes early humans taught abstract concepts of tool-making, digging, cooking, hunting and ritual life. Rather, he says, young people worked alongside older people for many years, watching, then repeating the actions, watching some more, repeating, and so on. As soon as you put it that way, of course he's right.[10]

You could call it the 'monkey see, monkey do' model of human intelligence. And grandpa and grandma would have been essential to that process. Across cultures, people are enjoined to respect wise elders and care for the elderly. It may be these are not just pieties, but the articulation of a theory of human evolution.

Among some animals, but not all, the care of the young may last only a few days or weeks. Even mammalian maternal love is limited in many species, but while it lasts it is fierce. In human society, care for the young is an important, typically lifelong, feeling. Shared caring also has had an enormous emotional effect on human society.

What happens with people is that love gets generalised across the species, and across time. Any member of the human species is equipped to care for and love the young. The young learn to love, in varying degrees, all those carers. Human beings are a loving, and a flexibly loving, species.

Shared caring had another effect. It diluted any natural emotional differences between male and female. Closeness with other males, and with other females, plays an obvious and central role in the lives of male chimpanzees. For instance, older brothers are close to younger brothers and sisters. But with human shared care, there is a qualitative shift. Love and empathy have been generalised and can extend far beyond our close companions.

Because Hrdy was a women's liberation feminist with langurs on the brain, she was able to notice something else about human evolution. She saw that among people there is almost no infanticide controlled by men, but infanticide controlled by the mother is surprisingly common. Once you start looking for it, you find it in many times and places, from the Kalahari to Brazil. Some of these groups are hunter-gatherers, some are farmers, and some live in cities in capitalist countries. Some are egalitarian, and many are not.[11]

This infanticide is not unfeeling, or without debate. It always takes place in private, away from the camp, village or city streets. In almost all cases among hunter-gatherers, it happens because it will be hard for the mother and her band to feed and care for another child. Perhaps because food is short, or the mother is exhausted, or the right carers are not available, or the birth has happened while the older child is still young. In these circumstances infanticide allows mothers to fit their rates of reproduction to their situation and environmental conditions. Human beings became a species which could control when to expand, and when to protect individuals in times of hardship. These decisions, and the relatively quick reproduction rates, meant that in good times human beings could populate whole continents quickly.

For many people the most uncomfortable part of Hrdy's brilliant insight is not that humans practise infanticide, but that the mother makes the decision. When Hrdy first published these ideas in 1974, they provoked controversy.[12] By 1990 the politics of abortion was making such an argument difficult in the United States. The central argument of the political right was that abortion was infanticide, and the pro-abortion feminists had been driven to deny this strenuously. In these circumstances any acknowledgement of human infanticide was politically dangerous. The idea that infanticide might be a woman's choice, not a man's, was doubly dangerous. It also contradicted what by then had become a very developed understanding that women were more loving and caring than men.

Hrdy, however, was a feminist of an older generation, and a scientist. She believed in facts. Moreover, the change she identified in infanticide marked a major shift from male power to female power. It was a crucial piece in the story of emerging human gender equality.

Among early humans, but not among other apes, the decision to raise a child became a woman's choice alone. Of course those women would have had easier lives, and easier decisions, if they had had access to birth control and abortion. Without those options, they did what they had to do. It is worth remembering that in many hunting and gathering societies, between a third and a half of children died before adulthood. The decision not to keep one child was also a decision to let other children live.

There is another reason that female control of infanticide represented an important increase in equality between the genders. This was not just true at the moment of birth. It was true every day. The woman did not have to be constantly anxious for the safety of her child. She could put down her infant and eat with both hands in peace. The end of infanticide by males, or by females other than the mother, was a crucial step in allowing childcare to be shared. Women could leave toddlers at home in the camp while they brought home food. That in turn increased the amount of food they could hunt and gather for their young and for the camp. And it opened for men a whole new world of love.

5

## HUMANS BECAME EQUAL BY SHARING ORGASMS

So, sexually, are we chimps or bonobos?

We're not chimps. Phew. We're not bonobos either. Damn. We are a third species, with our own, different and complex adaptation. As we have seen with baboons, gibbons, gorillas, chimps and bonobos, patterns of dominance and patterns of sexuality are part of a larger complex of anatomy, food, behaviour, environment and society. And so it was in human evolution, and so it is with us now.

We have argued that humans evolved as ambush hunters who shared meat, shared gathered food, and shared childcare. Here we show how our sexuality fits in with that adaptation. We begin with sex, and pay detailed attention to one particular kind of evidence— the ways human anatomy has changed and differs from that of other primates. We argue that those changes became established because they fitted humanity to a new kind of sexual politics which helped them survive.

Let's start with size. On average male humans are bigger than females, but the difference in size is only about 15%. This is about the same as chimpanzees and bonobos. This low ratio rules out social organisation dominated by an alpha male, like gorillas. It points to the possibility of either sexual equality, as we have seen with bonobos, or some sexual inequality, as with chimpanzees. It suggests, but does no more than suggest, that there was some inequality between early women and early men, but not a great deal.

Next, the male genitals. Biologists have now compared the penises and testicles of many primates. As a general rule, a male primate has a small penis compared to body size in a species where the female is unlikely to mate with another male. A silverback gorilla is a very big animal with a very small penis. The gibbon, smaller than the great apes, has a small penis. What do the two species have in common? They don't have to worry about sexual competition from other males. Depending on your point of view, it turns out that size does indeed matter, or it doesn't.[1]

Chimpanzees and baboons have long penises. Human penises are longer still, and bonobo penises even longer. Humans, indeed, are toward the top end of penis length for primates. Males of most of the other primate species with long penises have adapted to females who have larger swellings of the vulva when most fertile. In those cases, the male needs extra length to reach the cervix with his sperm. Humans just have the extra length, though men still average shorter penises than bonobos. These variations, and particularly the bonobo example, suggest that long penises evolve in response to female choice. In other words, it looks like early ancestral women did not wait around for an alpha male to triumph and claim her—she had a say in the matter, and could choose better penises. And she often had more than one partner.

The human penis also has a larger mass than other primates because it has a much greater girth. Other primate penises are long and thin. One explanation for our 'thick dicks' is that the human vagina has evolved to be much wider. As we know, women give birth to babies with much larger heads than other primates. This also suggests female choice. Probably early humans with wider vaginas tended to choose thicker penises.

There are, further, radical differences in the shape and feel of penises among different primates. As we saw in Chapter 2, the chimpanzee penis tapers to a point and has bristles on the end. While the bristles seem to cause females discomfort, males find them extremely sensitive. A male chimpanzee comes very quickly, often within seconds of penetration. Coming quickly may have evolutionary advantages to a male chimpanzee with only seconds before a more powerful male discovers what he is up to. Human penises either never had those sensitive bristles or have lost them over time.

Chimpanzees, and almost all other primates, also have a penis bone which helps maintain an erection. A human erection, by contrast, depends on chambers which fill up with blood. This means the penis carrier has to be more excited about the prospect of having sex.

Compared with chimps, men take much longer to reach orgasm—often ten minutes or more. This slow build to male orgasm is perhaps the most important anatomical change of all. We return to this matter soon. (See if you can wait.)

So, to sum up, the human penis is bigger around, smoother in the vagina, and simultaneously harder and softer. As Loretta Cormier and Sharyn Jones argue convincingly in their splendidly titled book, *The Domestication of the Penis*, this is a penis produced by female choice over a long period of evolution.[2]

But in one detail we find Cormier and Jones' ideas less than convincing. They assume that human males with slower orgasms have less pleasure than male chimpanzees who come quickly. Yet there are plenty of human beings around the globe who celebrate slow male orgasms that give pleasure for both partners.

Comparative testicle sizes among primates tell a somewhat different story about humanity than does penis size. Across a wide range of animal and primate species, large testicles occur when females have many sexual partners in any one cycle. The accepted explanation among biologists is that the male with the most sperm in each spurt has the best chance of fertilising the egg. So big-balled males are more likely to reproduce.

Among primates, gorillas have tiny testicles. Thanks to their size, male silverback gorillas live in, protect and dominate a small group, so they are not faced with constant sexual competition. Chimpanzees have larger testicles than humans, because their sperm are competing hard inside the female who mates with many males, one after the other, when she is fertile. Bonobo females mate with even more males, who have gargantuan testicles compared to human beings.

The medium size of human testicles suggests that our ancestors were not as faithful as gibbons, but not as adventurous as baboons, chimps and bonobos.

There were also changes in the human vagina. Humans developed labia. The labia majora and the labia minora work to cover and protect the vagina and help keep it moist. The vagina also grew longer. The clitoris acquired a hood which protected the sensitive tip. And the clitoris moved forward, away from the vagina.[3]

One consequence of the move of the clitoris was that sex without fingers or tongues stimulated the clitoris less. But it was probably based on a clear evolutionary advantage, to do with the dangers of childbirth for a bipedal human giving birth to a baby with a very big head. That combination produces a lot more trauma and tearing than among other apes. On balance, the evolutionary change seems to have guarded the clitoris against damage during childbirth and worked to protect a woman's subsequent sexual enjoyment.

Then there are all the secondary sexual characteristics. Humans lost almost all their body hair early on, so they were less likely to get heat stroke running across the savannah under the midday sun. But this leaves a puzzle: how to explain where and why human hair has been retained. The answer suggests it is the result of both male and female sexual choice. Beards in men, and head and pubic hair in both women and men probably functioned to attract the attention of the other sex. We know these preserved patches of human hair have an ancient history because each has their own distinct species of lice. One species is specialised for life in human pubic hair, and the other for head hair and beards.

Human female breasts, which are large in comparison with other apes, pose other questions. Chimps, gorillas and all other primates nurse perfectly well without them. Except, as it happens, female bonobos, who have smaller breasts than human females, but bigger than those of other apes. It looks like large breasts, too, are indicators of sexual choice, but this time by ancient male bonobos and ancient human men.

Humans are also vaginally active all their adult lives. There is evidence that humans are somewhat more likely to have sex around the time of ovulation. But only somewhat more. By contrast, among chimps and bonobos, 95% of male–female copulation occurs when females are ovulating, and their genitals are swollen. This is an enormous difference.

All these differences suggest an evolutionary change to females with more choice, and then those choices drove the anatomical changes. They also suggest a change for all humans to a society where sexual satisfaction played a far bigger role, took more time and lasted all year round. Which brings us to the mystery of the female orgasm.

*The Mystery of the Female Orgasm*

Most of our chapters on evolution are based on the work of other scientists and anthropologists. Here, however, we take some of these ideas further and suggest a new way of thinking about human orgasms.

## ... BY SHARING ORGASMS ...

Rather bizarrely, most primatologists find it a mystery why female humans have orgasms at all. A controversy rages about the evolutionary implications. The scientists' problem is this. Males of all primate species have orgasms. And no primatologist or evolutionary psychologist has ever had any problem understanding why men have orgasms. It's obvious, isn't it? The male orgasm exists as a mechanism for ejaculation.

Some of our male readers may be thinking, 'There is more to my orgasm than that.' Some of our female readers may be thinking the same thing. Hold those thoughts.

Primatologists agree that the females of most primate species do not seem to have orgasms during sex. Yet female primates clearly do experience sexual excitement and desire. Female rhesus macaques have been stimulated to orgasm by researchers, and it is likely that other monkeys can be too. Female macaques also have orgasms by rubbing their clitoris from behind against the rear of another female, and female bonobos certainly have orgasms by rubbing their genitals together.

All this is sure and agreed. Beyond this, there is disagreement among the experts. We side with Lucy Cooke in her recent book *Bitch* that female orgasms are common in monkeys and apes. There are quite a number of species where during sex the female 'shows' the lip smacking, the O-shaped open mouth, the hand clenching, the grunts, the 'vocalisations' and the shaking we have come to expect in pornography. And there is also the point Cooke makes—why do all mammals have a clitoris?[4]

Almost all of this marked sexual excitement has been recorded in macaques and other primates where an ovulating female has sex with many males. Obviously, the excitement helps the animal seek out many partners. The prevailing evolutionary explanation of why the female expresses so much excitement is a bit odd. The usual view is that they grunt and pant in order to impress the male so that he will remember them and not kill their offspring. In which case, you have to ask: why are female humans having orgasms? By and large women don't have sex with lots of men when they are ovulating, they have sex all the time and not just when they are fertile, and they do not fear male infanticide.

Primatologists have certainly tried to come up with explanations of the human female orgasm.[5] Early on, evolutionary psychologists favoured the explanation that female orgasms encouraged women to choose monogamy. Not surprisingly, this approach has since fallen out of favour. For one thing, the subtext was always, 'Oh Jack, you're such a stud in bed I would never look at another man.' For another, after the sexual revolution it occurred to many people that highly sexed women might have the same zipper problem as many men.

Other evolutionary psychologists have argued that orgasms help females to identify the best 'dominant male' to father their babies. This idea is called the 'Sire Hypothesis'. It assumes that the men who are more likely to make you come are of 'superior genetic quality'. The proponents of the Sire Hypothesis do not mean they have found the 'good at making women come gene'. They only mean that men who make you come will be of superior social status, which is doubtful.

Another explanation is that women use their orgasms to make themselves appealing to men and trap them into pair bonding. Conveniently, this provides an evolutionary explanation for why many women fake orgasm.

We are not making any of this up.

In 2005 the feminist philosopher of science Elisabeth Lloyd expertly demolished all these 'evolutionary' explanations in *The Case of the Female Orgasm*. Instead, Lloyd opted for what is known as a 'by-product' explanation. This by-product theory points to the example of nipples on male humans and other male primates. There is a good evolutionary reason for females to have nipples. There is no good reason for males to have them. Males just have nipples because females need to have them, and it's easier not to differentiate. Nipples do no harm, and it would have required extensive mutation and adaptation to produce a nipple-free male body. After all, nature usually works by providing one feature in both sexes, and then constructing some mechanism that turns that feature off in the other sex. In the case of male nipples, it is easy to see them as an inoffensive by-product. There are many other cases in evolution where something that serves no purpose, but does no harm, survives. For Lloyd, the human female orgasm is like that. Women have orgasms because men do, so why not? It's a lucky accident.[6]

Many evolutionary psychologists have understandably not been satisfied by Lloyd's argument. They have replied that there is a difference of scale between male nipples and female orgasms. It is unlikely, they argue, that something as spectacular as a female orgasm has no evolutionary use.

Cormier and Jones' work on the human penis is important here. They have demonstrated a whole complex of major changes in the shape, hardness, smoothness and length of the penis, and matching changes in the labia, vagina and clitoris. It beggars belief that all those changes happened as a by-product. However, Lloyd's by-product theory is still the dominant explanation among feminists who think about evolution.

We don't agree with Lloyd. But we don't agree with the earlier evolutionary arguments either. We think the question is being posed in a misleading way. What we say here is in keeping with the general argument of this book. We know that when people wish to justify gender inequality, they emphasise and exaggerate imagined differences between the sexes. Some of these differences are real, but most are not. The differences that do exist are by and large trivial. When there are differences, they are seldom binary and usually best understood in terms of continua. For all these reasons, our focus throughout our study of human gender relations is on the similarities rather than the differences between women and men. The same principle and starting point is appropriate to understanding human orgasms.

Four related ideas are useful here. First, biologists have found looking at differences between male and female reproductive strategies useful in understanding many species from langurs to ants. This is why they are inclined to pay particular attention to reproductive strategies among people. It is also why we need to make it clear we are not saying that sex differences are unimportant in animals across the board. We are saying that sexual differences are relatively unimportant among humans.

Second, the orgasms of human men and women are very similar. To investigate their evolutionary importance, it makes sense to treat male and female orgasms in the same frame and not separately as 'the male orgasm' or 'the female orgasm'. Behind this is an important principle of method. If you start by distinguishing your research subjects as male or female, you are always going to produce answers in terms of males and females. It's circular and intellectually sloppy.

Third, all biologists are conditioned to look for evolutionary explanations about how animals change to better pass on their 'genetic material'. So when faced with changes in sexual equipment and sexual behaviour, they immediately think of reproduction. We think that can be misleading. Sex has uses and consequences besides reproduction.

Fourth, we have been writing so far in this chapter as if all primate and human sex is heterosexual. It is not. Moreover, apes in any one species are not identical. Individual animals differ in their habit and choices, their social relations and the gender roles they play.

Gibbons, for example, are 'monogamous' and mostly live in groups of one adult male, one adult female and their juvenile offspring. Yet researchers have observed some units of two adult females and one male among gibbons of the genus *Nomascus* in China and Hainan. Some groups of white-handed gibbons in Thailand have two adult males and one adult female. Among the chimpanzees in one group at Gombe, an infertile female spent most of her time moving with the main group of males, and joined them in patrolling the borders of their territory. (She was the individual mentioned earlier.)[7]

On the sides of a volcano in the Virunga Mountains, Juichi Yamagiwa observed a stable group of six male mountain gorillas who had sex with each other. There were two silverbacks and four younger adult males. The sex bound the group together tightly, and they tended to avoid other groups. Each of the two silverbacks had exclusive relationships with two of the younger males. But if his overtures were refused by the younger gorilla, the silverback would then fight the other silverback, and the younger gorillas would intervene to make peace.[8]

This variation is not confined to primates. Bruce Bagemihl's *Biological Exuberance* is a 768-page treasure trove of examples of same-sex sex among many species of animals and birds. The biologist Joan Roughgarden goes further in *Evolution's Rainbow* and *The Genial Gene*. She deploys a wealth of evidence of transformations of sexuality and gender across many kinds of life to defenestrate Darwin's idea of 'sexual selection'. It is not an accident that Roughgarden is both a distinguished biologist and a trans person from San Francisco. We return to her important work in more detail in Chapter 17.[9]

## ... BY SHARING ORGASMS ...

*The Similarities in Human Orgasms*

With these four points in mind, let's look at the similarities in human orgasms. First, there are the similarities between a clitoris and a penis. Both the penis and the clitoris have a tip concealed by a flap. Directly above the clitoris, inside a woman, there is a large amount of soft tissue. That internal clitoris and the external penis are about the same size when they're erect. With sexual stimulation, all this tissue becomes engorged with blood, and tension builds until orgasm provides a sudden release.

Moreover, all human orgasms involve the whole body in a similar way. All the 'involuntary' muscles in the body, like the heart and the lungs, are unaffected. But all the 'voluntary' muscles, those that can be tensed or relaxed, from your toes to your lips, tense and then relax in one orgasmic burst. That's where the intense pleasure comes from.

There is evidence for some differences in male and female orgasms. Many, if not all, women are capable of repeated orgasms during a bout of sex. This suggests that women are capable of being more voracious than men. But we should also pay attention to our own knowledge that orgasmic experiences lie along a continuum. Individual women and men are in different places on that continuum, but so too are orgasms on different days with the same person, and in different years and decades, and depending on whether the children are asleep, or your mother is visiting. And sex with different people falls along a continuum too. But somehow all those different orgasms are also all one thing.

We have been writing as if human females can easily have orgasms. But both sides of the female orgasm controversy, the evolutionary adaptation side and the by-product side, start with an assumption that it is much easier for men to come, and much harder for women. The feminist philosopher Lloyd and the evolutionary biologist David Puts agree on this. For evidence, Lloyd and Puts both rely on the comprehensive surveys of sexual behaviour in the United States by Alfred Kinsey and his associates in the 1940s and 1950s, and a more limited survey of women in the United States by Shere Hite in the 1970s.[10]

These surveys did not deal with random samples. Kinsey combined asking people he and his associates met up with, and a lot of targeted interviews of prisoners. Hite sent out questionnaires to women, many of whom were early feminists, and only a tiny percentage of them returned the questionnaires. Neither survey can be taken as evidence for behaviour in the wider population.

In any case, these studies do not show that women have more difficulty reaching orgasm. They show something quite different, about mid-twentieth-century Americans, and not about women in general. They show that a large proportion of the women in their surveys did not usually reach orgasm when they had sex. They also show that a considerable minority of the women in their samples had never reached orgasm during heterosexual sex.

Moreover, Kinsey was adamant that women could achieve full orgasms in other circumstances. Shere Hite's respondents said they had no trouble reaching orgasm when they masturbated. Their problem was the ignorance of the men they knew.

Indeed, the main reason Hite did the research and wrote the book was that she thought women could have orgasms much more often, and should be encouraged to do so. She wanted to shout that from the rooftops, and her shouting had an effect.

Oddly enough, the way Lloyd and the evolutionary psychologists treat the evidence from Kinsey and Hite ignores the obvious fact that American women are more likely to have orgasms now than they were in the 1950s. Our evidence for this is anecdotal, but formidable, and hard won by the two of us and our associates. One reason for this change is more reliable birth control, which took so much of the fear of pregnancy out of sex. Another is the influence of feminism. The public celebration of the clitoris and vagina was an important, and very influential, moment in women's liberation.[11]

There is a great deal of evidence that other women, in other times and places, routinely expected to have orgasms from sex with a man. In 1929 the anthropologist Bronislaw Malinowski wrote a problematically titled book, *The Sexual Life of Savages in North-Western Melanesia*, that showed how and why this happened in the Trobriand Islands in what is now Papua New Guinea. In 1928 Margaret Mead had already reported the same satisfaction among Polynesian teenager girls in *Coming of Age in Samoa*. Mead and Malinowski were unusual in their time (and ours) in asking about sexual matters, and both became notorious because they had done so. In some places their books were banned, and in the 1960s Malinowski's *Sexual Life of Savages* could still only be read in the British Museum library by special request.[12]

Bronislaw Malinowski was the father of serious anthropology in Britain. During the First World War, his fieldwork in the Trobriand Islands transformed the discipline through a simple method. He lived in the village and learned the language. He listened and wrote down what everyone said. He liked to get the words right in every bit of gardening magic. He interviewed people, certainly, as anthropologists had before. But he also went to every ritual he could, and he sat and gossiped. There is a lovely picture of Malinowski squatting so he is on the same level as a group of children playing a game. He hung out—this is formally called 'participant observation'. And he was concerned not just with customs, but with whether people actually did what they said they did, and how often, and what happened when they did whatever it was, and whether people gossiped about it afterwards.

The basis of this method was respect. Malinowski found the Trobrianders very relaxed about sex compared to the people he was used to. The little children played all sorts of games, including a house game, where the boy and the girl lay together and had sex. Malinowski reassures the reader that girls in the game did not have penetrative sex before the age of eight. The parents heard about these games. When they talked to Malinowski about what their daughter was doing, they smiled, the way you do when your child puts on lipstick or pretends to cook.

By the time they were adults, they were pretty sure of themselves sexually. And Malinowski was impressed by how equal they were in their sexual lives, but also in the daily talk of husband and wife. He reports:

> Altogether the natives are certain that the white men do not know how to carry out intercourse effectively... Many a white informant has spoken to me about perhaps the only word in the native language which he ever learned, *kubilabala* ('move on horizontally'), repeated to him with some intensity during the sexual act...
>
> The natives regard the squatting position as more advantageous, both because the man is freer to move when kneeling, and because

the woman is less hampered in her responsive movements... Also in the squatting position the man can perform the treading motion (*mtumuta*), which is a useful dynamic element in a successful copulation. Another word, *korikikila*, implies at the same time rubbing and pushing...

As the act proceeds and the movements become more energetic, the man, I was told, waits until the woman is ready for orgasm. Then he presses his face to the woman's, embraces her body and raises it toward him, she putting her arms around him at the same time and, as a rule, digging her nails into his skin. The expression for orgasm is *ipipisi momona* = the seminal fluid discharges. The word *momona* signifies both male and female discharge. As we know, the natives do not make any sharp distinction between male semen and the glandular secretions of a woman... The same expression *ipipisi momona* is also applied to the (male or female) nocturnal pollution.[13]

Note four points here. Trobrianders use the same word for male ejaculations and female ejaculations. Both men and women have wet dreams. Men and women wait until both are ready to come. And sex lasts ten minutes or more.

Despite the shock their accounts provoked, Mead and Malinowski seemed to have it right. Then Mead's work on Samoa was discredited by the anthropologist Derek Freeman, who argued that her feminism led her to distort her field material. More recently Paul Shankman has vindicated her work in his forensic book *The Trashing of Margaret Mead*.[14]

The archaeologist Robert Suggs found the same routine expectation of female orgasms during careful research among Polynesians in the Marquesas in the 1950s and 60s. Similar accounts have now been gathered from many other places, including England in the seventeenth century.[15]

However, the English, Samoan, Trobriand and other examples do not mean that almost automatic male and female orgasms are more 'natural' than otherwise. All we really know is that for many women, at many times, routine orgasms did seem natural. This may be partly because those women assumed they would come, so they did. It may be partly because both women and men assumed that men would be skilled and considerate lovers, and so they were. It may be because women in those societies figured out how to diddle themselves during sex. It may well be a combination of all three.

These examples do not prove anything about orgasms among early humans in prehistoric times. Indeed, we know little about sexual satisfaction even among the egalitarian hunter-gatherers for whom we have records. More important, the present examples of sexual encounters come mostly from societies that had long been divided by class inequality. The Trobrianders and the Samoans had chiefs, and for most of the seventeenth century aristocrats dominated England. And there was gendered inequality in all these societies as well.

There is invariably gender inequality in class societies. And clearly this does not necessarily preclude female orgasms. Equally, however, female orgasms and sexual pleasure have been deliberately repressed in some class societies. One example is the often extreme forms of female genital mutilation. The idea and experience have also been inhibited psychologically in many societies, as we all know.[16]

The mistake those working from the American evidence make springs from ignoring the obvious—that the US is a society with extreme economic inequality and marked gender inequality. It is also culturally a particularly prudish society by contrast with, say, contemporary Europe or Latin America. And it is a society which assumes far less sexual desire among women. The United States is a bizarre place to look for examples of what is 'natural' about sex.

Moreover, Lloyd, the feminist philosopher, assumes that for the purposes of evolution real 'natural' sex is vaginal sex. She is not alone in doing so. Lloyd says, repeatedly, that the scholars who report orgasmic sex among modern human women are referring only to clitoral orgasms achieved with extra stimulation, and not to vanilla vaginal sex. Lloyd, and almost everyone else writing on the subject, assumes that although *Homo erectus* men and women could make clever tools two million years ago, they could not imagine using their fingers during sex. Indeed, these scholars seem to assume that even the people who did the cave paintings in Lascaux could not work this one out.

But if female orgasms are products, and not by-products—if they are linked to an adaptation, if they have an evolutionary purpose—what are the consequences of both sexes having similar orgasms most of the time? Put this way, there is an obvious answer. One consequence is increased equality between women and men. Let's explain why.

The evolutionary changes are several. Female people have orgasms from heterosex more easily than other female apes. For example, sex-mad bonobos reach orgasm easily in the female-to-female scissors position, and in mutual male masturbation, but females reach orgasm less easily with males.

In addition, human females have sex year-round, including when they are not ovulating. Male people also have orgasms far more often outside of the moments of female ovulation than male apes do. The comparison is striking. Many primates do have some heterosex outside of the period of ovulation, but the great majority of their heterosexual encounters happen around the time of ovulation. That's also true of bonobos.

Not only do humans have sex regardless of timing of female ovulation, it usually lasts longer than do sexual encounters among apes. All of which seems to mean that for human beings sex is likely to be important, and loom large, on any given day.

We mentioned earlier that most primatologists make an intuitive assumption that a desire for intense orgasms often disrupts pair bonding—the zipper problem. Certainly, there is a good deal of anecdotal evidence for this latter assumption. But there is also another possibility. We can just as easily suggest that human orgasms deepen and encourage all kinds of sexual relationships. They can reinforce both pair bonding and other sexual friendships. Sexual pleasure, day after day, may be what keeps two people together. And sexual pleasure as remembered, or anticipated, can be the glue that holds a whole band or village together. The Huaorani forest community in Ecuador described by Laura Rival and the Gond forest community in India described by Verrier Elwin provide good examples.[17]

Another consequence of wide, shared, constant orgasmic potential is that all human life becomes sexualised. It is not that everything becomes about sex per se, but that virtually everything has a sexual aspect, which may be more or less marked. This is true of the obvious things such as items of clothing, the shape of carrots and cigars, long yams, orchids, tent poles, water jugs and electrical sockets, but much more.

Indeed, all human relationships have a sexual aspect which may sometimes be conscious, sometimes unconscious, sometimes obvious and sometimes denied. This is so not just between lovers, but between mother and child, father and child, teacher and pupil, and in same-sex relations and friendships of all kinds. It is also true that every form of inequality, oppression and violence is saturated with sex. For orgasmic desire is not just about good vibes and kindness, it is about relationships and intensity however these are configured.

This is one of Freud's key uncomfortable insights, and it has become increasingly unavailable. So we need to be clear—what we are saying is not just that many things are gendered, but that they are also inflected with sexual desire.

The shared orgasmic potential can also deepen relationships between women and women, and between men and men. Precisely because human sex is not mainly about reproduction, it can energise many kinds of sex, and bring many kinds of people together. In each case, this equal orgasmic potential makes all individuals more equal. And that means, of course, it makes women and men more equal as well. Their desires are equal, their equipment is equal, and their practice can be equal.

We don't know which came first, hunting big game and the need to share meat, the dietary needs that led to shared childcare, or the extension of empathic love or human sexual passion. But there is an obvious synergy. As human relationships became saturated with sexuality, human sexuality could also become saturated with love. This does not mean people became monogamous. But it does mean we became a species where empathy, care and love of all kinds, and desire of all kinds, are intertwined in complex ways.

This leads us to a final thought about human sexuality. In almost every human culture on earth, people have sex where they cannot be seen by others. This is not true of any other primates. There are exceptions, of course. But those exceptions, like sex shows in Amsterdam or public sex in ancient Tahiti, were also exceptional moments in those cultures. They were, and are, exciting moments of transgression of an important rule.

In most cultures there is, typically, little comment about this rule. Social scientists haven't said much about it either. The rule is just there, obvious, and so invariant that it is probably part of our evolutionary heritage. But what is the evolutionary reason for this change?

The probable explanation is that it helped people to hide from any existing dominance hierarchy. Among chimpanzees, gorillas or baboons the dominant male spends a great deal of time on watch for other males having sex with a female he desires. Being secretive and hiding makes that harder. It is not that a potential dominant human male would not know. It is that the sex would not be in his face, an open challenge to hierarchy. Discretion and privacy around sex would fit with sharing meat and sharing childcare. They render any dominance hierarchy weaker, and females and males more equal.

Does that mean jealousy disappeared in human evolution? Give us a break. No. Accounts of contemporary and recent hunters and gatherers are full of male and female jealousy. There are plenty of women ranting and men muttering while they play with their arrows. But this jealousy is largely contained, because dominance and bullying are contained. The next chapter explains how humans faced the legacy of hierarchy and submission, which, in all but bonobos, favoured males. It was in the tension between these poles that humanity emerged. And we live with that tension now. The rest of this book traces how this has played out over time, paying special attention to the invention of 'natural difference' between humans, first and foremost on a gendered basis.

6

# HUMANS BECAME EQUAL BY OVERTHROWING THE DOMINANCE OF BULLIES

Now we come to a final important idea about evolution. Christopher Boehm is almost unique in writers on human evolution, in that he did his first fieldwork with European farmers in Montenegro, and his second with chimpanzees in Tanzania. The result is that he understands what both anthropologists and primatologists are talking about. The Montenegrins were by no stretch of the imagination hunter-gatherers. But his fieldwork meant that when Boehm came to write on human evolution, he paid careful, painstaking attention to the details of hunter-gatherer ethnography in a way that no previous primatologist or biological anthropologist had done.

Boehm came up with a new idea. Previous studies of primate and hunter-gatherer societies had asked whether humans were fundamentally peaceful and egalitarian, or fundamentally violent and competitive. Boehm said this was the wrong question. Instead, he saw chimpanzees, Americans, Montenegrins, and hunter-gatherers as all living with a constant tension between domination and equality. What human hunter-gatherers did, Boehm said, was confront this tension consciously and overthrow the alpha male.[1]

Boehm started by seeing that almost all primatologists had looked at domination, consciously or unconsciously, from the point of view of the dominant animal. But many male primates never become an alpha male. Even alphas have usually been dominated in their youth and will be dominated again once they lose their top ranking. Boehm said we had to look not just at domination, but also at submission.

If we look at what happens when primates submit, then we notice several things. First, these animals submit because they are afraid.

Habitual submission avoids fights, wounds and humiliation. But these animals resent having to submit to others. During confrontations they cry out, they shake, and they sit there afterwards in evident distress. They don't want to be bullied. And we have seen how chimps console their humiliated friends.[2]

Boehm suggested that what happened in human evolution was not that humans left behind the disposition to bully or submit to bullying. It was that humans overcame the system of domination. We became equal in the face of domination. And we did so by forming alliances with each other.

Forming alliances to compete for dominant status is common among primates. We have seen that it is a staple of male baboon and chimpanzee politics. A dominant male looks for allies to back him up in fights. A challenger also looks for allies to back him up. The successful alpha male at any one time is not necessarily the biggest, but the most canny.

What happened with early humans, Boehm says, was that the adults of a group formed a collective alliance against any possible alpha male. When any male tried to assert dominance over meat, cooked food, or sex, they stopped him. Boehm's suggestion explains a lot. We do know that hunter-gatherers in the last century were able to share meat without interference from an alpha male.

This is not a palaeo-fantasy. Neither Boehm nor we are suggesting that there was a revolution at one moment in prehistory and that society was different ever after. Rather, we are talking about a process that was repeated over and over again. It is a process evident from the new archaeology of early human societies. And we can see it continuing in the ethnographies over the last century.

Boehm has looked through the existing ethnographies of fifty groups of hunter-gatherers. For twenty-four of these societies, he has found cases where the community came together to kill a male bully. The way they do it is eerily similar across the world. The whole camp talks about it, quietly, in pairs or small groups. Then they decide, together, to do it. They always make sure all the man's close relatives are agreed, and all the men and women of the camp as well. Then they kill him, with weapons, by surprise. The killer is usually a close relative of the bully, but other camp mates sometimes join in.

## ... AND OVERTHROWING BULLIES

Boehm has found evidence of these killings in half the ethnographies. He suspects, and we agree, that with better records we would find such killings in almost all groups. As he points out, these killings were rare enough that they were unlikely to happen during the few months or years that an anthropologist was present. And an anthropologist would be unlikely to hear about what happened in the past unless he was looking for that kind of killing. Most ethnographers would not have thought to ask about such an event. Moreover, colonial authorities punished such killings severely, so people were well advised not to mention such matters to an anthropologist.[3]

Killing a bully is an extreme response to inequality. But other, more common habits also point to a constant tension between equality and hierarchy. In other words, the egalitarianism was not just the absence of domination. Hunters and gatherers constructed equality, insisted upon it, and kept harping on about it. They were explicit about this. They worked at making themselves equal.

In 1974, and again in 1996–7, the anthropologist Polly Wiessner recorded 308 different long conversations between groups of !Kung hunter-gatherers in the Kalahari. In 2005 she analysed those tapes, looking for occasions when people criticised someone present for behaving in an unequal manner. There were an average of seven people in each conversation, and those criticisms were designed to punish people for stepping out of line. Wiessner found that 193 of the 308 conversations included such collective criticism, sometimes about not sharing, but usually about what she called 'big-shot' behaviour.[4]

Richard Lee makes an interesting point in his ethnography of the !Kung.[5] One natural difference, Lee says, did threaten the equality that !Kung people valued. Men did the hunting of large animals. The problem here was not a divide between men and women. It was that a quarter to a third of men killed the great majority of the large game. Just as the distribution of athletic ability, hand–eye coordination and strength at your school was not uniform, so too some !Kung hunters were more physically gifted than others.

The !Kung had two main customary ways of dealing with this problem. As we saw earlier, one way of preserving equality was a system by which a hunter gave parts of the animal to his partner, her mother, and various other people. For the !Kung, this system effectively shared the meat among all members of the camp.

Second, the !Kung believed that men should never boast about hunting. Indeed, a skilled hunter was expected to return to camp and claim he had killed nothing. Then, under repeated questioning, he would admit that perhaps he had killed a small animal, but he was so weak he needed help carrying the game back to camp.

Others went with him to fetch the small animal. When they found his impressive kill, they would say things like: 'You mean you have dragged us all the way out here to make us cart home your pile of bones?' Or 'To think I gave up a nice day in the shade for this.'

The hunter should reply: 'You're right, this one is not worth the effort. Even a small antelope would be better than this mess.'

Then they all carry the animal home and eat their fill. As ǂTomazho, a famous healer, explained to Lee: 'When a young man kills much meat, he comes to think of himself as a chief or a big man, and he thinks of the rest of us as his servants or inferiors. We can't accept this. We refuse one who boasts, for some day his pride will make him kill somebody. So we always speak of his meat as worthless. In this way we cool his heart and make him gentle.'[6]

This deep commitment to egalitarianism was defined not in terms of equality, but against inequality. This makes sense. The !Kung lived their lives in opposition to the inequality of neighbouring farmers and the Botswana state. ǂTomazho was also aware that Lee, as an American and a white man, knew all about inequality. However, this sense of 'equality against' may also have been part of the values of hunters in a world of hunters.

Other groups of hunter-gatherers also had ways of cutting a tall poppy down to size. Around the world gentle ridicule was widely used to punish boasting or bullying. If that didn't work, brutal ridicule was used. Sometimes people were shunned. The anthropologist Jean Briggs wrote a wise book, *Never in Anger*, about how a band of Inuit on Baffin Island in the 1960s isolated her utterly because she was behaving like a pushy, bullying American. She describes how devastating that was, and how much she learned about how to be a decent person.[7]

It is also important that the !Kung and the Inuit raised their children to behave like equals. This did not mean that the kids were trained to assert themselves as demanding individuals. Rather, it meant children were listened and talked to, and gently educated into an understanding of mutual respect. Little children were almost never hit or physically disciplined. Rather, they were distracted in ways that made them attentive to others. None of these groups produced spoiled children. Quite the contrary, the children became tolerant and egalitarian adults like their parents.[8]

Crucially, in most hunting communities a child of six could move out of his or her parent's shelter to live with a grandmother elsewhere in the camp. A child could also move to her uncle's band elsewhere, or her aunt's, or his cousin's, for weeks or for months. Adults too changed bands for short or longer periods. Such free movement from one band to another was a crucial way of defusing tension and potential conflict. When things got heavy, people simply moved away. In most groups people had to have kinfolk to move to, but almost all bands they knew of included kin. Simply moving away also provided people with refuge when the food ran thin locally. And it made divorce easy. There was no ceremony—one partner simply upped and left.

The ease of leaving had deep consequences for the equality of women. Women and men owned nothing together, they had no bridal gifts to return, no land to divide and nothing to pass on to their children. Women could go when they wanted, where they wanted.

Of course, there were exceptions. Inuit in the Arctic found it extremely difficult to move for most of the year, because of the deep new-fallen snow and the terrible cold, and because the nearest neighbours might be hundreds of miles away. This may explain why the ethnographies of Inuit bands describe such careful controls on aggression, and such high levels of deadly violence when people snapped.[9]

Movement was one thing, but all these hunter-gatherers also shared. All the groups we know about shared all the meat of big game with everyone else in the camp. Typically, they did not eat in one big group. Instead, each household received a cut of raw meat and cooked it at their own hearth. In most places the meat was not simply divided—there were elaborate rules for who was given which pieces. These rules were a strategy against hierarchy. The highest status person did not get the best cut. So, for example, a Netsilik Inuit hunter would have eleven different 'seal meat' friends, each of whom was given one particular cut of the seal. In other societies, a man would give the kill to his wife's mother, who would then divide it up and give a share to everyone in the camp. In practice, of course, no actual camps contained the right number of mothers' sisters or seal flipper partners. But people worked around the rules to make sure everyone got some.

It is notable that this same insistent sharing is still found all around the world. People thank God for their daily bread, and would never eat in front of another person without offering them some. Sometimes when animals are sacrificed, a diagram of the distribution of the meat looks like a butcher's chart, with the prime cuts and tasty morsels given to people to mark special ties. On other ritual occasions, the important thing is to make a stew and make sure everyone is treated equally by eating out of one pot. Everywhere sharing food and drink is still ritualised. Equally, rituals depend on sharing food and drink, whether toasting the bride, blowing out the birthday candles, or sharing the body and blood of Christ in the celebration of Holy Communion.[10]

The sharing in hunter-gatherer societies was not simply generosity. People asked all the time for this and that. They complained all the time about the paltry share of meat they got, and what they had not been given. They often went on complaining the next day. The sharing was policed, but this was not a sign of oppression. Rather, it was a product of the commonly shared deep moral force behind it. And that moral force was mobilised collectively in conversation and gossip, not by any one individual. Within the household, over the one fire and the one pot, people did not share, in the sense of generosity and giving. They simply ate together.[11]

Much of the sharing in hunter-gatherer societies happens not because someone is generous, but because someone else is demanding. This 'demand sharing' is often reported by anthropologists, who almost always have more stuff than the hunter-gatherers they study, and who have not been raised to always share. Demand sharing also applies especially to goods from richer societies, like cigarettes and knives. The anthropologist Nicolas Peterson tells how an Australian Aboriginal friend showed him how to bury your cigarettes so your relatives could not find them. But demand sharing is common with food as well.[12]

## ... AND OVERTHROWING BULLIES

Among farmers and herders, too, vows, votive offerings and sacrifices have often been a formalised form of demand sharing. They create a moral obligation to share food by way of a spirit, saint or God.

Among hunter-gatherers, much else was shared between households too, and demanded, and grumbled about. Baldwin Spencer and Francis Gillen produced notable early accounts of the Aboriginal peoples of Central Australia. Spencer and Gillen complained that every time they gave a man clothes, the next week the man would be naked again, and his clothes would turn up on someone else, sometimes a day's walk away.[13]

In these societies, what you had, you gave. The idea of property was morally offensive. This was true of tools and weapons too. !Kung men, for instance, had special 'arrow friends'. In theory, the meat of big game belonged to the man whose arrow had killed it. But at any one time the majority of the arrows in a man's quiver would belong to other men, many of them a hundred miles away. So often an absent man was notionally giving the meat to an absent mother-in-law, while in fact the hunter's partner was sending her children round the camp in the dark with bowls of meat to be distributed. But men did go on long trips to visit their arrow friends, and those friends would take them in if times turned hard.

The ease of movement in and out of groups helped with equality in other ways. Colin Turnbull has described how among Mbuti pygmies people were constantly moving to join the band of a more skilled hunter. And then, at a certain point, the hunter and his partner would themselves move and leave them all behind, and the process would start again.[14] There was also, in many groups, a balancing out of rules about where couples lived. Among the !Kung, for example, and among the Hill Pandaram in Kerala, there were rules about the husband living in his wife's band and providing meat for her family. But there was often tension between the wife and the husband, each wanting to live near their own kin. In practice some couples lived here and some lived there.[15]

The constant moving served to produce equality. Young people might choose their own partners, or sometimes their parents would choose for them. But the young woman or man who did not like their partner could, and did, leave. Again, they held no property in common, and they could move because anyone could move. And because children could move from group to group, adults could either take their children or leave them behind with kin.

Some anthropologists, like Peter Gardner, have described such people as individualists, or as autonomous.[16] In one sense they are. They choose where they go, what they eat, what they spend their time doing each day and who they have sex with. From a young age, they are fiercely resistant to being told what to do. But in the usual meaning of the word 'individualist' in Europe, America, India or Australia, they are not individualists at all. They cannot refuse to share, ever. They are under constant supervision, not from their parents or their boss, but from everyone they know. They are expected to behave with decorum, dignity and consideration, and never boast.

*Language, Music, Brains and Equality*

Finally, there is one further kind of evidence to consider. If indeed people cooperated to control potential alphas, that would seem to be no small intellectual feat. The archaeologist Martin Jones dates the moment of the first 'feasts' to about 200,000 years ago.[17] It was then when people could cook food and eat it together, sitting around a fire in a circle in a group of ten or twelve. In a circle, he says, because there is a great deal of archaeological evidence that equal people sat in circles. We don't know why, but presume it was for the same reason Arthur's knights sat down at a Round Table. As Jones points out, if you sit in a circle, everyone can meet the gaze of everyone else.

We know that for any other animal, meeting the gaze of ten other animals is terrifying because it is too complex to keep track of. But for early humans, this became possible. Our brains were increasing in size as our social organisation became more complex, as hunting with weapons became more intellectually demanding, and as fire allowed us to spend energy saved in digestion on thinking instead. As our brains grew, we acquired the intelligence that enabled us to form increasingly complicated alliances to fight for power, until finally we had the intelligence to build broad alliances for overturning power itself.

## ... AND OVERTHROWING BULLIES

One might reasonably guess that language would be useful in forming and managing such a collective alliance, and that words were also important in creating a general agreement that people should be equal. Gossips could build that alliance with words, bit by bit.

Anthropologists do not necessarily disapprove of gossip. It's our bread-and-butter research method. Gossips can enforce oppressive discipline. But they can also share bedrock empathy. And with the coming of language, gossips with words could conceive of equality as an abstract principle.

Different writers have called such agreement 'morality' or 'culture'. We favour calling it 'ideology'. By ideology we mean any set of ideas used to justify a particular social order—in this case equality. We also mean a set of rules and moral prescriptions for how to behave to preserve that social order. Such ideas are expressed in stories, legends, proverbs, poetry, rituals and innumerable other ways. Such a shared ideology would have been immensely helpful in maintaining a collective consensus about the behaviours upholding equality.

Certainly, children in recent hunter-gatherer societies are taught to share. From a very young age, Aka pygmy children are taught to give food to other children and to ask for food. Among their first words are 'Give' and 'Take'. And in many places the children of hunter-gatherers are taught the self-reliance and sense of self-worth which are a central part of hunter-gatherer egalitarianism. This egalitarianism is consciously deployed against any dominant individual. It is also a way of insisting upon individual freedom, autonomy and constant sharing.

Besides language, and the abstract thought it encourages, the other striking intellectual achievements of humans are music, dance and art. Music and dance are collective activities in all hunter-gatherer societies. Among many groups there is singing many nights. When smaller bands come together in large numbers, it is party time. People eat great feasts together, and dance and sing through the night. Indeed, the neurological evidence suggests that we learned to sing and dance before we learned to use language.[18]

Robin Dunbar has suggested that music and dance also helped humans save energy. He points out that the most important way primates build alliances and hold groups together is mutual grooming. This means that many primates in large groups have to spend a considerable proportion of their lives in grooming pairs. With any more individuals in the group, this would cut into the time necessary to find food to survive. But several humans can sing and dance together, and by linking many individuals together at any one time, they have the possibility of forming larger alliances and groups. What song does for a pair of gibbons every morning it could do for a group of humans in the evening.[19]

Gibbon song and human singing have complex origins and are fundamentally different adaptations. But this doesn't take away from the fact that music, dance, ritual performances and trance states are an important aspect of our humanity. And religious—in the Latin sense of 'bringing together'—practices that bring us together, are found everywhere in human society. Many 'progressive' people have become hostile to religion, so it is worth taking a moment to explain the roots of religion in love.

We are social animals who have always depended on love for our survival. And when we lose this love, or when someone we love dies, we are bereft. Our loss is inconsolable. We are heartbroken and devastated that they are gone. And though we may learn to live with our grief, it never goes away. We remember, and relive our shared life with our child, our parent, our friend or lover who has gone for all time.

People everywhere and always have sought ways to cope with such loss: sometimes through prayer and memorials, sometimes through kindness to others, and sometimes through acts of terrible anger and revenge. Love, which we feel most acutely in the face of death, is the foundation on which our deep disposition to equality has been built. And it is a disposition we cannot escape because we cannot escape death.

Many Marxists, feminists and secularists are inclined to treat religious expression as a form of mystification. Or as offering solace in an unkind world, as the opium of the people and a form of compensation for oppression. Other people are happy to see spiritual experts commodify and retail bits of ancient wisdom in their search for well-being and mindful living.

Understanding religious beliefs and practices in such ways is not wrong. But it is wrong-headed. It downplays, and sometimes even denies, our need for love and the great pain we feel when love is lost. Nor do such critics do justice to the innumerable ways human beings try to manage their lives in the face of random luck and misfortune, happiness and sorrow. Dismissing religious practices does not help us explain the existence of good and evil, or inequality, or the fact that death is still with us.

How people die—peacefully in old age, tragically of illness, or of hunger, grief or violence—varies. So do the ways we explain these variations to ourselves. Of course, the details of how death occurs are gendered and hierarchical. So are our explanations of Why now? Why this way? Why him and not me? And, as we have all seen with the Covid-19 pandemic, in class societies the answers to these questions are stark measures of inequality.

But in the face of each death—our own, of someone close, or those we learn about from afar—we have the strongest evidence possible of our human disposition to equality. In the face of death, and in the rush of emotions which can overwhelm us, we are reminded of how important it is to share food with family and friends, and with hungry strangers; how important it is to cherish and care for the children in our lives and children everywhere; and how important it is to share laughter and tears and sexual pleasure.

*All in the Timing*

So, we have found plenty of evidence that human beings have, and have long had, a clear disposition toward equality. But what evidence can we offer that this—just like domination—is part of our hard wiring?

Is equality a recent conscious change? Or were these changes found among early humans long in the past? If the latter, there would have been time for egalitarianism to become part of our nature. A new way of doing things would, over time, have favoured a biological change towards humans who were generous and favoured equality.

Our answer is that we cannot be sure. The evidence of the fossil record simply does not tell us enough. And among the assorted experts, the jury is still out. There is also no consensus at all about when people began using language.[20]

# WHY MEN?

Of some things, however, we can be more confident. People have probably been cooking with fire for two million years. Sarah Hrdy is for pushing the change to shared childcare at least that far back as well. She argues that shared care was necessary to make the other adaptations of group hunting possible. From the records of hunter-gatherers and other human societies, it does look like shared childcare and the absence of infanticide by men may have become part of how humans 'naturally' did things.

It does seem from the anatomical evidence, and the evidence of prehistoric hearths and cooking, that ambush hunting, meat sharing, and sexual egalitarianism go back a long way. At least in some form, the mechanisms that enabled that combination must have been in place for at least 200,000 years, and perhaps for a million or more.[21]

Or perhaps less. Anatomically modern *Homo sapiens* developed in Africa about 200,000 years ago. But only 80,000 years ago there was a decisive moment in human history when modern humans left Africa and spread very rapidly across Asia, Europe and the Americas. It is possible that this was the moment when all the bits of the new adaptation came together.[22]

*Summarising the Egalitarian Argument*

Whatever else we know, we know that early humans adapted to a changing environment. They came out of the trees onto the plains, stopped relying on fruit, and became specialist ambush hunters. But they were not simply carnivores—roots, tubers, seeds, nuts, fish, shellfish and fruit were also important. They depended on a mixture of large game and more reliable foods.

The diet required both hunting *and* gathering. Because hunting big game was unreliable, humans were much more likely to survive if they shared meat within a band. But this sharing of food would have been far harder, probably impossible, in a world of silverbacks and alpha males. So people overthrew the domination that was their primate heritage. This was new. Even bonobos did not overthrow domination, just male domination.

Humans were also able to breed much more successfully because they shared childcare. Moreover, women, not men, controlled infanticide. That meant women of breeding age could be much more productive and raise more children in a lifetime than other apes. This again contributed to equality within the band. And it changed the emotional lives of early men to become more nurturing and more like early women. People lived longer and elders were valued for childcare and their wisdom and knowledge.

Humans changed sexually as well. Female and male orgasms grew more alike, and orgasms became continuously important to all humans. This too made men and women more equal, and it deepened emotional ties of many kinds.

These changes were both embodied and collective—people experienced their bodies together. Centrally, they shared food, childcare and sex, and all these were both sensual and social experiences. The greatest excitement and pleasure for people in most societies around the world is a party with food, sex, music, dancing and little kids running around.

This does not mean we became automatically egalitarian. Several features of hunter-gatherer societies suggest that it was not simply an absence of inequality, but an assertion of equality that made the difference. We have seen recent hunter-gatherers insist, again and again, on equality as a social value by saying that they will not allow one man to dominate. But perhaps they are also explaining equality as a continuing contest. For they also, again and again, have a whole panoply of habits that mock any attempt at domination. They tease, they ridicule, and they isolate. Because they can pick up and move, they do so to avoid bullies. And if necessary, they kill.

In short, it seems we did develop a disposition to equality, and we also created ideologies of equality. But we also carried with us a primate legacy of hierarchy and submission, which, in all but bonobos, favoured males. It was in the tension between these poles that humanity emerged. And we live with that tension now. The rest of this book traces how this has played out over time, paying special attention to the invention of 'natural difference' between humans, first and foremost on a gendered basis.

PART TWO

# THE INVENTION OF INEQUALITY

We have seen how human beings became equal. Part Two explains how, after the invention of agriculture, some groups of people were able to gain control of far more than their fair share of the food, leading to hierarchies of status and material comfort. We explain why that went hand in hand with male domination over women, a glorification of violence and competition, and multiple ideologies of 'natural' difference and superiority. And we also shine a light on the persistence of instincts towards equality and cooperation and how people in class societies have continued to resist.

7

## AGRICULTURE, PREDATORY ELITES AND CLASS

We have seen how we made ourselves equal in the process of becoming human. Then, starting 12,000 years ago, human beings invented agriculture in several different places. Agriculture and food surpluses made it possible for bullies to shape and dominate farming communities. One class of people, an elite, could enjoy the food other people grew and the goods other people made. And with food now tied to a settled place, there wasn't much those other people could do about it.

It took millennia before states based on grain agriculture dominated human lives around the globe. Over this long history many different class societies rose and fell. Like equality, inequality was something that people made. And with the material inequality of class societies, we find lasting patterns of gendered inequality as well.

The link between the rise of class societies, gender inequality, male dominance and all manner of 'isms' is central to our thesis. We address how and why this came about in the next two chapters. But our first task is to describe the character of class societies and dispel some of the myths around them.

The nineteenth-century Social Darwinian version of human evolution continues to dominate mainstream histories and popular media tales. That version posits stages of social development: hunter-gatherers domesticated animals and variously became herders, nomadic pastoralists and slash-and-burn agriculturalists. Only later did people invent grain agriculture, cities and civilisation. Social Darwinians believed that the economic stages coincided with stages of sexual control, from group sex to monogamous Christian marriage. And these stages were believed to coincide with a pro-

# WHY MEN?

gression from superstition and magic to animism, polytheism, the monotheism of ancient Hebrews, and finally Christianity. All this went with the idea that warfare was natural to men whose inherent aggression must be tamed by civilised rule.

What actually happened reverses this sequence. In reality, after thousands of years when all early humans were hunter-gatherers, agriculture began. Grain agriculture came first, and with it came cities, class and gender inequality. At first, farming was usually rain-fed, and began with the cultivation of grains. Then, once people had the idea that plants could be domesticated, they moved on to domesticate animals. Of course, dogs had become our friends long ago, but they were not kept for food. Nomadic pastoralists came later, and later still, some people moved on to slash-and-burn farming in the forests. And the to-and-fro between class and non-class societies was a feature of human society from the start. This oscillating history contradicts completely the Social Darwinian ideas about a straightforward and ever-upward march of progress.

Agriculture was independently developed in several different places, including:

— Some 12,500 years ago barley, wheat, emmer and flax were grown in the 'Fertile Crescent' in what are now the states of Turkey, Syria, Iraq, Iran, Lebanon, Israel/Palestine, Jordan and Egypt.
— Between 6,500 and 10,000 years ago sago and yams were cultivated in New Guinea. Exceptionally, there was no grain agriculture.
— Between 8,000 and 10,000 years ago potatoes and squash were cultivated in the Andes where the domestication of alpacas and llamas did precede farming.
— Some 8,000 years ago millet and rice were domesticated in China.
— And 7,500 years ago maize, beans and squash were grown in Mesoamerica, the name given to what is southern Mexico and the states of Central America.

From these early centres, the idea of farming spread around the world. But class society did not automatically follow. In some places, people sometimes farmed for thousands of years before they developed classes and states.

## AGRICULTURE, PREDATORY ELITES AND CLASS

The growth of class society was never straightforward, linear or simple. No group of farmers would tolerate the seizure of their crops if they did not have to. Rather, coalitions of bullies took food away from their neighbours and claimed elite status for themselves or their masters. But elites could lose control or be overthrown. Class societies rose, but they also fell. In forests, up in the hills, on islands or in the middle of swamps or deserts, people defended their equal societies. Exploited people constantly ran away, and landlords and states made regular raids into the hills and steppes to bring back slaves and prisoners. This to-and-fro process lasted 10,000 years. Remarkably, it is only in the last hundred years that people everywhere in the whole world have been brought under the control of class societies.[1]

While class society was not an automatic product of agriculture, farming and the control of food surpluses was crucial to this oscillation between unequal class societies and more egalitarian communities. Agriculture provided a surplus that an elite and their enforcers could easily get their hands on. Farmers are tied to the land, always captive to the current year's crop. They are also held in place by the labour they have invested over many years in clearing fields, planting hedges and building terraces, walls and irrigation channels. Unlike hunter-gatherers, farmers cannot easily flee when the soldiers arrive.

Class societies were, and are, particularly associated with grain agriculture. Grains are seeds, and seeds are a source of concentrated calories and nutrition. The main grains people grew in the early millennia of agriculture were wheat, maize and rice. Less widely cultivated were quinoa, barley, rye, millet and sorghum. Grain agriculture was particularly productive because farmers used selective breeding in two ways. Strains were selected that produced a larger number of seeds, and they were also developed so that the whole crop could be harvested all at once. However, harvesting an entire crop in one day, or even over two weeks, also made grain farmers vulnerable and more easily controlled than communities acquiring their food all year round through hunting, digging for tubers, gathering honey and foraging for fruit, seeds and nuts.

Storage was perhaps the most important element in this equation. Grains can be stored, often for years. On the one hand, farmers themselves sought the means to store their harvest, both to feed themselves and to ensure that they had seed corn for the following year. So, the farmers' own grain stores could easily be seized, and the harvest stolen. And when grain was stored by a feudal lord or local ruler, granaries became a form of wealth. That grain can be traded, but also hoarded to control hungry people.

The land used for agriculture was also crucial to the emergence of class societies. High yields, fertile lands and extensive irrigation systems all meant that more people could live in a smaller area. Larger and denser populations made enforcement and hunting down runaways easier. Riverine settings were important too. Armed parties, and whole armies, could move downriver, and even upriver, far more swiftly than they could move across land.[2]

*What Archaeologists Can Now See*

The archaeologists Kent Flannery and Joyce Marcus write powerfully in *The Creation of Inequality* about the rise and fall of class societies. They tell us what can be known from changes over time to burial practices, building sizes and styles, hearths and middens. Because class societies and agricultural production are so intimately related, prime locations near rivers and the rich alluvial soils of floodplains were often inhabited continuously for millennia. This means that archaeologists can literally dig down into the past, uncovering successively earlier layers, one below the other. Now, thanks to chemical microanalyses, DNA sampling and radiocarbon dating, it is possible to see something, if not quite the day-by-day lives, of earlier inhabitants, the changes they experienced year by year, and other changes over decades and centuries.[3]

One remarkable thing about such sites—the tepes and tells of Mesopotamia, or the iron-age villages and forts of Europe, or the great stone ruins of Mesoamerica—is the to-and-fro of their histories. Among the people living in a particular village, there may have been considerable inequality for a period of perhaps 300 years. Then, for whatever reason, the class hierarchy collapsed, and the lives of the people who remained were clearly far more equal. Then, after perhaps another 200 years, the pendulum swings back. The elite and their hench-folk again dominate the landscape, until they too eventually lose their grip, and another period of equality follows.[4]

## AGRICULTURE, PREDATORY ELITES AND CLASS

It is not a stretch to suggest that dramatic changes in burial practices are associated with dramatic changes in social relations. In some cemeteries everyone—children and adults, women and men—is buried in similar modest graves. Perhaps the body has been painted red, and a few tools or decorations buried next to it. These graves suggest a considerable degree of social equality. In another period, some people but not others were buried in rich clothing, next to piles of trade goods and sacrificed pets and retainers.

The size of buildings is another pretty sure marker of equality or hierarchy. Within the same village or town site, archaeologists may find that the houses are all of the same basic design, and much the same size. Then, at a certain point, they see new larger buildings appear. Sometimes the larger structure seems likely to have been a manor house, with a big dining hall. Sometimes it is just one big room with a small chamber behind. Archaeologists think these may have been temples with a vestry where the priests could change and store ritual paraphernalia. And sometimes, high walls surround the bigger buildings, or walls and palisades protect the town.

Other clues lie in the shapes of buildings. During periods of relative equality everyone lives in the same kind of small houses, and the floor plans are usually circular. But when larger buildings appear, these new buildings are often rectangular. At about the same time, the smaller houses around them often become rectangular too. The most likely reason for such changes had to do with how people ate together. As we saw, hunter-gatherers shared food, and ate together, typically in circles with no head of the table and no one set apart. Just as important, when people sit in a circle, everyone has a clear view of every other person. No one is hidden, no one is relegated to a corner. Equality was enacted and reinforced through commensality. And at feasts and on other occasions where larger numbers of people gathered, the same principle applied, and groups of people ate together in smaller dining circles.[5]

But the archaeology also affords us records of hierarchical feasts, and how commensality rules changed. Eating circles became, over time, meals where everyone ate, but in a rectangular room, with a top table which might be raised above the others. In such cases, while it seems clear that everyone in the community was included, what the archaeologists uncovered seems to suggest that an individual or a family were the host or owners of the feast. Then there comes a time when only some people are invited to a meal, and others are not. And when inequality is at a pitch, some elites are often screened off, or set apart, so others cannot see them eating.

Such are the signs in the archaeological record of class society. And there is one more. The people who are buried with lavish grave goods were often healthier, bigger and better fed than the people who were buried with little or nothing. For until very recently, power in class society was overwhelmingly power over food.

To be clear, we understand 'class' as those social relationships between people which are culturally elaborate and systematic, and in which some people use violence to get and control more than their share of the food.

*Power over Food*

Hunter-gatherers shared food. Fundamental to the understanding of social class is the idea that some people live off the work of others. For most of the history of class societies, the main product of that labour was food. Until quite recently, growing and processing food accounted for most human labour across the board. If you add in the work of building shelters, making basic farming, hunting and fishing tools and one or two sets of clothes, these products account for most human consumption too.

Because food production involved a great deal of hard work, until the nineteenth century and the industrial revolution, almost everywhere the great majority of people in a society, women and men, worked on the land—growing food, fishing or herding animals.

A small minority of the population constituted the elite. Perhaps they were royalty with an aristocratic circle and temple priests around them. Perhaps they were feudal lords, or khans, supported by vassals and smaller landlords. Whatever this elite was called, they and their families took a share of the crops that the farmers grew. They ate some of the food themselves. Some they used to feed the thugs and soldiers who enforced their power. Part of the crop they used to feed the expert craftspeople who made the weapons, textiles and trade goods they needed. And some went to the people who supported the apparatus of the fiefdom or state—the local priests, the scribes, judges, jailers, innkeepers, waiters, servants, jugglers, acrobats, poets, water bailiffs, stonemasons, carpenters, tailors and many more.

The surplus could be taken from the farmer through taxes, rent, debt, slavery, serfdom or sharecropping. The farming families' compliance was assured by their need to care for and protect each other—by the disposition to love that egalitarian adaptation had bequeathed to all humans. The exploiters also depended on nesting structures to keep control, so that overthrowing one landlord would not overthrow the system. The village landowner, the more powerful landlord who controlled several villages, and the great lord of a region all took their share. The king too might expect a share in the crop, rent or tax. A great king or an emperor could expect tribute from the lesser kings. Yet despite the class inequality we describe here, it is important to remember that the abiding paradox at the heart of our human nature also means that at each level, from top to bottom, from rich to poor, both men and women were invested in the system of inequality through love.

Farmers and other common people could pay over what they owed the great lord as a share in kind, in money, or in labour. We know from a wide variety of sources from different times and places—tax records, legal settlements, merchants' accounts, hagiographies and histories—that shares in the harvest, or their equivalent, were divided in many different ways. Sometimes as little as one fifth of the crop went to the farmer, sometimes a half or two thirds, while the landlord took the rest. In many places, there were small landlords who lived in the village themselves. They might work their own fields and let out a few fields to sharecroppers. Or employ one agricultural labourer year-round but hire gangs of women at harvest time. Such local landlords were very important to the defence of the system of exploitation because they knew everybody and saw everything. They knew which woman was outspoken and stirring up her neighbours, and which families were vulnerable and could be pushed further and harder.

In other class systems, slaves worked the land. But slaves were expensive to buy, to keep and to control. Serfs, tied to a village and forbidden to leave, could work three or four days a week on their own plots of land, and two or three days a week on the lord's land.

## WHY MEN?

Or tenant farmers could pay a fixed rent for the land, measured in so much grain, or three chickens and a piglet, or twelve long iron nails, or some fixed amount of money. Some people could work for wages: as a ploughman, milkmaid, shepherd, cowboy or harvest hand.

These different ways of splitting the crop were not stages in human progress. Here, rent might be dominant. There, agricultural labour might be done by serfs or slaves, or by women and men working for wages. But in most class societies of any scale, from ancient Mesopotamia on, we see that the elite use a mixture of forms of exploitation.[6]

There was, and continues to be, no end to the ways people can be taxed. There was corvée labour, when households or villages were expected to supply so many men or women for so many days to work the king's land, repair the irrigation system, fight locusts, build a road or carry loads for the army. There are tithes, sacrifices, Islamic waqf and Christian alms. Sometimes contributions to the church, the mosque, the temple or the priest were voluntary, but often they were backed up by brute force.

And there was debt, from the beginning of class society. A farming household may run short of food while they wait for the next harvest to ripen. Or they may find themselves with an unexpected expense and have to hire or buy an ox or a horse for their plough. They might want to finance a son's wedding or provide their daughter with a dowry. At such times people have to borrow, and when the crop comes in, they pay back more than they borrowed. This 'interest' sets up a cycle, and debt in every peasant society is a downward spiral. It is the way that small inequalities between peasant households, often accidents of inheritance or of the number of sons and daughters, are transformed into utter ruin. Debt is also, as David Graeber has brilliantly reminded us, a way that the brute force of exploitation becomes a moral obligation. At the end of the cycle, the peasant loses the land, and is sometimes forced to give himself, herself, or one of their children into slavery. However, serfs, slaves and anyone else who could, fled hierarchy and injustice.[7]

In short, in class societies from the beginning until the mid-nineteenth century, most people farmed and produced food. A minority took far more than their share of food. But to do this, the rich minority needed enforcers to bully people into giving up that

## AGRICULTURE, PREDATORY ELITES AND CLASS

food, or its equivalent in labour or goods, a body of armed men to put down uprisings and an organisation that held them together and represented their collective interests as a class. Whatever the elite were called—perhaps they were royalty, high priests, feudal lords, or a senate of great landowners—they needed the power of the leadership to be upheld through violence.

It was not just that the rich took more food. The new class order meant that the majority of people, adults and especially children, were much less well-nourished than people before the invention of agriculture. Archaeologists with many new technologies at their fingertips are now finding evidence of this from the bones and teeth of skeletons from ancient towns all over the world.[8]

*Weapons and Warfare*

In whatever age, from the beginning of class societies onwards, the force that kept class order within a state also created the possibility of that city-state or kingdom conquering others. It was rare for a chieftainship or kingdom to be stable for long and there was no easy way to avoid warfare being generalised over time and space.

The existence of warfare also drove two other processes whereby class societies changed over time. Innovations in weaponry and forms of military organisation enabled a city-state to conquer others, or perhaps just take some of their land. Such innovations often followed from other technologies which transformed warfare: first horses, then saddles, then stirrups; first wheels and then chariots. Axes and bows became lances, maces and crossbows; stone weapons became bronze, iron and then steel. Armour became the man on a heavy charger; stone walls then round towers; the war galley then the warship; gun powder then muskets, cannon and bombs. The kingdoms which first developed these new technologies came blazing across history. But their neighbours and their enemies soon learned to copy them and to improve and change their defences. But almost always, the movement of the technological frontier was in one direction—toward more killing.

The second dynamic introduced by warfare was the drive to create a greater surplus within each state. That surplus did not only go on the hobbies and pleasures of the families of the rich. The kingdom with a larger surplus could put more soldiers into the field. More important, they could use the surplus to raise more horses and bigger horses, and to mine more metal for smiths to forge into weapons. The longer the campaign, the further the reach of the armies; and the longer the siege, the more important were the logistics of supply, of horses and camels, carts and forage, bread and tents and camp followers.

The kingdom that could bring their innovations and their surplus to bear would take land and captives, win wars and even become an empire. This made innovations in work important. Of course, different class societies got to different places at different times in counting and geometry, sailing skills, irrigation, crop varieties, milling and the organisation of labour. But everywhere the need to win battles drove technological development in the economy as it does today.

Innovation fostered success, but so did brutal exploitation. As we have said, for a very long time, the majority of the population worked on the land, but yields were low, and this allowed only a small surplus. That meant constant pressure on lords and kings to squeeze more surplus out of those who did the work.

The impetus to warfare and to increase surplus foodstuffs rests on a constant contradiction. A ruler had to extort as much surplus as possible. But for much of the history of class society, it was not that difficult for people to run away. The obsession of rulers for centuries was not with the conquest of land, but with the conquest of people: captives and slaves who could be moved onto the land to replace the runaways. And the more brutal the rule and the exploitation, the more people would vote with their feet.

Even when people could not run away, they could rebel. The king and lords who pushed their people too hard could find themselves overthrown. Or peasants, slaves or shepherds dragged their feet and supplies ran out. The rulers of a cruel imperial power would find the neighbouring ruler conspiring to bring them down. Because the king or emperor relied on lesser lords, the king's younger brother or a king on the other side of the mountains could offer the lords a less onerous tax regime and entice them to betray their liege.

There was a constant tension in the politics of every class society. On the one hand, there was the necessity of raising fighting men, and procuring food and arms. On the other hand, the necessity of

# AGRICULTURE, PREDATORY ELITES AND CLASS

keeping the working people and the lesser lords on side. It is this tension that creates the constant succession of weak and strong kings and a chequerboard of kingdoms in every history. This dichotomy lies behind the endless Game of Thrones, for no ruling elite ever gets the balance right for long.

Some elites found it relatively easy to maintain their power with the technology and surplus they could command. And when kingdoms did splinter, new pretenders were often on hand to put things back together. But at other times, such struggles led to defeat. They could create a 'dark age', a label given by later elites to a period when ordinary people could escape tyranny and were able to keep most or all of the food they grew. On the scale of centuries, the rise and fall of kingdoms and empires has meant the arrow of history has never flown straight or only in one direction.

Increasing exploitation can be kept at bay, or rolled back, for generations. But over and above the constant struggle between hierarchical domination and egalitarian resistance, these first thousands of years of class society have seen it endure—and, ultimately, become near universal. One reason is that new knowledge is never really lost. Another is that the more efficient the exploitation and the more innovative the machinery of killing, the greater the reach of the empire. Over time, class society moved out from the great river valleys onto the plains and steppes, the lower hills, the nearer forests, and in from the coasts and harbours, across deserts and around the world. Over time, the logic of warfare was also inexorable. Militarisation and the accumulation of surplus have greatly accelerated in the capitalist era. Escape became harder and there were fewer places to hide. This meant that more and more people have had no alternative but to join the class struggle wherever they have found themselves.

*And Herders and Pastoralists—Where Do They Fit In?*

The Social Darwinian sequence of human evolution is familiar and accounts not just for ruling-class privilege and power but also for how the great unwashed have been scorned by elites since the beginning of time. The sequence is part of the naturalising myth of class societies. Abel was the couth youth and careful farmer, Cain, the

113

murderer, was red and hairy, an untamed hunter. However, the sequence is a fiction. If anything, the murderous antagonism worked the other way round.

The Social Darwinians also got the order wrong with respect to the relation between the rise of agriculture and specialist nomadic herders and mobile pastoralists. Except in the Andes, animal husbandry only evolved after farming began. Most herders and pastoralists, like cowboys and ranchers today, got at least half their daily calories, and usually much more, from food crops.

Many pastoralists were, and are, people on the margins. Reindeer herders in the Arctic, and the Nilotic cattle people along the great rivers of East Africa were remote from class control. Famously, many of the Nilotics were among the 'tribes without rulers'. They were warlike, fiercely egalitarian cattle-thieves with ideologies of male dominance, although gender relations in practice were blended and complex.[9]

Animal husbandry also figured in the lives of the people who used horses to hunt. The typecase here were the hunters of the North American plains. Their mobility was clearly envied, if we are to believe the indiscriminate branding of cars and trucks as Thunderbirds, Chieftains, Cherokee and Cheyenne. Their horses were, of course, domestic animals and they lived on a continent where there had been grain agriculture, hierarchy and empires for thousands of years. Like the Nilotic cattle, the horses invited theft. Where people cannot control a surplus, or a range, they can still steal cattle and horses. Native North Americans on the plains were mostly egalitarians with warfare and enormously varied ways of managing gender relations, a subject we return to in Chapter 14.

Finally, we need to mention the great pastoralist peoples from North Africa, the Sahel, Middle East, Iran, Afghanistan, Central Asia and Mongolia. Though culturally diverse, these specialists in animal husbandry are integral to class societies based on agriculture. Sometimes the pastoralists also have their own fields, sometimes they trade meat or milk for grain. Indeed, the anthropologist Emanuel Marx has argued that in the Middle East, most pastoralists have from time immemorial made a living by supplying meat to the cities.

In spite of the romantic images of veiled Tuareg men, Bedouin patriarchs and aggressive, orientalist brand names for vehicles like

# AGRICULTURE, PREDATORY ELITES AND CLASS

Nomad, Qashqai and Kadjar, these pastoralists haven't wandered over the face of the earth. Some move from well to oasis to well in a fixed cycle. Others may move vertically up a Himalayan peak in summer and come back down with the cold weather. Or they may cross great distances, feeding their animals in the lowlands in winter, then moving to high pastures in summer, only to return to the lowlands again in the autumn. Whether they move up and down one mountain, or travel hundreds of miles, they follow established migration routes, finding friends, trading partners and access to water and pasture along the way. Sometimes their mobility enabled them to elude the tyranny and taxes of states and empires. At other times, they became the frontier guards or recruiting ground for state or imperial troops. And it seems that gender relations within these pastoralists varied considerably, both along class lines and according to how tightly they were tied to the state.[10]

*Uruk*

We close this chapter with one example of an ancient state. Uruk was the leading city in the first civilisation in history. A 'civilisation' is usually defined as a city with a state, writing and full-time bureaucrats.

Uruk was one of a large number of small city-states in Mesopotamia between 3500 and 3100 BCE. Most of that region is now in Iraq. Mesopotamia literally means the 'land between the rivers'. In the north of Mesopotamia two great rivers flowed south to the Persian Gulf, the Euphrates on the west and the Tigris on the east. Between the rivers was land that provided the possibility of some rain-fed farming. But along the rivers irrigation made possible yields two or three times as great.

At the southern end of Mesopotamia the rivers came close together, and then spread out into a delta. Here the alluvial soil was very rich, and there were great marshes with shallow water and reeds. Uruk was on the edge of these marshes. It was just north of what is now the city of Basra. The sea level was much higher 5,000 years ago, and so the delta and the marshes were much further north than now.

In the twentieth century, the consensus view of ancient Mesopotamia was that class society had produced states there because irrigation made possible a much larger surplus. The cities, and the surrounding countryside, were dominated by temples. There was no market competition. In the extreme cases, these were powerful, entrenched, almost totalitarian religious states.

In the last forty years scholars have produced a new understanding. The reality was more complex. Uruk certainly was a place of rigid socio-political hierarchy and material inequality. But any such place will be filled with many more subjugated commoners than elite rulers—and there is evidence that the story of Uruk and ancient Mesopotamia was a tale not only of domination, but of the dominated fighting back.

Uruk became pre-eminent among the many little states because of a series of innovations. First, there was the increased productivity of irrigation agriculture. Then bronze was invented in about 3,500 BCE. Bronze is a mixture of copper and tin, and it provided much stronger and more useful weapons than copper ever had. From then on, history left behind the New Stone Age and became the Bronze Age.

For the ruling class in Uruk, the problem was that they did not invent bronze. Moreover, they had no copper or tin. There were small mines for copper hundreds of miles to the north, but much of the copper and all of the tin had to come from Herat, 2,000 kilometres away, and Badakhshan, 3,000 kilometres away in what is now Afghanistan. That meant they needed commodities to trade north.

They found a solution in the manufacture of woollen textiles. They grazed large herds of sheep, mainly for wool, and cattle, mainly for milk, in the marshes. The sheep and cattle both ate the reeds. The city also traded with pastoralists in the open steppe to the west and east of the delta.

The wool was then processed and taken to the weaving sheds, where women and children produced textiles. Guillermo Algaze, the leading historian of Uruk, writes that 'labor was provided by entirely or partly dependent women providing periodic services to the state-organized weaving establishments, or, most commonly, by fully dependent women and their children receiving rations, who laboured year-round in state-organized establishments under the supervision of overseers'.[11]

Fully dependent women and their children means enslaved women and children. Mesopotamian specialists are careful with the

## AGRICULTURE, PREDATORY ELITES AND CLASS

terms they use for different kinds of labourers, because they are not sure what the rules were. But there appear to have been more or less free labourers in the countryside. There were also partly dependent people, whose status was unsure, but may have been subject to forced labour part of the year. Fully dependent people were a lot like slaves. Some of these slaves were captives in war, and some were the children of slaves. But poor people could also find themselves enslaved for a period of years to pay off a debt, and poor parents also sold their children into slavery.[12]

There were four centres of ruling-class power in Uruk, and the other city-states. One was the main temple in the city. The second was the palace, the king and his army. The third were often family firms of long-distance traders. The traders were in competition with other traders, at home and in other cities, to make profits. The temples and the palaces competed to make goods more cheaply and wage war more successfully. The fourth main centre of power was the 'elders of the city', probably affluent men, traders and landlords. Andrea Seri, in a useful study of *Local Power in Old Babylonian Mesopotamia* suggests that a network of ruling-class families linked all these sectors, and she is probably right.[13]

Algaze's population estimates suggest that at the height of Uruk's power, about half of the population were working in the weaving sheds or in other jobs connected with preparing wool and textiles. By 3200 BCE, a good deal more than half of the population of Uruk were living in the city. Algaze also argues that Uruk became the leading power among all the city-states because the state and the traders were able to produce woollen textiles for export more cheaply than other competing centres. Other scholars of the period disagree with Algaze, but we find his evidence convincing, not least because he gives full weight to material and ecological considerations.

Algaze's understanding points to the importance of industrial competition, sheep, transport, rivers and long-distance trade. Uruk built and defended colonies for trading along the Tigris and Euphrates far to the north, to control the trade in copper and tin, but also an extensive trade in wool and many other goods. They exported expensive woollen textiles and clothing in return. For a period, the combination of trade and the textile industry made Uruk an enormously powerful city-state, all of it built on the labour of the women and children in the weaving sheds.

# WHY MEN?

And how did the women and children feel about this? It is hard to know, but we have some clues. There are some bits of evidence about how oppressed people in the same region felt later in history.

More than a thousand years after the zenith of Uruk's power, someone wrote down the story of Gilgamesh, a legendary king of Uruk. It begins:

> Gilgamesh went abroad in the world, but he met with none who could withstand his arms till he came to Uruk. But the men of Uruk muttered in their houses, 'Gilgamesh sounds the tocsin for his amusement, his arrogance has no bounds by day or night. No son is left with his father, for Gilgamesh takes them all, even the children; yet the king should be a shepherd to his people. His lust leaves no virgin to her lover, neither the warrior's daughter nor the wife of the noble; yet this is the shepherd of the city, wise, comely, and resolute.'[14]

'This is the shepherd of the city, wise, comely, and resolute,' is said with rage and irony.

We can also hear, echoing down the centuries, the voice of Hebrew captives in Babylon 2,000 years later. This is Psalm 137 in the King James translation of the Bible:

> By the rivers of Babylon, there we sat down, yea, we wept, when we remembered Zion.
>
> We hanged our harps upon the willows in the midst thereof.
>
> For there they that carried us away captive required of us a song; and they that wasted us required of us mirth, saying, Sing us one of the songs of Zion.
>
> How shall we sing the LORD's song in a strange land?
>
> If I forget thee, O Jerusalem, let my right hand forget her cunning.
>
> If I do not remember thee, let my tongue cleave to the roof of my mouth; if I prefer not Jerusalem above my chief joy.
>
> Remember, O LORD, the children of Edom in the day of Jerusalem; who said, Raze it, raze it, even to the foundation thereof.
>
> O daughter of Babylon, who art to be destroyed; happy shall he be, that rewardeth thee as thou hast served us.

## AGRICULTURE, PREDATORY ELITES AND CLASS

Happy shall he be, that taketh and dasheth thy little ones against the stones.

Well, there you have it! That's how the conquered and the captives in that part of ancient Mesopotamia felt about their overlords: happy shall he be who takes and dashes your little ones against the stones.

We also have one account of a workers' uprising in ancient Mesopotamia. It's a myth, and it's about the gods, but the people who told this story, and the people who listened, understood why workers would be angry and what their protests looked like.

The myth of Atrahasis was written down in Babylon in the seventeenth century BCE, 1,300 years after the fall of old Uruk. It begins with the story of the time before the existence of humans, when the great gods ruled and the lesser gods did the drudgery of work.[15]

The lesser gods worked in the ditches. They dug out the whole length of the Tigris River, and then the Euphrates. They dug the wells and the whole irrigation system, and they 'heaped up all the mountains'.

'Years of drudgery, and forty years, too much. Forced labor they bore night and day. They were complaining, denouncing, muttering down in the ditch.' Then someone said that they must 'take off their heavy burden'. They must march and to the house of the great god Enlil, surround him and pull him out of his house.

'Call for battle!' one of the ringleaders said. 'Battle let us stir up, warfare!'

The lesser gods burned their spades and workbaskets and marched off. In the dark of night they surrounded the house of the great god Enlil. 'But the god did not know.'

When Enlil did find out, he sent out his enforcers to instruct the lesser gods to go back to work. They refused and created a great din. The enforcers asked who the ringleader was, the instigator of war and hostilities.

'They were defiant, the labor gang.' They said: 'Every one of us has declared war. We formed our group in the ditch. Drudgery has killed us, our forced labor was heavy, our misery was too much.'

And so the great gods held a meeting, and decided they could not fight the lesser gods. Instead, they negotiated a solution. The great gods made men to replace the lesser gods as forced labour.

## WHY MEN?

But there was a twist. The great gods found out who the ringleader of the protest was—a lesser god named Aw-ila. 'They slaughtered Aw-ila, who had the inspiration in their assembly.' And then they mixed his flesh and blood with clay to make humanity.

And that's who we are, according to the myth of Atrahasis. We are the children of the marriage of clay and the leader of an uprising of slaves.

The Temple of Inanna

There is also one important piece of archaeological evidence, the fire at the temple of Inanna.

Most of what we know about Uruk at this time comes from the excavation of two sites in Uruk, an administrative precinct and the precinct of the temple of Eanna, or Inanna. All of the documents for the period come from these two precincts, and they are almost all cuneiform clay tablets used by the scribes of the temple and the government to keep records of the animals and people these institutions owned and the goods they traded.[16]

By far the most common object the archaeologists found was the 'bevelled bowl'. These were clay bowls, cheaply and roughly made, with bevelled edges at the top. They seem to come in a standard size, and they are everywhere. The consensus estimate is that they are probably ration bowls, filled with a day's grain for each partly dependent or dependent worker. For this reason, they are also sometimes called ration bowls.

The goddess Inanna is found, often under related names like Ishtar, across the history of ancient Mesopotamia. We say goddess, but that is to simplify. Inanna was certainly associated with sex, fertility and crops. There is controversy over whether she was also associated with the women who certainly did sell sex around the temples. She was also the god of war. In that capacity she was often depicted with breasts and hips, but also with a long beard of the type familiar from Assyrian statues. At some of the temple ritual celebrations, young men would dance in procession, the clothes and hair on one side of their bodies masculine, the clothes and hair on the other side feminine.[17]

But we should be careful of romanticising Inanna. Remember, the temple and the palace controlled the weaving sheds. And something strange happened to the temple of Inanna in Uruk somewhere around 3100 BCE, just over 5,000 years ago. The temple burned to the ground. It was not just a random fire. Everything burned. And after that, there was no temple on the site for centuries. The great power of Uruk was broken.[18]

Before the fire those bevelled ration bowls had been everywhere. After the fire, they are gone, nowhere to be seen. It is possible that the temple was burned by an invading force from another city. But a local uprising is also possible, and so is an uprising in solidarity with invaders. Whatever happened, and we cannot be sure, it looks like the slaves freed themselves after the temple burned.

8

# NATURALISING INEQUALITY

We return now to the question we raised in the Introduction. Why have all societies with class inequality had gendered inequality too?

In the Introduction we presented our argument about how elites in class society use gendered inequality to make all kinds of inequality seem natural. In this chapter and the next we present the argument again, in more detail.

As we saw at the end of Part One, it seems very likely that from very early on people used music and dance, language, collective rituals and religion to develop and constantly reinforce equality. In class societies the new elites could make the same capacity for complex coalitions and detailed ideologies work for them. Those who wished to live and benefit from inequality were also able to create their own legends and rituals to justify their superior place in the world. And this is where ideologies of difference and inequality came into their own.

Before class societies, there were of course gendered differences which were marked in a wide variety of ways. But there was no systematic or enduring inequality.

This is not to say all hunting and gathering societies were egalitarian. In Chapter 10, we describe the exceptional cases where slavery and class relations could, and did, develop among hunter-gatherers in some places where it was possible to control great concentrations of resources, like the salmon runs on the northwest coast of North America. We also have descriptions of farming communities which 'slash and burn' their fields and move on every few years. Some slash-and-burn communities tolerated considerable inequality, though people did not usually pass their unequal status down to their children.

# WHY MEN?

By contrast, most societies with settled grain agriculture, where people farm the same land from one year to another, have been class societies. In class societies some people are fed all their lives by the work of other people, and they are able to pass this privilege down to the next generation. And it is with the rise of class society that we see the rise of gendered inequality.

Let us mark the logic of this argument. It is important, because it goes against the contemporary tendency to focus on the exceptional example of capitalism.

Patriarchy and sexism—the systematic patterns of inequality between women and men in any particular setting—were around long before capitalism. So we cannot explain sexism in terms of capitalism alone. And explanations that blame individual men simply can't work, because there are men in non-class societies, but no systematic gendered inequality there.

We need a different sort of explanation. One which looks at causes and focuses on social change. That is, we need an argument which allows us to explain why, when and how relations between men and women, and between styles of masculinity and femininity, have changed through time. We need such an explanation because it makes sense, but also because we want to find ways to make things more equal.

Jane Collier described the problem with particular clarity some years ago:

> To understand conceptions of gender, we cannot look at what men and women are or do, but rather must ask what people want and fear, what privileges they seek to claim, rationalize, and defend. To understand gender, we must understand social inequality. And, if gender conceptions are idioms for interpreting and manipulating social inequality, then we should expect notions of femininity and masculinity to change when one organization of inequality gives way to another.[1]

## The Great Struggle

If the rise of systematic gendered inequality is associated with class society, the character of class society is certainly the place to begin. By class society, we mean that there is a ruling group who live for most of their lives off the labour of others. For most of the history of class society, most of the work has been growing food. Peasants or slaves grow the food, while the lord, the landowner or the king takes a third or a half of the crop in taxes or dues, and uses it to feed his family, priests, soldiers and servants. Nowadays things are more complicated, but almost all of us still work for them.

Class inequality is a *relationship* between two classes of people. We can characterise them as the leisure classes and those who work. Or as the rulers and those who are ruled, the haves and the have-nots, or the 1% and the 99%. The absolutely key thing about class inequality, and class privilege, is that it is *arbitrary*. By arbitrary we mean that those things that distinguish the ruling class from the subordinate peasants or workers who support them are contrived, socially constructed, and always open to question.

Elites are not privileged because they are smarter, harder-working, blonder, whiter or have better table manners. Since a particular ruling class's privilege is arbitrary, it is precarious, it can be challenged, and resisted and overturned. Elites can be replaced—dynasties change, ruling classes lose their grip and are overtaken by others. However, class itself cannot so easily be overturned. Revolutions happen, but revolutionary ideas of equality can be co-opted. Ultimately class privilege everywhere and always is kept in place by violence, and by ideology.

The violence is always there. Why the ideology favours men over women is an enormous question and one without the possibility of a definitive answer. However, it is certain that until the advent of weapons which require no brute strength—guns rather than swords and bows and arrows—the small differences in strength and stature made men the likely enforcers—as bodyguards, soldiers, or domestically—in any particular unequal society.

There was violence by feudal thugs and henchmen and a habit that those were jobs for the boys. Nowadays the gendering of class enforcers is more complicated. Men, and increasingly women, do these jobs—in the police and the army, and as overbearing managers and administrators of industry and corporations. And men, and increasingly women, run prisons, mental healthcare and school systems, and administer the institutions of the state.

Saying this puts violence right where it belongs—at the heart of class power. And it allows us to think analytically about violence.

Žižek's idea of distinguishing three types of violence—direct violence, anonymous violence and symbolic violence—is a useful way to start.[2]

Direct violence is where actors are known and can be named, where Tom bashes Harry, or a young woman slaps her child. Anonymous violence is part of the system, but it is hard to pin responsibility on anybody. Who is responsible for the drones which kill women and men in Afghanistan? Which British soldiers, which squaddies, which officers and which British politicians are responsible for the murder of Baba Musa in an Iraqi jail?

Third, there is symbolic violence—images of Jesus on the Cross, ancient stories and others like *The Hunger Games* and film series like *Terminator* or *Star Wars*. Typically, these remind us of the ferocity of the struggle between good and evil, the ruthlessness of a hated lord or the tyranny of a dictatorial regime. Violence of all kinds ultimately depends on coercive power, but day by day it is often enough for an elite to bully us and play on and manipulate our fear.

In the same way that violence is central to arbitrary class power, so too is resistance central to understanding the limits of arbitrary class power. Resistance is the other side of the equation. Resistance and power must be treated in tandem. They are aspects of an ongoing process and struggle which is the very essence of the class divide.

As we saw in Chapter 7, resistance to inequality is basic to who we are. Human beings are social animals, and therefore empathic. This means we can understand what other people are thinking, and what they feel, and we are able to see the world from another person's point of view.[3]

We know from the archaeological record, and from history, that ordinary people have always been able to see the commonalities between themselves and other people. A notion of 'common humanity' lies at the heart of all the world religion traditions. And other popular ideologies of fairness are always available.

Another, unnamed, universalising discourse allows people all around the world to shrug and say, 'There are good people and bad people, all kinds of people everywhere, but in the end, we are all human beings.' This offers scope for great decency in human relations.

Such universalising discourses share much history and common ground. Because they emphasise sameness and can appeal to the majority of the people at any one time and place, they are powerful ways to contest authority and confront power. In confrontations, the balance of forces between popular opposition and elite power determines the outcome of electoral contests, social movements, civil wars and revolutions. How you judge the outcome depends on whose side you are on.[4]

Because resistance is part of our makeup, the violence associated with class inequality is never just notional. It must also include real sanctions and sometimes terrible punishments for challenging class hierarchy. A fear of violence itself serves to discipline people. But to keep inequality in place, ordinary people must be made to understand that violence can become immediate and real. They must be taught that the ruling class will meet defiance with harm—perhaps by causing them physical and mental privation, or pain, or by turning to systematic torture and killing.

Over the long history of class societies across the world, what we see is that violence alone has never been enough to confront ideas of sameness and the disposition of ordinary people to favour, and fight for, human equality. To keep inequality in place, the ruling class also needs ideologies which naturalise difference and inequality, ideologies which divide and rule, ideologies which make inequality seem normal and right.

*Sexism, the Ultimate Ideology of Divide and Rule*

When something is 'naturalised', it is made to seem natural, as if it is God-given, 'meant to be', as something hard-wired, in biology or in our genes or built into the physics of our planet. When something is successfully 'naturalised', it seems wrong or impossible for ordinary people to challenge it or to want change. The class hierarchy is naturalised when we feel it is right and proper that the royals should live in palaces, and sad but inevitable that so many of us are homeless and others are struggling to pay for a roof over their heads.

Ideologies which naturalise inequality divide and rule by punishing and excluding people who are the wrong sex, or the wrong colour, the wrong nationality or religion. Such ideologies are shaped and propagated by the ruling class. After all, the ideologies benefit the elite. Which means we need to think clearly about this top-down process. And, of course, we need to understand that in practice we experience the harms and prejudices of gender, race, class, sectariansm and other inequalities simultaneously.[5]

As we saw in the Introduction, ideologies of inequality start as ideologies of meaningful difference. We all know how racism works. Racism isn't about shades of melanin, it is about someone making skin colour an issue, making it important, marking it and using it to oppress and exploit some people for the benefit of others.

We all also know that racisms vary. In South Africa, there used to be whites and blacks and a mixed-race category of 'coloureds' in between. In Brazil, racism works on a gradient of skin colour. In the American South, under slavery, one drop of Negro blood was enough to make an ostensibly white-skinned person black. These ideas are different, but they are all variants of the same kind of racist ideology. They are based on the same principle: that skin colour can be used to mark and sustain class inequality.

Just as racist ideologies naturalise inequality, so do sexist ideologies. And sexism does this ugly job better than racism because it creates a distance between each of us and every one of the people we love. It is new, and useful, to see sexism in this light.

Sexist ideologies are immensely powerful and have been since the beginning of class society. They are the most effective way ruling classes have found to naturalise inequality for one simple reason: gender goes deep.

All of our close relationships are gendered. The emotions we prize are also gendered—our capacity for feeling or expressing affection and joy, our passion, our energy and the thrill of sexual desire and pleasure. We know this. Yet consider also how both our closest relationships and our most decent feelings can be ruined by gendered neglect and hurt and anger and fear. The boundaries between sexual pain and pleasure are blurred, culturally specific, part of all our everyday lives and always up for debate. This is the stuff of great novels and soap operas, grand opera and country music—and the horror and tragedy of 'Kiss with a Fist'.

Sexism is a source of endless personal confusion for us all.

All our lives, all of us, every one of us, negotiate the contradictions between the love that our early adaptation to sharing, cooperation and equality has primed us to feel, and the sexist inequality that

## NATURALISING INEQUALITY

a dozen millennia of hierarchical societies have imposed on us as our 'true nature'.

Two brief examples:

These days most young couples know the sex of their child before s/he is born. From that moment the child is named, the whole pink/blue regime begins. If, however, you are a social liberal, and wealthy enough to be able to afford them, you may clothe your children in the new fashionable beige.[6] But gender trumps class in other respects. Little boys are handled more robustly than little girls, they're exposed to louder music and more noise and encouraged to take more risks, run faster and climb more trees. While surely you love your little girl and your little boy equally, your child's experience of gendered inequality started long ago in the womb.

A second example is romantic lovemaking. However exciting, magnificent a particular experience, however much you lose yourself in your lover, inequality is not far away. First, there are always lurking questions about who's on top, and who's come. And there are other nagging questions. Am I pretty enough, or rich enough, or smart enough, or kinky enough? And are you good enough for me? And what are your expectations—a fun fuck in the back of a car? Or silk sheets and breakfast in bed? And most important of all, who has to go to work in the morning? And who will take the kids to school?

Men and women are far, far more alike than they are different. But we can very easily forget this when we are in the grips of a sexist ideology. What sexist ideologies do is make it seem like women and men are absolutely different from each other, as if one is from Venus, the other from Mars.

Sexism, by which we mean systematic gender inequality, is when gendered differences—between 'women' and 'men' but also 'cisgender' and 'queer'—are marked socially in ways we can't ignore. In effect they are linked to a presumption that some sexual or gendered identities are more 'naturally dominant' or 'normal' than others—often as if men are more equal than women, straight is more equal than queer. Gender is marked in all those moments— from a fleeting gesture, or a single word to egregious sexual abuse— when someone, or something, makes you aware of yourself—not simply as a person, but as a woman, or a man, or as straight or cis or queer or trans.

Gender marking is a very useful idea. Gender marking comes into play when a class elite want to hide their privilege by encouraging us to focus and fight among ourselves. And in this process, we learn to doubt our feelings of compassion and our empathic concern for other people. The sexist conundrums, whether about parenting, romance or doing a job of work, are charged with emotional and intellectual confusion. They are also the enormously rich material from which the ruling class shapes various sexisms to fit their purpose. When inequality and difference are always intimately present—at home, at school, at work and at play—then it is much, much more difficult to question inequality and difference at a structural or societal level.

Approaching sexism in this way opens up an analytical space. Sexuality, violence and sexual violence are often treated as three quite different things. But we are embodied creatures, and our emotions, our desires and our fears, are not discrete, nor easily labelled and tidily packaged away. Our overlapping emotions are sometimes a source of pleasure and inspiration and sometimes of disgust or terror. And sometimes they are both at once—as any aficionado of BDSM, horror films, fairground rides or extreme sports can tell you.

Marilyn Strathern's definition of 'gender' and her important ideas about embodiment are useful here. For Strathern, gender is an open-ended category which draws upon sexual imagery as it characterises people, their paraphernalia and their activities.

And Strathern uses the notion of 'impingement' to discuss the effects people may have on each other. This has much to recommend it. It is descriptive, but it is a word that carries little baggage. Unlike the notion of 'power', impingement is not automatically associated with men or social dominance. Strathern also borrowed McKim Marriott's idea of 'dividual' people. This fits with our lived experience. Thinking of human beings as having permeable, changing boundaries is a good way of seeing how, and why, gender is fluid and situational.

In this respect it is useful to think of ourselves quite simply as 'partible people'. Thus, we are changed when we catch a whiff of perfume, when we are touched by another person, when we are

## NATURALISING INEQUALITY

fired by a new idea or when we hear another person cry. And vice versa, of course we change others—when we're happy, when we're anxious, when our feet smell bad.

In each of these encounters, there are real bodily changes: the chemical changes in our noses and brains are real when we smell something pleasant or noxious. So too do our eardrums vibrate when someone speaks to us, or shouts. Our bodies respond to soft stroking, and orgasms are real, semen and pregnancy and breast milk are real, but so too do our bodies bruise and break and other people can easily kill us.[7]

Seeing ourselves as partible people, the sheer complexity of the impact we have on others is quite astonishing. And people everywhere manage the anomalies and ambiguity our overlapping emotions and actions pose via rituals and rules.

Cross-culturally, these rules vary greatly. But everywhere they clarify what are acceptable behaviours between close kin, parents and children, brothers and sisters. Other rules clarify what are acceptable behaviours between possible sexual partners: who it is okay to fall in love with, to have sex with, and to marry—and who not.

In many places there are formal rules defining licit sex, legal unions, marital rape, autonomy within a relationship, the legitimacy of children, parental and domestic responsibilities, separation, divorce, inheritance rights and much else.

There have been many class societies where women ideally marry men of a higher status. Sometimes, too, men marry up. But mostly people marry—whether in heterosexual or same-sex unions—within their own class. As with class, formal and informal rules also govern relationships across race or sectarian divides. And class, race and sectarian inequality is often reproduced in extra-marital liaisons when powerful men have access to subordinate women. They may be mistresses, sex workers, graduate students, and sometimes a lucky Cinderella or Melania Trump. Such relationships may be benign. But mostly such relationships are exploitative and contain the seeds of sexual violence.

In class societies, confusions between love, attraction, excitement and desire simultaneously threaten class control *and* offer another means of class control. When class boundaries are blurred and rules are broken, what happens depends on who exactly is breaking the rules and who is charged with enforcing them. There are always questions of interpretation and relative power and resistance.

The slide from innocence to sexual violence can be both imperceptible and very nasty indeed. But what is certain is that however the arbitrary distinctions are marked they will be sexually charged. And when violence is used to mark and distinguish between intense, overlapping emotions in terms of what is licit and what is not, it becomes an extremely powerful tool of social control.

Consider only how until quite recently in the UK and the US, licit sex was strictly marked by wedding rings and wedding rituals. 'Fallen' women (but almost never their male lovers) were shamed, and often punished terribly for conceiving a child out of wedlock. Such was the story of Hester Prynne in Hawthorne's *The Scarlet Letter*, and the real and terrible fate of the young girls in Ireland banished to and enslaved in the Magdalene Laundries. Or think of the ways politicians, the police and other enforcers use homophobia, as they do racism and sectarian hatred, to claim legitimacy and power and justify violence.

*Some Rules of Thumb*

To make sense of sexism, and begin to escape its tyranny, we need always to keep in mind several rules of thumb. These rules build on each other and make it easy to ask good questions about gender and class.

First, it is important to understand that we are making an argument here that challenges every hint of essentialised sexual identity. In practice, of course, we all know that all 'women' are not the same, nor are all 'men'. Here we are emphatically saying something more: that there are no universals, neither biological nor cultural.

There is no uniform or homogeneous category 'Woman' which supposedly includes all 'women'. And there is no universal, uniform or homogeneous category 'Men', which supposedly includes all 'men'. At every juncture, we need to remember that when such boxes and labels are being used, they reinforce not just ideas of gendered difference, but also ideas of gendered inequality because the labelling is a tool of class power.

The second rule of thumb is that to make sense of sexism we need always think relationally. This is about logic. Labels only work as contrast sets. This means there can be no 'men' without 'women', nor 'straight' without 'queer'. The trick here is not just to follow the noise and hullabaloo, but always to ask about the unmarked, but typically dominant or superior, category as well.

When someone, or the media, is banging on about 'women' or 'gays', we need to consider the implications of what they are saying for straight men—and perhaps elite straight men in particular. Just as when someone uses racist terms, remind yourself what implications the comment has for those who are white, or who are otherwise assumed to be 'normal' and not 'different'.

The third rule is that we need to think comparatively and consider how ideas and practices (about marriage, or divorce, say) change over time. Looking at an institution or cultural habit which was once taken for granted, and now holds little sway, gives us an idea how ideologies naturalise particular social practices. This also allows us to think critically about causality and processes of social change.

Fourth, we need to think of relations hierarchically across the class divide. This means considering the relations between the boss and the people who work for him, or between the lady and her maid. The ruling class manages the rhetoric and practices of gendering between classes with ferocity and great care. After all, this is an important part of how their privilege is created and sustained.

Fifth, we need think about relations within classes as well. Within any class, men will mostly dominate women. However, because ruling-class men and women benefit enormously from class inequality, they have a very strong shared interest in managing sexism to their mutual advantage well out of sight of the *hoi polloi*. Sometimes, however, there is a breach case. Then things go awry, and ordinary folk get a glimpse of how sexism works within the ruling class. That's the Princess Diana story.

An *intra*-class perspective is also important when we think about a peasantry, or the working class. Here too gender hierarchies which privilege straight people over queer men and most women are likely to dominate people's experience. But it is also important to notice the subtleties of relative privilege: within any class, and within any gendered, or racial or socio-economic grouping, there will always be some people who are more successful, or more beautiful or closer to the dominant elite than others.

## WHY MEN?

In the case of gender hierarchies, in any given situation some men will conform more closely to masculine ideals than others, just as some women will be judged more 'feminine' than their sisters. And this means that men who can plausibly adopt dominant masculine styles are also likely to dominate others. Other men will find themselves in weaker social positions, as subordinates who are seen, perhaps as 'less masculine', perhaps as 'more feminine' than their superior fellows. And, of course, the same is so between women who dominate others and those who do not.

Unequal relations between people of the same socio-economic class—women and men vis-à-vis each other, among women and among men—are an intrinsic part of class society. And intra-class inequality feeds into and serves to naturalise class relations between an elite and those who work for them. Here too, sexism—systematic gendered inequality—is not something that has to be explained away or denied. Sexism is how the system works. And it distracts us from the inequalities in the system between the ruling class and the rest.

Clinging to Class Privilege

Class inequality is about the power to exploit the great majority of ordinary people who do the work in any class society. We have suggested that all ruling classes use violence, but also ideologies of racism, and especially sexism and homophobia, to legitimise privilege. The reasons they do so are economic.

As we said earlier, the ruling-class project in any era is to manage the economy to keep themselves in power. And when something important changes in an economy, the ruling class move to protect themselves as swiftly and effectively as they can. Ruling classes respond to the threat of competition in many ways. They may destroy the monasteries and steal their wealth or enclose the common land. They may invest in coal mines, railroads and hedge funds, or fight oil wars in the Middle East.

To protect their privilege, ruling elites are always looking for new sources of wealth and are quick to occupy positions commensurate with new forms of power. Watching political parties in the UK or the US scramble for donations is an object lesson in ruling-class manoeuvring. And we know that hanging onto class power is a ruthless business. Today the utter disregard for threat of climate chaos is a clear measure of that, as Naomi Klein so elegantly outlined in *This Changes Everything: Capitalism vs. the Climate*.[8]

We are arguing that the drivers of social change are material, and thus, economic. And as elites are forced to adjust class relations to retain their power, they also reshape gender relations—for themselves and for the rest of us—to better fit the new forms of inequality.

In Europe, for instance, heterosexual marriage strategies were a key to this process. One set of sexist ideas was tailored for the elites of feudal societies—the glorification of knights and ladies, and chivalry, the cult of thugs on horseback—but these ideas changed after the Black Death. They changed again mightily at the time of the early European empires, when Henry VIII could divorce and behead his wives, and Elizabeth I was the Virgin Queen. And elite marriage practices continued to change with changing forms of capitalist economy. Impoverished British aristocrats married parvenu industrialists' daughters and American heiresses. And later, as visible celebrity began to count, wealthy politicians and movie stars married trophy brides.[9]

But, it is not just among the elite that expectations and practices change to justify changing forms of the capitalist economy. Given the centrality of waged labour to capitalism, the changing patterns between women's domestic work and work for wages is not surprising. And at each turn, we see how ideologies of marriage, the family and women's autonomy have changed as well.

For instance, in late nineteenth-century Britain, the 'dutiful' wives of men of the new professional middle class were encouraged to become domestic managers, to care for their children and support their 'breadwinner' husbands. These were the invented ideas of gender difference and gender roles that dominated popular discussion at the time. But unless we look carefully, we are apt to miss seeing the many other young women of the industrial-capitalist age who were not housewives, but became mill girls or worked for wages as servants in the households of the new middle class. And if we look beyond London or Liverpool, we see the myriad of women working in the cotton fields of North America, on the sugar plantations of the Caribbean and the great armies of women in Africa and India whose work fuelled the British economy.

Or to tell another perhaps more familiar story: during the two World Wars of the twentieth century, governments responded to the demands of their war economies by moving men to the front lines and encouraging women to take up 'men's work' on the land, in the public services, and in factories. Then, particularly in the United States, abruptly at the end of the war, many women were forced back into the home and unpaid domestic work, so the returning soldiers could find jobs. However, during this push, other women managed to hold on to their jobs, in part because some rules, such as those barring married women from the workforce, were not reinstated, and from the 1950s onwards the proportion of women in waged work increased steadily. And by the 1960s, the unanticipated consequences of these changes shaped the resistance to the new forms of inequality, and women's liberation, premarital hook-ups, open marriages and then same-sex marriages followed in train.

In short, sexist ideas have been used to fit us for the changing forms of the capitalist economy. It was not their womanhood that led women to what was labelled 'women's work', but the structure of class relations in any particular period. And making the connection between the economy and class interests and sexism offers us a way to explain how and why gendered relations change, and so do the shapes and forms of resistance. This is an important general point.

Telling Stories

To naturalise inequality, and to engineer changes in gender relations to fit new situations, is not an easy task, given the contradictions inequality requires. This is why, even when a system of difference and inequality is in place, its ideological products—its culture, or its narratives, some might say—are not uniform, simplistic, or fully and solely in the service of that ideology.

Shakespeare explored every possible twist between men and women, aristocrats and common people, love and hate, envy and power—from Miranda accusing Caliban of rape to the anal rape of Richard II with a red-hot poker. From Coriolanus's monstrously proud mother and his tainted blood, to the tyrant Macbeth, his bloodthirsty wife and the murder of Macduff's family and his pitiful cry, 'All my pretty chickens and their dam'.

Then there are the fairy tales of Perrault and the Brothers Grimm. In the Ring Cycle, Wagner gives us the torment of Wotan, the patriarchal god, and the adultery, incest and tender love of Siegmund and Sieglinde. And there is Fricka, the jealous guardian of marriage, and Brünnhilde, the disobedient warrior daughter who sleeps behind a wall of fire until a true hero awakens her.

Just like human nature itself, these stories are complicated, full of both love and cruelty. So are their contemporary counterparts, in novels, plays and the films made in Hollywood, Bollywood and Nollywood. In many ways our recent myths are less bold, more prudish and prurient, than those of the ancients. But they are still about both competition and dominance, and cooperation and resistance, while the threat of sexual harm looms over moments of tenderness and love.

These recent stories are also about good and evil and licit and illicit power. From Aristotle to Freud and Lévi-Strauss, thinkers everywhere have sought to describe the effects of such dramatic stories.

> Are they cathartic? Yes.
> Do they justify inequality? Yes.
> Do they act as safety valves for dissent? Yes.
> Or do they excite resistance? Yes, that too.
> In practice, the balance of power and context is everything.

Labelling and Rubbishing People

The sixth rule of thumb concerns the binary categories so often used to label and judge people. Feminists have been challenging the 'binaries', as they are called, since the 1960s, but these categories are still with us all the time. We meet them continually in the media, in our legal systems and in everyday conversation. They are a key to understanding how elites can, with relative ease, manipulate relations of inequality and hierarchy to their advantage.

And they are ancient. They are stereotypes which have been around for at least 3,000 or 4,000 years, since Uruk and Sumer in ancient Mesopotamia. They are in the Bible. And versions of this way of thinking turn up in ancient Indian and Chinese texts, and in the Americas.[10]

And most important, but not always so easy to see, is how the binaries work in lockstep, so they can trap us in chains of association and circularities. Thus,

> Men are to women,
> as straight is to queer,
> as strong is to weak,
> as active is to passive,
> as rational is to emotional,
> as culture is to nature,
> as public is to private and domestic,
> as productive is to reproductive,
> as upper class is to working class,
> as white is to black,
> as the West is to the East,
> as Christian is to Muslim,
> and so on, and on, and on.

In effect, the binary categories are powerful, confusing and insidious. Such dualisms dominate so much of our thinking that it is almost impossible to avoid them, to think outside them, or around or past them.[11]

Feminists, anti-racists and others opposing ideologies of inherent difference now know to scorn the binaries, but it has taken a lot of thought and effort to get to this place. And because we all live in societies riven with division, it is only too easy to fall back on the binaries, often inadvertently, but sometimes deliberately to put someone in their place. Nowhere is this more true than with the gender binary, the most pervasive binary of all. We, your authors, know this only too well. In our struggles to think and write clearly, we too have sometimes found ourselves shrieking at each other in the immortal words of Monty Python—'Your mother was a hamster, and your father smelt of elderberries.'

Often the logic of the gender binary works such that if women gain, men lose—and if men gain, women lose. But the logic can also work as an add-on, without limits. Then it becomes easy to imply that there are no bounds to women's foolishness, or men's aggression.

## NATURALISING INEQUALITY

The stereotypes all too easily attach to our bodies, the way we talk, the clothes we wear and the cars we drive. These contrasts can be used to gender every single thing we touch, and everything we do. Indeed, the slippage between the binaries can account for absolutely any social configuration you might want to describe.

Sometimes gender is marked in ways which make us feel good about ourselves—a nice haircut, a smart suit, someone holding open a door, someone flirting with us. Then we are made to feel like 'a natural woman', or queer and sexy, or a cool dude. Such moments may be quite benign, but they are still moments when gender is marked.

More often—much more often—gender is marked in ways which make us feel bad, and even very bad, about ourselves. Even the milder forms of gender marking inscribe sexism deep in our souls. We feel bad about ourselves when we hear an unthinking homophobic remark, when someone jokes that 'all men are bastards', or someone says, 'you're behaving just like a woman'. It is the same when a bullying colleague sneers and makes us feel ugly, or stupid, or a failure. We all know those moments, and these feelings too—just like the positive ones—are a way of disempowering us, by getting us to function inside a lie.

Every ruling class has an enormous investment in gendered labels and boxes, and in the divide and rule tactics they make possible. But the labels and boxes are lies, just plain lies, whether they are about gender or about race or religion.

Our bodies are not differentiated in categorical ways. The differences between our bodies—the shape of my breasts compared with yours, or the length of your penis compared with his—these differences are not binary contrasts at all. We know that each and every one of us, and our bodies, vary. And we also know that, from one to the next, our bodies don't vary very much. Nor does our clothing, or our way of speaking, parenting, or making love. The sameness is our strength and anathema to elites because resistance is built on empathy, sharing, and collective recognition of each other as fellow human beings.

Elites are committed to a rigid interpretation of the essentialised categories—because that is how the stereotypes work. Things, and people, who blur the categories must be suppressed, because they show up the lies. Gays, trans and queer people, bossy, big-balled women, cuckolded or henpecked men—all the people who differ from the idealised norms, are ridiculed, and they are often punished, perhaps with violence or exile. And sometimes they are killed.

Categorical Power and Rituals of Resistance

The binary contrasts between men and women are powerful and essential to how sexisms work. No one fits the stereotypes exactly because the stereotypes themselves are full of contradiction. However, there are consequences for people whose lives challenge these categories in visible or dramatic ways. People who break the rules, cross boundaries and break taboos become vulnerable. They threaten the hierarchies that the labelling and stereotypes justify.

In unequal societies the apparently self-evident categories of 'women' and 'men' have ideological force precisely because they hide a greater truth: anatomy is not destiny. And whoever is doing the labelling is making a claim to power. Wrestling with these areas of ambiguity and anomaly is the very stuff of social life.

But there is nothing constant about how this process works. More often than not, ambiguity poses a direct threat to the powers that be, so redrawing boundaries is likely to be fraught with pain and oppression. Only think of the testimony of Christine Blasey Ford. Or read the rape stories Redi Tlhabi, Sohaila Abdulali and Roxane Gay tell.[12]

At different times, different kinds of gendered ambiguity, or anomaly, have been the focus of attention. Biological intersexuality has also sometimes been a 'problem'. Thus, the Romans borrowed the idea of Hermaphroditus, the child of the gods Aphrodite and Hermes, from the Greeks. There are many examples of gender fluidity in Roman myths and practices. But there was never one single response to intersexed people. Sometimes they were deemed delights, at other time monstrosities who violated the natural order of things and were, as the historian Celia Schultz reports, simply killed.[13]

Eleventh-century Muslim jurists responded differently. The judges' concern was to decide to which gender the hermaphrodite belonged. In a world 'where everyone had to be gendered, a person without gender could not be socialized. Such a person could not participate in ritual, in itself a profoundly communal and social activity, until it had been artificially gendered.' It was also important that the higher status of men vis-à-vis women be successfully protected, so when in doubt the jurists usually attributed an inferior status to hermaphrodites and gendered most of them female. This was sexist of course, but it was a largely benign process aimed at inclusion, so the hermaphroditic person could join the community of Muslims, and pray, honour their obligations to their kinsfolk and sometimes marry.[14]

Or consider the ethnography of the medical treatment of intersexed children in America. Katrina Karkazis tells the story of the minute and vicious cruelty practised by surgeons, doctors and psychologists who felt, from the 1950s until the fierce pushback by intersexed people at the end of the twentieth century, they had to make intersexed people unambiguously one sex or another.[15]

Similarly, sexualities may be framed by class and struggle. Queer or same-sex sexual practices have often been hidden because they disrupt an elite investment in strongly marked categories of 'women' and 'men' associated with heterosexual desire and practice. Transgendered people can present an even greater threat, and current debates about transitioning are often fierce and damning.

There have been other times and places in class society when same-sex sexualities have been barely marked. But this can change quickly in response to the interests of a dominant elite. In 1895, the trial and imprisonment of Oscar Wilde, the Irish poet and playwright, was a moment when same-sex relations in Britain suddenly became heavily marked to reinforce inequality.

Such a switch also occurred in Germany after the First World War. Socialists and communists were closely associated with a strong movement for gay equality. This was a time when gender was positively marked from below. When the Nazis came to power, they sent socialists, communists and gay men to concentration camps in a horrific reversal. The point is not that gay men were marked where before they had not been, but that now the marking was used to hurt them.[16]

Or, to take another example of when sex and gender boundaries were redrawn on a dime. Homosexuality was legal from the begin-

## WHY MEN?

ning of the Turkish Republic in 1923, and pop idols like Zeki Müren were flamboyant cross-dressers. Yet a hyper-masculine, military style was favoured by the state, and after President Erdoğan's election in 2014 conservatives have sought to ban expressions of gayness, as 'against the values of our nation'.[17]

Border crossings can also be thrilling and even sacred. The American rock & roll musician Little Richard was a great showman who cross-dressed and played up his gayness to counter racism. Cross-dressing men are central players in traditional Kabuki theatre in Japan, while cross-dressing women make the Japanese institution Takarazuka Revue exciting. And, for example, there are very old traditions in India of Hijra communities of queer and intersexual people. In the Arab Gulf, *xanith*, transvestite and transsexual men, have long been accommodated. However, Modi's government in India are now targeting Hijras, and in recent decades LGBTQ+ identities and queer sexual practices have been made illegal in the Gulf States.[18]

The danger and the excitement come from the same place. As Sartre wrote, 'we only become what we are by the radical and deep-seated refusal of what others made up'. This means resistance often follows the fault lines of the labelling process itself.[19]

A common form of transgression is to break the rules about sexual etiquette and modest dress. Sadhus, the wandering Hindu ascetics, offer an extreme example of boundary crossing between this world and another. For a traditional Hindu man of middle or upper caste, the rules and boundaries that frame his life are many, and breaking these rules can be socially dangerous. But sometimes men do just that. They leave their domestic and conventional public lives behind to become a sadhu who can wander from place to place half or fully naked, a begging bowl in hand as part of the costume of his role. Sometimes he is also sexually active in tantra, and he can always smoke all the hash he wants in public. He cares for nothing of the old rules, and in rejecting them for himself, he may feel he becomes far more a walking symbol of Hinduism than the householder who tries to conform.

Sometimes the resistance is aimed at gender discrimination. During the Women's Revolt against the British in Eastern Nigeria in 1929, women protested injustice by exposing their genitals.

## NATURALISING INEQUALITY

Women's liberation activists in the US had the idea of burning their bras, though whether any of them did it or not is an open question. 'Take Back the Night' and 'Slut Walk' demonstrators also aim to shock. In 2016 students at the Rhodes University in South Africa confronted the administration for protecting known rapists on campus. The administration called in the police. In a rage, some of the women confronted the managers and the cops bare-breasted.[20]

Human beings, everywhere, mark and ritualise changes of all kinds. In this sense we cross boundaries all the time. In rites of passage, young people attest their belonging to a faith community through a bar mitzvah or Catholic confirmation, or a Quinceañera when a girl reaches fifteen. And there are graduation ceremonies and others on becoming legal adults at eighteen or twenty-one. Weddings are celebrated, and thresholds are crossed, from home to work or abroad, from birth to death, from living to dead.

Rallies, religious revivals, pop festivals and big public demonstrations when crowds of people come together in great numbers are always exciting and transformative. But the meaning of such events depends on context. Sometimes they can work against hierarchies and reveal our common humanity. These are moments when we fully experience our shared passions. But as we know all too well, collective rituals can also be orchestrated to serve an elite, as at Hitler's Nuremberg rallies, Soviet military parades and the synchronised state displays of Chinese and North Korean citizens.[21]

Then there are the festivals of reversal. For a day or two, every social rank is turned upside down and a fool may become king for a day. The medieval carnivals in many cities in Europe, or the spring festival of Holi in India have such a character.

During the traditional Tibetan New Year celebrations in Lhasa before 1949, the Dalai Lama gave up power for two days to the poor monks of the largest monastery in the city. They invaded people's houses, demanding food, burlesquing the greed of the monasteries. A lord of misrule, a beggar from the edges of society, took power for a day. The next day the beggar was driven from Lhasa as a scapegoat for everyone's sins, and order was restored. However, after the 1949 Chinese invasion, Tibetan monasticism posed a threat to Chinese rule. In 1959, the working-class people of Lhasa, organised by the guilds, rose up against the Chinese occupation, but they were defeated and the Dalai Lama fled to permanent exile in India.

And reversal rituals are often great fun and hysterically funny to the oppressed. The title of Barbara Ehrenreich's social history, *Dancing in the Streets: A History of Collective Joy*, catches the spirit of such moments, and the great release of energy when boundaries are crossed. The human disposition to ritualise change carries a charge, and Ehrenreich also documents how increasingly people have been tamed, in Europe particularly, but in general around the world. Bawdy celebrations became sombre, gross references to farting and fucking were disciplined as class strictures tightened. The reason for such censure is plain. There lurks in all collective rituals the unspoken but screaming possibility that the social order will actually be overturned.[22]

# 9

## WHY MEN?

Violence is a constant feature of systems of class rule. And with class inequality comes patriarchy, ideologies of natural difference and cults of male violence. Why?

To recap, four things are most telling about our primate legacy. First, size. As a species, human beings display a (modest) degree of sexual dimorphism. That means that, in any particular community, the majority of men, on average, are somewhat larger and stronger than the majority of women.

Male ambush hunters of big game are also part of our long human history. And we can be sure that those able hunters understood weapons and killing. Nor did hunting cease with the advent of class society. Farmers continued to hunt in many parts of the world and still do.

Then there are primate hierarchies. Our primate cousins show two patterns. One is gendered equality in peaceful pairs, like gibbons, or occasionally squabbling groups, like bonobos. The other pattern is male domination of subordinated males and females. These are the societies of silverback gorillas and rampaging chimps. But as Frans de Waal has noted, what is striking is not the aggression of these alpha males, but the submission all males and females display during most or all of their lives. Humans, he says, are submissive animals by nature. In fact, our human primate adaptation falls somewhere in between living in peace with each other and being dominated by aggressive males. We can go either way.

Finally, humans are highly sexed primates and we're social animals who need love and care to survive. We are primates who take pleasure in masturbation. We delight in mutually pleasuring our sexual partners and sharing sexual joy. Choosing to make babies can also be part of the fun. Raising children well, laughing at their antics, watching grandchildren grow, are precious to us. And even when thoughts of making love may be far from our minds, our daily lives are saturated with sexual imagery and with respect, affection and love.

These gifts of sexuality and love are central to who we are. But for that very reason, they are also the places where we are most vulnerable. They can easily be traduced, sullied or stolen by those who would harm us.

For over 200,000 years, hunter-gatherers survived and thrived because they cooperated and shared and worked together to stop dominant men taking over.

Then, with the development of class societies, things changed. The die was probably cast when elites began to organise violence to control a surplus. And at that point they sought out men who were bigger, stronger and perhaps more belligerent than others to become enforcers and subordinate other men and women. Then many people faced the daily threat of violence. And unless they could run away and make lives for themselves in swamps, distant mountains or deserts, most men and women were forced to submit to violent men for most of their lives.

Indeed, size and strength probably mattered most in everyday village confrontations. Then the landlord's thug would need to move fast to hit an angry farmer and thereby cow the spectators gathered round. An overseer was often only one step above serfs or slaves, but three steps below his master. His relative privilege was precarious, and it was in his interest to be particularly brutal to keep the hierarchy in place.

And then there is sexual assault and rape. Women and men who are harmed in these ways often carry helplessness and fear with them for the rest of their lives. Children born after a rape may embody the assault. The man or woman who is forced to witness their child, parent, or lover being raped suffers terrible pain for being unable to protect the people they love. There seems to be no limit to the obscene, horrific ways such violence may be carried out. The extremes are the ends of continua, but less extreme forms of sexual abuse and insult—including the full spectrum of what's known as domestic abuse—carry this threat.

## WHY MEN?

Elite power lies in their control of food, their command of luxury goods, comfort and safety. And elites in class societies use gender ideologies and sexual violence as weapons of control. As with gendered differences, these ideologies and practices are constructed, and sexualised and gender-based violence and abuse are perhaps the most powerful form of class discipline elites have to control others.

Archaeological and historical records show that the invention of the cult of male violence was not a one-off event. Violence was gendered male early on, over and over, in many different ways, in different times and places. The fact of an enormous diversity of ideologies of male violence speaks to the fact that it was invented and resisted many times over. But the ubiquity of male violence in class society also speaks to the fact that it was necessary to keep class inequality in place.[1]

In this chapter, we explore three kinds of male violence, ubiquitous in the history of class societies: warfare, domestic abuse and sexual violence. Each traces back to gendered inequality and hierarchy. And we address two questions which could be seen to challenge our understanding of the link between class society and male violence: why do subordinate men also commit gendered violence? And why don't all men do so?

### The Glory of War and Other Stories

Warfare was an extension of the same dynamic. For most of the history of class society, warfare was a matter of at least some hand-to-hand combat. Guns and drones have been great gender equalisers, but they are recent. Earlier, size and strength mattered. Before gunpowder and modern arms, it was important that men were on average a bit larger than women. This is, of course, a continuum. Many women are stronger than many men. But with violence a prerequisite, it makes sense to put the men in the warrior slot and use gendered difference to further divide and rule.

Male violence was not just normal, it was celebrated. From the earliest written records, we can find warrior epics. The West Asian and European examples include *Gilgamesh*, Homer's *Iliad*, the Old Testament Book of Kings, the Norse Sagas and *Beowulf*, while similar cycles of myths and legends abound in Africa, India, China and the Americas.

## WHY MEN?

These great poems celebrated, but did not glorify, warriors. They entered into the world of the man who must fight and kill, who fears death for himself and slavery for his family, who lives in a world defined by honour and dishonour. These poems become great art precisely because they grasp, from the inside, the contradictions of the warrior who is both hero and monster. Homer is not blind to the destructive wrath of Achilles, and Snorri Sturluson knows the Icelandic feud is a tragedy. The centre piece of the *Mahabharata* is the *Bhagavad-Gita*, the 2,800 lines where Krishna tries to reconcile the violence of war and the kindness of spirituality.

But in these epics the gods and demi-gods mostly act with impunity. They are the elite of the elite, and serve as powerful models for human sexual predators, molesters and bullies. Ask yourself—what caused most problems in Greek mythology? And if you think about it, the answer is not hubris, or fate, or false prophecies, but that Zeus couldn't keep it in his pants.

However, the lives of heroes were distorted in the warrior epics. In real life there were always two sides to their story. As a muscular armed man he was celebrated as a soldier in the army of a feudal lord or king, but at the same time, he was an enforcer, and one of the three or four men who arrived to break the legs of the recalcitrant tenant. Sometimes he fought in war, but day by day he bullied. Most nights he sat at the table or stood in the shadows of the great hall ready to punish someone at the nod of the lord. This was his primary job. It was hardly ever mentioned in the epics because there was no honour in it.

Another silence in the epics persists in the accounts of archaeologists and historians. They concentrate on ancient states, not on class. The way the landlords and priests take from the harvest almost disappears. Instead, we have kingdoms, soldiers and wars. This is partly because the written sources and the material record (all the old coins and monuments) point that way. This is true of conservative and middle-of-the-road historians. But it also affects radical historians and anthropologists. The end of the Soviet regime and the celebration of capitalism in China has discredited the centralising Marxist models of social organisation which used to dominate in leftist circles in most parts of the world. However, this has created a space on the left for anarchist thinkers.

# WHY MEN?

We have relied in this book on the work of people like James Woodburn, David Graeber and James C. Scott. Their anarchism allows them to see the depravity and cruelty of ancient lords and kingdoms. The Stalinist Marxists who preceded them always had a soft spot for the development of the state and the productive forces. Anarchists, by contrast, show uncompromising sympathy with the underdog and hatred of the overdog. Yet, just like the conservative historians, Graeber and Scott are still mesmerised by the state. They pay more attention to power than to food. In the process, class struggle tends to disappear. And with it, so does the daily grind of male violence. That makes it harder to see the organic links inside the bodies and minds of enforcers between class exploitation and the violence of gendered inequality.[2]

There are other difficulties in seeing behind and through the myths. One persistent theme in the cults of male violence concerns beautiful young warriors who invite their own tragic deaths. The theme reappears in the contemporary myths of evolutionary psychologists. They argue that it makes more evolutionary sense for men to be warriors because young men can be spared, while the surviving women will be able to reproduce. A related argument that a disproportionate number of male babies are born after wars became popular during the nineteenth century. But both arguments are statistically flawed, while the most egregious mistake is that they assume that in war men are killed and women spared. This is not the case in the modern world, nor was it so in many earlier societies where fighting men killed men and women alike.

Another persistent thread in the myths and histories is about powerful men challenged by indomitable women. The hero is vulnerable because of a woman's frailty or her voracious sexuality. This is the story of Delilah's betrayal, Boudicca's heroic failure and the numerous warrior goddesses in pantheons around the world.[3]

## 'Domestic' Abuse

In class societies inequality is not just enforced on the battlefield and in the courtroom and the marketplace. Patriarchy is enforced constantly at home. Today this is usually discussed in terms of 'domestic abuse'. The phrase may describe forms of harm from mental anguish to brutal beatings, or a pathologically damaged sexist man strangling a woman. Such abuse occurs on a horrific scale. But calling it 'domestic' distorts what happened in human history until almost yesterday.

For most class societies, there was just violence. Violence within households was part of the larger pattern. In unequal relationships, the person in the dominant category was allowed to beat the weaker. Masters beat servants and slaves. Fathers and mothers beat their children. Husbands beat wives. Big kids beat up little kids. This was all normal, not pathological. In English, as we've mentioned, such beatings were called 'punishment' or 'discipline'. Those words also describe the ways armies, workplaces and communities are controlled. In class ideologies, such violence was and is legitimate, good and proper. 'Spare the rod and spoil the child', as the old English proverb has it.

Of course, there have always been people who went too far. Some men were known to beat their wives or children too severely. Other people would gossip about this. Kin might even take in a runaway wife or child. Sadism has often incurred popular censure, but the rule that you should not interfere has often held sway. 'A man's home is his castle', as another English proverb says.

In very recent history, in some places, this has changed. A teacher's former right to beat a child has been questioned and in some places is forbidden. Sometimes a parent's right to slap or spank a child has been stigmatised, labelled abuse and criminalised, while men who hit their wives are now committing 'domestic violence'. These enormous advances protect women and children. We owe them to women's liberation.

But there is a confidence trick in what has happened. 'Domestic violence' is now rarely seen as an aspect of society-wide custom, or even of patriarchy. It is now more often attributed to the failed character of a particular man. Pathologising and individualising violence in this way hides structural violence on a much wider scale.

We should also be wary of the tendency to read male violence backwards in history and tell a story of progress. 'In olden times, during the dark ages', the story goes, men were particularly violent and brutal. Then as people became more civilised, men became enlightened and less violent. Finally, we arrive at the 'new men' of our own blessed day. Reading history backwards displaces systematic violence into the past. Its analogue is the way systemic violence is displaced down the social scale as a practice, not of the elite, but of poor subordinate men.

Domestic abuse and gender-based violence are not individual failings. They are systemic in class societies. Mostly it is violence against women. But even when it is violence again men, it is a way of marking gender difference, perhaps literally with bruises and pain and scars. It is cruelty often disguised as love.

And of course, people resist, which is why—just as at the level of state control over common people—material force is not by itself enough. Relying on men's physical dominance to keep gendered inequality in place can be tricky within a household, or among close kin and friends. Some men may be weaker or older than the women they are supposed to control. If physical pain were all there was to domestic abuse, women could simply poison the soup or run off to a stronger and younger protector. Coercive control typically involves isolating the victim, destroying their self-esteem and autonomy, physical deprivation, lies, egregious, unpredictable violence to create suicidal anguish and an ever-present fear of injury or death.

However, physical dominance does not guarantee social dominance. Once a social system reaches a certain scale, the king, the landlord or the factory owner does not do his own violence. He says, 'Deal with him' to his knights, his guards, the goons or the foreman, and it is done. Indeed, the master would be seen as a lesser person if he deigned to do his own dirty work. Think only of Napoleon or Putin and the violence and number of deaths they are responsible for via a strategy of the mind, not the force of their sword arm. In a class society, doing violence is a way some ordinary men without power can get a job and three square meals a day. What gets you power is the ability to organise the violence of others, so you don't have to trade your kingdom for a horse.

None of this requires men to be naturally more violent than women. All it requires is that the people who run the system rely on *both* violence and a marked gendered divide to keep the hierarchy in place. And to do this they can call on aspects of our primate heritage we had once left behind.

# WHY MEN?

*Sexual Violence*

The processes we have been looking at also make sense of sexual violence. As we have seen, in the process of evolution we became a highly sexualised species. With humans, everything has a sexual aspect. As the modern proverb says, 'If it exists, there's porn of it.'

In the same spirit, a ruling class that honours violence will also sexualise violence. So will the men whose work and pride it is to perform that violence. Mustafa Khalifa spent thirteen years in Syrian prisons for telling a joke about the Syrian dictator Assad (the elder) to a fellow student in Paris. His memoirs describe endless torture, and worse. He tells of watching one guard beating the dead body of another prisoner, screaming:

> 'The president's the most powerful man in the world'—another blow—'The President will fuck your mothers'—another blow—'The President's got the biggest cock in the whole world'—another blow—'He'll fuck you and your sister one after the other!'[4]

Sickening fear is the right response to Khalifa's story.

At the other end of the continuum from such horror are the ways consensual sex may also become infused with violence and domination. There are the jokes: Is that a pistol in your pocket, or are you just happy to see me? Many find rich, powerful men, or a man in uniform, attractive. Watching men fight over you is a standard storyline. Romantic leads come with the intense eyes and smouldering brows of a Rhett Butler who sweeps you off your feet and carries you off to bed. There is the handsome quarterback, and there are gladiator movies. And all the homoerotic, queer and lesbian transformations of warrior sex.

The logic of class allows some men to take food from other men and women. Elite power is also often evident in their licence to indulge their sexual appetites and have sex whenever and with whomever they want. This is the logic of dominance hierarchies everywhere. We can see the extremes in military rape, in slavery in the Americas, caste domination in Indian villagers and when gangs become involved in prostitution.

The same class inequality is reproduced throughout a social system when men have access to people subordinate to themselves and when there is no recourse for the wronged woman or man or child. The secretary loses his job, the graduate student never gets her degree, and when the landowner has sex with a landless labourer, she and her husband may be killed if they fight back.[5]

And the other way round. In class societies, there is a mirroring in the gendered relations between rich and poor. Sex between subordinate men and dominant women may sometimes be treated as a joke—in British music hall comedy, cheeky builders on building sites whistle at pretty, posh women walking down the street, and milkmen are welcomed at the door by the eager housewives. But except in fairy tales, a poor man has no chance of marrying the princess. Not by coincidence, such liaisons are often the subject of obsessive fantasies and desire.

And, of course, the idea is transgressive and threatening to the elite. D.H. Lawrence's novel *Lady Chatterley's Lover* tells of a love affair between an upper-class woman and her gardener. The book was first published in the late 1920s, but for the next fifty years it was banned as obscene in Britain, Canada, Australia, India, the US and Japan for its explicit descriptions of the sex and the collection of sexy, aka dirty, four-letter words Lawrence used.

In practice, reversing class relations even when there is not even a hint of such a liaison may mean the poor man loses his work, his land and perhaps his freedom and his life. And adding caste or sect or race to the mix is often deadly. In the hundred years after the end of the American Civil War in 1865, thousands of black men, accused of offending a white woman, were lynched. In the notorious and horrific case of Emmett Till, the 14-year-old African American boy was kidnapped, tortured and killed in rural Mississippi because the white woman behind the counter in her family's grocery store accused him of being cheeky. Only in 2022, nearly seventy years after Emmett Till's murder, was a small change finally forced on the elite and lynching was made a federal hate crime.

What frames this pattern is an understanding that rape up the social scale should be punished as severely as possible. But rape by those who are wealthier or just more powerful than their victims is protected and their abuse covered up. This has been explicit in many class societies and remains the custom in almost all.

In 'Reading Ovid in the Age of #MeToo', Katy Waldman's clever piece in *The New Yorker* links—from ancient to modern—violent coercion, men's impunity and their victims' anger. There are three parts to Ovid's *Ars Amatoria*—the Art of Love, written in 2 CE. The first two instruct rich young Roman men in the art of seduction, the third 'winkingly advises the modern Roman woman how to resist the smooth advances of the modern Roman man'.[6]

Ovid's *Metamorphoses*, written some six years later, is a sex manual of another kind. As Waldman explains,

> Ovid's subject matter throughout the poem is a seemingly endless stream of rapes and sexual crimes. Hades abducts Persephone; Zeus impregnates Leda; Apollo pursues Daphne; Zeus violates Europa. The effect of all these attacks feels totalizing, as if women exist to be abused...
>
> It is hard to read this ancient tale without running into a web of #MeToo-era tropes and preoccupations: how men silence the women they violate; how women are made to feel complicit in their own violations and those of their sisters... And how female rage can overflow the banks of just-retribution, sweeping patriarchal taboos aside.[7]

Violent coercion, men's impunity and their victims' plight is also the pattern in what we now call 'workplace harassment'. The now notorious abuse of children by Roman Catholic priests, and the ways this was both accepted and covered up by their seniors, is one example of workplace violence. Or consider too how employers and managers use their power to hire and fire to threaten women into having sex or tolerate groping and jeering. This is also how the graduate student who refuses to sleep with her supervisor is punished. However, we also need to remember that sexual harassment can have another face and reveal again the deep contradiction in our human nature. Sometimes the secretary is promoted because she has sex with the boss. Sometimes the grad student marries the prof.

But more often the connections are sinister. There has been organised child abuse and child prostitution in Britain for a long time. In Rochdale the local MP Cyril Smith was at the centre of a ring of abuse for decades. And like the cover-ups and enabling of abuse by the Catholic Church in Ireland and across the world, all the rings of abuse and prostitution could not have continued without cover-ups by senior police officers, social workers and politicians.[8]

None of this means there is a rape and harassment free-for-all. There are always rules. Slaves may be fair game, or both slaves and servants. Women maybe be fair game, but not men. Children were fair game for paedophile priests, but adults were not. Working-class scholarship girls at university may be fair game, a sorority girl with an older brother in your fraternity is not.[9]

People carry contradictory ideas inside their heads as well. They excuse some rapists and despise others, while also being opposed to rape on principle. These contradictions, and the cover-ups that follow, go with the territory of class society. Cover-ups are not just about double standards. They are systemic, from the top down, and they are crucial to keeping any unequal economic system in place. Employers encourage managers to discipline and bully employees to make them work harder for less, and to make them more frightened and less able to fight back. Some managers—but not most—take advantage of this to use workers sexually. If the worker complains, the senior management reflex is to back the junior manager, because bullying is often a synonym for management.

Silence is where this comes together. The powerful want silence so that some of them can abuse. They also want to protect women of their class because that is a way of protecting a whole hierarchy of race or caste and class. Meanwhile, our shame also disposes us to silence, and is endlessly reinforced. The bottom line in all cases of sexual violence is never to say anything in public. And if you do, expect to be punished.

What Rebecca Traister writes about enforced silence and women's rage in *Good and Mad* is telling: 'Perhaps the reason that women's anger is so broadly denigrated—treated as so ugly, and so alienating, and so irrational—is because we have known all along that with it came the explosive power to upturn the very systems that have sought to contain it.'[10]

We all do know that if the worst bullies are punished, then other victims of bullying will take heart, and dare to organise to fight back. This is how the cover-ups in the Roman Catholic Church were first exposed.[11] And this is the story of Me Too. It was the courage and collective effort of a few Hollywood women that brought down Harvey Weinstein; it took the collective effort of several young women and dogged lawyers and reporters to break through the cover-ups and see Jeffrey Epstein and Ghislaine Maxwell jailed.[12]

# WHY MEN?

## And What of the Violence of Disempowered Men?

A conventional feminist view is that rape is not about sex, it's about power. But harassment, abuse and rape are about both. As a species our behaviour across the board is sexualised. So domination has a sexual aspect. Sex can be seen in Georgia O'Keeffe's flowers, or in the bodies of shiny red sports cars. It can be about both orgasms and power. Sex is not something naturally good and loving. It is something human, and nothing human is alien to sex.

Throughout this book we focus on the abuse by the powerful and the ways those who are vulnerable combine to save themselves. The reader may feel that we have avoided an ocean of evidence which discredits working-class men. That evidence is there, but our focus is deliberate. One reason is that the recent global movement against patriarchal violence and sexual domination has been almost entirely devoted to exposing abuse by powerful men protected by powerful institutions. The analysis we offer is one that makes sense of that kind of abuse.

Moreover, we argue that powerless men can only abuse because powerful men abuse with impunity. Systems of criminal justice and institutional practices that protect the powerful also protect subordinate abusers. There is a deeper logic at work as well that builds on the stereotypes and binaries which encourage us to believe that men lust and women are coy, that male violence is attractive, that male domination is natural, that sex is shameful, that bad sex is mortifying, and that the victim is the guilty person.

Another reason why men outside the elite may turn to gender-based violence is class itself. It is obvious that when the poor, and outsiders, migrants and the like, turn to crime, they do so because poverty or racism blocks them from other avenues. So too, the motives for abuse are to make money illegally. For example, in the twentieth century prostitution in the United States was largely controlled by Irish and Jewish gangs and the Italian mafia. This is why Tony Soprano is shown running a titty bar and why his life is full of 'goombahs'. This does not mean all Italians are the same.

Some poor young men in many places are involved in general violence as well as sexual assaults and rape. But among them violence and sexual violence is often policed by peers, and almost always takes place well outside the law. Most often, working-class violence and sexual violence is ignored by institutions of the state. When it does receive media attention, the report usually confirms elite values by reproducing class and racialised stereotypes about the urban poor.[13]

The best account we know of rape by the powerless is Kevin Denys Bonnycastle's *Stranger Rape*. Bonnycastle was a sociologist who did fieldwork with fourteen sex offenders in a Canadian prison. She sat with them through six months of intensive daily therapy. Afterwards, she interviewed them at length one on one. The main part of her book is the six chapters that tell the life stories of six of those men. All six were in prison for brutal rapes of women they did not know. All were working class. Each chapter is a tale of the loneliness, cruelty and suffering done to a child and young man. Bonnycastle is empathic and skilled, and it is impossible to read these stories without your heart going out to those damaged young people. Right at the end, Bonnycastle describes in one paragraph the offence that landed each man in prison. These paragraphs are horrific. In two of the cases, the man killed the woman during the rape.[14]

It could be argued that these men had been so deprived that what they did was fundamentally different from abuse by powerful and narcissistic men. That was not the view of the six men Bonnycastle knew. They thought what they had done was understandable, horrific and unforgiveable. Six months of all day work with their therapists and each other had made them strong enough to take responsibility for their actions, and to understand how they got to that point. They had also learned how to be open about their feelings in the hope they would never again find themselves in that dark place.

Yet, they explained to Bonnycastle, they had to close themselves down again in the months after therapy. They lived in a maximum-security prison, where the inmates were brutal and violent with each other. Only a tough and armoured man could command respect. To survive, they had to hide and forget much of the gentleness they had learned in therapy.

Bonnycastle noticed that all these men had attacked other men in rage before they raped a woman. One of them had violently beaten more than thirty other men before he attacked a woman. Which brings us to a related question. What are the motivations for rape? Or, to put it differently, why do some men rape and others do not? This is a difficult question to answer.

## WHY MEN?

*Why Not All Men?*

One partial answer invokes the example of Émile Durkheim's *Suicide*, the book which founded sociology. Durkheim looked for social rather than psychological connections to explain what he was seeing. This meant considering the social forces that affected the rates of suicide, not why this man or that woman killed themselves.

The implications of Durkheim's decision are easy to understand if you look at suicide rates in the USA today.[15] There men are more likely to kill themselves than women, single men are more likely to kill themselves than married men, and married women are more likely to kill themselves than single women. Middle-aged white men in the USA commit suicide more often than younger white men, native-born men are more likely to kill themselves than immigrants, gay teenage boys more likely to kill themselves than straight boys, and so on. Knowing these rates, then you can ask what social forces make this so.

By analogy, we could argue that we are not interested in why this corporate executive rapes and that one does not. Or why this working-class white man abused a child and that one did not. Instead, we could say that we're concerned with the social processes that make it possible for these men to get away with it, and thus make them much more likely to do it. After all, if we are concerned with prevention and want to stop rape, these are the issues that matter.

But we are not Durkheimians in that sense. We assume that a full understanding of rape will also mean taking account of individual psychology, shared cultural dispositions and national sexual politics.

Motivations for sexual violence vary within any one culture. For some men it is primarily a sexual event, and for others it is about power and domination. For yet others, it an expression of the rage of the utterly powerless, or a reluctant concession to peer pressure. It can be understood by the perpetrator as an act of punishment for defiant women, or aggression against their menfolk, or an entirely normal way for a gentleman to enjoy himself. It can be an act of torture, war or a desperate attempt to reach out for human connection. The damage done may well have little or nothing to do with the motivation. The act often springs from two, or several, of those feelings, in different combinations. What every act will have in common though, is that it is set in a framework of patriarchy and saturated with inequality and harm.

It's important, too, not to reduce gender-based violence and abuse to a statement that all men, or all fraternity boys or all gangsters, are inclined to do it. That is what the rapists and harassers want you to believe. 'Anyone would do that if they could,' they say. It's normal. But any adult woman or gender-minority person is aware of many times and places where they could have been abused, and a man did not take advantage of her. Or of other times when a man intervened to make sure she was safe. Individuals differ, and why they differ matters.

At the same time, focus on the individual alone not only makes healing impossible, it's also dishonest. We are social animals and share responsibility with others for the lives we lead. By beginning with the thread of class and impunity, we can hope to make fundamental social changes, and so prevent and heal.

*Women Warriors and Women Fighters*

But what then, you ask, about women warriors and women fighters? Well, yes, a word about them is needed. Women warriors are less troublesome to our argument than you might imagine, whereas women fighters turn up alongside men when ordinary folk are fighting for their lives and with the hope of resisting tyranny.

The pots that survive from classical Greece show one scene far more than any other. A soldier, or half man, half horse, spears a naked Amazon warrior woman. Many have celebrated this as important evidence for a long history of women fighters, challenging arguments that women have only begun waging war very recently and under the pressure of a 'politically correct' society either to erase the history of patriarchy or deny any importance to any biological differences between men and women. We can see how people get here, but we understand such imagery in a less optimistic way: as evidence of a long history of obsessively celebrating the sexually exciting murder of a woman who dares to fight back.[16]

There is, of course, no logical reason for some women not to fight in a mostly male army. After all, the belligerents in the chimpanzee war at Gombe included all the adult males and one childless adult female. Human women have the same primate inheritance as human men, and so they too can be cruel and brutal. We have the singular stories of women pirates Anne Bonny, Mary Read, Grace O'Malley and Ching Shih. And as archaeologists have recently understood, the number of women warriors may have been underestimated. In 2017 DNA analysis revealed that one chieftain in a well-known Viking ship-burial was a woman. She had first been excavated in 1888, but earlier scholars had simply assumed she was a man.[17]

But there is a completely different side to this picture of bellicose women. From an elite point of view, violence is supposed to work from the top down. Proper violence, we are told, is between equals, or when strong men are needed to stifle dissent or fighting men go to war. But none of this precludes violence from the bottom up. All over the world, peasants murder overseers and landlords and of course ruling elites brand such violence illegitimate. But when people are fighting for themselves, or for equality and better lives, or when they are fighting against tyrannous regimes in which they are in deathly terror, women are part of the fight. Some women may stay at home and wait, like Penelope; others keep the home fires burning, like the maid who sells her flax to buy her love a sword of steel. But there are also often women next to men on the front lines, or very nearby, covered in blood and guts.

Three brief examples are instructive. Rebecca Redfern's meticulous reanalyses of the human remains buried at the Maiden Castle hillfort in Dorset show the human cost of violence. The remains of the eighty-six individuals in one cemetery include adolescents and elders, women and men, all of whom seem to have been involved in deadly fighting which may provide evidence of popular resistance to the Roman invasion of Britain in 43 CE.[18]

We know from early seventeenth-century sources that tribes from the Iroquois Confederacy and their neighbours in eastern North America were egalitarian farmers, both democratic and warlike. Men and women were equal. Men were the warriors. The women tortured the war captives for hours or days before they died.[19]

In Afghanistan, in a feudally organised class society, Pashtuns, men and women fought off the British in three wars. In a story of mythic proportions, at the Battle of Maiwand in 1880, a young woman, Malalai, tore off her veil, rallied the Afghan troops and died in the battle. And in those battles against the British, as Kipling described, 'When you're wounded and left on Afghanistan's plains: The women come out to cut up what remains'.[20] Malalai is still a national hero for her part in defeating the British, and many Pashtun women carry her name.

In peasant revolts around the world, in the French Revolution, the Russian Revolution, on Mao's Long March in China, among the Vietnamese during the American War, among Sandinista guerrillas, Palestinian hijackers and Kurdish rebels, the women are there. And the women are as up for violence as men. These are class struggles, against powerful elites, and during such contests, sexism among allies is typically lessened for a period, or changed to accommodate the new ideas and demands of war. But just as no one knows at the outset how the struggle will end, neither is it predictable how gender relations will change after the war.[21]

The recent examples of systematic, top-down recruitment of women to fighting roles are cases of states and empires *in extremis*. About a million women fought in the Soviet army during the Second World War: 'They mastered all military specialties, including the most "masculine" ones. A linguistic problem even emerged: no feminine gender had existed till then for the words "tank driver," "infantryman," "machine gunner," because women had never done that work. The feminine forms were born there, in the war.'[22]

Weaponry and warfare have changed greatly in the past fifty years. Conscript armies are being professionalised, and governments have been forced to respond to popular pressure for gender mainstreaming. Women are now being allowed to join armies as combatants, as has been the case in the American army in Afghanistan and Iraq, and latterly as frontline fighters. Yet as we shall see in Chapter 16 on Abu Ghraib, neither such changes, nor those that are associated with wars of resistance, seem likely to greatly alter the relation between men and violence in class societies. Rather, sexisms may simply take new forms and the gender justification remains in place. Today's women soldiers have complicated feelings about why they are there.

Mostly, however, there has been a clear division of violent labour between men and women. And we should not be blind to the normalcy of most male violence in most of human history.

# 10

## SALMON, PIGS AND RITUALS

### ARE WE WRONG?

So far, we have been making a straightforward case for the association between surplus, class, gender inequality and violence. But since the 1980s, there has been much discussion among anthropologists and archaeologists of three exceptions to this generalisation. These exceptions will occur to any well-read anthropologist. They are important and not to be dodged.

The first exception is the Pacific coast of North America, where 'complex hunter-gatherers' lived in societies with chiefs, slaves, class and gendered inequality. The 'complex' bit of the label is problematic. All hunter-gatherers had complex cultural lives, it is just that some were equalitarian, and this lot were not. But problems with the label notwithstanding, by the 1980s, there was a consensus about hierarchy. The evidence the scholars drew on was manifold. It included accounts from Russian traders from around the 1750s, British traders from the 1800s, and many ethnographic accounts from the late nineteenth century onwards. But it was archaeologists who settled the debate by showing that there have been hierarchical societies along the Pacific coast of North America, on Sakhalin Island off the coast of Russia and in northern Japan for some 3,000 years.[1]

The second exception concerns the societies of the highlands of New Guinea, where slash-and-burn farmers had marked inequality between men and women but no class inequality. There is archaeological evidence of agriculture on the island for some 9,000 years, while the ethnographic evidence dates from very shortly after the

Second World War when the Australians re-established their administration of the island and set out to control the highlands. Within a few years, ethnographers were following the administrators inland and there are many excellent ethnographies drawing on fieldwork in PNG from the 1950s and 1960s onwards.

The third exception were Aboriginal hunter-gatherers of Australia who seem to have had economic equality but gendered inequality. James Cook made contact with the continent in 1770, and European settlement began in the 1790s along the coast of New South Wales and Victoria. However, there are many difficulties with the early ethnographies of indigenous Australian societies because they come so long—sometimes forty, sometimes one hundred years—after the frontier had moved slowly and brutally inland. And compared with what was done to the people in Papua New Guinea (PNG), the conquest of Australia was genocidal and utterly shattering. The effect of this violence cannot be underestimated and makes it virtually impossible to recover the character of the pre-conquest societies.

These three exceptions, taken together, seem like strong evidence that gendered inequality and the oppression of women are not a consequence of the invention of agriculture and the coming of class society. Or to put it more strongly, these three examples suggest that inequality has been with us always. There has been much careful work on these three exceptions; indeed, the literature on each case is enormous. It would be intellectually dishonest of us not to engage with that work.

These three cases could not be more different ethnographically, in terms of the detailed evidence that scholars rely on, the issues they raise and the tenor of arguments that surround them. This material may seem quite knobbly if you are coming to it for the first time. We have aimed to be succinct and clear as we join the discussion around these three exceptional cases.

As we shall see, the relation between economic surplus and class and gendered inequality seems quite straightforward in the case concerning the rich fisheries of the Pacific northwest. The arguments associated with the New Guinea example are more complex, in part because the sheer cultural diversity of the highland populations, and in part because the very notions 'class' and 'gender' are matters of debate among regional scholars. But as we argue, in the New Guinea case, the gendered division of slash-and-burn farming work and the existence of an economic surplus in pigs invites control, hierarchy and gender inequality.

The third exception is of a different order. At first sight the material on indigenous Australians seems to confound our basic argument. We suggest in this case that the very character of evidence itself is problematic, and we may be wrong.

Each of these three cases has received a great deal of scholarly attention and they often turn up as case studies in introductory anthropology courses. There are many reasons for this. In each case, the stunning art, mythic tales and sheer complexity of social organisation is dazzling. Warfare too played an important part in each of the three cases and added drama. And, of course, the totem poles and exotica, and the violence, fuelled racist stereotypes of the 'primitive'.

Two competing histories have driven public interest as well. As we discussed in Part One and will return to in Part Four, these exceptional cases have been foundational to the social evolutionary theories of Darwin and Engels and those of contemporary evolutionary biologists and psychologists. They are used as evidence that the invention of agriculture and the rise of class societies does not undermine a deep conviction that male dominance, violence and inequality are natural to our species.

But against such palaeo-fantasies, there is another history. The origins of social and cultural anthropology lie in the remarkable early ethnographies of societies of the Pacific northwest, the Trobriand Islands off New Guinea and Aboriginal Australia by Franz Boas, Malinowski, Radcliffe-Brown and others, while the numerous studies of New Guinea societies since first contact in 1950s have raised anthropological theory to a new level.

*Coastal Societies of the American Northwest*

We will take the hunter-gatherers with class first. Class societies, where most, but not all, people have to work for their food, rely on a surplus. However, there have been people who did not farm but did live in settled villages, stored surpluses, had classes and fought wars. They have been described as 'complex hunter-gatherers'. Their societies have been used as evidence that economic hierarchies are ancient among human beings.

The Chumash, for example, lived along the Santa Barbara channel on the coast of California before the Spanish conquest (the first Spaniards arrived in 1542), and until Spanish settlement began in earnest in the late eighteenth century.

The Chumash were fisherfolk with all the marks of a class society. They had minor chiefs, often several in one village, led by one of their number. The larger villages were regional centres, and their foremost chief would dominate the region. Chiefs wore special long feather cloaks and were accompanied by groups of armed guards. The common people provided food to the families of the chiefs who did not themselves work. Most chiefs were men, but women chiefs were not uncommon.

The archaeologist Lynn Gamble has written the standard work on Chumash society. She says that what made this style of chieftainship possible was the invention of the 'plank canoe', probably about 500 CE. These canoes were built of sawn planks of redwood, tied together, with the seams caulked by the asphaltum tar that is common in the region. Plank canoes were far more seaworthy than the alternative coracles and dugout canoes and were usually some 20 feet (6 metres) long, but could be longer.[2]

The plank canoe transformed fishing. The Santa Barbara channel was very rich in marine mammals, including several species of seals. The marine mammals were there because the waters were also very rich in fish. That meant big predators, swordfish and tuna, in deeper waters, and fishermen in plank canoes could hunt them too with spears.

The Chumash dried and stored the great fish. They had a considerable food surplus. But these were dangerous open waters, and many people drowned. Moreover, building seaworthy canoes required much skill and each one took approximately 500 person-days of work. The chiefs mobilised a specialist workforce, the 'Brotherhood of the Plank Canoe', to build the canoes. Once they were launched, the chiefs owned the canoes.

The canoes also made possible a regional trade network. People on the large islands in the channel specialised in manufacturing a shell currency, and acorns were among the goods traded with people from the interior. Acorns, like fish, could be stored in volume.

Along with the currency and the canoes came warfare. The archaeologist Patricia Lambert analysed 1,700 skeletons from thirty different Chumash burial sites over many centuries. The bow and arrow were introduced into the area about 580 CE. Before that, Lambert found a lot of bodies with skull fractures which had healed over, the person having later died of some other cause. This was consistent with a tradition of robust but controlled fighting with clubs between individuals, rather than warfare.

The shift to warfare followed two centuries after the introduction of the bow and arrow. From then on, for about six centuries, something like 10% of bodies were buried with projectile points inside them. After 1350 warfare continued, though not as intensely. The archaeological record also shows extensive evidence of defensive palisades, and of the burning of villages. There is suggestive evidence that the wars were fought for control of the central village in the largest community, and largest trade centre, on the coast.[3]

\* \* \*

The Chumash were not alone. There were many 'complex hunting-gathering' societies along the Pacific coast of North America. There were the Pomo and Patwin of northern California. In what are now British Columbia and Alaska, the Tlingit, Tsimshian, Haida, Kwakiutl, Bella Coola, Nootka and Coast Salish controlled rivers with enormous salmon runs, in addition to clam beds and berries. At the choke points on the salmon runs massive amounts of fish could be cornered, caught, dried and stored as surplus for year-round use.

Though without agriculture, these fisherfolk too had class societies with noble families, commoners and slaves, and marked gendered inequality too. There was polygamy among high-status men. 'Senior wives of polygynous chiefs supervised the labour of junior wives and slaves, and the creation of food stores.'[4]

The gendered division of labour meant that high-status men did the open-sea fishing and hunting for marine animals. Women, poor people and slaves were associated with shellfish found along the shore. And people's diets reflected these divisions and they were less well-nourished.

Madonna Moss, in a detailed paper on shellfish, gender and status, quotes one of the earliest ethnographic sources on the Tlingit. There we learn about a marriage in 1885 between a chief and a lower-class woman, a person of the beach. At the wedding the chief's aristocratic rivals sneered, 'no good could come of mating a chief with a clam digger'.[5]

The Dalles site on the Columbia River is an example of the great wealth from the fisheries. There were days, according to accounts from the late nineteenth century, when a small group of people could catch 100,000 pounds of salmon there. That was exceptional, and there was variation from site to site. But across the coast and the rivers, the better the stocks of salmon, the more class inequality is revealed in the archaeology and written accounts.[6]

The inequalities of wealth were often extreme. These people also had complex military technology, with great war canoes that carried large numbers of warriors and required many months for several men to make. The coastal peoples raided and traded with the egalitarian societies inland and upriver from them.

In some places, the archaeologists have found evidence of warfare stretching back 3,000 years. For most of this time, we assume that the cause was contests over control of food resources. Only after the massive epidemics and population decline that followed the arrival of the Europeans did control of the fur trade become more important than the control of food.[7]

In effect, these people were trapped by fishing places, just as farmers were trapped by their fields. And like farmers, storage was essential to these salmon fishers. For a long way back in the archaeological record, examination of their bones and teeth shows that between 40% and 60% of their annual diet came from salmon. The fish ran for only a few weeks, so that most of that diet must have come from dried salmon. Just as with farmers, environmental constraints and new technologies were opening the possibility of class society.

\* \* \*

However, some of the societies cited as 'complex foragers' were nothing of the kind (see, for instance, the Calusa in Chapter 18). Though the evidence about the Chumash, and the coastal societies of the Pacific coast of North America is striking, in fact, complex hunter-gatherer societies are comparatively rare in the archaeological record.

In 2020 Luc Moreau edited a collection of articles on *Social Inequality before Farming*. We recommend that collection. Because it's recent, the contributors are both archaeologists and anthropologists, and they put different sides of the argument carefully and honestly.

The decisive article is William Davies' careful explanation of why there were very few, and perhaps no, complex hunter-gatherer societies in Europe. Davies offers a detailed argument based on a wealth of archaeological evidence from the period of the Upper Palaeolithic onwards. His central point is that there was no reliable concentration of an abundant food source on the same scale as that of the salmon migrations of the North Pacific. Joe Jeffery and Marta Mirazón Lahr back this up by explaining why fishing along the coasts of Africa also did not produce class inequality.[8]

More important, the hierarchical hunter-gatherer societies of the American Northwest emerged long after the invention of agriculture. Indeed, the Chumash were contemporaneous with farming societies across the southwest, centre and east of what is now the United States, and they invented the plank canoe some 6,000 years after agriculture was invented in Mesoamerica.

*Tubers, Pigs, Big Men and Rubbish Men: The New Guinea Highlands*

Complex hunters and gatherers might seem to challenge our argument because they are foragers with class inequality. The New Guinea highlands examples pose an opposite challenge. For many, they seem to be farmers with marked oppression of women, but without socio-economic class. As we shall see, in great part the ethnographic puzzle hinges on how 'class' is defined, and by whom.

The people in the highlands practise slash-and-burn farming, sometimes called 'shifting cultivation' or 'horticulture'. Slash-and-burn methods are used in many places around the world. The farmers cut down the trees and vegetation in a forest to clear a field.

# WHY MEN?

Then they burn the wood and vegetation, and the ashes fertilise the field. The farmers then grow crops on the field for several years. After that the fields are left alone and the forest gradually regenerates. In twenty years, or thirty or forty, the farmers will return to clear the area again.

This is a sustainable method of farming, which can be used for thousands of years without destroying the environment. It differs in important ways from the permanent field method which is now much more common in the world. First, the total yields from any one region are smaller, because the land has to be left so long to regenerate. Second, permanent fields can support much larger population densities, which makes it easier for states and armies to exploit farmers.

Several rather different things seem to be at work here. A smaller yield avoids surplus, while a larger yield enables it. If a larger community can form, there are quite simply more likely henchmen to be called on and more elites to keep privilege going. And finally, slash-and-burn farmers can move off with less loss than grain farmers who may have put in years and years of dedicated work on fixed plots of land. This means that in many parts of the world people who have escaped from or resisted state oppression and violence are attracted to slash-and-burn farming.

These issues are all relevant to slash-and-burn farming in New Guinea, but the situation there is further complicated by another consideration. The arable land in the tight, heavily forested highland valleys is limited, which means the highlanders who are forced away from their farms by warfare, or who seek to flee for other reasons, often end up as dependents of the dominant group in the next valley over.

As we shall see, some slash-and-burn farmers have built egalitarian economies for themselves, with little or no exploitation. We look at four examples at length in the next chapter. However, in many parts of the world slash-and-burn agriculture has fed societies with economic and political inequality, and with gendered inequality as well.

Here we focus on those in the highlands of New Guinea, the third largest island in the world. The western half of the island is occupied by Indonesia. The eastern half of the island is the independent country of Papua New Guinea (PNG). Our interest is in the highlands of PNG, the mountains and high plateau in the centre of the country.

The people of the highlands lived free of any state control until the 1950s and 1960s, when they were conquered and became part of the Australian colony of New Guinea. In the twenty years after conquest, a number of anthropologists arrived to do fieldwork, and we have a pretty good picture of what life was like just after conquest.

The anthropologist Maurice Godelier arrived from Paris in 1966 to do fieldwork with the Baruya. In an ethnography published in 1982, Godelier said that the Baruya lived in a society without class, but that Baruya men strongly marked and enforced the subordination of women. He argued that this case disproved the claim that class societies led to gendered inequality.[9]

Godelier's argument was particularly influential because he was the most distinguished Marxist anthropologist in France. He was saying that his ethnography had shown him that the usual Marxist line, derived from Engels, about property causing the oppression of women was wrong. This mattered to him because he had been taught that the revolution would automatically end the oppression of women by ending capitalism. Now Godelier concluded that the revolution he desired would have to be much wider than that.

Godelier is clearly right about masculine competition, warfare and sexism among the Baruya. And there is a sense in which the Baruya and other highlanders did not have class. But the Baruya certainly did have economic inequality, political inequality, economic exploitation, and an ability to store and accumulate a surplus. Furthermore, our interest in inequality and gender is both broader and deeper than what may or may not be called class. We suggest, quite simply, that the particular form of gendered inequality Godelier describes is associated with the great economic inequality between some Baruya men and others.

* * *

Our explanation begins in the Kuk Swamp, near what is now the highlands town of Waghi. People invented slash-and-burn farming there between 6,500 and 10,000 years ago. For technical reasons, estimates vary, but the best guess is probably about 9,000 years ago.

## WHY MEN?

Archaeologists have found evidence in Kuk that people began cultivating three crops: sago palm, taro and yams. They also built irrigation channels to flood and drain the swamp as needed.[10]

Unlike farmers in much of the world, though, the highlanders did not go on to build states. It seems that for the next 9,000 years local groups managed land collectively. The crops they grew are an important reason for this difference.

In ancient societies where people grew grain, the crop was harvested all at once and could be stored for years. That made control by landlords and kings easier. Taro and yams are tubers. They are bulky, hard to transport, and left in the ground until they are eaten. The highlanders also ate the pith of the sago palm. But that can only be harvested when a tree is felled. Unlike grains, none of these crops are harvested at the same time. And, in each case, the nourishment per kilo is less than with grain.

That meant the farmers were thinly distributed across the rugged terrain of high passes, steep, forested valleys, and low-lying swamps. Geography and the nature of their crops seem to have precluded the emergence of kingdoms and states.

Then sweet potatoes reached the highlands some several hundred years ago. Sweet potatoes are ideally suited to wet weather and high elevations, and they became the most important staple crop in the highlands. But sweet potatoes were also tubers, like sago and taro, and were left in the soil until needed. Still, they produced more calories per kilo.

In the years before the Australian conquest, farming all over the highlands was organised in similar ways. The division of labour was highly gendered. A man would cut down trees and clear bush to make a farm for his wife. Wives planted, weeded and harvested the tubers in the fields, called 'gardens' in New Guinea. Unmarried and divorced women usually cooperated with their brothers.

Men also hunted, and women raised domestic pigs by feeding them sweet potatoes. The pigs reproduced and the herd grew. In practice, pigs were how people stored any surplus.

Land was worked in common by local communities. Individual men did not permanently control any land. Rather, each man controlled the land he had cleared for as long as the garden lasted. Then it was allowed to return to forest and regenerate. This system depended on there being enough land for all men in the group.

People lived in small communities, each of which controlled some land. They would be enemies at war with some neighbouring communities, and at peace with others. In these wars, local groups would often drive out other groups and work the land previously used by the defeated community. Within any valley, there was often a hierarchy of dominant groups and dependent, conquered or refugee groups. People could not steal food, but they could fight over land.[11]

One consequence of the greater nutritional value of the sweet potatoes was an increase in population in some favoured parts of the highlands. And with the increase in population, pressure on the land also increased. And the greater the population, the more likely was war.[12]

Within any local group there was also inequality between men. A minority were 'Big Men', the majority 'Rubbish Men'. These are not translations. Rather, they are the words used in Tok Pisin, the national language, a creole based on English.

Big men gained status in three related ways. One was through bravery and prowess in war. The second was through the ability to dominate discussions and the decisions men made about politics and war. This ability came with wisdom, clarity, rhetorical skill and the ability to build coalitions. But it also relied on physical confidence and skill at bullying weaker and younger men.

The third route to Big Man status was through organising exchanges with other big men in neighbouring villages and valleys. The important exchanges took place at feasts where one local group hosted another. The two groups might be allies, but they were often groups who had been, or would be, enemies in war. These feasts were a way of making peace for a time, and of keeping routes open for trade and marriage.

Big Men were at the forefront in organising feasts. At feasts, they also made very public gifts of shell ornaments and other valuables to Big Men in other groups who were their special trade friends. Whole communities attended feasts which lasted several days. Large numbers of pigs were slaughtered to feed guests, and Big Men contributed more pigs than other men.

Preparing for a feast was demanding and a Big Man relied on the help of Rubbish Men to pull it off. There were invariably more Rubbish Men than Big Men. Although Big Men did not pass on property to their brothers or sons, their prestige and competitive nous did, by association, benefit the next generation.

So, contrary to Godelier's findings, there was in fact inequality of social status and material and dietary wealth within highland societies. And this was present alongside the marked gender inequality which Godelier did identify. Among many groups, there were separate men's houses and a series of sacred men's initiation rituals which lasted over years. There were cults of warriors, courage, semen and the sound of flutes.

Above all, women feared and experienced violence at the hands of men. Yet if Big Men needed Rubbish Men, they needed women even more. The women managed the pigs. And in some areas, but not in other areas, in order to marry, men gave pigs as bridewealth to other men. These pigs too were managed by women. Below, we show that this gender inequality not only existed alongside the overall hierarchy of social and economic inequality between men, but it was also inextricably linked with it.

This was the picture that anthropologists found when they came to do fieldwork in the twenty years after the first Australian arrived. But this may have been an exceptional period. Two aspects of contact with other cultures may have skewed the ethnographers' accounts. The first was that as soon as the Australian district officers arrived in a valley, they suppressed warfare.

Second, the people the ethnographers met had obtained steel axes through long-distance trade networks between ten and thirty years before the Australians arrived. Pacification and steel axes may well have meant that there was a lot more feasting and a lot more economic inequality than before. And these went together in a curious way, and they may also have contributed to gender inequality.

In the 1960s the anthropologist Richard Salisbury measured the difference in work time that steel axes made. He asked older men who had grown up using stone axes for help. Each of them cleared some land with a stone axe, and another patch with a steel axe. Salisbury found that what took five days with a stone axe could be done in one day with steel.[13]

In the time of stone, men had done five days of clearing while women did five days of tending the crops. Now men did one day's work and women still did five. Men could sit around chatting. They could migrate to the plantations on the coast to work for wages. Or Big Men could marry more wives.

The limits on a Big Man's power and control of resources had been the hard labour of clearing land. Now one man could easily clear land for two or more wives. And the labour of the first and second wives could raise the pigs that would allow a Big Man to give bridewealth for another wife. For those men, the accumulation of a surplus in pigs enabled by the introduction of technology which only benefited men's work could combine with increased political influence. An increase in status allowed a Big Man to control more cleared land, giving more crops, allowing him to 'buy' more female labour and so more pigs, and so more feasting.

Confusions about Sexism

The debate among New Guinea specialists about sexual antagonism and male domination is confusing for several reasons. One is that, from the early twentieth century onwards, ethnographers like Boas, Malinowski and Evans-Pritchard sought to protect the people they knew from the stigma of First World voyeurism and the racism directed at these 'newly discovered primitive peoples'. This meant explaining strange, unpalatable PNG customs in ways that were acceptable and made sense to their Western readers. This is indeed what anthropologists do, but it can be overdone.[14]

Another, problematic impetus was an indirect effect of women's liberation. Male ethnographers who had focused on prestige, men's public cults and ceremonial exchanges now became defensive. As Margaret Jolly put it, tongue in cheek, 'The problems of Highlands men became the problems of male anthropologists—how to preserve the maleness of groups in the face of threats, intrusions and allurements from women.'[15]

And there is a third consideration. In this book we have drawn deeply on the work of the feminist anthropologist Marilyn Strathern. Her definition of gender—as moments when a person, object or an activity is characterised in terms of 'sexual imagery'—is the one we have adopted here.[16] And *The Gender of the Gift* is Strathern's veritable encyclopaedia of gender relations in New Guinea. In this dense masterpiece, she argues that gender inequality in the region has been massively overstated by ethnographers who have not understood local categories and ways of thinking. We are partly persuaded. But as Strathern also recognises, 'the strength of Big Men depends on small women who carry the burden of registering his size'.[17]

There is a lesson here. Because people have to live, there are contradictions crawling all over the underside of any dominant ideology—in this case about sexual antagonism. It seems that Strathern, to counter the extreme stories of male violence, has focused on the underside, on the stories the New Guinea women and subordinate men tell themselves to get by. So they fill their lives with confusing stories and tie themselves in knots. These are the stories that help them pretend that power politics, coercion and control are unimportant, and it matters little that they are also being beaten and used to grow pigs.

These are the stories that fill Nora's head in Ibsen's *Doll's House*. These are the stories that anyone living with a violent man tells herself. So too does Strathern make old problems disappear, and 'builds on old insights by extracting from them entirely different messages from those intended'.[18] In effect, Strathern fully understands the complexity of any ethnographic project.

At the very beginning of *The Gender of the Gift*, she notes that much of the symbolic activity in Melanesia

> deploys gender imagery. Since the same is true of Western metaphysics, there is a double danger of making cultural blunders in the interpretation of male–female relations.
>
> The danger stems not just from the particular values that Western gender imagery puts upon this or that activity but from the underlying assumptions about the nature of society, and how that nature is made an object of knowledge.[19]

There are many good ethnographies of these highland communities. To step back in time and leave Euro-American truisms behind, Gilbert Herdt's ethnography of the Sambia is probably the best place to begin. What Herdt describes for the Sambia is not quite a class system, but inequality between men and men was closely associated with inequality between men and women. And in many areas across the highlands, though not all, marked economic inequality was associated with marked gender differences and gender inequality.

In his earlier books you can see how much Herdt liked the Sambia and how taken he was with the ritual homosexuality between teenage boys during initiations. Herdt, an American, was himself gay and what fascinated him was how different this homosexuality was from what he knew. He says at one point that a small minority of Sambia boys and men were deviants: either because they were unable to have oral sex like other boys, or because they were unable to make the transition to live as heterosexual adult men. The density and sophistication of his economic and symbolic descriptions is important. But so is the change in his later work where he begins to understand fully just how frightening and emotionally painful the world of warfare and masculine competition and cruelty was for many of his friends.[20]

The perfect complement to Herdt is Lisette Josephides' *The Production of Inequality*. In a careful analysis, she shows how Big Men among the Kewa used the labour of women and subordinate men to produce pigs and feasts for exchange. She is particularly good on how the Kewa egalitarian ideology of exchange concealed the reality of inequality in production, and how a cooperative ideology of family life concealed the labour of women.[21]

Josephides provides us with the key for understanding the relationship between gender and inequality and a counter to Maurice Godelier's argument that Baruya men oppressed women but had no class.

Godelier's argument is a bit tricksy, because he uses a special definition of class. As a Marxist, he says that class is when some people own the means of production, and others do not. This definition works reasonably well in an industrial-capitalist society. But among the Baruya, as Godelier points out, the only privately owned means of production are hoes, axes and netbags.

Even in these terms, there is a sense in which the Baruya and their neighbours do not have class, because the status of Big Man is not inherited. It is not tied to land ownership, since land is only ever controlled by a particular community for a period of time, rather than being the property of an individual. Yet inequality and violence are everywhere.

The highlanders of New Guinea are a good example of why we have been careful all through this book not to define class in terms of ownership of the means of production. Though we repeat ourselves, it is worth saying again that we understand 'class' as those social relationships between people, which are often ritualised, culturally elaborate and systematic and in which some people use violence to get control of more than their share of the food.

One reason to look at unequal economic relationships rather than ownership is that, as any anthropologist can tell you, ownership is a very special ideological construct in modern capitalism. People are said to own things. But look a bit more closely, and the house is mortgaged to the bank, the exporter cannot move their goods without paying value added tax and customs duties, the state holds the right of eminent domain to force people to sell their land, and so on. There are literally thousands of laws, and thousands of pages of trade agreements, that qualify the meaning of ownership.

What we do see in the examples from the New Guinea highlands is the importance of violence in creating economic inequality and the association of male violence, economic inequality and gendered inequality.

Warfare is the method of inequality between groups, by which some people take control of land they did not previously farm, and some groups become dependent refugees. Warfare is also one of the central ways young men can become Big Men. Women are afraid of the violence of men and disciplined by it. Big Men dominate women, but they also dominate the majority of other men, the Rubbish Men. Big Men control the distribution of food. The labour of women and men grows tubers, and the labour of women turns those tubers into pigs mainly controlled by Big Men. So, like the Pacific fishing societies, the slash-and-burn farmers of the New Guinea highlands aren't such a challenge to our arguments after all. But now we should turn to the 'counter-case' which is trickiest to unpick: Aboriginal Australians.

*Indigenous Australians: Rituals and Marriage*

All accounts agree that traditional Australian hunting societies showed the same pattern of economic equality, personal autonomy and constant sharing that are found among other hunter-gatherers. But much of the anthropology literature, early and late, suggests three important forms of inequality between men and women. One was a great deal of domestic violence. The second was that men dominated ritual affairs. The third was that older men exchanged younger women as their wives.

Together these have been taken to mean that in societies without class, the oppression of women is still possible. Moreover, the Australian case depends on the history and ethnography of no single, small and isolated band. Until recently, in Australia everyone on the continent lived by hunting and gathering. In this respect, it is a key test case.

In this final section of the chapter, however, we question this picture of Australian sexism. But we are not trying to wish away the evidence. We began working on this section knowing that the ethnographies of indigenous Australians presented the most stubborn case to our argument. So we settled on rereading the ethnography and asking questions. And in the process we met two very considerable obstacles to understanding the lives of people in preconquest Australia.

The scale of the genocidal violence of the European invasion and conquest of the continent is the first and most daunting obstacle. The second shock was realising the extent to which the discipline of anthropology in Australia has been affected by conservative and racist values. Indeed, it is only very recently, and in part in response to Black Lives Matter and Me Too, that many Australian public secrets—those things that everyone knows but cannot say—are being exposed. This has encouraged us to reconsider the early fieldwork of three ethnographers, whose flawed research has informed many of the assumptions about indigenous relationships to gender and violence.

Before we take a closer look at the complex and troubling realities obscured by this early ethnography, it is useful to start with a researcher who *did* perceive those realities during her fieldwork: the feminist anthropologist Diane Bell, author of *Daughters of the Dreaming*. Bell did more than two years of field research between 1978 and 1983 in the Northern Territories, mostly at Warrabri, about 220 miles north of Alice Springs. The women Diane Bell lived and worked with were originally from two communities, one to the south of Warrabri and one to the north.[22]

## WHY MEN?

One of the great virtues of Bell's work is that she places the relationships between the genders within the context of the violence that flowed from British colonialism. The people to the south of Warrabri were the first in the region to encounter the white conquest, in the form of the men pushing the telegraph line northwards across Australia in the later nineteenth century.

Bell quotes Arthur Ashwin writing about the 1870s in Warumungu country in central Australia:

> I let six staghounds go, and away they went towards the rising morn. Then we heard a stampede like a mob of cattle breaking through the scrub; then a native yelling for about five minutes; then all was quiet. About ten minutes later the staghounds came back to camp and were tied up again. They were covered with blood. Milner said, 'Aye, mon, Arthur! They have done good work. I think the fear of God will be with the natives to-night.'[23]

Bell reports that there was also chronic warfare as the white colonial pastoralists moved north with their cattle. (Pastoralist is the word used in Australia for a cattle or sheep rancher.) There was one white woman to every ten white men on the frontier. The pastoralists tried to exterminate the Aboriginal men, both to stop them fighting for their land and to ensure that white men had access to Aboriginal women.

Bell says that the toll of such attacks and counter-attacks on the Aborigines was great. She quotes one report of 1898 from the Frew River area, 'where 45 bucks and 460 gins remained alive'. (Bucks was the ugly word for an Aboriginal man, a gin was an Aboriginal woman.) We have no statistics with which to compare these numbers with previous decades, but the implications of the sex imbalance, even if overstated, are horrendous.[24]

The historical memory of the men Bell did fieldwork with was unequivocal. They said the wars between white and black and the massacres by whites were attempts by white men to gain control of Aboriginal women. In this case it seems likely that white settlers had killed 90% of the men, and they did so to get access to Aboriginal women.

Several of the older women Bell knew in the 1970s still remembered a series of massacres by pastoralists in the 1920s. As children, they had heard news and rumours of the massacres, and several of them had witnessed and survived a massacre. As old women, they were very reluctant to speak of these events to Bell, but they also could not help compulsively mentioning them.

* * *

In 2017 Professor Lyndall Ryan and her colleagues at Newcastle University in New South Wales released the first version of their online map of frontier massacres in Australia between 1788 and 1930. They have updated it regularly ever since. By 2022 they had reasonably reliably found accounts of 403 massacres of Aborigines. They supply all the details they can for each of these cases. Ryan and her colleagues only count instances where more than six people were killed, and almost all their body counts are estimated round numbers, such as 10, 20, 30 or 100 dead.[25]

They found several peaks in the number of massacres, first in Tasmania in the 1820s and then in the 1840s across New South Wales, Victoria, South Australia and Western Australia. 'From the 1860s when the frontier shifted to Northern Australia, massacre peaks took place in Queensland in the 1860s and 1880s and [from] 1880 to 1930 in the Northern Territory.'

The last really big killing was a coordinated series of massacres in 1928, when 'several hundred Walpiri, Anmatyerre and Kaytetye people were killed in reprisal for killing a [white] dingo trapper'.[26] These were the massacres that Diane Bell's older friends could not talk about and could not stop thinking about forty years later.

Ryan and her colleagues have found a total of 403 massacres of Aboriginals by whites, with 10,925 dead. They have also found 12 massacres of white colonists with 152 dead. That is 72 times as many Aboriginal dead as white settler dead.

About half of the 403 massacres of Aboriginals were done by agents of the state, police or soldiers, often with help from settlers. About half were done by settlers on their own. Ryan says that almost all the massacres were planned ahead of time, and usually designed to drive Aboriginal people off the land settlers coveted.

These statistics are approximate, and they must have missed many cases. Perhaps more important are the killings of fewer than six people at a time by police and other settlers.

## WHY MEN?

The men, women and children who survived these killings were driven off the land and forced to live with others in refugee communities, in most cases without work of any kind and minimal welfare payments. And it seems from the experience of native North Americans as well that there is something especially hard about remaining after such death-dealing as the poorest and most despised people on land that was once yours. If there is much about their lives in those camps in recent years that reeks of a sexism that fits with the settler society, this is not surprising.[27]

Accounts of the forced settlement of hunter-gatherers on other continents also suggest lives blighted by alcohol and violence. That tells us nothing about how people had lived before.

Even amid the horrors of forced settlement, however, people can and do build lives. Many Aboriginal communities are not blighted by drink. Some are collectively teetotal. Not all Aboriginal people are lost. Bell describes in considerable detail how the ritual lives of the women she knew kept them whole and sane.

\* \* \*

Ryan's anti-racist work documenting the massacres is admirable but it comes late after the shameful history of racist anthropology. After about 1920 cultural and social anthropologists in many countries saw opposition to racism as the intellectual heart of their discipline. Their mission was to prove to the world that people of colour were as intelligent as everyone else, and that every culture and way of life was valuable.

Australia was different. From 1894 to 1926 Sir Baldwin Spencer dominated anthropology there. A professor at Melbourne University, he became the government's official Protector of Aborigines. He believed and said that Aborigines were savages, racially inferior and would eventually pass away. Spencer made it a particular focus of his work that 'half-caste' children in Aboriginal camps should be taken away from their families and never have anything more to do with camp life. He was the official national Protector during many massacres, and seems to have done no protecting.

Spencer did most of his work jointly with Frank Gillen, who lived in Alice Springs and was the official Protector of Aborigines there.

## SALMON, PIGS AND RITUALS

In his letters, Gillen said that protectors 'should have two objects firstly to ... collect and record the customs, habits, etc. and secondly to make the path to extinction—which we all agree is inevitable and rapidly approaching as pleasant as possible'. The anthropologist Diane Austin-Broos adds that, 'On the basis of this logic Gillen, like Spencer, supported the removal of "half-caste" and orphan children from their aboriginal kin.'[28]

Then, from his appointment as the professor at the University of Sydney in 1933 until his death in 1966, the Anglican clergyman A.P. Elkin dominated Australian anthropology. He did not believe that Aborigines should die out, but he did believe that their culture would die away and that they should all be assimilated into mainstream white society.

In the next generation, Elkin's student M.J. Meggitt was one of the stars of the profession. One of the central arguments of his book *Desert People* in 1961 was that the Walpiri with whom he did his fieldwork were sufficiently advanced to be good candidates for eventual assimilation, unlike other groups who could never hope to achieve that status.[29]

In this atmosphere, there was a great deal that could not be said. After 1950 it was understood that the government would ban anthropologists who were also communists from doing fieldwork in indigenous communities. A brilliant history of the Sydney department of anthropology makes it crystal clear that anyone who wrote or spoke about settler or government cruelty would never get research permission or a university post again.[30]

* * *

This official code of silence explains something a bit odd about the ethnographies of indigenous Australians. Consider, for example, W. Lloyd Warner's 1937 classic *A Black Civilization*. Warner did three years of field research in the far north with Murngin people between 1926 and 1929. Warner was not a racist, as the title he chose for his book makes clear. As a student in his native California he had been an active socialist. After Australia Warner would go on to write eleven books about inequality in the United States. But in his 1937 book on the Murngin he said nothing about white behaviour.

## WHY MEN?

In the second edition, twenty years later, there was a twenty-page appendix on social change. Almost all of it was about the Malay traders who had been coming to Murngin land for a few months of every year for a long time, probably at least a century. In that appendix, Warner permitted himself one remark about white settlers, writing that all the indigenous people

> speak very highly of the Malay traders, for they always mention first their generosity and immediately after this they say, 'They let our women alone'. In the same breath that they tell a white man whom they consider to be their friend, that the white and Japanese traders are 'no good' because they are stingy and always trying to rape their women.[31]

Though he readily acknowledges the apparently widespread reality of colonial sexual violence and economic exploitation, this is all Warner has to say about it: a short mention at the back of the book, in isolation from his findings on the Murngin way of life, and only added decades after his research was first published and became influential.

Even this reluctant, minimised recognition from Warner can help to corroborate what others have found about the impact of European contact on indigenous ways of being. Lauriston Sharp, who spent a year in the 1920s with people just to the north of the Murngin, wrote about the shattering effects of the way that steel axes destroyed the old trade in stone axes long before the settlers arrived. And he wrote poetically about the way that rich and violent invaders were causing people's deepest faiths to collapse.[32]

It is a similar story in the semi-arid Kimberley region in the north of Western Australia where the feminist anthropologist Phyllis Kaberry did her research. Kaberry's *Aboriginal Woman, Sacred and Profane* was based on some eighteen months of research between 1934 and 1936. The people she stayed with spent part of the year in hunting camps, although some of the men also worked on cattle ranches. Kaberry provides the best account we have of what women's lives were like in a semi-traditional society.[33]

In the years before Kaberry arrived, there were at least seven massacres in the Kimberleys: at Mowla Bluff in 1918, Auvergne Station in 1918, Bedford Downs in 1922 and 1924, Sturt Creek in

## SALMON, PIGS AND RITUALS

1922 and 1925, and Forrest River in 1926. Several features recur in the accounts of these massacres.[34]

A posse of police and settlers would seize men and women as a collective punishment. As was usual in police work in the area, the white men rode on horses and their prisoners walked in lines, with chains connecting the shackles around their necks. The prisoners were shot or poisoned and then burned to destroy the evidence. Firewood was scarce in an arid land, and the settlers and police often had to kill only a few prisoners in one place, and then march the rest to another place where there would be more firewood. Sometimes the prisoners were forced to gather the firewood themselves before the executions.

The official story put about by the posse was that Aboriginals had speared a cow or a camel for food. In many cases, however, it was widely known in the area that the real source of tension had been a pattern of sexual abuse and rape by a particular pastoralist. The Forrest River massacre in 1926 began because Frederick William Hay sexually assaulted Anulgoo. Her husband, Lumbia, fought back. Hay attacked Lumbia with a stockwhip and then fired his revolver. Lumbia killed Hay with his spear. The posse then rounded up, killed and burned twenty-three men and women.[35] That was too much. A courageous missionary made public accusations until a Royal Commission was appointed to make a report. The proceedings were national news. But no one was ever convicted.[36]

In 1934, eight years after that massacre, Phyllis Kaberry began her fieldwork at Forrest River. The older women who were her main informants must have told her about the massacre. She must have known about the Royal Commission. She never mentioned any of the massacres in her book. Such was the silence.

The massacres associated with the rape of Aboriginal women and the racist anthropology present great obstacles to understanding the lives of pre-conquest Australians, though they do make it easier to understand the considerable violence reported in some twentieth-century Aboriginal communities and the extent to which that violence was gendered.

\* \* \*

There is, however, a great deal we can say with some confidence about the second kind of 'evidence' for sexism among indigenous

## WHY MEN?

Australians: the claim that men dominated ritual affairs and that women had impoverished ritual lives in comparison with men.

Indigenous Australia was an intensely thoughtful civilisation. There are many, many accounts of their subtle, but also mind-bogglingly complicated ways of thinking about their lives and the world around them. These were people obsessed with intellectual concerns. Two fields were particularly important. One was a very complex system of ritual, dreams, geography, history, myths, art, music and dancing. The other was the system of kinship and marriage.

Some idea of the complexity can be gleaned from the fact that in many areas, proper ritual activity by an older person required the knowledge of four complete languages, two contemporary and two archaic. This is of course common enough now among a small minority of learned religious professionals in Buddhism, Hinduism or Christianity. What was different about Australia was that such knowledge was very widely distributed in small communities, although limited by age because it took decades to learn. And, of course, all this knowledge was handed down orally, with no system of writing.

The extensive knowledge connected with the ritual system was also closely guarded. Women were careful not to share knowledge with men, and men with women. Everyone was careful not to share with whites, but also not to share with people from neighbouring groups. Today any anthropologist who is eventually trusted and given ritual knowledge has to promise not to share the specifics of that knowledge with her readers.

Up until the 1970s most anthropologists reported that men had very complex ritual lives, but women did not. The exception was Phyllis Kaberry, who insisted that the women she studied had their own complex rituals, song, dance and knowledge. Kaberry said it was just that the rituals and knowledge of men and women were kept separate. She writes fiercely, 'there can be no question of identifying the sacred inheritance of the tribe only with the men's ceremonies. Those of the women belong to it also… The women with regard to the men's rituals are profane and uninitiated; the men with regard to the women's ritual are profane and uninitiated.'[37]

It is not clear if the other early ethnographers were suffering from male bias. Perhaps they were merely reflecting what they were told by men who wanted to respect the secrecy of women's rituals. Probably it was both.

But Diane Bell, in the late 1970s, was clear that she was only really able to find out about the ritual lives of women because she was a divorced mother with two children. The fact that she had children, and had been married, made her a grown woman like the women she got to know. The fact that she was divorced meant she would not tell their secrets to some man. Still, it took the women a long time to decide they could trust Bell. Once they did, however, they let her see how much their ritual lives in the compound were central to their existence. She argues, convincingly, that their ritual system was as complex as the ones reported earlier for men.

\* \* \*

Let us turn now to the third vexed question: whether or not women were oppressed in marriage. To second guess ourselves about the changes that must have followed from conquest and settlement, we have to go as far back in time as we can. Here too, the key ethnography is Phyllis Kaberry's *Aboriginal Woman, Sacred and Profane*.

The traditional anthropological view was first set out in 1931 and elaborated in 1949. This model said that Aboriginal men lived in patrilineal groups and exchanged women in marriage with other groups.[38]

The model was mistaken. Later work has shown that groups were local, not patrilineal, and they did not exchange women. The Aboriginal people did have complex kinship systems. In most places this meant that any individual man or woman was only permitted to marry between a quarter and a half of the likely people nearby of the opposite sex.[39]

But crucially, these marriages were arranged by older people. This happens, of course, in many parts of the world. It happens among the egalitarian !Kung, and among the Huaorani, and in many unequal societies as well. In these societies, the parents of the groom and the parents of the bride come to an agreement, usually with at least the grudging consent of their children.

What seems to be exceptional about the Australian system was that though people were economic equals and shared food and other goods, the older men could, and often did, arrange marriages for themselves with much younger women. In effect, there has been a consensus among anthropologists that in spite of material equality, there was gender inequality before the conquest, and competition among men over the control of women's marriages. We are not so sure.

Kaberry was a feminist. She was concerned to rescue Australian women from the condescension of a male-dominated profession of anthropology.[40] She argued that women had far more autonomy than they had been given credit for and were far more equal. She did not argue, and this is important, that women in the Kimberley were the equals of men. She argued only that they were much less oppressed than they were portrayed.

Her account of what happened in marriage is different. Kaberry was clear. The older women she knew told her that they were involved in the negotiations and decisions over who their daughters married. If the mother rejected a possible candidate, he would not have her daughter.

More important, a betrothal was a long-term agreement about work and food between the groom and the mother of the bride. The way it worked was that a man would approach the mother of a baby girl soon after the child was born. If the mother agreed, the groom was then obliged to give steady gifts of meat he had hunted to the mother. These gifts lasted for years as the girl grew up. The central economic relationship, day by day, was between the mother and the groom. Of course, she shared the food with her relatives, neighbours, the groom and indeed her daughter. If the groom did not keep up his end of the bargain, the engagement was over. And he had to keep bringing meat to his mother-in-law long after the marriage began.

These facts do not entirely settle the matter. The male anthropologists were right that the men said they arranged exchange marriages with other men. But Kaberry was also right that the mother said: 'That man came to me and asked if he could marry my daughter and I said yes.' Both men and women were pointing to different aspects of the same system.

How do we know which aspect was more important? Well, we know what Kaberry thought was more important in practice, and she was a splendid ethnographer.

## SALMON, PIGS AND RITUALS

Just as important, the girl had control of her own body. Soon after beginning sex with her husband, she moved rapidly to dalliances and affairs with other men, mostly men much closer to her in age. It would be wrong to say she was entirely free in doing so. Husbands got jealous. But she had ample opportunity.

The husband might become furious. But fights between men and women were not one-way. The anthropologist Eleanor Leacock says of Kaberry's work:

> References to women of recent times fighting back publicly in a spirited style, occasionally going after their husbands with both tongue and fighting club, and publicly haranguing both men and women bespeak of a continuing tradition of autonomy...

In relation to 'those reciprocal rights and duties that are recognized to be inherent in marriage,' Kaberry writes:

> 'I, personally, have seen too many women attack their husbands with a tomahawk or even their own boomerangs, to feel that they are invariably the victims of ill treatment. A man may perhaps try to beat his wife if she has not brought in sufficient food, but I never saw a wife stand by in submission to receive punishment for her culpable conduct. In the quarrel she might even strike the first blow, and if she were clearly in danger of being seriously hurt, then one of the bystanders might intervene, in fact always did within my experience.'

> Nor did the man's greater strength tell in such a struggle, [Leacock says], for the wife 'will pack up her goods and chattels and move to the camp of a relative ... till the loss of an economic partner brings the man to his senses and he attempts a reconciliation.'

To which Leacock adds, quite brilliantly, that what may be called the 'household economy' in our society is the entire economy among hunter-gatherers.[41]

The sexual freedom of young women was central to what made marriages in the Kimberley equal. The marriage did, however, determine paternity and which kinship section her children belonged to. They belonged to their father's section, and their mother's husband was their father. This was true without regard to who she was actually having sex with. Moreover, divorce was easy and common, and most women who married young chose a younger husband when the old one died.

This pattern of young women having relatively free sex lives was found in many other parts of Australia as well. It was not a simple matter, though. As we have said, husbands could and did become angry.

Among the Tiwi of northern Australia, for instance, affairs between young women and young men were common.

The Tiwi live on the twin Melville and Bathurst islands separated by a narrow strait, and about 50 miles off the northern coast of the continent. The first anthropologist to do detailed ethnographic work on the islands was C.W.M. Hart, in the 1920s. Hart, and his later collaborators, Arnold Pilling and Jane C. Goodale, continued the work in the 1950s and 1980s.[42] Hart is our best guide to 'traditional' life, because his fieldwork was early, but he writes with little respect for the Tiwi. Still, Pilling and Goodale largely agree with him.

Hart's informants told him that in the past, when older husbands became jealous, they could challenge the young man to a duel, in which the aggrieved husband threw spears at the young man which the young man dodged. Then, they said, it was considered good form, and respectful, for the young man to eventually allow a spear to connect, creating a graze or flesh wound. Then honour would be satisfied. If the young man persisted in defiantly dodging the spears, the old men would all stand with the aggrieved husband and together they would kill the offender. But no such killing had happened since the white conquest fifty years before. When people were killed under European colonial rule, the killers were arrested and sent to prison in Darwin. So when Hart was there in the 1920s, the old men only threw sticks which did little damage.[43]

What's more, Hart, Pilling and Goodale are agreed about the basic features of Tiwi marriage. While Hart offers a sneering, cynical view of Tiwi women—who 'as daughters and wives were quite thoroughly subordinate to the wishes of their fathers or husbands, and Tiwi wives were as frequently and as brutally beaten by their husbands as wives in any other savage society'—he also goes on to explain at length that

> Old mothers with influential senior sons were extremely powerful. Any affront to an old woman was an affront to her sons, and some of

the strongest alliance networks were alliances of several senior brothers, in which the old mother seemed the mastermind and the senior sons largely the enforcers of that the old mother and her middle-aged daughters (their sisters) had decided among themselves.[44]

Hart argues that this was not a marriage system dominated by old men, but a system dominated by old people.

Hart, Pilling and Goodale, writing together, also note that the Tiwi marriage system was unusual for Australia. Other communities certainly had old men who arranged marriages and had multiple wives. But some old Tiwi men had many more wives than in other groups, and many Tiwi men never had any. Moreover, in other groups a man would begin marrying in his twenties, and Tiwi did not begin doing so until their thirties.

This difference is important, but as with the research of Bell, Kaberry and Warner, we know that the Tiwi too were dealing with the consequences of conquest. And in this exceptional case, there were yet other things in play.

Though the Tiwi were not conquered by white Australians until the 1880s, the inlands had for centuries been the object of slave raiding, usually called 'blackbirding'. These raids began from the Dutch-controlled island of Java about 1600, and from Portuguese Timor in the eighteenth century. Hart, Pilling and Goodale speculate that the Tiwi islands may have been unusual because for such a long time so many of the young men had been enslaved each year.

When the slavers came, the old men, the women and the children stayed far from the shore in hiding. The young men went down to meet the slavers, who were also sometimes traders. The young men were driven to do so because they wanted iron which they used for spears and fishhooks. And they learned from the slavers and traders how to make dugout canoes and bark canoes so they could hunt the dugong and sharks offshore.

Hart, Pilling and Goodale propose another explanation as well for the power of old men. In other places, like the Kimberleys, women who were oppressed by their husbands could and did leave. In the Tiwi islands there was no place for an unhappy woman to escape. There were two uninhabited islands where people could stop if they tried to make the trip to Darwin on the coast in a dugout canoe. But even resting on one of them, the shortest leg of the voyage was still 25 miles.

There was another factor that may also have changed gender relations among the Tiwi. When Hart did his fieldwork in the 1920s, the Tiwi were divided between ten different 'countries'—local groups. Three 'countries' lived in the traditional manner by hunting and gathering. And they operated a kinship system in what seemed to be a traditional way. The people of another four 'countries' were dependent on the Christian mission, which gave them food, raised the girls inside the mission, and then arranged the marriages of the girls to young men. Finally, the people of the remaining three 'countries' lived under the patronage of Japanese pearl-diving ships, which had been coming for centuries. The divers gave the Tiwi food and other goods in exchange for sex work.

\* \* \*

Some readers will be thinking that the Indigenous Australians were not in fact hunter-gatherers but farmers. This idea comes from a brilliant book by Bill Gammage in 2012, *The Biggest Estate on Earth: How Aborigines Made Australia*.[45] Gammage's book was popularised and extended by Bruce Pascoe, whose influential book *Dark Emu* provoked the fury of the racist right.[46]

Here, however, we want to concentrate on Gammage's book. He made ingenious use of a variety of evidence to show that Aboriginal people used fire to manage the landscape before the European conquest. He showed how they used firesticks to start many small fires and transform much of the continent from forests into rolling parkland. This was skilled work, requiring a complex knowledge of how fire can be controlled, and of the ecology and growth patterns of many species of trees, plants and animals.

Gammage demonstrates convincingly that Aboriginal people were not hunting and gathering in a pristine, natural environment. This was a landscape transformed and shaped in great detail by human management. It was an achievement as impressive and far reaching as the invention of agriculture. But it was not agriculture as we know it in Asia, Africa or Europe.[47]

For our purposes here, what matters most is the ways in which Australian land management was similar to hunter-gatherers in the rest of the world. Aboriginal Australians did not gain power by controlling a stored surplus. Everyone shared food, and land. People kept up relationships with other people over great distances because the ability to move in times of drought or distress was crucial to survival. What they did was to transform the landscape, and then hunt and gather in that new landscape.

\* \* \*

The case for gender inequality in Australia has three main pillars. The first is the high levels of domestic violence in many contemporary communities. This is the result of a colonial history and present-day economics, and in no way proof that is how things were before. The second pillar is the inferiority of women's ritual lives. Kaberry, and especially Bell have put that to rest. The third pillar was that men were exchanging women. As we have seen, that is not what Kaberry reports.

But there is another reason to be careful here. The evidence for traditional inequality between men and women may be lacking. But that is not the same thing as clear evidence for traditional equality.

Both Kaberry and Bell are careful to say that while the women they knew were of much higher status than anyone outside had given them credit for, they were not the social equals of men. Like white Australian or Norwegian women, they were oppressed. We simply do not know for sure, on the evidence we now have, whether or not there was gender equality before the conquest.

Indeed, we must really ask ourselves, what with rape, sex work, genocide, poverty and racism, what honestly can we know about people's pre-conquest lives? The recorded massacres, after all, must have been only the tip of an iceberg. On a daily basis, individual murders, beatings and whippings would have meant that people were trapped in communities saturated with fear and humiliation. Historians glimpse the sexual violence of the settlers at the moments of heroic resistance that led to massacres. But the daily reality of settler sexual exploitation must have had a deep influence on relationships between Aboriginal men and women.

These were communities of survivors, of people living with a deep history of trauma. But there are two sides to the frontier conflicts. The accounts that tell us of massacres are also records of an unending resistance over two centuries by people who defended their access to land for as long as they could, who kept spearing the livestock on the land that had been stolen and resisted rape at enormous collective risk.[48]

There have also been collective resistance to the labour regime on the cattle stations and the long fight for land rights.[49] But perhaps the most important form of resistance against such odds was that people have survived, raised their children, and hung on to their languages, their rituals, myths and oral histories, and above all the traditional stories that give people a moral right to the land.

# 11

# EQUALITY AMONG REBELS IN THE MOUNTAINS AND FORESTS

Over the last few chapters, we have made and defended our argument that what led humans to discard their gender-equal origins in favour of patriarchal domination was the arrival, thanks to farming, of class society—that male violence and power marked a bigger shift, away from the egalitarian and cooperative side of our nature and towards the dominance and hierarchy so evident in our primate heritage. But that more peaceful, more equal side of our nature has endured also. Here, in the final chapter of Part Two, we tell the story of four societies where people have fought for and maintained equality between men and women. For there was always another world beyond the farmed river valleys where states and class societies flourished.

All over Europe, from early medieval times onwards, wooden stave fences called the pale marked the borders between 'civilised' people who knew their place and the unruly, feared and free savages. Before the pale, there was Hadrian's Wall and Offa's Dyke, and in China, the Great Wall, and yet others even before those. The trick is to know whether the pale was to keep people in, or to keep people out. Often it was both.

In this chapter we are particularly interested in a three-fold association: rather than grain agriculture, development of class hierarchy and male dominance, we can see that process's hopeful mirror in the links between slash-and-burn agriculture, flight from class hierarchy and egalitarian gender relations. The association is not inevitable, and as we saw in the New Guinea highlands, slash-and-burn farming is sometimes associated with hierarchy and gender inequality. Mayan slash-and-burn farming at certain periods of that civilisation's long history was another example. And so is the Yanomamo case we discuss in Part Four.

However, what we want to show in this chapter is that gender equality did not cease everywhere with the invention of agriculture. For some slash-and-burn agriculturalists living beyond the pale, gender equality was and is a reality. This may seem hard to believe. Yet it is an important part of our human story. To see what that means we look in detail at how four groups of our tribal contemporaries manage gender equality, though in very different ways: Lahu villagers in Southern China, Huaorani of Amazonian Ecuador, and the Pemon and Piaroa people in Venezuela. These are not the only slash-and-burn farmers who live in an egalitarian way. We chose three of these examples because of the strength and beauty of the ethnographies, and because, in each case, the ethnographer makes different, important analytical points about gender equality. We chose the Pemon example because we've been there.[1]

Three of these groups are slash-and-burn farmers. (The Huaorani are farmers some of the time and hunter-gatherers the rest of the time.) Slash and burn is a way to support yourselves. But it is often also a way of fleeing beyond the cruelty of states based on rice, wheat or maize. Slash and burn is particularly common in tropical forests where intensive farming will not work. This is for a non-obvious reason. A tropical rainforest looks, and is, lush. But cut down the bigger trees, and the topsoil bakes or washes away.

Slash and burn allows the soil to regenerate. But it is also usually much less productive than farming grain in constantly replenished soil along the riverbanks in the forest. Which is another way of saying that slash-and-burn agriculture is hard work. And before steel axes it was very hard work indeed. So is slash and burn on steep rocky hillsides. Both are far less productive than permanent farming on richer, more even ground.

Nonetheless, in many parts of the world there are people to whom slash and burn appeals strongly. These people are willing to put up with thin soil and backbreaking toil if they can stay out of reach of the soldiers and landlords. It may be easier to grow a bushel of rice down on the plains, but not if the landlord comes and takes half that bushel. In the forest or on forested hills you may have to work twice as hard for the bushel, but without a landlord, you keep all the rice. And in the forests and hills, you can keep your dignity and self-respect.

That can mean extraordinarily different things among different people. In the rest of this chapter, we turn our attention to four groups of egalitarian slash-and-burn agriculturalists living in the hills and in forests apart from today's class societies.

Farming without class exploitation, where farmers were equals, and where there was gender equality as well, is a proposition you may find hard to believe—or even imagine. Our best chance of understanding how farming and gender equality can go together in practice, and how it feels, comes from ethnographies of particular remote slash-and-burn agriculturalists doing their best to elude the agents of neighbouring states.

Meanwhile what we learn from those slash-and-burn agriculturalists who were egalitarians holds many surprises.

One of these surprises is about warfare. We have been arguing throughout Part Two that male violence, whether individual, societal or waged by a patriarchal state, is a tool for enforcing inequality. But slash-and-burn farmers often pursue a special kind of war that was called by twentieth-century anthropologists 'primitive warfare'. However, there is nothing primitive or ancient about it. It arises partly from the population pressures of slash-and-burn farming, and partly from resistance to encroaching class societies.

A corollary to the notion of 'primitive warfare' is worth keeping in mind. The societies of the Lahu, Huaorani, Pemon and Piaroa cannot be understood in isolation. These societies of backwoods and hill people have been built in a relationship with the farmers and states of the river valleys, and with the local states and colonial rulers. In the same way an account of the culture of the Apache or the Sioux must include the contact history of Native Americans with fur traders, gold prospectors, the railroads and the United States Cavalry. As it was on the American plains, so it has been in many places in the world. For the people whose lives we describe here, the gender equality and the warfare of these peoples are ways of living together, but they are also conscious forms of defiance.

It is strange which anthropologists do, and which do not, emphasise gender equality among hunters and gatherers, and among some slash-and-burn farmers. The anthropologists who have done research on the ground are unequivocal. These people are equal, they say. Most feminists, including feminist anthropologists, are sceptical.

*Power Couples: Real-Life Equality Among the Lahu*

Shanshan Du is one of the believers. She did fieldwork with the egalitarian Lahu in southern China, and she makes an important point. No society is ever perfectly egalitarian, Du says. But that does not mean it is not egalitarian:

> In the process of struggling for gender equality in their own societies, some Euro-American feminists have turned to other cultures for hope and inspiration. Accompanying the heated debate over the universality of female subordination in the mid-1970s, the search for gender-egalitarian societies also reached its peak. Ironically, by projecting diverse utopian ideals into cross-cultural studies, the declaration of the non-existence of gender-egalitarian societies became a self-fulfilling prophecy. After all, there is always an unbridgeable gap between a utopian fantasy and a real society because the latter never operates on seamlessly coherent principles. While not a single existing society on the planet can possibly match just one utopian model, it is even more impossible for a society to live up to the expectations of *many* utopian ideals, some of which hold conflicting standards for measuring gender equality. Not surprisingly, no agreement has been reached on vesting a single society with the title 'gender-egalitarian'...
>
> The different impacts of idealistic approaches on cross-cultural studies of women's status correspond to the different assertions denying the existence of gender-egalitarian societies. A society is sometimes classed as 'male dominant' despite the fact that its ideology and institutions are predominantly gender-egalitarian.[2]

Indeed, Du says, in some cases egalitarian societies have been classified as sexist on one trait only—they isolate women who are menstruating. So let's see what equality between women and men looks like in practice, rather than in perfect theory.

The Lahu are a classic example of a much more general pattern identified by James C. Scott in his 2009 book *The Art of Not Being*

# EQUALITY AMONG REBELS

*Governed: An Anarchist History of Upland Southeast Asia*. The book has rapidly become influential because it is marvellous. Scott's examples range across Southeast Asia from the Philippines to Burma. He argues that upland tribal peoples did not live in some antique style. Rather, he says, the ruling classes along the rivers in the lowlands built kingdoms and empires based on rice cultivation in irrigated 'padi' ponds. It was impossible to grow padi above a certain altitude, or without enough irrigation water. Where padi was possible, the lowland kingdoms had enough surplus to feed landlords and a state. Above that latitude, farmers turned to slash and burn.[3]

In different parts of Southeast Asia, the people of the lowland padi fields would go by one name—Thai or Han, Khmer or Vietnamese, Shan or Burmese. The people who farmed by slash and burn were the 'mountain tribes' with other names—Kachin, Lahu, Hmong and dozens of other groups. Each of these groups spoke a different language, had different customs and sometimes a different religion. But people changed groups all the time. When the lowland state conquered them, they became Thai or Burmese. When the lowland Burmese fled into the hills, they often became Kachins.

The Lahu studied by Du are one of these hill peoples. There are 650,000 Lahu now in the hills along the borders between China and Myanmar. Some of the Lahu people were once settled farmers who fled Thai and Chinese state taxes and oppression. Some of them were the descendants of Han Chinese peasants who had rebelled against the empire and lost. The Lahu, indeed, have a long tradition of revolts led by prophets—mostly Buddhist monks, but more recently Christians too. Since 1725 there have been dozens of Lahu uprisings led by prophets.[4]

Shanshan Du studied one of the more 'traditional', and therefore more egalitarian, Lahu villages in South China. She first met these Lahu people when she was a student in China. Du loved what they did. When she did a PhD at an American university, she went back to the Lahu for her fieldwork.

There is more than one way to have gender equality, Du says. People can have gender complementarity, like the Iroquois or the Ashanti. Men and women are different, but 'the different attributes and role assignments of the two sexes are equally valued'. Or they can treat gender differences as real, but trivial, like the Vanatinai islanders of Papua and the Aka pygmies.[5]

## WHY MEN?

The Lahu do it a third way. They have gender unity, and they mark and value the unity of couples. The key to this was lifelong marriage of a man and a woman. Divorce was rare and difficult, adultery was uncommon and fraught, and the villagers told Du they had not heard of any cases of homosexuality in the village.

Within a marriage, Du found men and women were equal. This was not simply a custom, there were also legends. It was a project the Lahu were intent upon. Men and women did the same work, in the fields and the kitchen. Some tasks needed particular strength. When the man was stronger than the woman, he did those jobs. But when the woman was stronger, she did those jobs.

The Lahu had two sayings they repeated often to young people. 'Chopsticks only work in pairs' explained why marriage was necessary. 'Work hard to eat' expressed their other central value, and both spouses did that. The couple made decisions and plans together. In a few couples one partner worked hard but was not confident at making decisions. People pitied the husband or wife who had to do that on their own. In a few cases, a wife or husband was lazy, drank or took heroin regularly. (They lived along the drug route from Myanmar to China.) In those cases, the couple were judged severely, not the individual.

The Lahu understood, of course, that women gave birth. But they tried not to use the female-tinged Lahu word for 'give birth'. They used a more gender-inclusive word which meant raising children. In an unusual custom, the husband usually acted as the midwife for their children. At the first birth he was inexperienced, so both grand-couples, her parents and his, would move in several days before the birth to make sure they were on hand to help. The grandparent with the most experience would gently teach the father the art of midwifery.

The Lahu protected internal village affairs by electing a chief who dealt with outsiders and the government. That chief was a couple and was elected because both husband and wife were trusted. If one died, or became infirm or an addict, the couple retired. In one especially traditional village, there were four offices, each filled by a couple— the chief, the village spiritual specialist, the village Buddhist monk and the village blacksmith. God, too, was a couple. That couple was one person, not two, and was a marriage of identical twins.

## EQUALITY AMONG REBELS

The ideal person, man or woman, was kind and gentle. The Lahu word for such a person also meant 'soft'. Bad, immoral people were 'harsh'—loud, angry, pushy and dominant. But the Lahu were not pacifists. Their prophets had led armed uprisings. They were both warlike and gentle.

Some people were left out of this world of happy, equal couples. Some were stuck in unhappy marriages, or their parents had persuaded them to marry someone they did not like. Some, we can assume, may have wanted something beyond heterosex. There were also legends about lovers who killed themselves because they could not be together. These remained largely legends, told in songs, until the middle of the twentieth century.

Then, in the 1960s, the Chinese state forced the Lahu to join people's communes. Traditionally, and now, the couples go to the fields together, and work in the home together. But during the Cultural Revolution, people worked as individuals, and many were sent long distances to work on different projects. In the process they left their husband or wife behind, and often found a new lover in the new place. But since they were married and Lahu, they could not divorce. These new lovers would sing to each other in the firelight at night the old songs of suicide couples. Their friends around the fire would sing with them softly. Many times, the lovers would kill themselves because it was the only way they could be together. Du counted the cases for the village she studied. During the Cultural Revolution thirty-six couples—seventy-two people—killed themselves from a village of only 2,000 souls.

As Du says, the Lahu are not perfectly equal. Particularly among chiefs, who have to deal with the state, men often now do more of the work. The children now watch Kung Fu movies and *Baywatch*, and that too distorts their views of gender equality.

But sometimes the Lahu seem to go out of their way to emphasise gender parity. In their language, the gender of a big mountain is female, and a small rolling hill is male. A raging torrent of a river is female, while a placid brook or a pond is male. There is a sense, reading about them, that they are being absolutely systematic in building a society that is clearly differentiated from the dominant Han Chinese people of the plains, and the difference is that men and women are equal.

201

# WHY MEN?

*The Huaorani*

Let us turn to our second example. The Huaorani are egalitarian, gender egalitarian, warlike and homicidal. Huaorani men are warriors. But they are also the survivors of a long holocaust, taking care of each other in the forest. Men and women are different, but equal, just as men are equal, because being a warrior does not entitle you to tell someone else what to do.

The Huaorani live in the Ecuadorian part of the headwaters of the Amazon. Their ethnographer, Laura Rival, says that they have been under attack from outsiders for at least 200 years, and probably much longer. Until recently, their response was to hide in the rainforest. They lived mostly through hunting and gathering. They also relied, however, on supplies of palm wood and from sites where their ancestors had done slash-and-burn farming. From time to time they stopped to grow manioc in these sites for a few months.[6]

After the arrival of European colonists, the Huaorani hid from Spanish-speakers and cultivated a reputation for ferocity. Many Amazonian groups believe that white people are often cannibals. When Joanna Overing first lived with the Piaroa (see below), they assumed that the tinned meat she carried with her was human flesh. The Huaorani, however, take this one step further. They believe that all other groups, both Spanish-speakers and other indigenous tribespeople, are cannibals.

The Huaorani live in small longhouse groups of ten to thirty-five people. Each longhouse is a long way from the nearest neighbours. At any one time there will be groups of three, four or five longhouses linked by marriages and living at peace with each other. Beyond that, they are potentially at war with the other Huaorani longhouses, other natives and whites.

Rival first arrived to do fieldwork with the Huaorani in 1989. At that point, most of them had been living for some years not in longhouses but in larger settled villages, under the patronage of American missionaries. There they sent their children to school. After Rival arrived, one group of villagers went back into the forest, and she went with them. They did not make war, but they were wary, and sometimes homicidally angry. She was also aware of a few longhouses of people who had never come into the villages, and tried to kill anyone who contacted them, including other Huaorani.

The memory of war was still very much alive, Rival says:

> A great number of narratives, including myths, reiterate one fundamental fact: there is neither beginning nor end to the Huaoranis' flight from predation and destruction. It is often difficult to differentiate historical narratives that recall true violent encounters with non-Huaorani attackers (Zaporos, Naporunas, white explorers, colonists or traders, military, and so forth) and those that depict the cannibal attacks perpetrated by dangerous demons... A story I recorded, for example, started in the mode of reportage and recounted a raid carried out by inhabitants from the town [high] on Coca ... in the early forties, but quickly turned into a fantastic epic of savage slaughter [by ...] half-human, half-animal, imaginary beings, who dove from their hiding places in trees onto passing Huaorani, cracked their skulls to eat their brains, sucked their blood, and carved up their dying bodies into pieces to be roasted on big open fires.[7]

These were fantastical descriptions, but the battles they were describing were real, and not in the distant past. Whenever they talked to Rival about war, which they did with great energy, they always showed her their actual scars:

> Scars are bodily imprints reminding whoever sees them that spears are weapons purposefully designed to cause suffering and to kill. Huaorani spears are nine-to-ten-feet-long pieces of hard palm wood. Double-handed, they end in two fire-hardened heads of a triangular shape. The heads, one of which is usually notched, are as sharp and cutting as metallic blades. They can be sharpened again but generally break off in the victim's body... [They are] thrust fiercely and designed to kill by inflicting deep wounds at close range, tearing organs, and spilling blood in profusion, they are left in the bodies of dying enemies. As I learned from demonstrations on dummies, the barbed points, aimed primarily at the lower abdomen, are moved to and fro to cause maximum internal haemorrhage.

The wounded bodies are left with several spears in the body to die and rot:

> The suffering inflicted on the speared body culminates in the excruciating pain and slow death of moribund victims, unless they are

found by compassionate kin and co-residents who dig a fairly large and deep grave, and bury them alive. When the victim is male, as is most often the case, female kin line the grave with bamboo mats on which they lay the dying body to hasten his death and put an end to his suffering. There are many stories of dying fathers buried alive with one of their children, usually the last one, so, I was told, 'the father does not leave the land alone, so he does not feel lonely in the afterworld.' My classificatory sisters once showed me how this was done, and as they were putting a young infant on the pretend grave, they explained to me that the [body-soul] of a buried spear victim who dies by suffocation does not go back to its birthplace but stays right there. The burial place, with its trapped 'body-soul' becomes a place vividly remembered.[8]

Notice that the victims of war are usually men, but sometimes women. However, the central importance of war created a difference between men and women. Men had to be brave and must have been very afraid. What made it worse was that they believe that all deaths, except those of the elderly, are caused by sorcery. When a man lost someone he loved, he was enraged, and began to gather weapons with other men for a revenge expedition. The men would usually calm down at some point in the next few days. But there was always the threat of a special kind of rage, called *pii*. In former times, people told Rival, 'If someone in the longhouse became sick and died, the men would get angry to the point of being driven to murder someone, anyone.'[9]

Some enraged men had to be excluded from the community permanently. Legends are told about them, men 'mythologized as fierce, perfectly autonomous individuals who live kinless and without society, alone with the trees, and drinking his own urine'. Such men, people say, have become orphans.[10]

So men have to become warriors, afraid, emotions boiling, hyper-masculine, and potentially dangerous to all around them. But they do not oppress women. There is another side to life in the longhouse. Rival writes lyrically of the longhouse as a haven of love and sensuality. All the people in the longhouse share their food. They sleep together. They are always touching each other, stroking each other. In time, the Huaorani say, even if people are not related, they become of one substance:

## EQUALITY AMONG REBELS

> Sensual bonding, as diffuse as food sharing, unfolds as one aspect of the pleasure of living in each other's company. Everyone partakes in everyone else's care and well-being, the more people spend time together, the more they become alike.
>
> Sensuality in this culture is not centred on genitalia, nor is the exclusive domain of adult heterosexuality... Huaorani culture does not eroticise sensuality, nor does it differentiate genital pleasure from other bodily pleasures. For example, no distinction is made between the pleasure and contentment felt during sexual intercourse, the pleasure and contentment of a 3-year-old caressing the breast of the woman from whom she is feeding, the merry feeling of someone stroking gently the body of a caressing companion ... or the pleasure of being deloused by someone's expert hands... By contrast, sexuality is never used in Huaorani society to create power differentials.[11]

The backbone of a longhouse is usually an extended family group of a woman and her daughters. Men move out of the longhouse they are born into, because a husband is supposed to provide food for his wife's mother. As we saw in the last chapter, Aboriginal grooms in many parts of Australia did the same for the first years before and after marriage. But for a Huaorani husband this is not 'bride service'; he does it for the rest of his life. So the longhouse community is built around the woman, her daughters, their husbands, and their children.

After a woman marries and her husband moves in, her sisters often marry her husband as well. The sisters are very grateful for the chance to do so, because it means they can be certain of staying in their home longhouse. Everyone also praises the kindness of a man willing to marry one or two more sisters, because everyone knows it means a lot more work for the man.

Brothers and sisters usually stay in touch from their different longhouses. When possible, they arrange marriages between their children. But the announcement of a marriage is always a tricky moment. The older people will plan a marriage and tell no one. Instead, one longhouse decides to hold a drinking feast, and invite another longhouse, without saying why. This is a big event. The hosts have to settle in one place for months and grow enough manioc to make the drink. Then all the people of the other longhouse come to the party. Everyone drinks all night. Towards morning, the old people who have planned all this grab a young woman and young man and tie them up together. Then the old people sing long, loud songs at the couple about how they must work hard for the rest of their lives.

At this point the tension becomes acute. These are small communities, and everyone has some idea of who might be getting married. But the elders who arrange the marriage tell no one beforehand. So, when the engagement is announced, someone could easily take offence, wanting one of the couples to marry someone else, perhaps themselves. Huaorani tell stories of memorable drinking parties where that led to pitched battles in the longhouse, and to wars afterwards.

No one consults the young couple beforehand, or on the night, or at least it is said that no one does. The next day the man confirms the marriage by going hunting and bringing back at least one piece of game to give his new wife. She confirms the marriage by cooking it. Sometimes either he or she refuses to do their part, and the marriage is cancelled. But that is their decision because, after all, people are equal, and autonomous, and no one can tell anyone else what they should do. The important thing is that their actions do not lead to fighting.

\* \* \*

Rival, writing in 2016, is surprisingly upbeat about what has followed her first fieldwork. The Huaorani are now active in national politics. As Rival says, they bring 'a new vital intensity to Ecuadorian culture by participating in it from a position of radical difference'. They have accommodated to the oil companies and the Ecuadorian state. And 'the Huaoranis' unique way of knowing nature and understanding the ecosystem' meant that they did not see the forest as 'a pristine environment external to society'. Instead, they saw that both forest and society were 'regenerated through the business of ordinary life'.[12]

*The Sacred and the Hilarious Among the Piaroa*

From the Huaorani in the eastern Amazon basin, we turn to the Piaroa and Pemon who live in the relatively isolated hills and forests

## EQUALITY AMONG REBELS

around the headwaters of the Orinoco and the Amazon. The Piaroa, like the Lahu, insist upon pacificism with each other. In many other ways too, these people are like the other rebels of upland Southeast Asia described by Scott.

But we must be careful here. There is evidence that many of the surviving groups of indigenous tribespeople in the South American forests are descended from settled farmers who fled before the European invaders. However, it is equally likely that some of them are descended from people who were hunter-gatherers, or slash-and-burn farmers in the forests long before the invaders arrived. As in Southeast Asia, we are not saying that all 'indigenous' people are refugees. Some are, some are not, and all are mixed together in different ways.

The Piaroa too are egalitarian slash-and-burn farmers. About 7,000 Piaroa live over an immense area in Venezuela. Since the eighteenth century they have been fighting or fleeing the Spanish and then the Venezuelan state. When the anthropologist Joanna Overing arrived in 1968, they lived by slash-and-burn farming, hunting, fishing and gathering. In their small villages everyone slept together in one longhouse, half a day's walk from the next village. Their main crop was cassava, also known as 'bitter yucca'.[13]

As anthropologists so often do, from here on we describe the Piaroa of 1968 in the present tense. Anthropologists call this the 'ethnographic present'.

The Piaroa believe strongly in equality and say so. They also believe in the autonomy of each individual man, woman and child. They value independence and non-violence. No person is allowed to tell another what work to do, or even to suggest that maybe it would be better to go out hunting now. Such remarks occasionally happen, but they are regarded as extremely rude. No one controls the labour of another person, and no one owns land.

The Piaroa do not just 'have' gender equality. Like the Lahu, they make gender equality. In fact, they insist upon gender equality.

Children are never hit, adults never hit each other, and children never hit each other. Piaroa can certainly imagine such behaviour. Neighbouring peoples do it, the Spanish speakers in Venezuela do it, and Piaroa mythology is full of violence. But they regard it as wrong. Overing says that the definition of a fully adult male is that

# WHY MEN?

he is able to control his emotions and live in tranquillity with others. The definition of a fully adult female, Overing says, is that she is able to control her emotions and live in tranquillity with others.

Overing points out, however, that many anthropologists would say that the Piaroa have male dominance. This, she says, is because anthropologists often make two mistakes about gender and power. First, they assume that the customs and symbols which mark women as inferior in European society also mark them as inferior in other societies. Second, they assume that where difference is marked, inequality is automatically being marked as well. They are assuming that inequality arises from difference, not from exploitation.

Overing gives a useful example—the dangers of menstrual blood. In Europe and many other places, menstrual blood is shameful, polluting and sometimes dangerous and linked to the inferiority of women.

The Piaroa tell a myth about the origins of menstruation. As you read this, remember that the Piaroa act out their myths as they tell them, and that this story is intended to be both sacred and hilarious. Shamans tell it to young women when they have their first period. It begins:

> The wives of Wahari, the creator god of the Piaroa, played on a swing in the jungle every day after working in their gardens. They swung over a ravine between two hills, each taking their turn.
>
> Buok'a, Wahari's older brother, who had no wife but was very successful with women, found Wahari's wives at the ravine and played with them. One after the other, the women took turns on the swing, sitting on it, bottoms bare, inviting Buok'a to make love with them. Each time a woman swung across the ravine, Buok'a, from the far bank, made love with her. He had a very long penis which he normally wore wrapped about his shoulders, and he could therefore make love from a great distance and very often. The wives adored him.
>
> Wahari, finally irritated by his brother's success, transformed himself into a beautiful woman and joined his playing wives at the ravine, where he took his turn on the swing. He swung across, legs spread wide apart. Buok'a sent his penis out to Wahari and tried to penetrate him—but he found no opening. The penis hit Wahari on the belly button, looking for an opening, on the thigh, searching.

# EQUALITY AMONG REBELS

When it hit Wahari's thigh, he rapidly cut Buok'a's penis into five parts with a knife until it was shaped down to normal size.

From the end of Buok'a's shortened penis blood flowed, and he became sad. Thus, he isolated himself in a small hut set apart from his regular house. He lay in his hammock there with his menstruation, and brooded—just as a woman does with her first menses when she has to stay in such a small hut for a week.[14]

Wahari's wives could not figure out what had happened to their lover. They 'moped and refused to work. They stayed in their hammocks and wept.'

Wahari went hunting. He stopped off to visit his brother in the hut and was shocked to find that Buok'a was menstruating. 'What is to become of us?' he wailed. If his brother wanted to menstruate he should go off to the hills of the northwest Amazon, where it was normal for men to menstruate.

The story continues: 'Wahari arrived back home with all of his hunt. He had all types: toucan, peccary, pheasant, lapa. But his wives were still sad, and they refused' to cook for him. At that he got angry and said he was the one who should be upset:

'I encountered my brother today, and he was menstruating! Men should not menstruate!'

The women leapt to their feet and asked in chorus, 'Where is he? From where is he menstruating? From the head? The ears? The mouth? From the point of his fingers? From the knees? From the feet? The anus? The penis?' They did not yet know about menstruation.

The women dressed themselves up for their lover. They put on leg bands, necklaces, and they painted themselves. Then they went to Buok'a's house where he quickly made love with each—and that is how they received menstruation.

The story goes on, but we can stop here. We would guess that in the hands of a master storyteller, the two funniest lines would be 'from the ears?' and 'The anus?' On the other hand, acting out tying your enormously long penis around your shoulders, done right, might be even more hilarious.

But this is also a serious story. Remember, a shaman tells it to a girl at her first menses. This is not simply a Just-So story about origins. It is part of her education as an adult woman. The Piaroa believe that all knowledge comes from other worlds, either past worlds or alternative worlds, and that knowledge has a dangerous power that must be tamed by the calm responsibility of the person who learns. The main knowledge women learn is how to control and enact their fertility, and they learn this at first menstruation.

The equivalent knowledge for boys is the knowledge of sorcery, or shamanism. Only some boys embark on learning and controlling this knowledge. It is dangerous, and the shaman in training must take strong hallucinogens and travel long distances in the dark across space and time, visiting other places and other worlds. A boy who throws tantrums, for instance, would never be allowed to train as a shaman. It would be foolishly dangerous for all concerned.

When an established shaman begins training a young apprentice, the power of the knowledge comes from the same source as the power of women. The established shaman tells the apprentice the same story of the origin of menstruation. And the apprentice has to menstruate. As it happens, almost all shamans are boys and men. It's not a rule. Piaroa say that women can do it, and Overing heard of one case.

Luckily for the men who set out to be shamans, there is one way men can menstruate as they start out on their long journey. The shaman pierces the tongue of the boy with the spine of a sting ray, and the menstrual blood comes out of his mouth. It is not actually his, the shamans say. It is the menstrual blood of the women he lives with in the longhouse, and he has acquired it by being close to them.

The Piaroa know perfectly well that there is no such thing as men's menstrual blood. But when the apprentice bleeds the blood of the women he knows, he has the same power to learn and control himself that they do.

The Piaroa believe that menstrual blood is dirty and dangerous. More important, they think it is poisonous. And they think men and women are different. But, Overing says, this does not mean they think women are inferior. They think women are powerful, but men can be powerful too.

*Egalitarian Pemon*

Some readers may find it difficult to believe Du's description of the Lahu, Overing's of the Piaroa or Rival's of the Huaorani. Perhaps you feel these ethnographers are being starry-eyed, romantic and happy-clappy. That scepticism is understandable. We might feel the same way, if we had not had first-hand experience of the Pemon.

The Pemon are also egalitarian slash-and-burn farmers living where Venezuela, Brazil and Guiana come together, at the headwaters of the Orinoco and the Amazon, not far from the Piaroa. Jonathan spent three months in 1997 teaching English in a secondary school in a Pemon village in Venezuela. He was there to research a play for junior schools in the outskirts of London based on Pemon mythology. Nancy had a chance to visit briefly.

The Pemon are pacifists now, but they were once a warlike people. In 1750 the Spanish authorities and Capuchin friars began serious penetration of Pemon territory. By 1772 some of the Pemon had guns, obtained from the Dutch colony of Surinam. Father Benito de la Garriga, on an exploring expedition up the Caroni River, reported that 'they kill each other frequently, and we found empty houses, in which hammocks hung with bones of dead people and heads broken by wooden clubs'.[15]

The Capuchins had already begun capturing large numbers of Pemon to work as unpaid labour on their mission ranches. The friars found it increasingly difficult to locate any tribespeople, as the Pemon had moved away from their usual homes along the rivers far into the forest. The Capuchins were eventually driven out by Venezuelan revolutionaries fighting for independence from Spain.

Then the Pemon were mostly left alone by the Spanish-speakers until the middle of the nineteenth century. By that point, explorers said, the Pemon were wild looking but not warlike. Today, they enjoy a reputation among Spanish-speakers as gentle, pacifist 'Indians'. What is important here is that the recent pacifism is a choice.

\* \* \*

To help us understand the Pemon we have a careful, even brilliant book, *Order without Government*, by the anthropologist David John Thomas. What makes it special is that Thomas describes an unusual way of ensuring equality in a society. He did his field research in 1970 to 1971, and again briefly in 1975. At that time, he said, equality was beginning to change, but still largely structured the lives of most communities.[16]

## WHY MEN?

The Pemon were slash-and-burn farmers, living mostly on manioc, a root crop. Manioc is poisonous, and it takes a lot of labour to get rid of the poison, but (unlike the Huaorani, who are occasional dabblers) most Pemon ate manioc bread almost every day. People were spaced very thinly on the ground, with a population of 4,000 on 12,000 square miles of savannah and rainforest. That is one person for every 3 square miles. Moreover, almost all settlements held no more than fifty people, and eighty was a very big village. That meant it was easy to deal with serious conflict by walking away and moving to another settlement. When the going got tough, Thomas says, there was always a backdoor in Pemon society.

The most common form of inequality was between older and younger siblings. This inequality was not gendered. An older brother might be superior to his younger brother, but he was inferior to his older sister. However, when they grew up, both sisters and brothers tried as hard as they could to continue to live with each other. And the heroes of Pemon mythology, trapped on some nightmarish mountain or forest with a Jaguar mother-in-law or a King Vulture father-in-law, are always longing to return to live with their mother.

Women and men are equal, Thomas says. Just as Overing says of the Piaroa, Thomas says that the work of Pemon women and men was complementary:

> The complementary nature of the male–female relation was rather vividly brought home to me in observing a joking discussion between a sister and her brother's wife on the one hand and her brothers on the other, during some festivities where the men had brought in a deer and a tapir after being out on a three-day hunt.
>
> The discussion started out with the brother avowing that meat was really important food, and that it was, after all, men who brought in the meat. But who, his sister shot back at him, prepares the manioc cakes and *cachiri* [manioc beer] that give the men the strength to go out and hunt? And who, the brother replied in turn, cuts the forest so that the manioc can be planted? And who, the sister and her sister-in-law asked, tends the plots so that the manioc will not be swamped by weeds, and who brings it home and grates, squeezes and bakes it? Who, said the brother, makes the manioc squeezer so that the manioc will be rendered edible?

# EQUALITY AMONG REBELS

Round and round it went, for the space of half an hour or so, till finally the discussion left off in a few joking barbs and the grudging admission on both sides that one thing supported another, ad infinitum. (Everyone was quite agreed that that no meal was really complete without meat (or fish) and manioc cakes.)

What intrigued me about the repartee was not only the theme but its joking nature and its outcome—no one could be topped, there was always a comeback for every one-upping line which preceded it. The result was not just a draw, but simply that there was no end to the trade-offs.[17]

The idea that people in some jobs should be paid more than people in other jobs is a key part of modern capitalist ideologies. So is the idea that inequality happens because men and women do different kinds of work. The Pemon did not think that way, nor did the Piaroa, and nor, probably, did our ancestors on the savannah.

* * *

The Pemon in 1971, Thomas said, had three central social values that promoted equality. A person should not lie, should not be angry, and should not be stingy. Thomas points out that these values were phrased in negative terms. There is indeed a word in Pemon that means 'generous'. It is just almost never used. In many cultures people are praised for being honest, friendly and generous. Among the Pemon they were not. That was merely the background state of being. It's how normal people were supposed to be all the time. And by and large they were, but not all the time.

People did have reasons to be angry, jealous or fearful. But when they felt that way, they were strongly encouraged to be quiet, not to say or do anything. This did not mean that people had to sit in a corner and sulk. Thomas says that large, aggrieved men would be pretty upfront on social occasions, standing there silently in the middle of everyone. And people let them be that way.

Generosity included sharing food. But households generally cooked and ate their own. What people mostly shared was manioc beer. Calling it beer is a bit misleading, actually, because in our experience it has a kick like a horse. But not sharing beer was the

## WHY MEN?

classic example of being stingy. That was often, Thomas says, because a household did not have enough workers in the prime of life—economic inequality was reconfigured as a character flaw. Characterising failure to share as that—a failure—and passing down a compulsion to share both constantly flattened inequality.

People, particularly some men, did try to be important. An older man would try to bring his younger brothers and sisters and their spouses and children to live in a hamlet around him. He could also try to marry more than one woman. Even better, he would encourage an unrelated person or two to live with them too. But of course the spouses of your siblings always wanted to go home and live with their own sisters and brothers, and were probably nagging about it. So you had to keep everyone happy. And especially you had to be careful never to exploit the unrelated people, always to allow them their equality and autonomy, or they would move on.

Still, some people could not be silent. There were men who beat their wives. This was appalling behaviour. Everyone felt very upset. But no one outside the couple could intervene. There were also people, often men, who shouted and sometimes even hit each other. Again, it was appalling behaviour, but the only way to stop it was by the force of gossip. People would talk, and then they would talk to the close relatives in the hamlet of the angry men and the wife beaters. Once the man's relatives agreed that he had gone too far, more and more people in the hamlet would stop talking with him, and pointedly stop sharing beer. At that point the angry man, or woman, would leave and go live with relatives elsewhere.

Thomas heard of only two cases of murder, one recent and one in 1920. In both cases there was no revenge, no ritual and no formal judgement. But the murderer had to leave.

There was also supernatural power, for both good and evil, and this was another potential source of individual domination which Pemon people struggled to control.

Women had always been shamans. Thomas knew two of them, one widely regarded as dangerous. But most shamans were men. An important shaman, which meant a man of great spiritual knowledge, could use that skill to try to become influential. Most male shamans, unlike most other men, had more than one wife. Thomas knew of one case where a shaman had tried to take a third wife, by threatening to use sorcery if he was refused. But the courage and determination of the woman he had eyes on and her father stopped that, and the hamlet forced the shaman to move away.

Early in 1971, in one river valley with a population of about 300, thirty children under the age of fifteen died of measles in the space of two months. Because the adults who got sick did not die, there was no question but that it was sorcery. And everyone suspected a local shaman who had been throwing his weight around. The influential older men called an assembly, where they confronted the shaman's mother. They gave speeches, begging her to make her son stop. She denied that he had done it, and we have to assume she was right, for that is not actually how measles kills. But as the deaths continued, several grieving fathers came together and plotted to kill the sorcerer. They never managed to do it, but shunning forced the shaman to leave for a hamlet far away.

Thomas points out that this was an extreme case, but it makes a larger point. There was little you could do to stop a bully if their brothers or sisters would offer refuge. But those who were devious, angry or stingy found themselves lonely.

* * *

Pemon mythology is another window on their egalitarian values. In many different ways, they tell the story of a little guy, a Pemon or an animal, faced with a dangerous and violent monster. We said earlier that the distinction between older and younger siblings was the main form of hierarchy in Pemon society. One of the main strands of the mythology is the stories of the sons of the Sun. Older Brother is a grownup, a plodder who follows the mainstream, does the right thing and is always trying to help out the younger.[18]

Younger Brother is a trickster, who often changes size, but mostly appears as a small boy, a toddler, a chigger or some other kind of insect. He is endlessly inventive, intelligent, cheeky, naughty and sometimes really bad, and he outsmarts his older brother every time.

In one story Older Brother whittles a toy shotgun for Younger Brother to play with. Quietly, his back turned, Younger Brother picks up the wooden shavings and uses them to build his own shotgun. When Older Brother finally sees what's happening, he reproves the kid and says that gun will never work. Younger Brother fires it off with a tremendous bang.

In another story Younger Brother is a toddler who persuades Older Brother's wife to take him down to the river and wash him, as anyone would wash a baby. When they get into the water, Younger Brother reveals his enormous penis and they have enthusiastic sex. They do the same on many more occasions. But one day the family Dog follows them and sees everything. Dog goes back and tells Older Brother, and then Younger Brother works magic so Dog can never talk again. And that is why even to this day, dogs can't talk.

There are many such stories. Like the Piaroa menstruation myth we looked at earlier in this chapter, they are hilarious and they carry wisdom. And the biggest lesson they teach is that somewhere there is a world where the little guy always wins.

\* \* \*

Thomas says that Pemon society was changing when he began fieldwork in 1970. He traced a weakening of egalitarian values back to the re-establishment of the Capuchin mission in the 1930s. After that some Pemon worked for the mission, some women went to work as maids in the city, and some men and women went to the gold fields on the edge of Pemon territory.

By 1975 Thomas had seen two cases where a Pemon temporarily employed another Pemon to do work and paid them wages. One of the employers was a woman and one a man. Thomas knew that practice would spread and end in general degradation.

By 1996–7, when we were in Pemon territory, the pressures for inequality were growing. One result was that the women in Kavanayén were organising to ban the import of beer into the village. Bootleggers in a pickup, pretending to be fish peddlers, were smuggling in beer. The problem was not the drinking as such. Drinking homemade manioc beer had been central to Pemon culture for centuries. It was far stronger than the bootleggers' beer, which was brewed in the city and sold in cans. But manioc beer had been shared by the whole family, men and women, and all the neighbours. Now men were buying canned beer and drinking it in small groups with other men, proud to show each other their sophistication—and that they could afford to buy a beer. The women were furious, because this was not shared with them, and worse, because subsistence farming families had only tiny amounts of cash. The fury of the women and the pride of the men were tearing families apart.

Externally, too, equilibrium has increasingly turned to conflict.

In the years since 1998 the Pemon began to organise to defend their land rights as part of a broader movement supporting the government of Hugo Chávez. But then they turned decisively against his successor Nicolás Maduro. In 2016 the government declared a 'National Mining Arc' that covered land near the Brazilian border, one eighth of the total area of Venezuela. Most of that was Pemon land. In 2017 the government began to open all of that land to mining for large reserves of gold, copper, diamonds, coltan, iron and bauxite.[19]

The politics of what followed were complicated. There were several massacres of miners, many of whom were Pemon. The central conflict, though, was between Pemon defending their land and the soldiers of the National Guard opening that land for mining. In 2017 the National Guard sent 300 armoured vehicles down the highway through Pemon country to the Brazilian border. Pemon fighters turned out and blocked the highway. Over the days that followed the soldiers opened fire on crowds and killed between twenty-five and eighty Pemon.

The Pemon are no longer peaceful people.

\* \* \*

But some of the old values survived. When Nancy left to go back to her job in London, the two of us took a bus from Pemon country to Ciudad Bolívar, on the banks of the Orinoco. It was an all-night journey in a rickety-rackety bus that stopped only briefly at the desperate wild west towns of the gold miners, Eldorado and Kilometre 88. We shared the long bench seat across the back with Maria, a Pemon woman, and five of her children, aged between about two and nine. The two older children sat facing us, pressed up against each other, silent, stoical, not complaining, for ten hours. Throughout the journey, Maria held the youngest child, while the older children took turns holding the other two babes on their laps. These were not children being cowed or 'good'. This was active kindness.

(Jonathan stayed on. He writes:) Because I was teaching English, I learned little Spanish and less Pemon. But I remember the day, towards the end of my stay, when I learned something very important. I lived in a ground-floor room in the Catholic mission attached to the school, and my window opened onto the playground. In those three months I had never heard an angry word, a shout or a crying child from the playground. In London I once lived across the road from a school playground, and the constant roar during playtimes was angry and upset. The contrast could not have been greater. Then suddenly, one day, I heard a Pemon child wail outside my room. I felt something must be terribly wrong, and leapt from my bed, pulling on my shirt as I went through the door. There, right outside my door, in the covered passageway, was a girl of about five. The rain was pelting down on the roof, a tropical downpour. I understood immediately. The sudden rain had cut her off from friends and kin. She was alone, and therefore afraid. I held out my hand and she took it. We did not speak. In a few minutes the rain stopped and she ran home.

No Pemon child made another child cry. Ever, as far as I could see. Only the rain.

PART THREE

# HUNGER GAMES AND POPULAR RESISTANCE

The next five chapters share true tales from across time and space of how male-dominated class hierarchy meets with resistance by the marginalised. In a global history of sexual and gendered difference, class society, violence and resistance to these power structures, we might be expected to provide a general survey of how capitalism developed and how hierarchies of gendered identity changed on a world scale. But that would be deeply misleading. There are no such one-to-one connections. Instead, we look for similarities of process, for which a general and synthetic history would be useless. So we use extended case studies. In other words, we tell stories. Each chapter in Part Three does three things. First, it shows how patriarchal violence in that time and place was enabled and defended by a class elite.

Second, we explore a process. When the form of economic inequality changes, elites seek to reconfigure patterns of gender to justify and fit with the new forms of class inequality. But this is never straightforward. Invariably, elite plans excite protest and resistance against the privation they seek to impose.

Third, we want to show how our approach can cast new light on well-known stories and can generate new ideas. Each of the five chapters focuses on a ritualised enactment of violence designed to enforce the power of a patriarchal ruling class. Each is a theatre of cruelty, performed in public to terrify those whose lives the elite seek to control.

The stories are not new, but reframing them through our gendered lens is novel and shocking, and reveals the mechanisms of power. And we see how, in response, resistance to such tyranny is also deeply gendered. In these five chapters we write about human sacrifice, aka murder, executions and torture, and focus the sexual and gendered identities of both the victims and victimisers, Our examples come from a Viking funeral on the Volga, a mass grave in North America, the death of Joan of Arc, the trial for sodomy of two sailors in the British Royal Navy, and torture at Abu Ghraib prison in Iraq in 2003.

What makes our gendered lens so very effective is that at the same time we also keep a sharp eye on our sources. The problem is twofold. As the archaeologist Alice Kehoe has explained, 'archaeological inference proceeds from a drastically pauperized database in regard to cultural knowledge ... and from the archaeologist's own natal and professional enculturation'.[1] And the biases of historians can be no less distorting. So in each case we ask: how have we come to know these stories? Who was telling them, to whom and for what purpose? And why are we retelling them now? And in answering these questions, the relationships, past and present, between class power and patriarchy become stunningly clear.

12

WHO WILL DIE WITH HIM?

In our first story, we witness the ritual murder of a young woman as part of the elaborate funeral of a Viking chieftain through the eyes of an Arab envoy in the tenth century, an encounter which takes place on the peripheries of empire along the Volga River.

Human sacrifice was common in the early centuries after class rule was established, in the kingdoms of Europe, Asia, Africa and the Americas. Sometimes the victims were mostly or all men, and sometimes, mostly women, as in Chapter 13 about the city-state of Cahokia, in what is now the American Midwest a millennium ago. And as we shall see, the gendering matters.

We are taught to think of human sacrifice as an aberration, as a practice which human beings left behind as they became 'civilised'. But exactly the opposite is true. Human sacrifice has been surprisingly common throughout the history of class societies. The English word 'sacrifice' comes from the Latin. For the Romans, often considered in Europe as the founders of advanced Western 'civilisation', a human sacrifice was an offering to the gods of a human life. 'Ritual murder' is now perhaps the more usual term for the whole range of rituals requiring a human death to mark them off from what might be called profane killing.[2]

Here we use the terms 'sacrifice', 'ritual murder' and 'murder' interchangeably, but to respect the likely point of view of the person murdered, not the person performing the sacrifice or ritual killing. And we ask what exactly is the difference between killing someone to please or placate some god, and killing someone legally in our more secular times? How do we judge those who have the power, and ultimately the right to kill? What makes capital punishment, or the killing of women or gays or political dissidents or Jews or terrorists or enemy combatants licit and laudable, and to whom?

Human sacrifice and 'civilisation' go together, begging a series of difficult, and murky questions about those who rule, and those who are ruled. These are questions most of us seek to avoid, yet they lurk behind any investigation of the gendering of death.

*Held in Honour? Our Human Sacrifice Blind Spots*

Bruce Trigger, a distinguished archaeologist of Ancient Egypt and the Huron, published a major work of synthesis in 2003, *Understanding Early Civilizations: A Comparative Study*. Trigger took seven examples: Old and Middle Kingdom Egypt (2700–1650 BCE), southern Mesopotamia (3800–2000 BCE), the late Shang and early Zhou in northern China (1600–1000 BCE), the Classic Maya (750 BCE–900 CE), the Inka kingdom (1300–1572 CE), the Central Valley of Mexico (1–500 CE), and the Yoruba states and Benin in West Africa (1100–1700 CE). These are seven very different societies, relying on a range of different staple crops, with a range of forms of class exploitation, at very different times. Though Trigger himself doesn't make anything of the coincidence, by searching the index of his book one finds that human sacrifice is important in all seven societies.[3]

And other examples of necropolitics abound.[4]

The Mesopotamian exhibits at the British Museum begin with an account of 'The Queen's Grave and the Great Death Pit' in what was the Mesopotamian city of Ur, now in modern Iraq. (This is the city of Ur, not the city of Uruk where the temple burned down.) The display is a celebration of the crucial advances and development of Sumeria, the world's earliest known civilisation. As the display label says, 'The objects in this gallery illustrate the beliefs, achievements in writing and art, and the international connections of the Sumerians and Babylonians.'

But the objects also illustrate the Sumerian and Babylonian disposition to human sacrifice, though the label leaves this unsaid, and thus contributes further to both the museum curators' and the punters' blindness to human sacrifice.[5]

Leonard Woolley excavated the Royal Cemetery at Ur dating from around 2500 BCE. Ur and Uruk were both kingdoms in south-

## WHO WILL DIE WITH HIM?

ern Mesopotamia, about 50 miles apart. The sacrifice we are about to describe happened about 500 years after the probable revolt in Uruk, which we described in Chapter 7. According to Woolley,

> Queen Puabi's body was covered with fine jewellery and objects lay with three attendants within a stone and mudbrick tomb chamber situated to the east of the death pit. A ramp led down to the pit, which was about 12x14 meters in size. The bodies of 5 with copper alloy daggers lay on the ramp and at the base were the remains of a sledge with 4 oxen and 4 more men.
>
> At the southern end of [Puabi's] pit the bodies of ten women wearing elaborate headdresses were laid out in two rows, with musical instruments ... in the centre was a huge decorated wooden chest surrounded by a large quantity of objects.

As for The Great Death Pit, it deserved its name, though there was little evidence remaining of the stone tomb chamber that it belonged to. In the pit were the bodies of six guards or soldiers with weapons and sixty-eight women. According to Woolley:

> Most of the women lay close together in rows but four of them were grouped around four musical instruments including the silver lyre... All the women wore elaborate headdresses, necklaces and earrings, and their clothing was decorated with beads. Two statues of rams were found in the corner of the pit... [The women] were disposed in regular rows across the floor, every one lying on her side with legs slightly bent and hands brought up close near the face, so close together that the heads of those in one row rested on the legs of those in the row above. Here was to be observed even more clearly ... the neatness with which the bodies were laid out, the entire absence of any signs of violence or terror.[6]

Different historians have produced different scenarios for how the women died. Leonard Woolley imagined the nicest possible form of sacrifice. He thought it was 'most probable that the victims walked to their places, took some kind of drug—opium or hashish would serve—and lay down in order; after the drug had worked, whether it produced sleep or death, the last touches were given to their bodies and the pit was filled in'.

## WHY MEN?

From their elaborate headdresses, fine jewellery, and the fragments of red wool cloth found among the dead women, Woolley says that 'clearly these people were not wretched slaves killed as oxen might be killed', but

> persons held in honour, wearing their robes of office, and coming, one hopes, voluntarily to a rite which would in their belief be but a passing from one world to another, from the service of god on earth to that of the same god in another sphere.

To Woolley, apparently, the mass killing of women was unproblematic if the ten musicians and sixty-eight others in the Death Pit were of high status and offered themselves up willingly for the sake of their religion. Following Woolley, the museum labels also gloss over the mass killings and simply seem to take for granted an unchanging relation between patriarchy and power.[7]

But there is no place for such an automatic assumption. Political economies change and then gender relations change as well. Thus, sometime after the mass burials in Royal Cemetery, Ur collapsed into a number of smaller city-states. Then, later, Akkadian outsiders became the new rulers of the new trading empire of Ur.

The imperial history of Ur is immensely complicated, but the feminist archaeologist Rita Wright offers some hints at how such political and economic changes might have altered relations of class and gender at a later period in Ur's history. Wright describes the complex social processes behind new technologies of weaving and textile manufacture. The new skills, she says, were exploitable and created opportunities for the elite to appropriate surpluses and control the production process itself. Wright uses legal documents and other records detailing the conditions of work and payments to show the gendered division of labour and the class differences between an elite who wore and traded these lavish goods and the workers who made them.[8]

The British Museum exhibit is conventional in its focus on an elite and their luxury goods. Two things are obviously missing from the picture. One is the wider focus on economic and political change that Wright offers. The other is any insight into the ritual process behind the sacrificial deaths. Who did ritual benefit and how? Who was harmed, and why? What was the ritual meant to mean, and above all, did it work?

# WHO WILL DIE WITH HIM?

*A Viking Funeral at the Edge of Empire*

An account by Ibn Fadlan, an envoy from Baghdad, the capital of the vast Abbasid Empire, gives us an exceptional, unmediated, insight into the past and a European example of human sacrifice by the Russiya/Viking slavers in 922 CE on the Volga River.

The place to start is with the violence Ibn Fadlan describes, and why it can't be separated from his own presence there. The Vikings he met were slave hunters who aimed to dominate the lucrative slave trade at a time when the alliances between the states and empires of the region were facing drastic economic changes and deadly political struggle. The rape and murder of a young girl in front of Ibn Fadlan and the rest of the embassy from Baghdad may well have been in part designed to shock the Abbasid authorities into agreeing to new terms of trade.

Ibn Fadlan wrote:

> When a great man dies, the members of his family say to the slave girls and young slave boys:
>
> 'Which one of you will die with him?'
>
> One of them replies: 'I will.'
>
> Once they have spoken, it is irreversible and there is no turning back ... usually it is the slave girls who offer to die.
>
> When the man I mentioned above died, they said to his slave girls: 'Who will die with him?'
>
> One of them answered: 'I will.'
>
> Then they appointed two young slave girls to watch over her and follow her everywhere ... Meanwhile, the slave girl spends each day drinking and singing, happily and joyfully.[9]

Ibn Fadlan was a civilised man. He often found the various tribes he travelled among dirty, ignorant and savage. But he did like to see what was going on. The dead man would be arranged on his boat, on a mattress, and cushions covered with Byzantine silk. An old woman they called the 'Angel of Death' came down to the boat. 'She is in charge of sewing and arranging all these things', Ibn Fadlan writes. 'And it is she who kills the slave girls. I saw that she was a witch, thick-bodied and sinister.'[10]

The dead man had been buried under some earth and wood to preserve him. Now his people took him out and dressed him in his funeral clothes. 'I saw that he had turned black because of the coldness of the country... The dead man did not smell and nothing about him had changed except his colour.'[11]

They laid him on the mattress in the boat, with a drum, fruit, basil and other food. 'After that, they brought in a dog, which they cut in two and threw into the boat. Then they placed his weapons beside him. Next, they took two horses and made them run until they were in lather, before hacking them to pieces with swords and throwing their flesh on to the boat.' Then they killed two cows, a cock and a hen.

'Meanwhile, the slave girl who wanted to be killed came and went, entering in turn each of the pavilions that had been built, and the master of each pavilion had intercourse with her, saying, "Tell your master that I only did this for the love of him".'[12]

That's a nice touch.

Certainly, Ibn Fadlan writes of the willingness of the girl to die, a detail picked up in more recent accounts. Bruce Chatwin goes further when he writes that 'the slave woman ... made love to each of the companions'.[13]

But 'love', as we know, is a tricky notion. Timothy Taylor suggests that it is misplaced romanticism to say that the 'slave girl chooses her pagan death freely, for the highest motive: love'. Certainly Taylor is having none of it: 'Regimented submission need not necessarily be "willing"... Coercion, hierarchy and mind-altering substances would have been interwoven with inner metaphysical convictions to the point at which the word "willing" falls wholly short of reality.'[14]

Then they take the girl down to the boat, where she meets the 'Angel of Death':

> Next, came the men with shields and staves. They handed the girl a cup of *nabīdh* [a wine made from grapes or figs]. She sang a song over it and drank. The interpreter translated what she was saying and explained that she was bidding all her female companions farewell. Then they gave her another cup. She took it and continued singing for a long time, while the old woman encouraged her to drink and then urged her to enter the boat tent and join her master...

## WHO WILL DIE WITH HIM?

> Then the old woman seized her head, made her enter the pavilion and went in with her. The men began to bang on their shields with staves, to drown her cries, so that the other slave girls [would not be frightened and] try to avoid dying with their masters. Next, six men entered the pavilion and [lay with] the girl, one after another, after which they laid her beside her master. Two seized her feet and two others her hands. The old woman called the Angel of Death came and put a cord around her neck in such a way that the two ends went in opposite directions. She gave the ends to two of the men, so they could pull on them. Then she herself approached the girl holding in her hand a dagger with a broad blade and [plunged it] again and again between the girl's ribs, while the two men strangled her with the cord until she was dead.[15]

This part of the ceremony was not public, so we do not know if Ibn Fadlan had special permission to watch, or that he based his description of the weapons and tools he saw people carrying on the people entering the pavilion and the sounds that followed.

The ritual moved to the public burning of the boat. They placed the bodies of the girl and her master on the boat, then built a pile of wood under the boat. Then the closest male relative of the dead man came forward and took a piece of wood which he lit at a fire. He then walked backwards towards the boat, his face turned towards the people who were there, one hand holding the piece of flaming wood, the other covering his anus, for he was naked.[16]

He lit the fire, and then many people came up, and each threw a lighted piece of wood onto the fire. The wood burned, as did the boat, the tent, the slave girl and her master.

Because Ibn Fadlan was curious to see things for himself and because his careful description has survived, the Viking ritual is much less opaque than it might be. The difference this makes is enormous.

Among other things, the Viking ritual is clearly a celebration of both wealth and the slave trade. The goods burned with the master—the boat, silks, cows, horses and weapons—were not cheap. The woman burned was also property, part of his wealth. Burning all this showed that his relatives too could afford to destroy such things.

The ritual was also a celebration of a certain kind of masculinity. The burning of a slave, and the suggestion that she volunteered, are important here. The sheer cruelty of the event recapitulates the larger cruelty of the slave trade. Look at us, the Vikings are saying, we burn people. We are warriors and the slave trade is as much about war and violence as it is about money.

Notice too all the sex. And notice that the ritual is conducted as if she wants all the sex. Each of the other masters lies with her in the days before her death. And each, ritually, tells her to tell her master in the afterlife that they do not mean to offend him. The prior claim of another warrior is honoured, even as they share the woman. Then, just before she is killed, six men rape her while she is in a drunken stupor. And we might assume, it is they who bang their staves on their shields.

Neil Price, writing more widely about Viking mortuary rituals, makes several striking points about Ibn Fadlan's account. Of the rape just before the slave-girl's death, he writes that

> This primarily concerns power rather than desire, and it is very hard indeed to see any kind of 'celebration' in raping a screaming girl on the same bed as a ten-day-old corpse. Not just a matter of modern moral sensibilities confronted with alien values of the past, these events concern people who are *all* constrained by rules... The 'Angel of Death' is a funeral director, and together with everyone else she is clearly following an agreed procedure. The sexual themes appear central here and they take on a repetitive overtone with respect to the girl. Ibn Fadlan mentions that the female slaves were sexually abused by their owners. This role is amplified significantly after the slave-girl is marked for a funerary death, and the entire mortuary process is in fact punctuated by sexual acts.[17]

Price perhaps makes too much of the difference between power and desire. Power and violence are both far more likely to be sexualised for some, if not all, of the participants and onlookers. However, he offers an excellent description of how overwhelming and involving the ritual must have been. Thus, he points out how violent are the deaths of the animals and the importance of actual violence to the spectacle. He suggests that 'too little thought has been given to what these events would have looked, sounded and smelled like'.[18]

At the time of the burial the cremation ship 'must have been dripping with blood. How did the animals react after the first of their number was killed? It is not difficult to imagine the noise, to visualise the gore covering ship, objects and onlookers, and the scent of blood and offal.'

Price adds, lest he be misunderstood: 'This is not an exercise in gratuitous melodrama, but an attempt to recapture an integral part of the funerary experience for those who were there... This whole ten-day process is continuously accompanied by chanting and music ... one could do worse than to focus upon social inclusion, expenditure, effort, violence, intoxication and not least sexual performance—all of these in considerable quantities and expressed conspicuously.'

And there is the final touch. Let us not forget the naked son or brother of the dead man, carrying the lighted wood, showing his penis to the assembled crowd, while covering his anus so no one can see it. His cock, his sex, is part of his boasting, his wealth and power. We cannot know from this account the meanings of the anus for these men, but we can assume it represents his vulnerability, and perhaps something that is not masculine.

Neil Price is categorical: the Viking death rituals are 'about power and the use of power—they are spectacles with a message and a purpose'. He finishes his survey with a quote from an American journalist on the genocide in Rwanda: 'To a very large extent power consists in the ability to make others inhabit your story of their reality—even, as is so often the case when that story is written in their blood.'[19]

It is difficult for archaeologists and anthropologists to say that human sacrifice is the sort of thing that happens once you have social class inequality. And it is hard for the rest of us too. It is easier to massage such an awkward fact into obscurity.

## 13

## CAHOKIA

### FREEDOM AND EQUALITY AFTER 'COLLAPSE'

We know that early class societies were often grossly unequal and cruel, and that the cruelty was deeply gendered. This seems also to have been the case in the indigenous kingdom of Cahokia which flourished between 1050 and 1200 CE in what is now the American Midwest.

Cahokia is now a UNESCO World Heritage Site, celebrating the 200-year history of its wealth and power. The richest finds from the site come from Mound 72, where probably upwards of 300 people were buried, among them four separate mass burials in which 19, 22, 24 and 52 young women had been killed in one go. It is an appalling example of gendered inequality.

But the Cahokian state did not last all that long. By 1200 CE, some villages and towns had burned and people were leaving. By 1400 CE the site was completely empty. Then, for the next 400 years, many Native Americans in the region lived in egalitarian societies without any state organisation. And in the historical period, we see that equality has been associated with a remarkable fluidity of sexual practices and the ways that people were gendered.

In this chapter we write of the rise of Cahokia and these terrible deaths, and of the fall of Cahokia and the egalitarian societies on the Great Plains that followed. And we consider the biases—the racism, classism and misogyny—which make writing about Cahokia difficult.

There are no contemporary accounts of Cahokia, and the paucity of sources limits greatly what we can, and cannot, know. And of course all histories and ethnographies are coloured by the politics and prejudices of their time, a truism that applies to our writing as well. Later scholars will no doubt uncover our unconscious biases, while we bring an explicit socialist feminist perspective to the arguments of this book.

In Part One on early human history, we were highly critical of the sexism of the Social Darwinists. And we have touched on the male biases of archaeologists in several places, most notably in Leonard Woolley's ugly fancy that the seventy-eight young women and the few men who were buried with Queen Puabi of Ur died happy deaths because they were buried without any 'signs of violence or terror'.

In Chapter 11, we considered how the genocidal racism of the European colonists was reproduced in the contemporary racism against indigenous Australians, and how, at the same time, most accounts of traditional Aboriginal societies focused on men and ignored or dismissed the beliefs and practices of women.

In the Cahokian case too, a genocidal conquest history, the continuing racism towards Native Americans and the well-documented sexism of some archaeologists have been the most important impediments to clarity.[1] The second difficulty is intrinsic to archaeology which traditionally focuses on elites, because elites are the ones who leave behind the most impressive material records—their cities, their trade goods and prestige paraphernalia, their beads and bones. And because of the very gender biases of modern patriarchal class societies many of the dead were (or were presumed to be) elite men—kings, warriors and the like. For the same reason, compared with the attention archaeologists have given to the rise of the Cahokian city-state, they have paid much less to its fall. Another bias, somewhat surprisingly, stems from a hostility to class analyses full stop. This is North American exceptionalism, which sidelines the comparative histories of the Maya and Aztecs and others to the south, and which, during the Cold War period, saw a tendency within the American academy to privilege certain narratives.

In this chapter we are also wrestling with a basic, but largely unaddressed, moral question that lurks behind any telling of human history: how do we judge the value of human behaviour and social organisation? Are class societies, for all their inequality and violence, better simply because they are hierarchical and 'civilised' and technologically advanced? And are egalitarian societies morally depraved and 'primitive' because, being organised around notions of compassion and fairness, they lacked the firepower to protect themselves from aggressive invaders? If we buy into this binary, consider what we are likely to miss about gender and, more generally, oppression in the 'advanced' society, and about gender and, more generally, freedom in a 'simpler' society.

*The 'Big Bang': A Cahokian Elite Invents Inequality*

The World Heritage Site of Cahokia lies some 10 miles east of the Mississippi River and the city of St Louis. The official site is enormous. There are more than 120 mounds scattered over the 2,200 acres. There were many other mounds nearby, including many now destroyed. Cahokia is the most extensive mound complex in North America, built by people still sometimes known dismissively as the 'Mound Builders'.[2]

People in North America had long had the habit of building mounds. They piled thousands of tons of earth into great heaps across the east of the continent and up and down the Mississippi and its tributaries. Some of the mounds were used for rituals of state and sites of government. This was probably the case with Monks Mound, the giant platform mound at Cahokia. (Monks Mound was named after the French priests who farmed there and were associated with the small village of Cahokia founded by French settlers in 1670.)

In size, Monks Mound is often compared to the Pyramid of the Sun at Teotihuacan near present Mexico City, and those in Egypt. Others across the east and centre of the continent were burial mounds filled with grave goods which, in each epoch and locality, had their own distinctive cultural style. Some, mostly far to the north of Cahokia, are called effigy mounds. When seen from the air, these are like giant Andy Goldsworthy sculptures of serpents, birds and abstract environmental art.

There has been plenty of debate about Cahokian origins. By 900 CE people around Cahokia had been farming squashes, some grains and sunflowers for many centuries. Combined with extensive hunting and fishing, this provided a nourishing diet. But it took a great deal of labour for people to feed themselves, and there was not much of a surplus left over.

Then came rapid economic and political change, due, surely, to a combination of factors. First, there was an agricultural breakthrough. The people around Cahokia had long grown small amounts of one variety of maize. Agriculture did not change radically but intensified and people moved to a diet that relied heavily on new strains of maize with higher yields than the older crops.[3]

Some say just having an ambitious leader was enough to initiate growth, or perhaps Cahokia grew as a pilgrimage centre. Certainly, prominent archaeologists have long favoured an understanding that it was 'a sudden event, archaeologically speaking'—Cahokia's Big Bang—and a dramatic growth in population around 1050.[4]

This seems over-enthusiastic. There is reason to think the impetus for the city-state came from an influx of migrants. At much the same time that the population grew, a new politics, along with new cultural styles, science and technology also seem to have been brought north by people coming from areas in what are now the states of Arkansas and Oklahoma.

These newcomers—perhaps a third of the population was not from the immediate area, but probably from not very far afield either—somehow contrived to raze to the ground the original Cahokian settlement of about 1,000 people. Almost immediately, a new planned settlement went up and work building the mounds began. Archaeologists have focused on the genesis of the city-state, and there is more than a hint of pride and identification in Timothy Pauketat's comment that these events were 'the first government-sponsored urban renewal project on the continent'.[5]

There is an assumption that people flocked to the site, coming together voluntarily to build the huge mounds as a way of celebrating some connection with the sacred. Maybe. But as the new arrivals clearly had the power to destroy the original settlement and rebuild a planned city, they might well have been able to coerce or enslave others in this process.

Early on, some 200 farmers, probably themselves from the south and west, were 'relocated' in settlements on the high ground to the east of Cahokia. Then around 1100, another 3,000 farmers arrived in the upland villages. A central depot for grain storage was situated

# CAHOKIA

between the settlements. It may also have been used as an observation post for keeping an eye on the workers.

Susan Alt, the doyenne of Cahokian archaeology, suggests the depot and observation post was a place of 'renewal and fertility'. A place of 'spiritual power that mediated the worlds of the living and the dead'. Perhaps it was those things for the elite. But, as we shall see, the farmers were clearly less than happy with such supervision and control.[6]

In the end, little is known of the Cahokians themselves, not even what language they spoke. The military history of Cahokia, the extent of the state and its rulers' imperial ambitions are also unknown, though the energy of the polity is not in doubt. At its zenith from 1050 to 1200 CE (AD), the city had a population of perhaps 12,000 people, with as many as 40,000 people in the hinterland. In size it rivalled some of the early cities in Mexico and Peru. And as it grew, new farming hamlets and villages appeared and a series of 'Cahokianised' towns soon appeared all along the rivers in the Midwest.

Nor do we know how the city-state was organised, though it was a class society with considerable inequality between peasant farmers, craftspeople, and a ruling elite. Certainly, Cahokia grew into an urban centre much like the city-states of Mesoamerica in what is now Mexico and Guatemala. Those states too were built on the labour of men and women growing maize.

\* \* \*

Big Bang or not, Cahokia's efflorescence undoubtedly had a great deal to do with the environmental geography of the place. The land around Cahokia lies just below the confluence of the Missouri, the Illinois, and the Mississippi Rivers, and forms a region known as the American Bottom. Some 150 miles downstream, the Ohio River also joins the Mississippi. Together, this huge river system drains half of the present contiguous United States.

Over many centuries the rivers at Cahokia have meandered and ox-bowed, leaving lakes and marshes full of fish and other wildlife, and laying down rich, deep topsoil. In 1000 CE there was no more fertile, or better connected, place than Cahokia for a thousand miles in any direction.[7]

## WHY MEN?

The Cahokians seem to have taken full advantage of the geography of the site. Their large wooden canoes gave them access to the vast river system and to trade routes which stretched across much of the continent and down to the Gulf of Mexico and the sea. At the time of the Cahokian state, people undoubtedly walked long distances, and for sure travelled up and down the rivers and along the coast. Yet in much of what is written about Cahokia, undue weight seems to be given to the great distances involved and little attention paid to the ease of travel by water.

How trade was managed is unclear, but the grave goods associated with the early burials suggest it was well established by 1050. As for what the Cahokians had to offer, there was copper to be had nearby, a hard, valuable pipestone, and fine Burlington chert from the Crescent quarries was worked into knives and hoes. In exchange, in trade or tribute, Cahokians obtained obsidian from the Rocky Mountains, copper from Lake Superior and mica from the Great Smoky Mountains. Beads and other ornaments were made by skilled workers from thousands upon thousands of shells from the Gulf of Mexico.

No trade goods from Mesoamerica have been found at Cahokia, apart from one dubious bit of Mexican obsidian. Perhaps this is not surprising as less than 1% of the site has been excavated.[8]

But the spread of domesticated maize, the distribution of trade goods and cultural habits all suggest connections with Mesoamerica. Centuries later, when the first descriptions of Cahokia were sent on to Washington by European American travellers, they remarked on the similarities between Cahokia and the Mesoamerican city-states. But because of the absence of direct material evidence, and the complex politics of the discipline of archaeology (on which much more later), from the early 1960s until quite recently modern mainstream scholars had little to say about the cultural similarities.

The Olmec, Mayan, Toltec, Aztec and other ancient kingdoms of Mesoamerica were astonishingly complex, sophisticated and violently hierarchical states. Culturally, Cahokia shared with them a number of similarities. There is a special game played with stone discs, known in North America as *chunkey*, huge wooden henge structures apparently aligned like astronomical dials to mark the rotation of the earth, a wide ceremonial plaza, and the mounds and an elite whose leader may have been a sky god and lived on the highest pyramid.[9]

And human sacrifice.

*Mound 72: Rituals of Gendered Violence and the Misogyny of the Experts*

The story of Cahokia's rise and fall has a direct bearing on the main arguments of this book. And though we do not know what happened exactly, by reflecting on the burials in Mound 72, we can get some idea what it was like during the period of Cahokia's rapid growth.

In the late 1960s a small ridge-top structure, now known as Mound 72, caught the attention of the archaeologist Melvin Fowler. He was fascinated by its uncanny alignment with sunrise at the winter solstice and sunset at the solstice in summer. Fowler and his site supervisor soon recognised that what they had found was 'in some ways, comparable to the Royal Cemetery of Ur in Mesopotamia'. In effect, Mound 72 has become 'critical in shaping a present-day understanding of Cahokia … a society that featured social inequality, political theatre, and human sacrifice'.[10]

The Cahokia Museum and Interpretive Center is surrounded by parkland. Pride of place is an exhibit from Mound 72. A glass case contains a model, not the actual remains, of a well-built man found in Mound 72, buried between 950 and 1050 as the kingdom was rising.

The man lies on his back surrounded by luxury goods and seems to have died a natural death. Near him were found 700 finely worked arrow points, made from a variety of valuable stones in different styles. They were arranged in lots, almost as if someone had anticipated their display in the museum. The man and his paraphernalia were buried on a bed of 20,000 beads made from shells from the Gulf of Mexico, 900 miles away. He was clearly a man of considerable wealth. And given that his death is closely linked with the beginning of the Cahokian polity, perhaps he, and the vast collection of valuables buried with him, came from elsewhere.

The shells were thought to have been laid out in the shape of a falcon, so archaeologists called him 'The Birdman', as he is named in the display. Whoever he was, he was the key figure of the 'Beaded Burial' group. He was, it seems, a young man. Another young man,

# WHY MEN?

also on his back, was buried under him. Nearby are several male–female couple burials, and what other archaeologists describe as 'retainer burials', some six individuals 'sacrificed', including one man, wearing jewellery, who was perhaps thrown down, and 'not quite dead until reaching his final position'. Next is a group of young men and women with grave goods heaped upon them.

A lot of other people were also buried in Mound 72, including four groups of young women.[11]

Bill Iseminger, the Deputy Director of the Cahokia Museum, managed the difficult job of writing an accessible book for museum visitors which avoids sensationalism while being sensitive to the complicated politics of doing archaeology at a Native American site.

Iseminger, working from the original excavation reports, tells us that in two pits there were 'twenty-two burials oriented east to west, piled in two layers. Those that were identifiable were females.'[12]

A second pit 'contained nineteen burials oriented north to south also in two layers. Although preservation was especially poor, it is likely that these were also female burials.' And above this pit was another one filled with 'dedicatory offerings' and a treasure trove of over 36,600 marine shell beads. There was also another cache of arrow points, 451 of them, and six broken pots 'that looked like they had been smashed against the edge of the pit'.[13]

Iseminger turns to Melvin Fowler, who supervised the original excavation, for a disarmingly bland explanation: 'Fowler believes these two burial groups were part of ceremonies dedicated to the central group at the charnal structure.'[14]

Whatever the ritual, it was simultaneously about wealth, young women and death.

A third pit was dug in Mound 72, 'and twenty-four women were buried there in two layers at right angles to the pit orientation... Mats lined the pit and covered the burials, and then a platform was built over it with ditches along the sides.'[15]

Finally, in another area there was

> a unique burial ... four men with their arms interlocked and their head area oriented to the northeast—but their heads and hands were missing and have not been found. They ranged in age from twenty to forty-five years. The reason for removing the heads and hands is unclear—and they were never found—but it is not likely

that this was a punishment, or they could not have been given this special burial in this special mound.[16]

Punishment or not, this same style of killing has also been found at another site in what is now central Illinois. There is no way we can know what it meant.[17]

Next to the four headless men, 'at the bottom of a large pit were fifty-three skeletons of women [fifty-two young and one older woman] laid out in two rows, two deep'. Because of the state of the bones, archaeologists found it difficult to be precise about the bodies, but most 'had female characteristics and an age range averaging from fifteen to twenty-five years old', except for 'an older female laid at a right angle to and on top of the others along one edge of the pit'.[18]

Iseminger continues: 'The limited age range and the gender is indicative of human sacrifice, since disease is not quite that selective to such a narrow window of a population; the same is also suggested for the female burial pits.' The hint of sarcasm about young women's untimely deaths also turns up elsewhere, and, to us, it is a clear indication of the archaeologists' discomfort at what they are seeing.[19]

Though we can know nothing about Cahokian beliefs, we can be sure that whoever was doing the killing had an explanation for what they were doing. We can also be sure the deaths produced a similar depth of feeling among the people of Cahokia as the slave girl's brutal death did among those who witnessed the Viking funeral— though with different meanings of course. And as an accompaniment to whatever belief system the elite purveyed, what better way of exercising control, and suppressing unrest and thoughts of revolt, than by killing young women wholesale?

Iseminger's own conclusions are circumspect. He reminds us that 'when one is treated differently in death, it reflects differences in life as well', adding that most of these ritual burials happened during 'the early stages of Cahokia's explosive expansion around AD 1050'. However, he does not draw any conclusions about the relative status of men and women shown by the repeated choreographed mass killing of women. Instead, he concludes that the ritual burials, 'appear to have been commemorative events focusing on certain structures or burial groups, maintaining the honor and memory of those who had passed on before'.[20]

## WHY MEN?

Iseminger points to 'the activity of Mound 72 as a form of theatre—public display and ceremony reflecting their belief system, mythology and cosmology'. And in this way, the killing and mass burials of 22, 19, 24 and 52 young women simply disappear from Iseminger's bland summary. He does not ask, 'Why women?' and ignores the great fear such violence surely inspired.

\* \* \*

Whence the blindness to the glaring gendered aspect of the human sacrifices at Cahokia, when this ritualised violence clearly indicates a society organised in a gender hierarchy? We know that among many professionals, misogyny and an Indiana Jones machismo ruled. Neither women nor Native Americans were welcomed into the scholarly fold.

And there was another element to the misogyny. For complex reasons, Cahokian scholars have also been reluctant to write about class and status hierarchies and to move on to the global world-systems and big history approaches that have been familiar in Old World archaeology from the outset.[21]

In Mesoamerica, the turn to big history in the study of civilisations like the Maya or the Aztecs has offered a powerful perspective on class society, state control of sectors of the economy and an emphasis on the 'exploitative nature of that control. Elites are seen as selfish agents who exert control to benefit themselves at the expense of commoners, rather than altruistic representatives who assume the burden of control to benefit the entire society.'[22]

But such hard-headed materialism has not found much favour in discussions about Cahokia. Perhaps this is because Mound 72 looms so large in the history of the site and gendered violence is tough to digest. Or perhaps scholars felt, but could not argue publicly, that the cruelty of Cahokia was insignificant in comparison with the oceans of blood spilled in the American genocide of native people.

In his book *1491*, Charles Mann gives a vivid account of the rise and fall of the Mound Builders across the eastern woodlands and at Cahokia. He notes that the practice of human sacrifice across North and South America has been treated in two diametrically opposite ways. One is to say that human sacrifice was never practised, but the myth stems from post-conquest racist lies used to justify the conquest. The second response suggests that the appetite for blood in the Americas was fundamentally different from anything known in Europe.

As Mann points out this serves to deny the similarity between human sacrifice in the Americas and the public hangings in Europe, the heretics, like Joan, burned at the stake, and the criminals drawn and quartered by European rulers. But of women as opposed to men, and the women murdered in Cahokia, Mann himself becomes casual and inaccurate. It seems that the institutionalised sexism in early class societies is so taken for granted that even the extremes become unremarkable.[23]

Mainstream histories now often nod towards feminism. But the presumptions of patriarchy and heteronormativity and the accounts centred on men and male privilege still sweep all before them. So alternative histories need to put questions of sexuality and gender front and centre.

Alice Kehoe is also deeply angry about the sexism in the profession, the 'facking fuckulty' as the archaeologist Sally Rosen Binford put it. Rita Wright, in her introduction to *Gender and Archaeology*, argues that there is clear evidence that 'the restructuring of gender relations is a key to the centralization and institutionalization of state power'. Some studies, she notes, show how elites reshape gender relations to serve their purposes, others describe how peasants and other common folk resist such interventions. This way of seeing changing patterns of gender relations is very close to our hearts.[24]

But for many of the gung-ho early women activists this posed a problem. When the detailed work at Cahokia got under way in the 1960s, any focus on the women's deaths worked against the anti-racism of the Civil Rights struggle and the American Indian Movement.

In another complication, it is instructive that Sally Binford wrote fiercely against the early radical feminists, including Dianne Feinstein, Gloria Steinem and others associated with *Ms.* magazine, who turned to archaeology to anchor their belief in an original matriarchal society. Binford, writing of myths and matriarchies, noted how religious beliefs can rationalise the status quo, how groups invest a mystical past from when they were powerful and strong, and how notions of an original matriarchy deflect attention away from gender inequality.[25]

## WHY MEN?

Kehoe also scorns what she calls the cookbook approach of the early 1990s when women's activities are itemised and catalogued without due attention to ethnography and ethnohistory—the ideological context in which these women from the past carried out the activities and roles we've been able to identify, and how that context changed over time.

And Kehoe is equally acerbic about how 'male archaeologists seem to be fixated on the idea of worshipping female fertility'.[26] With nothing much to go on, some Cahokian archaeologists turned to the present-day beliefs and practices of Native North Americans as a kind of pick-and-mix of apt illustration. 'Religion' has always been the black hole of archaeological and anthropological explanation. Projecting isolated details of religious belief and practice back 1,000 years is a way of making the past seem familiar—but it is mistaken.

* * *

The sexism of ancient Cahokia seems incontrovertible. Research on the strontium levels in the teeth and bones has shown that the young women were not local. We are told they may have been captives or perhaps offered as tribute to the Cahokian rulers.[27]

Maybe. But we have to be wary when the notion of 'captives' turns up as an explanation of ritual killings. It can also be a way to avoid confronting the issue of social class. What is sure from the Cahokian skeletons, is that the men who were buried, but not sacrificed, ate more animal protein than the sacrificed young women. The skeletons of the young women offer evidence of the 'dietary dimensions of social inequality' and are a testament to their low status. They ate mostly maize, they had many dental caries and were nutritionally stressed.[28]

Despite the echoes of Artaud's Theatre of Cruelty and Foucault's *Discipline and Punish*, Pauketat writes in a chapter on 'American Indian Royalty', 'Even female sacrifices, while taboo in some cultures, might have been considered culturally appropriate, or even in some way "normal" at Cahokia.' Pauketat is aware of the generalities he is purveying as a way of trying to make human sacrifice somehow acceptable rather than horrific. And it is notable how this keeps us focused on the Cahokian state and not its demise.[29]

# CAHOKIA

Like Pauketat, the Cahokia expert Susan Alt, in her recent book, is concerned to normalise the women's deaths, and she concludes with an admonition, that 'we must put aside personal feelings and try to understand the original intent and meaning of sacrifice'.[30]

She is right, but there is a difference between putting aside personal feelings about ritualised murder and putting aside the ability to see patriarchy within it.

\* \* \*

Not long after we began reading about Cahokia, we found Amanda Padoan's paper, 'Who Will Die with Him?' We have borrowed her title for our Chapter 12.

Padoan begins with great ferocity, 'Could we even recognize a prehistoric gender issue if we saw one?'

> Mound 72 ... towers over the field of gender archaeology. Inside it, fifty-three women were found stacked like matchsticks. All but one were young, mostly teenagers. They were strangled, but not by hand ... [probably] with a rope or a strip of cloth which leaves no trace on bone. Five sacrificial retainers crouch beside [the Birdman]... The fifty-three matchstick girls share the wider mound, but little else. Birdman died of natural causes; they did not. Their remains, juxtaposed, recall a time not far removed, when life was cheap and women's lives were cheapest. In contrast to the girls, the honoured life and well-provisioned afterlife of Birdman practically caws hegemonic exploitation.[31]

But how do we cope with the time-warp, and the intrusion of our own feminist morality? Perhaps, Padoan suggests, such ancient atrocities are so fascinating because it's safer to confront violence against women in the past than in the present? And with these prehistoric murders, we do not know how they were spun—as community service, chosen martyrdom? Or, to put it more bluntly, why were they killed?

We simply cannot know. And there are many other questions we can ask about how exactly the gendering might have worked. Was it transferable, and perhaps additive? Did the women's deaths enhance the Birdman's maleness? Was he perhaps fifty-three times more masculine in death than in life? And what of the girls? Were

# WHY MEN?

they, as Padoan asks, 'afforded a more understated personhood, or none at all'?[32]

Putting women in the picture is one thing, putting gender in the picture is another. And putting both poor women and poor men in the picture is yet a third, particularly when the voices of peasants and slaves are liable to be inaudible at the best of times. But the four pits of sacrificed women are not the only burial pits found at Cahokia—the last two, and other archaeological evidence from the site, tell a related, but different story: one of an oppressive class society, and of an underclass offering resistance.

*Things Torn Apart? Class and Resistance at Cahokia*

The last two burial pits of Mound 72 are different. They are one on top of the other and they are not the resting places of women sacrificed in a death rite for an elite man. Instead, they suggest the possibility of an insurrection put down with great brutality. We know that the people in the two pits were not strangers to each other but belonged to the same gene pool.[33] Let us follow Iseminger again:

> [T]hirty-nine males and females between the ages of fifteen and forty-five ... the majority were males, but fifteen were not able to be sexed. They were apparently standing on the southern lip of the pit and were clubbed to death, falling into the pit in various positions, three face down, three on their sides, and the rest on their backs. They were not respectfully placed, as seen in the other burial pits. A couple of them may have not died immediately, as they were lying face down with their fingers digging into the pit floor; three were decapitated and one partially decapitated, probably with a heavy stone axe or mace, and the heads were placed with them. Two burials had arrow points in the body cavity area that could have been related to their death, or they may have been unrelated old war wounds.[34]

This is a description of a massacre.

Several layers of matting were placed over these bodies, and then a second group of fifteen people were interred. Some of these had cedar poles laid next to them, probably from litters used to carry them to the grave. This was a mixed group of women and young children together with at least one man. Some of these bodies had been wrapped up before they were buried, and some had probably begun to decompose before they were brought to the site. These people had not died good deaths either, but they were less likely to have been the political enemies of the city-state than the people buried below them. The illustration in Iseminger's book is particularly grim—below are the jumbled bodies of the thirty-nine people massacred and above them are the fifteen people each buried with care.[35]

At the end of his chapter, 'The Mysteries of Mound 72', Iseminger acknowledges that there may be 'many potential interpretations of what all of this means'.[36] This is true, but we also find that one interpretation of the massacre pit—that this was an attack or uprising that the elite successfully put down—and when taken together with other archaeological finds from the later history of Cahokia, makes far more sense than any other.

Stories of the rise and fall of rulers have been part of the history of class societies from the beginning. Urban centres can take off and expand with surprising speed. But inequality and class divisions bedevil hierarchies, and rulers can be, and are, deposed or overthrown. And when regimes come to an end, the people do not vanish but live on, as in the case of Cahokia, without the burden of a cruel ruling elite.

This understanding of the rise and fall of class societies challenges the notion that cities, empires and civilisations 'collapse', as the popular, but quite mistaken writer Jared Diamond has claimed. Diamond's implicit assumption in *Collapse: How Societies Choose to Fail or Survive* is that if you abolish hierarchy, a state and dictatorship, then everyone dies. He's wrong. Collapse may well be catastrophic from the point of view of the ruling elite. But that is unlikely to be a point of view widely shared by those who have been exploited and oppressed. And the dire narrative of ecocide that Diamond has pushed—of the mismanagement of the farmland, the forests or floodplain by the people themselves—is simply not part of the Cahokian story, though climate cooling may have been an element in the state's demise.[37]

Archaeology, and what we can and cannot know about Cahokia, has changed radically in the past fifty years. Lidar, DNA and other kinds of microanalyses of organic and non-organic objects mean archaeologists can make a great deal of sense of passing moments, a day's feasting, and the ephemera of campsites and faecal residues of human and animal waste in sediment.

These new techniques have also had an important bearing on what we can understand about more recent Native American history, and sites which are less than monumental. But even so, the jump from the demise of the Cahokian state to the lives of Native Americans today is tricky, not least because many of the issues are less technical than sentimental.

As for what actually happened, there are some important clues.

Around 1150 CE, within a century of their arrival, the farmers, who were probably migrants and unfree workers, abruptly left the upland villages after the depot-cum-observation-post burned to the ground. This points to resistance and a successful insurrection, though Alt is reluctant to let go of her faith in the city-state and writes of 'ceremonial burning as part of a planned politic-religious event'.[38] Indeed any hint of political struggle is hidden in her consideration of the small differences in the 'assemblages' of material goods at house sites as evidence of people's 'diversity' and 'hybridity' which is also a tidy way of avoiding a discussion of class and socio-economic hierarchy.

It seems unlikely that the insurrection was benign, isolated or without a class dimension. Indeed, it may have begun, or perhaps spread, to the urban centre and mounds in what is now East St. Louis where, at much the same time, an extensive settlement was sacked and destroyed by fire.[39]

About this time too, Monks Mound and the centres of other towns began to be fortified. At Cahokia itself, few signs of conflict have been uncovered, but the weaponry that was available throughout the history of the city-state is deadly and technically superb. Though there may have been some fear of external attack, the archaeologist Thomas Emerson makes a telling point: 'It's interesting... At Cahokia the danger [for ordinary people] is from the people on top; not other people [from other tribes or locations] attacking you.'[40] What Emerson means is that the weapons were more likely used by the elite to control the Cahokian underclass, than to fight off enemy attacks or to aggress against outsiders. But maybe it was both. Certainly, the extensive palisades around the giant Monks Mound suggest both a gated elite facing internal unrest as well as a desperate concern to keep hostile neighbours at bay. After all, internally precarious states are likely to be vulnerable to external predation as well.

Throughout the next century there are other signs of unrest, and perhaps even endemic warfare. Other villages further afield also burned, and both men and women seem to have been targeted equally.[41] There was a massacre around 1300 CE of some 260 people whose remains have been found at the Norris Farms Cemetery not far from Cahokia in the Illinois River Valley, and another massacre at a large settlement at Crow Creek, along the Missouri River in what is now South Dakota around 1350 CE in which some 480 people were killed and their bodies mutilated in an overwhelming attack.

As Pauketat and Alt write, 'As it happened, by 1350 all the residents of Cahokia had departed, dispersing in every direction. Political or military mishaps, an uptick in organized violence, a loss of faith, and crop failures might all have been to blame—possibly in that order.' By 1400 Cahokia and other settlements in the region had been abandoned completely. Archaeologists describe the region at this time as a vacant quarter.[42]

In all this—and we do not seem to know a lot more—there is perhaps quite a simple explanation for Cahokia's decline and fall. Where people gain power over others, there is corruption and dynastic privilege and licit forms of violence as we saw both with the ritual sacrifice of women and with the massacre of a mixed group who must have been problematic to the elite in some way. In all this, the ordinary people of Cahokia may have been fascinated and cowed by spectacular violence, and they may also have been outraged by whatever else kept them enthralled and the hierarchy in place.

Certainly, the earlier killings would not have been possible without a practice of cruelty and intimidation, and an ideology of inequality reinforced daily. Then some event may have made the ruling elite look vulnerable—a defeat in battle, an unexpected failure of the rains, a bloody falling out within the ruling family that either enabled or prompted those they ruled to cease recognising their authority. Or the people around Cahokia may have just had enough, risen and got rid of the tyrants themselves and left.

Either way, what we do know is that Native Americans in this region did not just reject an oppressive regime. They built an alternative.

*After the Fall: Equality and Resistance on the Great Plains*

In this book we explore two related ideas: first, that there is close association between class hierarchies, violence and marked gender inequality. The second idea is that the converse is also true—that without policed hierarchy, class categories, identities and conformity imposed from the top, cultural expressions of gendered differences and sexualities vary enormously.

With respect to both these ideas, Cahokia seems to be a case in point. When the Cahokian state came to an end, the people who scattered created for themselves egalitarian societies with a great diversity of practices and ideas around sex and gender.

By 1250, Cahokia was in decline. Meanwhile, Mississippianised tribes and others the archaeologists now call the Oneota were on the move. Some were farmers, some hunters, and some moved between the two at different times of the year. And within a century, by around 1350 CE, the Oneota began to thrive not far from Cahokia in what is now central Missouri.[43]

The Oneota were hunters; they had no temple mounds but enjoyed the niceties of permanent villages, gardening and pottery. Perhaps the Native Americans who lived on the eastern plains and along the great rivers of the Midwest were descendants of the Oneota culture, and before that Cahokia. What is certain is that for four centuries after Cahokia's demise, local people lived in quite a different way.

A striking aspect of the later history of the Plains was their inhabitants' determined egalitarianism in the face of European hierarchy. At first it was a history played out at a distance, long before face-to-face relations began. After the Spanish invasion of Mexico at the end of the sixteenth century, horses were gradually traded north. This made possible a new economy on the prairies. Because horses were valuable and could easily be stolen, the people of the plains did a lot of raiding, but they mainly used horses to follow and hunt the buffalo. Because no one could ride more than one horse at a time, accumulation was difficult, and it was possible to keep their societies fiercely egalitarian. Between their mobility and determined economic equality, relationships were relatively equal between men and women. The mixed-gender people we write about below were more or less equal too.

Over several centuries, Native Americans were slowly propelled into the capitalist system. They faced colonial onslaughts from Spain and Mexico to the south and west, and from France, Britain and then the United States to the north and east. The Midwest, though far from the coasts, became from the outset a 'shatter zone' changed by the chaotic impact of living on the 'free' side of a frontier with colonial powers.[44]

However, dramatic cultural differences remained. Tribal groups had varying definitions of statuses and roles and degrees of hierarchy, but they were all careful not to have chiefs who told people what to do. Sometimes they chose peace chiefs without any great power, and almost never did they have a 'war chief' to coordinate them in battle.

Indeed, only at the end, just before Custer's Last Stand in 1876 at the Battle of the Little Bighorn did the Sioux tribes give in to military necessity and choose Sitting Bull as their war leader. The three reasons they did this say everything about the class and gender order they were defending. First, Sitting Bull was recklessly, almost insanely, brave in battle. Second, men and women liked him because he sang all day long as he went about his business. And third, he was admired because he was kind, generous and humble and spent so much time every day playing with the small children of the camp. So they made him war chief.[45]

Among the many different tribes of semi-nomadic hunters of the Midwest and Plains, the social differences that were marked related not to roles considered inherently natural to one or another group, but to individual talents and skills. To illustrate how this might have worked elsewhere, Alice Kehoe draws on her recent ethnographic work with contemporary Native Americans. She describes how Blackfoot men's and women's roles could be clearly defined without men dominating women, 'widows and independent-minded women might hunt, and men knew how to cook and sew'.[46]

And certainly, the many different tribes of semi-nomadic hunters of the Midwest and Plains knew and accepted a great variety of gender roles and sexualities. The variety of arrangements concerning sex and gender is the subject of Sabine Lang's immensely scholarly compendium, *Men as Women, Women as Men: Changing Gender in Native American Cultures*.[47]

In North America, the word 'berdache', from Arabic via French, has long been used to refer to 'people who partially or completely take on the culturally defined role of the other sex and who are classified neither as men nor as women, but as genders of their own in their respective cultures'. 'Berdache' has also been a term of opprobrium and used to stigmatise Native Americans. This is hardly surprising given the sense of moral superiority and sexual prudery of the early colonists. But things do change. Now most Native Americans, among those who wish to be known as queer, are eager to leave the notion of 'berdache' behind. They prefer to use the idea of 'Two Spirit', or 'Two-Spirited' persons, to refer to the range of historic, but now lost, mixed-gender statuses and roles.[48]

Like people everywhere, Native Americans had to come to terms with intersexed individuals, but Two-Spirit people were not these. Lang quotes Margaret Mead's interest in cultural variation, noting that sexual dimorphism notwithstanding, 'many cultures place at the disposal of each biological sex several gender role alternatives'. Mead was happy to conceive of gender role change as an alternative 'sex career'.[49]

This is a useful insight. Two-Spirited people are those with unambiguous external genitalia who, in some places, took on the roles and statuses of the opposite sex. In others, they formed an intermediate or third gender. In some places, the gender mixing was sometimes construed as cross-dressing, in other places as cross-acting. It was typically chosen voluntarily, and often remained lifelong.

Starting from external appearance, there were an enormous variety of gendered categories, identities and sexual practices in different parts of the North American continent. All of them were closely connected with other aspects of the social life of each tribal group. The range of possibilities was very great. There was men's work performed by men-women, and women's work done by women-men, boys raised as girls, and girls raised as boys. Each of these combinations was named and accepted. Among some groups, gender roles were defined very clearly but carried out with great flexibility. In others, gender roles and statuses were defined in ways that left some areas of social life un-gendered, or uni-gendered, allowing for maleness and femaleness to be experienced as unitary, mixed, or overlapping.

Individuals who were female in external appearance lived and dressed as male hunters and warriors. Other individuals who were male in external appearance enacted degrees of intersexuality, dressed as women and even simulated female bodily functions, including menstruation and childbirth. There were other people whose appearance was deliberately androgynous. There were manly-hearted women, and men whose bodies were adorned with women's tattoos. Many different kinds of transvestism and cross-gendered behaviours were unique to Two-Spirit people, from shamans and medicine women to women-men who took part in lacrosse games as women players.[50]

Long-term partnerships were mostly heterosexual, and also widely varied. Most unions were between a woman and a man, but others were polygynous unions between a man and several women. Yet other people practised forms of polyandry, involving unions between a woman and several men. But these forms of marriage didn't preclude other kinds of coupling: between women and between men, while most Two-Spirit people had anatomically same-sex sexual partners.

A great range of sexual practices were also known and accepted: chosen abstinence, heterosexuality, bisexuality, lesbianism and homosexuality. And there was a tolerance of both promiscuity and male and female prostitutes.

Two-Spirit identities of both women-men and men-women were neither default identities nor a status of some kind of social abnormality. They were people held in high regard. And gender equality and bravado styles of male violence do not preclude each other. In spite of a Euro-American bias that says they do, the bias comes from not seeing the association between macho violence and gender inequality as part of class relations.

In parts of North America without class hierarchies, there was no widespread or consistent pattern of male dominance, or ultra-masculinity, or its opposite. Some tribal groups were organised in terms of a clear gendered hierarchy and pronounced male dominance; others strongly favoured gendered equality. Both dispositions—toward hierarchy and male dominance or toward equality between the genders—were found among widely disparate groups. Gender hierarchies characterised the social organisation of some groups of warlike Plains Indians, while other equally warlike hunters strongly favoured gendered equality. Similarly, some horticulturalists, people who relied heavily on gardening, were organised in terms of gendered hierarchies, but others were markedly egalitarian in their gendered and sexual arrangements.

As significant was the cross-cultural variation across the continent. In different tribal groups, the range of possibilities was different. But there was a great deal of contact between tribal groups, much individual movement from one group to another, and a broad exchange of knowledge between them. This suggests that a wide variety of possible arrangements of gendering, and sexualities, were known and tolerated across vast distances.

*Gender Fluidity in the Shatter Zone: The Osage*

To take one example, the Osage were one such prairie people among many. The Osage territory was enormous, extending from the eastern forests and mountains to the prairies and plains across the present states of Missouri, Kansas, Arkansas and Oklahoma. That brought them into contact with a great number of other tribal groups. Yet paradoxically, the Osage are far less widely known than other native nations, probably because of the central role they played in the contact history of the region.[51]

From contact histories from the early nineteenth century onwards, we know that the Osage, who spoke a Dhegihan Siouan language, were fierce egalitarians like the other hunters and horticulturalists of the region. Men were hunters, raiders and horse thieves—they were fine riders with splendid horses. Bravery was much admired. Women were house builders and potters. But throughout the summer, almost everyone left the large settlements and villages to live in tepees and to hunt for bear, buffalo and deer.[52]

The Osage settlements varied in size and composition and changed throughout the year. In the spring and fall, ten or fifteen kinfolk lived together in longhouses in large villages. Smaller villages and camps were circular, and their houses had wood frames, covered in mats or hides. Their gardens formed an outer ring around the settlement, while the chief's house, only slightly larger than the others, was inside the circle.[53]

They were healthy and prosperous. George Catlin, the artist and explorer who knew the Plains Indians as well as any outsider, wrote in 1834:

> the Osages may justly be said to be the tallest race of men in North America, either of red or white skins, there being very few indeed of the men, at their full growth, who are less than six feet in stature, and very many of them six and a half, and others seven feet. They are at the same time well-proportioned in their limbs, and good looking.[54]

The Osage governed themselves with considerable discretion. They were unusual among Plains Indians in the formal complexity of their clan and political organisation and its ritual entailments. Both men and women could acquire 'the seven degrees of clan knowledge', and both played an important part in religious ceremonies.[55]

According to the historian Kristie Wolferman,

> A select group of elder warriors, known as the Little Old Men, served as the keepers of tradition. They set the standards of conduct and were the actual government body of the tribe. Each Osage village had one or two chiefs, who were leaders rather than rulers. Chiefs inherited positions from their fathers, but they had limited power. The Little Old Men could remove them from authority if they proved to be unworthy.[56]

Further, as the Osage historian Louis Burns explains, 'A band chief's power was limited only by the people he led. Since he led only by consent of the governed, if he abused his power, he had no people to lead. The consent of the people he led could be withdrawn simply by their choice to follow another leader.'[57]

The Osage were divided into two patrilineal groups, the Sky People and the Earth People. Marriage partners were chosen from the opposite group, thus 'recreating symbolically the universe and hence the Osage people'. But couples usually lived with the wife's family and dwellings belonged to women. Young people often enjoyed a series of relationships in their twenties, before settling down. Marriages were sometimes, though rarely, polygynous. It has been argued that polygyny, though never widespread, occurred as a consequence of contact: because of the numbers of men's deaths in warfare, the demographic effects of epidemics, and the work involved preparing furs for trade. In any case, divorce was easy and not uncommon, though there was often great affection between spouses, and children were 'very much coddled and adored'.[58]

As we have seen, Native Americans knew and accepted a wide range of gender roles and sexual practices. Among the Osage, the Omaha and others from the eastern plains, were *mixu'ga* people, or women-men. These were boys and men who, having had a vision, adopted the clothing and occupations of a woman for life.

Lang draws on the unusual history of one young Osage warrior described at length in an early twentieth-century account. Unfortunately, the young man was not named, but we learn that he fasted and had many visionary dreams. Then, as he and several followers returned as a successful war party, he acted in ways that led people to understand that their leader was a *mixu'ga*, the kind of person who did not normally go to war: when he got home, he put on women's clothing and adopted women's speech patterns. But he did not relinquish his role as a warrior. Later when he went to war, he would take off his women's clothing and dress as a man. Though he married and had children, he continued the cross-dressing and cross-acting at home for the rest of his life.[59]

As the story of the Osage warrior makes clear, different degrees of gender-role change were possible within a single community and varied according to the circumstances of the person concerned.

With the coming of the Europeans, this acceptance and celebration of sexuality and cross-gendering became an excuse for colonial censorship and oppression. Catlin, the missionaries and many others deeply disapproved of Indian domestic arrangements. They pressed for marriage laws to control such unacceptable practices. As Lang suggests in her careful review of the twentieth-century anthropological literature, the study of gendering in Native North American societies is particularly revealing of the preconceptions and prejudices in more recent Western scholarship.

\* \* \*

The Osage were the largest and most powerful tribal group in the central Midwest. They played a key role in the politics of what has been called 'the Shatter Zone' for several centuries, as part of a history in which Native North Americans are not seen simply as victims of imperial and capitalist violence, but as 'people who lived and participated in the colonial world [and] contributed to and sometimes created colonial violence'.[60]

Certainly, the Osage managed, and sometimes prevented, Spanish access to the Midwest. From the other direction, they controlled French, British and American access to the West. Later the colonists themselves arrived, coming for furs and slaves, gold and silver, and eventually for the land itself.[61]

In his memoir, William Waldo, a mountain man, fur trader and sometime 'Indian fighter', addresses with a kind of fury the 'good, pious people [who] deny the Aborigines of America possess human souls, and think they should be slaughtered, and exterminated from the face of the earth, without regard to age, sex, or condition; and they go so far as to quote Holy Writ to justify their faith'.[62]

But such tolerance on the part of the white colonists became increasingly rare. Indeed, American President Thomas Jefferson, determined to break Osage power, ensured that the Lewis and Clark expedition up the Missouri River in 1804 was large enough to withstand them. From then on, traders and trappers also organised themselves on a military scale to travel through Osage territory. The historian Anne Hyde reports that by 1840,

> the Osages had lost most of their hunting domain, but they had not taken up reservation life. ... They could see no advantage in such a life. An Osage warrior, Big Soldier, observed that Anglo-Americans needed to 'possess the power of almost every animal they use'. He warned them: 'You are surrounded by slaves. Everything about you is in chains, and you are slaves yourselves'.[63]

Certainly, the Osage were a stubborn bunch, and until very late they refused to farm, to learn English or become Christians, and they set up their own constitutional government.[64]

> One of their leaders in the 1860s and 1870s, Chief Shonka Sabe (Black Dog), was 'known to the government agents as a "blanket Indian" because he refused to give up his Osage ways'. You can see

WHY MEN?

this in George Catlin's splendid portrait, one of many he painted of the Osage.[65]

But, of course, the story does not end there. David Grann's impressive book, *Killers of the Flower Moon* (2018), tells of the good fortune of the Osage when, in 1894, oil and gas was found on the reservation, how great wealth and tragedy followed and how the Osage were scorned as 'red millionaires'. Grann's book ends with a quotation from the journal of an early missionary describing the Osage as 'the happiest people in the world ... they had a sense of freedom because they didn't own anything and nothing owned them'.[66]

The irony alone could break your heart.

*Not Knowing: The Erasures of History*

Agnotology is the study of how not to know things, nor see things hidden in plain sight. And how to ignore painful emotions and ugly facts. In this respect, our concern is not just with Cahokia. Archaeologists and historians, whether writing about China, Mesopotamia or Europe, often have difficulty seeing the hunger games of male power and violence for what they are.

In a telling phrase, the anthropologist Arjun Appadurai described the past as a scarce resource. As individuals, as members of local groups, nation states and communities of scholars, we use and misuse the past. Indeed, all politics rest on contested versions of history. And we know that the myths and histories we hear most often are the ones told by the people on top, the people who have the resources and time to tell their own stories and compel the agreement of others. And these stories often do an excellent job of hiding class divisions, virulent racism and deep misogyny.[67]

Rebecca Solnit begins her exquisite essay on silence with the following words:

> Silence is the ocean of the unsaid, the unspeakable, the repressed, the erased, the unheard. Silence is what allows people to suffer without recourse, what allows hypocrisies and lies to grow and flourish, crimes to go unpunished. If our voices are essential aspects of our humanity, to be rendered voiceless is to be dehumanised or excluded from one's humanity. And the history of silence is central to women's history.[68]

Such silences, imposed from the top down, have a bearing on how we understand what followed Cahokia's fall. The lives of those who moved along woodland tracks between campsites, fishing holes and garden plots can seem like small beer compared with those who built huge mounds and left behind mass graves rich with spectacular grave goods. Yet this is a great pity, not least because this fixation has worked to reinforce contemporary biases and simultaneously project them back onto the ancient state. And the fixation also makes it puzzling, and difficult, to understand both the emphasis on equality and the ideas and practices around gender and sexuality which followed. But the elites of American history-writing (to whom we'll return) have not been the only ones motivated to obscure the fact that the Cahokian state built a deliberate structure of violent, gendered hierarchy, when things could have been otherwise.

There are two possible approaches to the story of the rise and fall of Cahokia. One is to celebrate the fact that Native Americans were able to build a dazzling and complex civilisation. The other is to take delight in the fact that after the cruel state collapsed many Native Americans went on to form much more egalitarian communities. Both approaches fit the history.

We prefer the latter emphasis because it makes us think hard about the relation between class, gender, inequality and resistance. Many Native Americans however prefer the first approach. Growing up as an Omaha, Marisa Miako<sup>n</sup>da Cummings heard a great deal about Cahokia from her father.

> He was part of a new generation of educated Natives ... in an era of self-determination, Cahokia signified and affirmed that we were more than wandering savages. It gave us pride in the fact that our people built cities and created trade networks that baffled anthropologists... My father used Cahokia as a reference of cultural pride and identity.[69]

There are also very good reasons for thinking of Cahokia this way. They have to do with genocide and the violence, racism and lies that the survivors have had to face.

The central fact of the recent history of the United States is the systematic and sustained killing of the native peoples by European colonisers. It is the largest genocide in the history of humanity. The other great injustice in the history of the Americas, slavery, now looms large in public discourse. It is widely understood as a historical wrong, and as foundational to the kind of society that the United States is now. The prejudice, massacres and broken treaties of the 'Indian wars' are of course also known, but they are far less often seen as a central process in the making of the United States.

To understand the enduring power of grief, let us look more closely at what is known as the Ghost Dance religion which, after 1870, swept across the Great Plains. Many people know about the massacre of nearly 300 Lakota people in 1890 near Wounded Knee in South Dakota. Fewer people know why they were massacred. It was because they had left the reservation and headed into the free grasslands. They left because the US Army forbade them to practise the new religion of the Ghost Dance on the reservation. On the plains, they could dance.

Ghost Dance was an unfortunate name for the new religion because it makes the Native Americans sound superstitious. From the 1890s onward, it was the term widely used for a spiritual movement that had many local names. The anthropologist James Mooney began his remarkable 1896 history of the Ghost Dance:

> The wise men tell us that the world is growing happier—that we live longer than did our fathers, have more comfort and less of toil, fewer wars and discords, and higher hopes and aspirations. So say the wise men; but deep in our hearts we know they are wrong...
>
> As with men, so it is with nations... And when the race lies crushed and groaning beneath an alien yoke, how natural is the dream of a redeemer, an Arthur, who shall return from exile or awake from some long sleep to drive out the usurper and win back for his people what they have lost. The hope becomes a faith ... and the dream a religion, looking to some great miracle of nature for its culmination and accomplishment. The doctrines of the Hindu avatar, the Hebrew messiah, the Christian millennium, and the Hesûnanin of the Indian Ghost Dance are essentially the same, and have their origin in a hope and longing common to all humanity.[70]

The new religion spread through Native American communities across the West and Midwest because it spoke so powerfully to the survivors of massacres and epidemics. The people danced for hours, or for days, until exhaustion and hunger transported them into a trance state. And in that trance, they saw all the people they had loved who had died. They sat down with the departed, in peace and sunlight, and all around the grass grew high and the buffalo still grazed, and they were happy together again.[71]

But the killing did not stop. As we were working on this chapter, the indigenous First Nations community around Kamloops, in British Columbia, announced in May 2021 that archaeologists working with the tribe thought they had found the graves of 215 children. Those children had all been students at the Kamloops Indian Residential School between 1890 and 1978. No records had been kept of their deaths.

Across the rest of Canada, more than 6,000 such graves have been discovered, and many more will be. In the residential schools, students were forbidden to speak their own languages, were chronically cold and hungry, and routinely brutally beaten and sexually abused on a massive scale. The last point is not surprising, given that most of the schools were run by the Catholic Church for which 'disastrous error' and 'evil' Pope Francis recently apologised.[72]

The purpose of those schools was to stamp out the native language and culture and turn out people who had lost their culture. The reason for this was that First Nations communities still existed and were still fighting to defend their land.

The United States too had residential schools, for much the same purposes, though so far much less of the horror has been exposed. This is likely to change drastically as the sites of some fifty residential schools are due to be excavated. In those schools too, generations of Native American children were told that their traditional way of life was savage, and that they were poor because they were stupid and ignorant.

Of course, writing history is never neutral, but it is much more difficult to be wise in the knowledge of such heartbreak and suffering. When this is your history, is it any surprise that some of you may want to hold on to and emphasise anything that can be thrown back in the face of the institutions and the state telling you that you had no culture and no history of civilisation?

For some Native Americans who wished to lay claim to an older ancestry and history and oppose the tyranny of the Europeans, letting go of the Cahokia means letting go of a pride in their ancestry and the remote past and the achievements of the state. For centuries most Native Americans have been fiercely egalitarian, yet their devotion to freedom and equality was a world away from what must have been the hierarchy and values of the elite who governed Cahokia.

This understandable impulse—to embrace Cahokia, despite its injustices, over the less 'monumental' or 'civilisational' post-Cahokian societies of the Plains Indians—has chimed all too easily with archaeologists who have been attracted to and find it hard to let go of 'large, deep sites at the expense of smaller, less artifact-rich ones'.[73]

Unfortunately, however, the bias of European and US commentators on the history of Cahokia does not stop at an attraction to the big, rich and powerful and ignoring the egalitarian societies which came after its fall. Historically there has also been a political, or specifically a class, imperative involved.

With Native North Americans, the issue was never, as with plantation slavery, the ownership of labour. As Thomas King argues in *The Inconvenient Indian*, it was always about the ownership of land. Those who would not leave the land or tried to return were killed.

What makes it worse is that the Native Americans owned their land collectively—in other words, they had a kind of socialism. That ownership could not be allowed to stand in the past, nor now.[74] It had to be erased from historical recognition, or else explained away as a matter of primitive savagery. As Olúfémi Táíwò says of settler colonialism more generally, the Aboriginal inhabitants 'were treated as flora and fauna to be cleared out of the way'.[75]

Opening the eastern part of the continent to European settlers was a central aim of the American Revolution. President Thomas Jefferson's 1804 Louisiana Purchase then opened the lands west of the Mississippi. By the middle of the nineteenth century, many thousands of white colonists understood that their 'manifest destiny' was to farm and to spread Christianity, democracy and a capitalist economy west to the Pacific.[76]

When the new Americans arrived, they found the mounds awesome and inexplicable, but cared little about their history. The mounds were attributed to all sorts—Phoenicians, the lost tribes of Israel, the Vikings, the Welsh—anyone but the Native Americans.

Though many of the new Americans were running from tyranny and class inequality in Europe, few seemed to think that the Native

Americans they met might also be people who fled hierarchy, aka 'civilisation', to find a more equal way of living. Nor were the land-hungry immigrant settlers looking for such a model. They were usurping the land of desperate 'savages'. They had no reason to revere the ancient landscape, and without conscience, they looted and levelled the mounds.

And there was a further embarrassment. Whoever the Mound Builders were, they were clearly outdone by the indigenous pyramid-builders in what are now Guatemala and Mexico. This, at a time when the United States aimed to dominate the politics of the Americas, made such comparisons invidious and helped to create an ideological and geographical border between the United States and the Spanish-speaking south well before Texas joined the Union.

The racism of the genocide has also been compounded in the United States because Lewis Henry Morgan, the father of North American archaeology and anthropology, was a racist.

Morgan was a scholar of the Iroquois nation, and of kinship systems. And, at the end of his life, he did some fieldwork in the American Southwest. In 1877, he published *Ancient Society*. From then, until very recently, his ideas and those of other social evolutionists such as Herbert Spencer and Edward Tylor held sway among American archaeologists and anthropologists. And in another twist that we discuss in Chapter 18, during the 1970s many left-leaning feminist anthropologists picked up on Friedrich Engels' *The Origin of the Family, Private Property and the State*, which leaned heavily on Morgan's work.

Morgan proposed that human beings progressed through stages on the evolutionary ladder from savagery to barbarism and civilisation. The archaeologist Stephen Lekson tells the story succinctly:

> Morgan was utterly convinced that no New World society, Aztec to Iroquois, ever achieved the status of a state—the golden ring at the end of his global evolutionary schema for human societies. Not everyone was enthusiastic about Morgan's social evolution, but many welcomed his conclusions about Native America. Restated, he presented an America untroubled by kings and emperors. All government was communal and quasi-democratic. ... Morgan's communalism sat well with the young republic... But Morgan's argument was racist: he believed Native American societies were

communal because Native Americans themselves were racially incapable of achieving civilization (his term) or states (my term). ... Mexican archaeologists dismissed Morgan outright, but American archaeologists bought his beliefs hook, line and sinker. ... No states existed north of Mexico. That is, no Native societies within the continental United States ever had Kings or governments or any of the trappings of state-level politics.[77]

In Morgan's train, the notion of class was absent, and there was little discussion of violence or the use of force even when grave goods included axes and arrowheads. And as Lexson underlines, Morgan's ideas fit well with the colonial advance.

Leslie White, the founder of the anthropology department at the University of Michigan, was key to the transmission of this social evolutionary theory in the United States. White's focus on Pueblo society added a particularly North American myopia to his ideas, and the next generation of scholars were dominated by White's students.[78]

Other slights of mind displaced the brutality and violence of the dispossession onto victims themselves. Thus, the Sioux, Apache and others became ideal types of Native Americans. They were warlike, brave and fought every inch of their centuries of retreat. But they were also 'Indians' and could be stigmatised as stupid, subhuman and cruel. 'Bloodthirsty savage' was a cliché. While the blood was real enough, the thirst was in other throats.[79]

\* \* \*

Morgan's racist legacy did not go away with the Cold War, quite the opposite. In the 1960s, what became known as the New Archaeology was promoted by Lewis Binford, and for the first couple of years, his then wife, Sally Rosen Binford. They were theoreticians but also did fieldwork, including at Cahokia in the early 1960s.[80]

The New Archaeology became a movement which emphasised research methods which were narrowly focused on science and technology. It was research designed to attract National Science Foundation funds and build up overwhelming US military might.[81] And in emphasising the close adaptation of 'Indians' to nature and the environment and treating violence as innate to the human species, the New Archaeology became another version of the evolutionary psychology we have described in Part One.

And as latter-day McCarthyism, the New Archaeology stymied socialist and Marxist critiques of hierarchy, class divisions and violence. There was an ideological clamp-down and left-leaning thinkers were silenced. Thus Preston Holden, described by Timothy Pauketat as 'the best and most passionate archaeologist to be sucked into ancient Cahokia's vortex before or since', was red-baited, black-listed and fired from his university post.[82]

After she parted company from Lewis Binford, Sally Rosen Binford wrote a memoir entitled 'From Tight Sweaters to the Pentagon Papers'. In it she described how the CIA infiltrated the academy. 'During the early Sixties, when the big boys in Washington decided the Third World was where the action was, a lot of funny grad students started turning up in anthropology ... what better cover could anybody have, for working in the 3$^{rd}$ World, than being an anthropologist.'[83]

On the other side of the political divide, North American exceptionalism and chauvinism created problems for the archaeologists and anthropologists who hated racism and respected the Native North Americans. Wanting to see them in an admirable light made it difficult for well-wishers to admit there had been anything wrong with Cahokian society. So this contradiction too had to be hidden.

Between Morgan's racism, the New Archaeology's determined disinterest in big-picture structural analysis, and the impulse among some Native Americans and their scholarly allies not to acknowledge the cruelty baked into Cahokia's system, class analyses disappeared from the academic mainstream. Early on Alice Kehoe described Cahokia as a state 'hiding in plain sight'. And in her 2022 autobiography, *Girl Archaeologist: Sisterhood in a Sexist Profession*, Kehoe describes the New Archaeology as a 'pseudoscience'.[84] Yet Susan Alt, who deplored the minimalist New Archaeologists, still thought those who identified Cahokia as a city-state were 'exaggerationalists'.[85]

As for what came after Cahokia, between the European colonial drive to erase Native history and Native ways of life altogether and the Native drive to recover a history of 'greatness', there has sometimes been little room left for another side to this deeply complex truth about Cahokia: the Native history, not of greatness, but of quiet cooperation and relaxed identity categories.

In short, there have been many ways to make the 1,000 years between Cahokia and the present disappear. But there are signs that the way we approach the history and archaeology of Cahokia, and Native America more generally, is changing for the better. The most striking evidence about class and gender at Cahokia comes from Mound 72. That is to say, the evidence comes from graves. And in the shadow of a genocide, people have strong feelings about death and graves, as Chip Colwell's sensitive and important book, *Plundered Skulls and Stolen Spirits*, describes.[86] After sustained campaigning by many native communities, in 1990, the United States Congress finally passed the Native American Graves Protection and Repatriation Act (NAGPRA). Since then, no researcher can excavate Native American graves without the approval and cooperation of local Native American communities. In most cases, this permission has not been forthcoming. At Cahokia, the excavation of graves has stopped. As Alice Kehoe, the feminist archaeologist, iconoclast and rebel, has said, NAGPRA 'upset the apple cart of white supremacy in American archaeology'.[87]

The archaeologist Madonna Moss tells the story of two Native American graves. In Alaska there was close cooperation between archaeologists and the local Tlingit community, and everyone was proud of what they discovered. But in Washington state the archaeologists had no connections with local Native American communities, and were determined to have things their way. After eight years of litigation, and a cost to the federal government of more than three million dollars, 'the case has taken an incalculable toll on the reputation of archaeology in Indian country'.[88] Moss' point is simple. These are the ancestors of indigenous people. The best way forward for serious and productive scientific work is for archaeologists to work with, and for, native peoples—and to be clear that power to make decisions lies with them.

From beginning to end, the Cahokia story is an example of how historical biases from different eras and cultures have been blended and merged to make it difficult to see that a ruling elite used gendered violence to create and sustain gross class inequality, and that such an elite was not inevitable: that, in its absence, a different egalitarian and gender-fluid space emerged.

## CAHOKIA

Empathy is difficult. It can revolt us, and broach the unthinkable, while reminding us of the sexism and violence we live with today. But understanding how the 'sacrifices' must have terrified observers also makes it easier to understand why Cahokia fell—and what was able to flourish in its wake.

# 14

# THE COURAGE AND CLOTHING OF JOAN OF ARC

Joan of Arc was a fifteenth-century French peasant warrior and prophet who won the love of a mass movement. In this chapter we explain how the events of her life were part of a class struggle played out in a battle over gendered categories. And we show how transgression of identity binaries can offer a powerful and deliberate challenge to established order and class hierarchies.[1]

Joan of Arc, the hero of our story, grew up in the village of Domrémy, in what is now northeastern France, and began to have visions when she was about 13 years old, in 1425.

Like most people in France at that time, and indeed most people across Europe, Joan was a peasant. In 1425 the basic productive unit of French rural life was the peasant household. The luckier households, rich enough to own two horses or two oxen, ploughed their own land. The poorer households used hoes and worked part of the time for others who had more land.

Peasants paid a part of their crop to the king, and part to a local lord who owned their land. The base of the lord's power, and the king's, was a retinue of thugs on horseback, commonly known as knights. This was the age of 'chivalry', from 'cheval', the French word for a horse. Possession of battle armour and a charger big enough to carry that weight and race into battle required wealth. Assembling a force of such armour and horses required great wealth.

To understand this society, think *Game of Thrones* (the books, not the TV series), and you will not be far wrong. George R.R. Martin did his homework on fourteenth-century and early fifteenth-century France and England, the two kingdoms whose war brought Joan to the battlefield. The brutality, pride, cruelty and desperation of his noble families are on the mark.

## WHY MEN?

But this was also a time of great peasant revolts across Europe. Class power was shifting and unstable. The key event was the pandemic of the Black Death across Eurasia, peaking in Europe between 1347 and 1351. Estimates of the death rates vary greatly. Some authorities say that a third of the population in Western Europe died. Others say that such death rates were limited to particular areas. Whatever the rates of death, there is little doubt that contemporaries viewed it as a time of catastrophe.

Within England and France, the Black Death had two important effects. One was that in the first generations afterward, there were simply fewer people. Feudal serfs in many places had been bound to the service of a lord. But after the Black Death lords had all the land they needed and not enough hands to work it. That made it easier for peasants to play one lord against another, and to work for wages or rent land from neighbouring lords.

The other effect is not as often remarked upon by historians. But we suspect that the great death discredited the legitimacy of both the lords and the priests whose rule had failed to protect their people.

There were great risings too. In 1381 a peasant army marched on London. According to the historian David Green:

> The citizens of the capital who shared their grievances opened the city gates, and for a few days in 1381 it appeared that the rebels would take control of the city and the government... The rebels' demands, articulated by their leader, Wat Tyler, were truly revolutionary. There were, as one would expect, demands concerning wages, rents and landownership, but much more remarkable was the call for the disendowment of the Church—all ecclesiastical property was to be handed over to the people; there was to be an end to serfdom; and, most extraordinarily, an end to all lordship save that of the king.[2]

Green repeats a telling story:

> The rebels also broke into the Tower of London and ... into the bedchamber of the king's mother, Joan of Kent. There they were said to have jumped up and down on her bed and waved what the chronicler coyly described as 'their filthy sticks' at her. Although a minor incident, it shows the complete breakdown of central authority and of the barriers between social classes.[3]

France had not seen a peasant uprising on the same scale since the Jacquerie of 1358. But in 1413, when Joan was about 1 year old, the common people of Paris rose up in an attempted revolution. The leaders came mainly from the guild of butchers, the guild of skinners and the teachers at the University. Among them was the *écorcheur* (skinner) Simon Caboche. The leading contemporary historian of the Hundred Years War, John Sumption, comments that 'Caboche, whose low status and brutish nickname, symbolised for many the excesses of the plebian revolution, shortly gave his name to a whole movement'—the Cabochions.[4]

The butchers and skinners were joined by all the other trades, and many of the poor. A massive crowd stormed the Bastille, arrested more than a hundred royal officials and courtiers, and began public executions and a reign of terror. Thousands of rebels invaded the royal court, and the meeting of the estates that the king had summoned to enable him to raise taxes. The common people presented the king and the Dauphin with more than 200 demands, all of which were passed into law. The royal family were held prisoners for weeks, and most of the important officials were sacked and replaced by the 'base and low born' men nominated by the crowd. The rebels had thousands of white cloaks made, like those of the White Friars, the Carmelites who had taken an oath of poverty. And the king, all his family and all his officials were forced to don them.[5]

The similarities between this uprising and the great French Revolution of 1789 are striking. The movement of 1413, though, was eventually defeated by an alliance of all the warring lords of Burgundy and France. But everyone among the courtiers and lords of France would have remained acutely aware of the danger from the common people.

By the time Joan was born in 1412, most of the suitable arable land in northern France was already being farmed. Intensive cultivation was depleting the land and the more marginal fields were reverting to wasteland or pasture. Peasants found it harder to meet the rents, tithes and taxes levied by the lords, kings and church. As receipts fell, the lords and kings turned the screw harder on the remaining peasants, for the lord who could not put men and horses in the field was in danger of losing his own land and position.

The historian Guy Bois has analysed the dynamic of the terrible century that followed in *The Crisis of Feudalism*. His book tells, in

## WHY MEN?

careful detail, the story of Normandy. Joan was from the east of northern France, and Normandy was in the west, but the situation would have been similar. The kings of France and England had been at war for most of the previous eighty-eight years. Later historians would call it the Hundred Years War, and it raged back and forth across what is now France. The alliances between the great lords and princes of feudalism kept shifting. But when Joan was growing up, the Burgundian lords of northern France and the low countries were allied with the kings of England, and the Armagnac lords of southern France were allied with the kings of France.

According to Bois, the impositions of the lords and kings, the falling returns on less fertile fields, the carnage of a long war, and the epidemic of the Black Death all combined in an apocalypse. By the time Joan entered history, the population of Normandy was half what it had been a century earlier, and worse was to come.[6]

The century after the Black Death, between 1350 and 1450, was a period of open class conflict between lords and peasants across much of Europe. The landlords and the nobility were able to put down the largest peasant rebellions, but they were on the defensive.[7]

In Normandy both English power and peasant resistance was strongest. But the surging wave of peasant confidence went far beyond the partisan war there and lasted well after Joan died in 1425. The fifteenth-century Norman chronicler Thomas Basin describes a peasant uprising against English lords in 1436:

> This great crowd of peasants spread out in disorder near the gate of the moat. Then two or three hundred English horsemen hurled themselves upon them and made great carnage. They were peasants fighting on foot, almost without weapons, and who only relied on their almost infinite numbers... The English pursued them, slashing them down with swords and exterminating without mercy.[8]

Such was the power of men on horseback. And the depredations of war that had begun with the Black Death pressed hard on Domrémy as well.

*Joan's Mission*

Joan was a peasant in an age of peasant revolt. But her message was not directly about class. It was about war and nationalism. The bor-

# THE COURAGE AND CLOTHING OF JOAN OF ARC

der between the lands controlled by 'France' and 'England' ran through the middle of Joan's village. Domrémy lay along one bank of the river Meuse, where a small stream flowed into the river. That stream divided French lands from English. The house of Joan's family was just north of the stream. Two miles to the south, across the stream, was the church where Joan went to pray most days after her work was done.[9]

Over the eighty-eight years, and all through Joan's childhood, the wars would start, and stop, and start again. When they started, the armies would sweep across the border. When the soldiers came, the villagers would flee with their cattle and hide in the marshes. All soldiers were dangerous, but these villagers lived in special fear of the brutality of the English and Welsh archers and men-at-arms. They feared death, of course, but they also feared rape and losing their cattle.

If war was dangerous, peace was worse. The English soldiers were paid in wartime. But they were mercenaries, and in times of peace they roamed across the countryside in bands, dependent on raiding to stay alive.[10]

All the boundaries Joan crossed in her life would have one purpose, to move the border that ran through the middle of Domrémy away from the village. Her mission was to end endless war, by winning once and for all. With this aim she ignored all the old feudal alliances and lordships and spoke of countries. Her purpose was to move the English out of France.

\* \* \*

When Joan was sixteen, the voices that spoke to her grew urgent. She must go to Charles, the son of the last king of France. He had not yet been crowned, for the English and their allies controlled the only cities where his coronation could convincingly take place. Those voices came from God and they told her that she would lead Charles' soldiers into war against the English and see him crowned.

But first Joan had to get to Charles. She was nobody. However, wandering women and men with such visions and prophecies were not so unusual. Great lords listened to them, and large crowds attended their open-air preaching. That part of Joan's mission was not new. But she proposed to lead an army, and that was something only great lords did. The overwhelming majority of men were not allowed that privilege. And she was not just a woman—she was a manual worker, a herder of cattle and still not much more than a child.

Joan could not get access to Charles' court directly. So she went to the captain of a local garrison, 10 miles north of her village, and asked him to take her to Charles. He refused. But more and more local people began to talk about Joan, and Charles was growing desperate at the prospect of losing all his lands. When she returned to the captain several months later, he sent her on to court.

Before Joan set out, she cut her hair and changed her clothes. 'She was given a horse to ride and an outfit of men's clothes—tunic, doublet, hose and breeches, all in black and grey, as a replacement for her rough red dress. When she left, with a black woollen hat pulled down over her cropped hair', her escort was entirely male.[11]

Her rough dress was gone, and now she had a horse. She was beginning to change class. And she was becoming man-like. But at the same time, she was absolutely not a man. She never called herself Joan of Arc. That was an aristocratic style, ridiculous for a person like herself. When she spoke, and when she dictated formal letters, she called herself *Jeanne la Pucelle*, Joan the Maid.

*Pucelle*—maid—was a word loaded with meanings. The most obvious was 'virgin'. At key moments, Joan's virginity was tested: before she set out for the court, before she was presented at the court of Charles, and before the English put her on trial for her life. Each time, Joan would open her legs and a woman of noble birth would peer down and stick her finger in Joan's vagina to feel for the hymen. Joan passed those three tests. If she had not, no one would have paid her any mind.

Another meaning of *pucelle*, however, was a girl who would soon be married. In this meaning, the word was playful, sexy, flirtatious. Maids were desired, and they were desirous of others. Peasant maids, shepherd girls like Joan, were known to be fair game and easy targets for soldiers, lords and passing strangers. It was this meaning Joan had always had to keep at bay. When the church tried her, the words they used were 'heretic', and 'sorcerer', and 'witch'. But the word the English soldiers shouted at her again and again, on the road, and from the walls of besieged Orleans, and in her dungeon cell, was 'whore, whore, whore'.

# THE COURAGE AND CLOTHING OF JOAN OF ARC

There was always the threat of rape. Joan travelled with escorts of men, and only men. She slept out with them on rough ground. Especially at the beginning, when she first rode off to the court, she was enormously vulnerable. Many years later, the men who served around her would remember a miracle—she was beautiful, but they felt no desire for her. Two of them reported seeing her as she changed her clothes, and feeling no desire, though, one said, her breasts were beautiful. Maybe they felt less awe at the beginning, and maybe a bit more desire. But there was something in her manner, her forthright way of speaking, her way of standing, that kept men from thinking of her as a sexual being. The clothes were an essential part of this defence.

There was a third possible meaning of *pucelle*—the holy virgin herself, Mary the mother of Jesus. Joan never laid claim directly to this mantle. But she began her formal and public letters 'Jhesu Maria, I, Joan the Maid'. About her there was always a hint of the popular religion of Mary, beloved of the common people, and of women.[12]

In 1429 Joan came to court and persuaded Charles to honour her vision. He gave her a force of soldiers and she led them to the relief of the city of Orleans, garrisoned by the English and their French allies. Now Joan wore armour that gleamed in the sun and torchlight. Light armour, though, not thick enough to protect her from swords. Armour that was easy to move in and made specially for her slender frame. She wore a sword, but she did not draw it in battle. Instead, she still led her troops from the front, with a white banner, signalling purity, clutched in her right hand. Joan said later, proudly, that she carried a banner so she would not kill any man. But she led the soldiers into battle. She arrived at Orleans and took a few outlying fortifications. Then she threw herself, and her troops, at the city wall. The English soldiers yelled 'whore' down at her, but the people of Orleans opened the gates, and the English and their allies melted away.

The maid was a prophecy made flesh. It was the utter impossibility of her, the virgin dressed as a man, the peasant leading an army, that made her power possible. She embodied miracle. Each step of the way the support of the common people gave her power too. She was one of their own. The great lords had fought over the fields and the bodies and bones of the common people for generations, and they were venal and cruel. That was why the people around Domrémy and the neighbouring villages talked up her policy, and why they raised the money for her first set of clothing and the horse. It was why other common people opened the gates of Orleans. And that faith of the common people was why the English soldiers and their French allies fled. They were not sure what to think, and their officers said she was a harlot, but so many people countered and said that the Maid came from God.

Her gender transgression was not separate from her class transgression. Each gave power to the other. You may have been wondering how becoming a political voice and a military leader within a monarchical system, in support of a king, could amount to resistance to feudal lords as a class. Does transgression to one's place in the pecking order necessarily mean resistance to the order itself? Not always, but in the social turmoil of the times, the very fact that Joan was present carried a threat to a whole system of hierarchy. And after the taking of Orleans, the road lay open to the cathedral at Rheims, where French kings had been crowned of old. Joan led Charles there, and stood next to him at the coronation, her armour shining, the white banner in her fist. He was crowned through the grace of God, and Joan.

Which was a problem, and not just for Charles. In effect, he now shared power with a 16-year-old girl. The coronation ritual had dramatised that. She was not, and could not be, admitted to his council. But she had a very definite idea of what he should do, which was drive the English back to the sea, and of how he might do it. Joan's solution did not fit his complex, shifting feudal negotiations with the other lords. And it was probably not militarily possible. But more important, a peasant girl's power was unprecedented. Such a thing had never happened before in human memory. It was an inversion of the entire class order that sustained every lord in the control of his land.

Joan could not be allowed to grow in power. She insisted that she should be given forces to take the English stronghold of Paris, the largest city in France. Charles gave in but did not give her enough men. She led her men at the walls of Paris, an act of military madness, in the hope that God would intervene or that the people would open the walls. Neither happened. She was seriously wounded and carried from the field.

# THE COURAGE AND CLOTHING OF JOAN OF ARC

When Joan recovered weeks later, her army had already fallen back from Paris. To get Joan out of the way, Charles sent her to command a small force against a minor lord in Brittany. There too she led soldiers from the front and went up the ladder placed against the city wall, only to be taken prisoner at the top.

She assumed Charles would ransom her, as he would have done one of his own lords. He did not. Instead, he allowed her to be sold to the English as a prisoner.

The English took her to the port of Calais, the part of France where their grip was strongest. They threw her in a cell, and organised bishops, lawyers and priests to try her in a church court. The politics were complicated here, and Joan had a hand to play. The English royal family, led in Calais by the Duke of Bedford, wanted to disprove Joan's royal mission. But there was general agreement that her voices were real. The question was, did they come from God, or from Satan?

If Bishop Cauchon and his church lawyers could prove it was the Devil speaking, that would confirm the right of the young king of England, Henry VI, to rule both England and France. However, the church lawyers had to prove this to public satisfaction. In one sense, their verdict was a foregone conclusion. But burning Joan without proving her wrong would not prove their case. Moreover, it seems clear from the way that Joan's jailers treated her that they were not at all sure about the source of her power.

Joan was tried by the church but held in a cell by English soldiers. This made her vulnerable. It was crucial that she retain her male clothes if she was to maintain the aura that protected her from abuse. Those clothes were also a central part of her heresy. As the judges wrote at the beginning of her trial, 'The report has now become well known in many places that this woman, utterly disregarding what is honourable in the female sex, breaking the bounds of modesty, and forgetting all feminine decency, has disgracefully put on the clothing of the male sex, a shocking and vile monstrosity.'[13]

Indeed, there were five separate charges of wearing male dress at her trial. One read:

> The said Jeanne put off and entirely abandoned women's clothes, with her hair cropped short and round in the fashion of young men,

275

> she wore shirt, breeches, doublet, with hose joined together, long and fastened to the said doublet by twenty points, long leggings laced on the outside, a short mantle reaching to the knee, or thereabouts, a close-cut cap, tight-fitting boots or buskins, long spurs, sword, dagger, breastplate, lance and other arms in the style of a man-at-arms.[14]

In the detail of these charges there is a class rage as well as a gender rage. It is not just that she is like a man, it is that she is like a warrior, and an expensively dressed warrior at that. Notice the 'twenty points', and the 'tight-fitting buskins'. This is not an ascetic boy, they are saying, this is an upper-class man showing off his body and his wealth.

The thirteenth article in her charges develops the point. It accuses her of wearing 'rich and sumptuous habits, precious stuffs and cloth of gold and furs'. And:

> Not only did she wear short tunics, but she dressed herself in tabards and garments open at the sides, besides the matter is notorious since when she was captured she was wearing a surcoat cloak of cloth of gold, open on all sides... And in general, having cast aside all womanly decency, not only to the scorn of female modesty, but also of well instructed men, she had worn the apparel and garments of most dissolute men, and, in addition, had some weapons of defence.[15]

The judges asked her to put aside male clothes, and she refused. They asked her repeatedly why she refused to take off the clothes, hoping she would say God or the saints had instructed her to wear such dress, and then they would have her for obvious blasphemy. Repeatedly, Joan refused to say why. But she stuck to her clothes, and the forty to sixty clerics who judged her at different times did not dare take them away.

### Defiance

Let's step back for a moment and return to some of our earlier concerns about categories. Some writers have treated Joan as a precursor of today's trans people. Leslie Feinberg, in *Transgender Warriors*, treats Joan as a trans hero. Was she?[16]

In one sense, we have to say no. Running through this book has been an argument that there are many ways to experience gender, and that these are situational and often fleeting and fluid. Trans is one way the categories of gender are divided now in many countries. We don't know, and can't know, what gender Joan preferred, or secretly knew herself to be. To say she wanted to be a boy, or was a boy, would have put her life in grave danger. It would have destroyed the complex balancing act whence came her power. Joan was certainly pushing the boundaries. But she was equally clear that what she wanted to be was a maid who wore men's clothing. To make her a trans hero is to ignore the specifics of her life, and of her time and place.

In another more literal sense, of course she was a trans hero, because she took her life in her hands to challenge the gendered conventions of her time and try to change the known world.

And she was also a peasant hero. The trial proceeded for months, with several days of interrogation at a time, punctuated by weeks of delay while the prosecution tried to work out a more convincing strategy for breaking Joan. She endured hours of questioning, firm, wily, and outspoken in rooms where a hundred great men were against her and no one on her side.

Her heroism is astonishing. But being a peasant was also a source of strength. Outside the walls of Calais, a class resistance against the English lords had been growing for fifteen years. The English army under the Duke of Bedford had occupied the Norman countryside for ten years, from 1415 on. Many areas were laid waste, devoid of people. The English lords increased their demands for levies, and enforced them more brutally, for they had to fund their own war.

Bois writes:

> The domination indeed encountered growing resistance, the social base of which was the rural masses: the military framework was supplied by elements from the minor Norman nobility... 'Partisan war' took shape at the start of the occupation... Bound together by oath, [the partisans] organized themselves into 'companies' that kept to the countryside or forests. These outlaws obtained weapons and were sometimes mounted. Their action was directed exclusively against the English and their servants: sergeants, receivers of aids, collectors of taxes: for these country folk the enemy was as

much the soldier who seized provisions from the farm houses, as the agent of a fiscal administration, heavier than in the past. So the petty local functionaries they captured were ransomed. On the other hand, they conscientiously paid for the commodities they obtained in the villages where they still had ties. This was therefore an armed, conscious, organized and tenacious struggle. A century earlier, it would have been inconceivable. But what changes had taken place in rural society since then! The most important of these was the decay of [the] seigneurial authority [of the lords], eroded on all sides, with its corollary, the strengthened influence of the rural communities. Because of their enhanced social role, the peasants had acquired a new dignity, reinforced their cohesion, and gained a certain autonomy: racked by the hardships of war and insecurity they had learned to handle weapons. They no longer behaved like poor passive wretches whose somnolence was broken only at rare intervals by sharp bursts of rage—terrible, perhaps, but ephemeral. Behind this Norman resistance is a surging wave which carries the peasantry forward, making it more demanding in every sphere.[17]

That class resistance was why Charles had to betray Joan. It was why Bishop Cauchon and Lord Bedford had not just to burn her, but to break and humiliate her. And it was part of the reason Joan was able to be so brave.

Bishop Cauchon called her to a hall, filled with all the instruments of torture in the city, and the silent torturers standing beside their machines:

> She had been shown the proof of her errors many times, the bishop told her sternly, and in response she had lied and lied again, and denied the truth despite the efforts of my [the bishop's] many learned scholars to teach and advise her. She left them no choice but to put her to the torture, in order to lead her back to the path of righteousness for the good of her soul and body which she had exposed to so much danger.

Joan looked at the bishop and the torturers for a time, and then she said, 'In truth, if you were to have me torn limb from limb and my soul separated from my body, I still won't tell you anything more. And if I did tell you anything else about this, afterwards I would always say that you made me say it by force.'[18]

# THE COURAGE AND CLOTHING OF JOAN OF ARC

She had called the bishop's bluff. He dared not torture her. In the end, the church court found her guilty, as everyone had known they would. Then they begged her to admit that she had lied. If she did, she would be discredited and the English would have destroyed her power. She would also be a prisoner for the rest of her life. If she did not recant, she would be turned over to the English and burned.

Joan, confident in God, refused to recant. The soldiers took her to the place of execution, and a cleric asked her one last time to recant. She could see God would not save her now. Eighteen years old, just a person, like you or me, she said that her voices were not real.

She was taken back to her cell. Joan had been tried by the church, but now she was a prisoner of the English, watched over by their soldiers. She was given a dress, and she put it on. And then her English guards grew less and less afraid of her. She was just a girl, and utterly at their mercy.

At this point, her guards provided her with men's clothes, and urged her to put them on. She, and they, knew that if she did that, she would be a relapsed heretic, and would be burned. She resisted their urgings. But on the Monday, after four days in her cell, she put on the men's clothes.

Why? Many years later, Charles and the church staged a retrial designed to exonerate Joan of the charges of sorcery and heresy. At that trial, three witnesses, a master mason and two friars, testified that Joan told them that her guards had abused her sexually:

> Among other [witnesses] is one called Pierre Cusquel, a burgher of Rouen who, apparently, was a master mason in the service of the 'master of masonry works in the castle'; for, he says it was by that officer's permissions that he twice entered Joan's cell and was able to talk to her. He declared: 'People were saying that her condemnation had no other cause excepting that she had resumed men's clothes; and that she had not worn and was not wearing this male attire excepting in order not to give herself to the soldiers with whom she was. Once, in the prison, I asked why she was wearing this male attire and that is what she answered me.'

> [Friar] Martin Ladvenu's evidence is in the same sense: 'As for knowing whether anyone approached her secretly at night, I heard it from Joan's own lips that a great English lord entered her prison

and tried to take her by force. That was the cause, she said, of her resuming men's clothes.'

Again, there is [Friar] Isambart de la Pierre: 'After she had renounced and abjured and resumed man's clothes, I and several others were present when Joan excused herself for having again put on men's clothes, saying and affirming publicly that the English had had much wrong and violence done to her in prison when she was dressed in woman's clothes. And in fact I saw her tearful, her face covered with tears, disfigured and outraged in such sort that I had pity and compassion on her.'[19]

It is unclear from this evidence whether she was actually raped. Maybe, and maybe not. It is clear that she understood that if she did not resume male attire, sooner or later she would be raped.

The bishop and the English were immediately informed that she had put on the clothes of a man. The next morning, dressed only in a white shift, she was burned alive in the public square.

We have suggested that this was a form of human sacrifice. It could be argued that we have pushed an analogy too hard, that this was a form of punishment for religious transgression, not a sacrifice to God. But the similarities are real. This is an execution sanctioned by religion, and by priests. A young woman, a virgin, is led through the crowd dressed only in her underwear and tied to a stake. She is watched by a crowd who expected to be moved, each in different ways, by fascination, terror or sexual excitement.

We are calling attention to these similarities because we want to make a simple point. The public festivals of sexual cruelty that we have seen in a Viking camp, in Cahokia and here in medieval France, and that we can find in thousands of places throughout history, are not signs of savagery or barbarism. They are the marks of societies built on material inequality, male domination and a brutal policing of the ideas keeping everyone in their place.

As the flames grew around Joan, she called the name of Jesus, over and over, in a clear, strong voice.

* * *

And then something strange happened, or probably happened. And here, perhaps more than anywhere else in the book, we need a

## THE COURAGE AND CLOTHING OF JOAN OF ARC

trigger warning. What follows is brutal, and you may want to skip to the next chapter.

We know about this from the private journal of a man historians usually call the Bourgeois of Paris. No one knows his name, and he was probably a priest or monk, but not a bourgeois: he may well have been a teacher at the University of Paris.

Historians return to his journal again and again, because for this period it is perhaps the most reliable source about what ordinary people in France were thinking and doing. It reports the word on the streets and in the markets. It is true that much of what he repeats is rumour. But in places where people live under autocrats and censorship, rumour is often the most reliable news. That said, the historian Colette Beaune points out more generally that the Bourgeois had a weakness for rumours that contained sexual fantasy.[20]

Certainly, the Bourgeois was in the habit of writing down interesting pieces of news in his journal, which is what he did when he heard about the execution of Joan in Calais. His entry ends:

> [She] was tied to a stake on the platform (which was made of plaster) and the fire lit under her. She was soon dead and her clothes all burned. Then the fire was raked back and her naked body was shown to all the people and all the secrets that could or should belong to a woman, to take away any doubts from the people's minds. When they had stared long enough at her dead body bound to the stake, the executioner got a big fire going again around her poor carcass, which was burned up, flesh and bone reduced to ashes.[21]

The Bourgeois is saying that as soon as Joan died, the fire was put out and her naked breasts and genitals were shown to the crowd. Is this story true? Technically, it is certainly possible. Death by fire kills swiftly because it cuts off the oxygen. But the obvious question is: can we rely on this account?

One might discount this story as propaganda against the English. The fact that the Bourgeois believed it, however, makes it more likely it was true. The Bourgeois was a strong supporter of the Duke of Burgundy, an enemy of the Dauphin of France and at this point an ally of the English. This meant that he was hostile to Joan. And if he was a man of the church, he would have sympathised with the clerics who convicted and executed Joan.

## WHY MEN?

So his account may well be true, but possibly not. Either way, it shows how strongly the clerics and English lords who executed Joan needed to establish that she was a woman. We can understand from the earlier parts of the story just how much the clerics and lords might have wanted to humiliate and degrade her body. We have seen also how desperately important it was to draw an uncrossable line between men and women. And the story shows something else which is not visible anywhere else in the historical record. Many people in the crowd, and among both her followers and her enemies across France, must have believed that Joan was somehow both masculine and feminine.

15

## MUTINY IN A TIME OF REVOLUTION

This chapter tells the story of a mutiny on HMS *St George* in 1797, when sailors tried to save two shipmates accused of sodomy. Again we see a theatre of cruelty and we see resistance. More than a hundred ships in the British Royal Navy mutinied that year, in the midst of a wave of revolution across Europe and the Americas. In our story here, as at Cahokia and with Joan of Arc, gender is at the heart of both oppression and resistance. But this time the gendering revolves around two men who made love with each other, and those who would defend them against all odds. In this chapter we see how policing and ideologies of gender were put to the service of empire in the face of slave rebellion and popular revolution.

*Power and Revolution*

In the eighteenth century the dominant fuel was wind, and the most important technology was the sailing ship. These were the biggest machines of the age, with thousands of moving parts. They were owned by people with capital, and represented a massive investment of money. The workforce were mostly highly skilled manual labourers who worked for wages.[1]

The largest ships of all were the great warships, literally known as 'men of war'. They used the technology of the sailing ship as a platform for the technology of artillery. These ships and guns were dependent on the knowledge of engineering and mathematics, and on large numbers of workers. Only great empires had the wealth and the industries to produce a fleet of 'men of war'. And those fleets, in turn, were dependent on the expertise and the numbers of seamen produced by a great trading empire. Through the eighteenth century they fought what seemed an endless war, interrupted by periods of peace, for control of the Americas, the coast of Africa, Europe and India.

The eighteenth century is often described as an era of 'mercantile capitalism'. In the usual telling of this narrative there were not yet factories or an industrial working class. Instead, there were just great 'merchants' who owned ships. But this view is mistaken. Those merchants were only a tiny part of the great mass of humanity whose working lives were associated with the sea. The merchant seamen, the shipbuilders, the sailmakers; the shipyard workers, the foundry men making the guns and cannon balls, the male and female mineworkers who dug the coal that fed the foundries; the navigators, the naval seamen, the dockworkers, the stevedores, the carters, the slaves and the vast army of port women who cooked and served in the bars and sold sex for a living—each of these groups far outnumbered the merchants. It was their labour that produced the profits.

The profits were reinvested into more, new, faster, bigger ships, and drove an expanding global trade, which in turn drove expansion of new industries back in Europe. Capitalism began above all as a mover of goods and people, especially enslaved Africans.

As the triangular trade of the Black Atlantic grew, the more people were enslaved, the more free wage labourers worked alongside them on the slave ships, supervising. This took place on the merchant ships too, as well as in the armies and navies.

\* \* \*

The owners of capital required a state and society that was run for their profits. They needed power to control the national economic decisions and make the laws. In many countries, still dominated by landowners and lords, that would not happen without a revolution.

The first of these successful revolutions was that of the Netherlands against the Spanish empire, which won effective independence by 1581. That made possible the Dutch empire, a new kind of global capitalist trading empire, dominated by businessmen. Then came the English Civil War of 1640–9, a fight between the aristocracy on one side and the merchants and the common people on the other. After that, capitalist farmers dominated the British countryside, and capitalist merchants the cities. And like the Dutch, they proceeded to build an empire dominated by businessmen.

The decisive battle in Europe came with the wave of revolutions that began in North America in 1775, and spread across Europe and its colonies from the 1789 French Revolution onwards. In Germany, Italy, Ireland, Poland, Romania and most of the West Indies the revolutionaries lost. In Scandinavia, the Netherlands and Haiti the revolutionaries won. These revolutions were not presented as a simple tussle between big landowners and capitalists. Rather, the fight against the landlords was presented as a fight for all humanity, or in the language of the day, the rights of man. Those ideas had the power to mobilise all ranks of society.

France and Britain were the two great powers in Europe, the Americas and India. The British government were men of business already. But they saw in the French Revolution a challenge to the system of slavery, property and every kind of inequality. In 1793 Britain assembled an alliance of every monarchy in Europe to crush the revolutionary movement threatening to reorder human relations around the globe. The war that followed lasted twenty-two years.

With the coming of war, there were 100,000 seamen in the Royal Navy. A seaman could earn three times as much in a merchant ship, so volunteers were in short supply. The Navy made up the difference with press gangs who roamed the streets of port cities, seizing men who looked like sailors, but never taking gentlemen. As a result, seamen in the Navy were seldom allowed on shore, and were unwilling workers who were constantly beaten or whipped to make them work. This was in addition to the formal, ritual brutality of flogging in front of all hands.

These sailors had a tradition of strikes—there had been a national strike in the merchant fleet in 1792. And at the end of the eighteenth century Britain was on fire with the ideas of liberty and the French Revolution.[2]

The year 1792 also saw the birth of the London Corresponding Society, a mass working-class organisation calling for political reform. Thomas Hardy, the secretary of the Corresponding Society, was a shoemaker, the son of a sailor who had died at sea. In 1794 Hardy was arrested for treason and taken to the Tower of London.

There he was interrogated several times by a collection of the most powerful men in the land: the prime minister, the home secretary, the lord chancellor and the king's privy council. It was a sign of the balance of power that one man who worked with his hands faced all the great men of the country. And because of the strength of public feeling, at Hardy's trial a jury of twelve men acquitted him.[3]

In 1795 the Corresponding Society organised a mass open-air rally in Islington, with 100,000 to 150,000 people in attendance out of a total population of a million in London. Three days later 200,000 people surrounded the opening of parliament, shouting 'No War', 'No King', and throwing stones at the king's carriage. The next month 200,000 attended another rally in Islington. And there were mass demonstrations in towns across the country.[4]

This was not yet actual revolution. But we know that by the spring of 1797, the United Irishmen were organising the uprising that would begin the next year. A third of the Royal Navy were Irish. Revolutionary ideas were common among the English and Scots too.[5]

In April of 1797 the sailors in the Channel Fleet, anchored at Spithead off Portsmouth, went on strike for a rise in wages. They took over the ships and put ashore more than a hundred cruel officers. They elected two delegates from each ship to a committee to run the fleet and press their demands. They refused to go back to work until they had a pay rise and a pardon for every man, passed by both houses of parliament, with a copy signed by the king's own hand delivered to every ship in the fleet. To us today these are astonishing demands. And more astonishing yet, all these demands were actually met.[6]

The sailors were men. But when a 'man of war' was in port there were always several hundred women on board, some of them wives and relatives of the seamen, more of them sex workers. For all the days of that April and May when the ships remained under the control of the men on strike, those women stayed on board. And after each ship's captain read out the king's pardon on each ship, the women and the men rowed ashore to march together in drunken, dancing triumph through the streets of Portsmouth.

From the fleet at Spithead the revolt spread to the fleet moored in the Thames estuary, to the *Hermione* in the West Indies, and to the Mediterranean fleet, then just off the Straits of Gibraltar. That's where the story of mutiny became entwined with a case of sodomy.

# MUTINY IN A TIME OF REVOLUTION

*Two Men Embracing on the Deck*

On the evening of 27 June 1797, a bit after 9 pm, the British naval ship HMS *St George* lay at anchor off the coast of Spain. With ninety-eight guns, the *St George* was one of the largest ships in the Royal Navy, with about 700 men aboard.

The sailors called themselves the Georges, and said they were 'the people of the ship', not just the crew. They slept below decks in rows of hammocks, each man with a space 18 inches wide, his hips touching the men on either side, so they rocked together with the movement of the waves.

The Georges were part of the Mediterranean Fleet, blockading the main Spanish fleet, which was trapped inside the port of Cadiz. Many men were already in their hammocks, and some were asleep. But John Tippett heard two men 'breathing very short and very quick in the dark'. It sounded like sex to him, and he thought it was 'unnatural'. Tippett went up to find a petty officer to investigate.[7]

There were hundreds of men around him that night, and quite a few of them could hear the two men. None of them went to fetch a petty officer. Only Tippett.

He found the captain's coxswain, who sent someone for a light.

When the light came the coxswain and Tippett could see two men lying on the deck below the swinging hammocks. Both were able seamen, and both were 25 years old. Philip Francis, from Dorset, was lying on his right side. John Benson, from Ireland, lay on his left side, facing Francis. 'Philip Francis had hold of John Benson's privates with his left hand and John Benson's right hand [was] over Philip France's neck.'

In other words, the two men were embracing as they made love. Both men had their trousers down around their knees and their privates and buttocks bare. They were clearly very drunk and utterly absorbed in each other, paying no attention to the light.

A man called Thomas Playford 'took the light and turned Philip Francis's face up to know he was'. After that Playford 'went away with the light' to another part of the deck. It seems he was protecting Francis.

As this was all happening several people standing around in the shadows were telling Francis and Benson to get up, in vain. It seems

## WHY MEN?

probable that the bystanders were urging them to sneak away into the darkness before they were apprehended and punished.

Seven or eight minutes later a boatswain's mate arrived with another light. Tippett testified later that 'then I saw Philip Francis lying on his belly and John Benson on top of him, making motions with his body as though he wished to have connections with him'.

Benson and Francis were sent to the admiral's flagship.

Confusions about Sodomy

Admiral St Vincent decided to send both men for a court martial on a charge of sodomy, which carried the death penalty. This was extremely unusual.

Seth Stein LeJacq has read all the accounts he could find of naval courts martial for sodomy between 1690 and 1900. LeJaqc finds records of eighty-one cases in the 105 years before the trial of Benson and Francis—an average of less than one court martial a year.[8]

Only thirteen men were hung for sodomy over these 105 years. Two of them were tried for having sex with animals, in one case a sheep and in the other a nanny goat. This leaves eleven men actually hung for sodomy with another man or boy, about one a year.

Even then, nine of the eleven sodomy cases that made it to a court martial involved cases where officers had sex with a man or boy of lower rank, or where a rank-and-file seaman had sex with a boy. Very few admirals and captains believed that men should be hung for consensual sex with their equals. The cases they tried were ones suggesting that a powerful man had forced themselves on someone of lower rank. In effect, what we would now think of as both sexual harassment and rape.[9]

In other words, before the court martial of Benson and Francis in 1797, only two seamen had been executed for what we would understand as consensual sex.

\* \* \*

We also need to understand the complexity of attitudes toward homosexuality on board ship. There was a great deal of a nod and a wink in daily behaviour, and a great deal of bitter denunciation in print. There were many cases where captains and officers avoided punishing men for sodomy, but also cases where men were severely punished. On board ship, people had complicated private feelings and felt differently in different situations.

First of all, what the Navy called sodomy was not exactly what we now call homosexuality. The word sodomy evoked two kinds of offence. The first was very serious, and mystically dangerous, associated with Satan. The reference point was the men of ancient Sodom in the Bible, who attempted to rape one of God's male angels. By law this kind of sodomy included sex with animals.

Such appalling and unspeakable sodomy was the kind of anal sex which preachers and writers condemned in print. It was unnatural sex. In theory it also included anal sex with women, though in practice this was never prosecuted. It did not include any other kind of sex between men.

The other legal kind of sodomy was ordinary, everyday anal and other sex between men. In the eighteenth-century Navy this was usually called buggery. It was often the cause of rough, sometimes relentless, teasing. But for practical purposes, most officers and sailors seldom thought of ordinary buggery as sodomy.[10] The connotations of 'buggery' were complicated, but it was not then the straightforwardly rude word it is now.

Presented with a possible case, officers and captains did everything they could to avoid a trial for sodomy. They could avert their eyes, or pass over the events with a reprimand. They often got rid of the problem by informally encouraging men to desert. They also flogged men with a dozen or three dozen lashes for 'uncleanness', an offence which could mean many things, but usually did mean love between men.[11]

A Travesty of Justice

Benson and Francis were caught having sex on Tuesday night. Their court martial for sodomy began on Friday morning.[12]

What we said above bears repeating. There had only been one previous case in which two consenting men of the same rank had been tried and convicted of sodomy, and that had been in 1705, ninety-two years before. So it is clear that Admiral St Vincent must have had strong reasons to court-martial.

The court martial was held on the *St George* itself. A vice-admiral and eleven ships' captains sat as judges. The law required that every captain present in the fleet attend, and they did. The proceedings show just how strongly these senior officers needed to stage a hanging.

The crucial question was whether the two men had had anal sex. The legal definition of sodomy was entirely clear and known to all: one man's penis in another man's anus. Without penetration, there was no crime. The court asked every witness if they had seen such 'a connection' between the two men.

All the witnesses—even Tippett—said no, they had not seen a connection. Some were categorical. Others said that they could not tell. The ship's surgeon, Mr John Frazer, testified that, when he examined the two men the morning after the incident, 'I saw nothing that led me to suppose that there had been a connection.'

The judges considered their verdict. Benson and Francis were then called back into the court room and told that they would be hanged by the neck from the yardarm at such time and place as the admiral would decide.

This was a travesty of justice. And that, too, was very unusual in British naval courts martial: as the late eighteenth- and early nineteenth-century transcripts show, these trials were fairer than many countries' courts martial today.

Of course, the penalties were cruel. But the captains who sat in judgment had a deep respect for both the rule and the letter of the law. Again and again, they acquitted on what we would regard as a technicality. They expected officers to tell the truth, but they knew that men from the lower deck often lied to protect their shipmates, and they made allowances for that. Of course the judges did convict at least one defendant in almost all mutiny trials, but the evidence was always quite clear.[13]

The judges who convicted Benson and Francis wanted to make an example. But the court was sitting in the captain's cabin of the *St George*, and the people of that ship were outraged by the trial. The captains may also have reasoned that once St Vincent had started the process, an acquittal would itself encourage unrest.

## What Was Propelling This Theatre of Cruelty?

To answer that question, let's look at that moment from the point of view of Admiral St Vincent.[14]

## MUTINY IN A TIME OF REVOLUTION

John Jervis, as he was born, came from a relatively modest home, and went to sea as a midshipman in the Navy at the age of 13. In 1783 he, like many serving naval captains, had been elected to parliament. Jervis supported the Whigs, the more liberal party, whose leader was an acknowledged friend of the common people and enemy to the Tories and the king.

Then came the French Revolution in 1789 and the Haitian Revolution in 1791. War began in 1793. Jervis found himself in command of a fleet in the West Indies. His flagship was HMS *St George*.

At first Jervis and the Georges were successful in taking the main city of French Guadeloupe. But in February 1794, the revolutionary government in Paris abolished slavery, and in May the new governor of Guadeloupe began a Black uprising that overwhelmed and drove out the British. Jervis sailed home, defeated. He had strong reason now to hate and fear revolutionary ideas and common revolt.

In 1795 Jervis was appointed to the command of the Mediterranean fleet. During the course of 1796, French troops, revolutionary ideas and popular uprisings spread down through Italy. Then Spain declared war on Britain in alliance with France. Jervis's fleet was driven from the Mediterranean. They blockaded the Spanish fleet in Cadiz, which is where we found the Georges at the start of our story.

In February of 1797, Jervis won a signal victory against the Spanish and was made Earl St Vincent. He continued the blockade, without which the Royal Navy would be heavily outnumbered. Jervis was entitled to feel that the fate of an empire was at stake.

When the Spithead mutineers won their demands in May, without punishment of any kind, the Admiralty in London began to send the most militant of the ships to the Mediterranean fleet. If anyone could subdue those crews, it would be St Vincent, a strict disciplinarian.

St Vincent's correspondence and actions through June show a man constantly on edge, looking for any way to restore order. This was why he was driven to prosecute Benson and Francis. A direct attack on the former mutineers from Spithead was risky, after assurances had been given that those who surrendered and returned to the fleet would not be punished. The 'buggers', on the other hand, he must have considered vulnerable. He could still set in motion the awful majesty of a formal hanging to intimidate the rest.

St Vincent was acting to defend his career, his country, his empire and the rule of gentlemen over the common people throughout Europe and the Americas. Those were the pressures bearing down on Benson and Francis. We may surmise that Admiral St Vincent had to hang someone, and he did not dare hang the mutineers. So he went for two isolated, defenceless 'buggers'. Only they turned out not to be defenceless.

## The People Come Aft for Mercy

Friday night, after the court martial of Benson and Francis, two men came up onto the quarterdeck of the *St George*, the sacred officers' territory in the rear of the ship, where the captain's cabin was. They were carrying a piece of paper.[15]

John Anderson was a very junior petty officer, 25 years old, from Durham. Michael McCann was also 25 years old, an able seaman and an American from New York. Early in the war he had been captured while serving on a republican French privateer, a sort of legalised pirate ship. He had been enrolled into the Navy without punishment, for everyone knew that privateers were the elite of seamen. But this is perhaps a clue to his political sympathies.[16]

Hundreds of sailors walked silently behind Anderson and McCann, until they filled the quarterdeck. In ordinary times, no man was allowed there unless specifically ordered.

Such conduct was part of how things were done in the Navy when the people of the ship felt seriously about something. Sometimes such a protest by all the Ship's Company ended with justice from the captain and the admiral. Sometimes with the arrest and hanging of the ringleaders. Sometimes, as recently at Spithead, with the people seizing control of the ship.

Anderson and McCann handed the paper to the first lieutenant. 'This a petition for mercy on behalf of the prisoners sentenced to death,' they said. 'We request you to give it to the captain.'

Captain Shuldham Peard wrote to Admiral St Vincent that night, and St Vincent replied. The next morning, just after breakfast, Peard had all hands mustered on the deck. Peard stood on the quarterdeck looking down upon the people, and read out loud to them the Naval Articles of War, with all their dreadful punishments for every offence. The twenty marines on board, in effect the ship's police, would have stood alongside him, their guns at the ready.

Peard told them that the admiral had confirmed the sentence. He said that the death warrant was in his pocket, and that 'the unhappy men would certainly suffer at 9 o'Clock of the next morning. I ... dismissed them with a caution to ... not suffer themselves to be seduced into any impropriety.' Then a chaplain led prayers and gave what Peard thought was a 'most excellent sermon'. The captain was content that his firm measures 'had put down the refractory spirit, and felt no apprehension on that account'.

But the Georges began to organise below decks. We cannot tell who all the leaders were. We know Anderson and McCann were among them. So were two more men, both also able seamen, and both from Cork in Ireland. John Hayes was 26. James Fitzgerald was 38.

They sat down to draw up a paper for all the Ship's Company to sign. They discussed the drafting of several articles. The first was that they all swore to stick by each other. The second was that they would seize the arms and take the ship by force after dark that evening.

Sailors came in groups and someone read the articles to them. One by one, the men put their hands on a book, probably a prayer book, and swore an oath to stick by his shipmates.

Then each man signed the articles. When a man could not read, the organiser held the pen and wrote the name, then the man made his mark. As the day wore on, men moved through the ship to find men who had not yet signed and urged them to do so. Do it to save the two men, McCann said to one man.

This was not a new way of organising. The drawing up of articles was what the people at Spithead had done in May. Taking an oath to be true to each other had been done many times before.

Peard, when warned, moved to secure the ship. He had only twenty marines, but he happened to have 100 soldiers of the 251st regiment on board.[17] As the sun set, Peard 'took the opportunity of mustering the watch', and threatening that the soldiers would open fire on any mutineers.

At some point after that the people began to assemble on the main deck. Peard did not in fact call upon the marines or the soldiers to fire. He must have been aware that a slaughter would provoke a mutiny of the entire fleet.[18]

When Peard, standing directly in front of the crowd, was ignored in his command to the sailors to disperse and return to duties, he

## WHY MEN?

could have ordered the marines and soldiers to charge the crowd. That would have meant hand-to-hand fighting, and the Georges might well have won. What happened next was utterly unexpected.

Captain Peard and the first lieutenant, and only those two men, 'rushed into the crowd' and 'resolutely seized' Anderson and McCann, 'dragged them out by main force, and put them in irons, without experiencing any opposition from the remainder of the crew'.[19]

There were more than one hundred courts martial for mutiny from 1793 to 1815. The transcripts show only one account of an officer touching a mutineer, violating separations of hierarchy.[20] What Peard and his lieutenant did would have astonished everyone, and it worked.

The people of the ship were stunned. They dispersed. The mutiny was broken.

\* \* \*

Anderson and McCann were sent in irons to the flagship that night; two others, John Hayes and James Fitzgerald, were arrested the next day. On Monday morning the lovers Benson and Francis were hanged on the *St George*, with the entire Ship's Company forced to watch.

The court martial of the four mutineers took place later that week. The proceedings were swift, evidence was presented only on a limited part of the events, and all four men were sentenced to hang.

St Vincent set the executions to take place the next morning, Sunday. This violated tradition. The vice-admiral, a committed Christian, protested publicly on the quarterdeck. St Vincent relieved the vice-admiral of his command and immediately put him on a ship back to England.[21]

In the Navy a man was hanged by a rope run up through a pulley. The prisoner stood on the quarterdeck, surrounded by officers, soldiers and marines. A noose was placed over his neck, and then sailors pulled on the other end of the rope, so the prisoner was lifted forward and upward off the quarterdeck. People who were hanged in those days were very lucky if they died instantly. Usually they hung for several minutes, slowly being strangled, jerking wildly. And during all that time, the crews watched. The ritual was meant to terrify. But the helplessness was as important as the fear.

Almost always, however, they were spared the extra humiliation of having to haul on the ropes that killed their own shipmates. By custom, that work was done by men from other ships. In those years there was deep moral power of solidarity between shipmates—not a solidarity with officers, but of the people below decks with each other.

But on Saturday night St Vincent wrote a memorandum ordering that

> The sentence is to be carried into execution by the crew of the St. George alone; and no part of the boats' crew of the other ships [in the fleet], as is usual on other occasions, is to assist in this painful service; in order to mark the high sense the Commander-in-Chief entertains of the loyalty, fidelity, and subordination of the rest of the fleet.[22]

\* \* \*

There are two lessons to be learned from this story. The first is about gender and the purposes of imperial power. The historian James Dugan writes that immediately after the execution of Benson and Francis,

> The yellow flag [for execution] was hardly down before the red flag went up on [the flagship. St Vincent] ordered the fleet into battle. He sailed inshore and bombarded Cadiz. The military justification was to provoke the Spanish fleet to come out and give battle. Part of it did so. The larger purpose was, as St Vincent wrote, to 'employ the minds of the seamen and divert them from following the mischievous example of the ships in England' and 'to divert the animal from these damnable doctrines which letters from England have produced.'[23]

The second lesson is about gender and the purposes of common people in an age of revolution. In extraordinary times, several hundred working sailors were prepared to rise up to defend the rights of two men to love each other and give each other pleasure.

# WHY MEN?

Their leaders were martyrs in the long struggle for what we would now call queer liberation. But let us remember too John Benson of Dorset and Philip Francis of Ireland, their bodies embracing each other.

# 16

# THE GENDERING OF TORTURE AT ABU GHRAIB

In this chapter we come close to the present, to an American-run prison in Iraq in 2003. There are three points to this chapter. The first is that hunger games are still with us. There is nothing backward or barbaric about theatres of gendered class cruelty. They are not something we have left behind. The second is that the victims of sexual violence include men as well as women. The third is that military rape, the paradigmatic expression of patriarchal violence, does not spring naturally from human masculinity. Generals decide to encourage or forbid rape.

Military rape holds a special place in the literature of sexual violence. In 1975 Susan Brownmiller published the pathbreaking feminist book on rape, *Against Our Will: Men, Women and Rape*. That was an important and influential book because it broke a silence with a roar of rage.

It was also deeply problematic. As Angela Davis argued at the time, it was a racist book. The American police arrested proportionately more black men than white men for rape. Brownmiller took this as evidence that black men were in fact more likely to commit rape, not just as evidence that the police were prejudiced. And unforgivably, she half-justified the infamous lynching of 14-year-old Emmett Till after he whistled at a white woman in Mississippi.[1]

However, Brownmiller, quite rightly, paid a lot of attention to military rape, to the times when armies rape hundreds of thousands or millions of women over months or years. It was important that she highlighted those horrors, and it is important that since then no one has quite been able to put them back in the box. Sadly, however, Brownmiller said that this was evidence that all men were rapists, proof of what men were.

## WHY MEN?

What she glossed over was that military rape, like all sexual violence, is sanctioned from the top down. In any army there are always a few soldiers who rape. But systematic rape, on a large scale, only happens when commanders encourage it.

Given that military organisations are meant to win and protect an elite, it is not surprising that they seek to maximise their power over their enemies. Sexualised male violence used as a means to humiliate male opponents is a powerful way to break them and render other men powerless. Sexual humiliation mirrors hierarchies in place in the wider society. This means that gendered violence and humiliation certainly mirror the sexisms and homophobia in the wider society, but also the racisms and religious prejudices which help the elite to divide and rule.

The men tortured in Abu Ghraib were despised and brutalised because they were Arabs and Muslims. Colour racism and Islamophobia, prejudice and hatred were jumbled into other orientalist and sexualised stereotypes of weak men and homosexuals, of poor men, 'ragheads', savages, and of aggressive braggarts, macho men who neither protect their women nor themselves. Their punishment mirrored relations in the wider society, the class and imperial the power of the tough, white, Christian warriors and virtuous Americans who had every right to attack and occupy Iraq. And it also mirrored a history of thousands of years of sexual violence against the powerless in class society—including victims of war.

*The Decisions Generals Make*

There are many examples of the simple proposition that generals decide whether or not soldiers will rape.

It is now well-known that in 1945 the Soviet Red Army raped hundreds of thousands of German women, in large part because the Soviet generals wanted to terrify the German population. By contrast, the Soviet army fought in Afghanistan for seven years in the 1980s and raped almost no one. This was not kindness—the Soviet army killed between half a million and a million Afghans. It was a strategic calculation on the part of the Soviet generals who knew that wholesale rape would so outrage the Afghan population that the Soviet Army would lose control of the cities.[2]

# THE GENDERING OF TORTURE AT ABU GHRAIB

Or take a contrasting example. American generals in the Second World War wanted the support of the civilian populations in Italy, France and Germany as they fought their way to Berlin. It is probably not a coincidence that the American armed forces raped few women in Europe, compared with their record in other twentieth-century theatres of war. Yet the way the generals guaranteed this outcome was shocking and ugly. The American historian Mary Louise Roberts has written an important history of the sexual lives of American soldiers in Normandy in 1944, right after D-Day. *What Soldiers Do* tells a complex story, carefully.[3]

Roberts describes how before D-Day the American officers and the American press told their soldiers that French women would be 'easy', and grateful for liberation. In practice it was not that simple, and there were a significant number of rapes. Many French people in Normandy were also outraged by the prostitution around American camps. Some local French mayors complained.

The senior American officers did not want trouble with French civilians. They came up with a creative solution. They swiftly tried and hung twenty-five African American soldiers and four white soldiers for rape. This was not a mass trial, but a series of different trials. Roberts looks at the cases in detail and concludes that some of the black soldiers hanged may have been guilty, although many would have been found innocent in any fairer setting. The American army staged the hangings in public and put notices in the local press inviting French villagers to attend.[4]

This solution drew on the rich American tradition of lynching black men accused of rape. For decades before the Second World War, those lynchings were an important part of the terror that enforced racial segregation. They were often public events, with hundreds of white people in attendance, including families and children, and with vendors selling snacks. Many brought souvenir postcards of the bodies later. Most people lynched were men, but some were women. Most were in the South, but many were in other parts of the country. Almost no one was ever punished for lynching. And beyond the public killings there were far more judicial lynchings where the criminal justice system killed black men, often on flimsy evidence, for supposedly raping white women.

In Normandy, the American generals' intention was not particularly to terrify black people, however. The executions were useful

299

## WHY MEN?

because they gave a clear message to all American soldiers, while not provoking the kind of backlash back home that hanging more white soldiers would have produced. There was little rape after that by American soldiers in France, and very little in Germany.

That was one war. But in Vietnam between 1965 and 1972 the American armed forces raped large numbers of Vietnamese women. This time the generals wanted to terrify rural civilians and drive them out of the countryside.

More recently, in the oil wars in the Middle East, American soldiers in Afghanistan and Iraq have raped very few civilian women. This is not because the American generals have grown kinder. Rather, like the Soviet generals before them, the American generals knew this would be a mistake.[5]

However, these same American generals continue to tolerate sexual violence within the American military. The semi-official 2014 RAND survey, *Sexual Assault and Sexual Harassment in the U.S. Military*, was based on a large sample, but not a random one. The study produced an estimate of 10,600 men sexually assaulted each year in the American armed services, and 9,600 women. Women were more likely to be assaulted, but there are many more men in the services.

The survey found that 5% of service women and 1% of service men reported being sexually assaulted in the previous year. Rates were higher in the navy and the marines. But people are often reluctant to answer questions about rape and abuse in surveys, so we can assume that these figures under-report the actual rates for both men and women. At a reasonable estimate, at least 10% of American service women in Iraq and Afghanistan were sexually assaulted each year.[6] Their commanding officers tolerated this, understood it, and their inaction effectively enabled sexual cruelty.

* * *

There was another reason that American generals could not tolerate their soldiers raping in Afghanistan and Iraq. In 2001, after the great shock of the 9/11 attack on the World Trade Center in New York, everything changed. President Bush's immediate response was to wage a war of terror in Afghanistan. His decision met with widespread approval among Americans who, like their president, wanted revenge. And Bush also garnered immediate support from Tony Blair, the British prime minister, who was eager to join Bush's war.

The war began on 7 October, but it only took a few weeks after for the extreme violence of the American bombing campaign to repel many people. A vastly unequal war of revenge doesn't look very good in the eyes of the world, so better to be doing something of virtue. And to this end, little over a month into the war, Bush and Blair had a public-relation epiphany.

Bear with us here, because what comes next is the perfect exemplar of our idea that powerful elites, when they fear trouble, turn to issues of gender to sow confusion, misdirect people's attention and twist their feelings of love and concern.

In anticipation of the American Thanksgiving holiday, on 17 November 2021, Laura Bush, the president's wife, loudly lamented the plight of veiled Afghan women. Cherie Blair, the British prime minister's wife, echoed her sentiments in a public statement a few days later. These wealthy warmongers' wives were using the full weight of the orientalist paradigm to blame the victims and justify a war against some of the poorest people on earth. And from then on, 'Saving Afghan Women' became the persistent cry of many liberal feminists to justify the American war. It was an argument that worked very well for the Americans, and for Britain and the NATO countries who joined in the Afghan War, and it continues to resonate well in the West.

This was a new version of the racism Gayatri Spivak described years ago as 'white men saving brown women from brown men'. Riley speaks this egregious expression of feminist Islamophobia as a form of 'transnational sexism'. It domesticated and effectively displaced the ugly truths about a grossly unequal war in several ways. It separated the notional 'women to be saved' from the thousands of actual Afghan women, and men and children, killed, wounded, orphaned, or made homeless and hungry by American bombs. It also precluded comparisons between the undoubted sexist rule of the Taliban and sexism in the United States and elsewhere. And it staved off international criticism from other power states by making it easier for the governments of Russia, India and China to attack Muslims at home.[7]

## WHY MEN?

The rape of Afghan and Iraqi women by American soldiers on any scale would have obliterated this justification for the wars. But it was still possible for American men in uniform to harass and attack American women in uniform. And it was also possible, as we shall see, for American men and women in uniform to sexually violate Iraqi male prisoners.

*Sexual Assaults at the Prison*

In the spring of 2004, a few dozen photos were leaked to the media showing American soldiers abusing inmates at Abu Ghraib prison in Iraq. One photo became iconic—a hooded man, standing on a box, his arms spread, with electric wires attached to his fingers. He had been put there to stand all night without sleep before his interrogation the next day.

All the photos from Abu Ghraib were shocking, and there was an outcry. Eight American prison guards, three of them women, were court-martialled for mistreating prisoners. The highest-ranking defendant was a sergeant. Seven of the eight were sentenced to prison. No interrogator, no commissioned officer and no CIA agent was punished.

The sociologist Ryan Ashley Caldwell worked as a research assistant to an expert witness for the defence at the court martial of one of the female prison guards, Sabrina Harman. Harman was a lesbian, but Caldwell's *Fallgirls: Gender and the Framing of Torture at Abu Ghraib* does not start by looking at women, or men, or LGBT people. Instead, Caldwell looks at gender as an aspect of all social relations. She asks question after question about knitting, makeup, tattoos, lovers, homosexuality, underwear, women prisoners, toilets, women officers, masturbation, skin, phone calls, who holds the leash, who takes the pictures and who becomes the scapegoat.[8]

The answers to her questions about gender tell us much we could find out in no other way. They shine light into hidden horror. They tell us something important about the US military and the wars in Syria and Iraq. And they tell us something important about ourselves.

Gender, Caldwell says, is something we perform all day long, all the time, in every word and gesture. In that performance we try to occupy the highest place we can in an unequal world, or we try to challenge that hierarchy, or both. Gender is always, and all the time, about power. The more unequal any relationship, the more the gender inequalities will be marked. Abu Ghraib prison was terrifying and unequal, and torture is always all about bodies. That is why everything in the prison was saturated with sexuality, and gender was heavily marked.

On 20 October 2003, Sabrina Harman wrote an email from Abu Ghraib prison in Iraq to her partner, Kelly Bryan, back home in the States. Harman was a military policewoman in the US Army. She was working night shift as a guard in the prison. Part of her job was softening up prisoners at night before their interrogation and torture the next day. She told Kelly that the night before it was time to 'mess with' the Military Intelligence prisoners.

> But it went too far even I can't handle what's going on. I cant get it out of my head. I walk down the stairs after blowing the whistle and beating on the cells with an asp [baton] to find 'the taxi driver' handcuffed backwards to his window with his underwear over his head and face. He looked like Jesus Christ. At first I had to laugh so I went and grabbed the camera and took a picture. One of the guys took my asp and started 'poking' at his dick. Again, I thought, okay that's funny then it hit me, that's a form of molestation... I took more pictures now to 'record' what is going on. They started talking to this man and at first he was talking 'I'm just a taxi driver, I did nothing.'

Another prisoner, she told Kelly, 'had been so fucked that when they grabbed his foot through the cell bars he began screaming and crying. After praying to Allah he moans a constant short Ah, Ah, every few seconds for the rest of the night. I don't know what they did to this guy.'

Harman was deeply upset:

> Not many people know this shit goes on. The only reason I want to be there is to get the pictures to prove that the US is not what they think. But I don't know if I can take it mentally. What if that was me in their shoes. These people will be our future terrorist. Kelly, it's awful and you know how fucked I am in the head... I thought I could handle anything. I was wrong.
>
> Sabrina[9]

# WHY MEN?

In the next few weeks Harman took a lot of photos to record what was going on. The other guards started taking snaps on their digital cameras too. This was before cameras on phones. Between them, they took 16,000 photos, of which only a few dozen have been released. Everyone presumes the still secret photos are worse.

*Why Abu Ghraib?*

Harman's email to her partner was sent six months after the US invaded Iraq. We need to explain a bit about that invasion, because one of our purposes in this book is to put stories of patriarchal violence and inequality in their wider context.

On 11 September 2001, Al Qaeda activists had attacked the Twin Towers in Manhattan and the Pentagon, killing almost 3,000 people. The Bush administration knew they had to retaliate. The attacks were also a humiliation for the American military, and very public punishment was required in order to restore American power in the Middle East. The first step was the invasion of Afghanistan two months later.

Crucially for our story in this chapter, along with the invasion, a campaign of kidnappings and renditions covered many countries, and delivered tens of thousands of Afghans and other Muslims to secret terror prisons run by the CIA.

The second step, two years later, was the invasion of Iraq. That was not about 9/11, nor about restoring American power. It was about oil. In the 1960s and 1970s governments all over the Middle East had taken over the oilfields owned by the Western oil multinationals. This happened in Iraq, Iran, Libya and Saudi Arabia. President George Bush and Vice-President Dick Cheney, oilmen both, wanted those oilfields back. Privatisation of publicly held companies had been central to the neoliberal project all over the world since 1980. And if the American government could get control of Iraq and force the next government to sell off the oilfields, that would be the largest privatisation of all.[10]

This is not wild-eyed Marxist conspiracy thinking. It was widely understood at the time. Evan Wright, for example, was embedded with American soldiers fighting across Iraq in the early weeks of the invasion. He says those professional soldiers understood that they were fighting for oil.[11]

## THE GENDERING OF TORTURE AT ABU GHRAIB

Most Iraqis understood the same thing. From the first days after the fall of Baghdad, the American military met widespread guerrilla resistance. They had not expected this. The situation was chaotic and frightening for them. They could not impose American control on the streets of Baghdad. The military reacted by setting up prisons and torture sites in many parts of Iraq. They rounded up suspects in night raids, or pulled them off the streets, usually innocent people, but sometimes part of the resistance. It was an ad hoc, seat of the pants attempt to gain intelligence and to impose control through fear.[12]

The US Army took over Abu Ghraib, one of Saddam's prisons. The new prison was chaotic. The night shift had a constant problem with lighting. The Americans had not fixed the national electricity grid that their bombing had destroyed.

Generators were supposed to produce electricity on site. But the generators did not work and were not repaired, and the fuel supplier never came. Many nights the Americans lined up all the army trucks to face the main block of the prison and left the engines running and the lights on. There was no other light inside the prison at night. There were similar problems with the portable toilets. The company with the contract to empty them did not come, and they overflowed. Guards and the prisoners shat where they could.

The sheds where the interrogation and torture happened were outside the main block. Military Intelligence worked there. So did what everyone called OGA—Other Government Agencies. Sometimes this was a euphemism for the CIA. But there were several other US intelligence agencies involved, and lots of civilian contractors, so the American guards could not keep track of who was who.[13]

The guards looked after the prisoners when they were not out in the sheds being tortured. Because the Pentagon was saving money, there was usually only one American guard on shift for every 150 to 200 prisoners.[14] Meanwhile, the area around Abu Ghraib was largely controlled by the Iraqi resistance, which sometimes shelled the prison. The guards heard gunfire and explosions many nights.

In other ways too the job was unreal. The prisoners were called 'detainees', because if they were 'prisoners' either the Geneva Convention or Iraqi law would have to apply. The detainees had been picked up in sweeps by US troops. Everyone involved knew the great majority of the prisoners were not part of the resistance. But someone had to be tortured, so someone was.

Caldwell, the sociologist who wrote *Fallgirls*, attended two of the court martials of guards for abuse of prisoners. She noticed that witnesses kept mentioning the women and children in the cells. But no one ever asked what those women were doing there. If they had asked, Caldwell says, someone would have had to say. So no one asked.

Caldwell did ask, and she discovered the women and children were not detainees, or prisoners. They were housed in cells interspersed among the men's cells. They had been picked up in sweeps by the American military, alongside the men, often from their homes. So many of the men and women were related. But the women and children were not assigned numbers at Abu Ghraib, so there was no paperwork on them.

Javal Davis was one of the guards court-martialled. He told the journalist Philip Gourevitch, 'If we can't get the insurgent leader, we took their kid. "OK, Akbar, I have your son—your son is in jail, turn yourself in, and we'll let your son go." I call that kidnapping, but that's what we did.'

The youngest child in the prison was 10 years old. As Harman said: 'A little kid, he could have fit through the bars he was so little.'[15]

Caldwell also asked why Harman wrote 'rapist' on one of the prisoners. Harman explained that they often wrote on the prisoners' naked bodies. The records were utterly chaotic, Harman said. No one was keeping track, and the prisoners were naked all the time. So the guards wrote a lot of information on the prisoners' bodies just so they would know the basics of who they were dealing with.

And why were the prisoners naked, Caldwell asked. One reason was they didn't have any clothes. The army took away their clothes when they were arrested, and then no one supplied them with prison uniforms. Captain DiNenno kept asking his superiors for orange uniforms, as it was getting cold with winter coming on, but by early November there were still not enough uniforms.

Another reason the prisoners were naked was that there were Iraqi civilian guards working in the prison alongside the Americans. They were left over from when it was a civilian prison. The

Americans did not trust the civilian guards, who did not have uniforms, which meant the Americans could not tell the guards from the prisoners. It was safer to keep the prisoners naked in order to distinguish them from the Iraqi guards.

But none of this goes any way to explaining the panties. Caldwell asked Harman about that: 'Why in the world were there so many women's panties at Abu Ghraib? I mean, they are in so many photos and they are continually referred to at the trials. What is going on here with women's panties?'

Harman said,

> The panties were there when we got there so I have no idea. Getting supplies for the prisoners was not easy. Soap, shoes, towels, Korans, you name it, it was hard to have the amount needed for all prisoners that kept piling up. I don't think they ordered them to put them on the heads of prisoners, but then again you never know.[16]

But *that is* what they used the panties for. Sometimes they kept the men naked with their own underwear tied on their heads. But mostly the guards tied women's panties on the prisoners' heads. They even sent soldiers into Baghdad to buy the panties. This was to humiliate the prisoners, but of course it was also exciting for some of the guards.

Caldwell calls attention to how much 'homo-eroticism' there was in the abuse. This is important, though we would put it a bit differently. We don't think it is so much that the prisoners were men, as that they were naked, helpless, human bodies. The excitement among the guards was probably mostly simply erotic. We don't need to fit it into a box as a particular labelled kind of sexuality. As we saw in Part One, human sexuality is endlessly fluid and social, and intense feelings have sexual aspects. Sexual violence is about terrifying people and about control. But it is also about sex.

Later, when they finally began to get uniforms for the prisoners, the Americans gave them panties to wear as underwear. One of the things Caldwell noticed was that they gave the women in the cells men's boxer shorts at the same time. Maybe this was just because they had run out of women's underwear from the PX shop at the barracks. But for whatever reason they were given boxers, and boxers did exist to be given, but they were not given to the men prisoners.

# WHY MEN?

Four days after Harman wrote the email we quoted earlier, there was a 'riot'. Several men in the cells protested about the food. The guards knew the prisoners' food was often inedible, and assumed it was because of corruption on a contract. So on many nights the guards gave the prisoners American army rations. But first the guards had to pick out all the pork and bacon, for religious reasons, and all the Tabasco sauce, in case it was used to make a weapon. All this was very time-consuming, and the army hierarchy kept telling the guards not to use the rations in this way. So that night there was a protest about food.

This is resistance, again, in the most difficult and terrifying of circumstances, and it was met with sexual violence to make it stop.

Some guards dragged several protestors to the central corridor between the cells. They were forced to make a pyramid of bodies, bound and naked, writhing on top of each other. The guards punched them hard, ran their heads into the wall, and then forced them to masturbate. The guards took a lot of pictures.

Matthew Wisdom, another guard, arrived on the floor a bit later. He told Gourevitch: 'When I arrived, I saw one prisoner on his knees with his mouth open, and another prisoner masturbating with his penis in the prisoner's face on his knees. Both of the prisoners were entirely naked. ... Sergeant Frederick ... turned towards me and said, "See what these animals do when we leave them alone for two seconds."'[17]

Harman went off for an hour while this was happening and made a long phone call to Kelly back in the States. The next morning Harman wrote to Kelly:

> Something bad is going to happen here. ... No one would believe the shit that goes on. No one. The dead guy didn't bother me, I even took a picture with him doing the thumbs up ... they said the autopsy came back 'heart attack'. It's a lie. The whole military is nothing but lies. They cover up too much. This guy was never in our prison. That's the story... If I want to keep taking pictures of those events—I even have short films—I have to fake a smile every time. I hope I don't get into trouble for something I haven't done. I'm going to try to burn [copy] those pictures and send them out to you while Im in Kuwait—Just in case.

# THE GENDERING OF TORTURE AT ABU GHRAIB

I love you and I hope to see you in the next day–

Your wife–

Sabrina[18]

## *The Fallgirl*

Sergeant Ken Davis and Specialist Joseph Darby eventually blew the whistle on the abuse. Davis was persistent—he went to his congressman and gave Harman's photos to the media. The army was forced to do something. So they court-martialled eight guards.

Let's pause a moment here and ask a question. How did Joseph Darby get those photographs? None of our sources say, but there is only one possible answer. Sabrina Harman gave the photographs to him, knowing what he would do. She could not say this at her court martial. The punishment would have been fierce. But the military prosecutors must have known.

Moreover, Harman's photos had a shattering impact. US military and intelligence services were torturing thousands of people in those years. Darby's report, and those of other whistle-blowers, would have been brushed off without the photos. Once seen, no amount of lies could make them unseen.

But the court martials were not about justice. Only eight people were tried. None of the prison authorities even had to testify. The prosecutions were part of the cover-up. So it was fitting that Sabrina Harman was to be punished.

This is a point with relevance far beyond this one story. We have lost track of the number of times we have read of a survivor of rape saying that her questioning by the police, her appearance in court, her testimony and her cross-examination, felt like she was being raped all over again. This is not accidental. There is an element of justice to rape trials. But equally, there is an element of intimidation. The rituals of the courtroom are also part of the machinery of cover-up.

When Harman was tried for mistreating prisoners two years after the abuse, there were many elephants in the room. Harman's wife, Kelly Bryan, was one of them. Bryan testified, not in the regular trial, but in the sentencing hearing. There was a lot of evidence about their relationship in emails, and phone records, and how

## WHY MEN?

Bryan kept Harman's letters by her bedside in a special box. No one mentioned that the two women were partners.

But, once again, Caldwell's book fills the gendered silence. She asked Harman how the other soldiers in the unit in Iraq treated her, given her sexuality. It was 'Don't ask, don't tell' in the US Army then. But soon after she arrived in Iraq, Harman's commanding officer took her aside. He said that her girlfriend was really hot—a way of saying he knew and approved. All the other guards she worked with closely knew too, and none of them made her feel bad.

The army brass was different. The soldiers who attended or testified at Harman's court martial all told Caldwell privately that the brass were killing 'two birds with one stone'. They could have a scapegoat for the photos, and they could rid the army of a lesbian.

Makeup and Skirts: The Power Game Continues

Another thing Caldwell noticed in court was how much time Captain Patsy Takemura spent on her makeup. Takemura was one of the two attorneys for the defence at Harman's court martial. She was considered good looking, the only woman in the whole long story to wear a skirt as part of her army uniform. During breaks in the trial she spent a lot of time ostentatiously fixing up her makeup in the well of the court.

Why? Caldwell's answer is that Takemura was a good lawyer. As part of the defence, Takemura had to explain why Harman had taken so many photographs to record what was happening without ever telling her superior officers.

The 'dead guy' Harman mentions in her email to Kelly was another elephant in the room. The photograph of Harman with the corpse in ice is the most disturbing of the photos that had become public at the time of her trial. Harman is smiling happily, giving a thumbs up to the camera, her head right next to his. His face is emaciated, and full of suffering.

The photo was the strongest evidence they had against Harman. But the prosecutors did not use it. Caldwell thinks it was because if they had produced the photo at the court martial, someone might have asked how the man had died.

In fact, he had been brought in the same day he died. A CIA operative had him taken into the shower and hung up there with his arms stretched out spread-eagled above his head. The guards called this the 'Palestinian hanging position'.

They left the man in the shower, and when they came back he was dead. Harman came, saw him and had her picture taken. According to Gourevitch:

> Later that evening, Harman returned to the shower with Frederick to examine the body more carefully. This time, she looked beneath the ice and peeled back the bandages, and she stayed out of the pictures. 'I just started taking photos of everything that was wrong, every little bruise and cut,' she said. 'His knees were bruised, his thighs were bruised by his genitals. He had restraint marks on his wrists. He just had bruises everywhere. ... I just wanted to document everything I saw. That was the reason I took photos. It was to prove to pretty much anybody who looked at this guy, 'Hey, I was just lied to. This guy did not die of a heart attack.'[19]

Had the prosecution produced the photo of Harman smiling, she would have said that in court, and might have produced her photos of the body.[20] But they didn't.

Takemura asked many soldiers who testified during the trial if they had been afraid at Abu Ghraib. All those men said yes, they had been afraid in Abu Ghraib. There were a total of eight court martials of the scapegoated guards. Yet nowhere else in any of those court martials did any man say he was afraid. But the witnesses on the stand in open court all told Takemura, with her gentle femininity and her careful cosmetics, about their fear.

Takemura did not go on to ask them what they were afraid of. But in context it is clear. They were afraid that if they reported what was going on, they would be killed. They were afraid of their sergeants, their officers and the interrogators. Thus, Specialist Israel Rivera answered Takemura's question as to why he was afraid to report abuse: 'It seemed like I would be compromising my own safety ... because if they were willing to do that to a detainee, why would they not do it to me?'[21]

Caldwell also asked Harman about her tattoos. Harman said, 'My first one was when I came home on leave in November 2003 and it's of me in a straitjacket with tape over my mouth and my eyes wide open, meaning I can't talk about what I was seeing. The next one I got during my trial was the bad apple. Thanks Bush!'

# WHY MEN?

Most of the eight defendants in the trials got bad apple tattoos to protest the army's insistence that the problem was not a systemic one of an institutional culture built on violent male power. Rather, the army said, this was a question of a few bad apples— aberrant individuals whose behaviour was not representative. Harman continues:

> A skull with tape over the eyes, means trying to forget what I saw. Another is two girls facing each other hiding knives behind their backs, meaning don't trust. And two angels, one protecting the other, it's not finished yet. Also a puppet (me) in a prison suit with my jail number hanging from a string controlled by a hand, which is the government. And a peace dove riding a missile with the Iraq colors. Oh, and I did have a tattoo of [a prisoner] on a box but I just had it covered with a gas mask because I didn't want people asking what it was.[22]

After she got out of prison, Sabrina Harman was in a bar with her partner. A woman came up to her and, trying to be supportive, said that all those prisoners in Iraq deserved what they got. Harman started crying and could not stop.

PART FOUR

APOLOGISTS FOR INEQUALITY

Part Four tackles the mainstream of the apologists for violence and inequality by looking at several key thinkers. We start with Charles Darwin and show how his theory of human evolution elegantly knits together the fact-based science of natural selection, a sexist fantasy, racism, class arrogance and imperialism. The result has been a conservative intellectual movement of apologists for inequality.

Next we consider the radical apologists for inequality. We focus on the work of Friedrich Engels, the author of the first and most important attempt to explain the origins of sexism. He linked the rise of class society with the oppression of women, as do we. But we argue that his approach was deeply flawed by the racism and colonialist fantasies he borrowed from Darwin, from Darwin's followers and from Lewis Henry Morgan, the 'father' of American anthropology we met in the Cahokia chapter. Yet his theory was long influential on the feminist left.

Then we fast forward to our own era, and return to the debate around a bestselling apology for inequality, *The Dawn of Everything*, by David Graeber and David Wengrow.

In the final chapter in Part Four we consider two of the leading lights among apologists for male violence and warfare: the evolutionary psychologists Napoleon Chagnon and Steven Pinker. They have repackaged Darwin's idea for a more liberal age. But the central ideas remain the same. War, Chagnon and Pinker say, has always been part of human nature, and that is because men are naturally more aggressive, warlike and competitive than women.

# 17

## DARWIN, RACISM AND SEXUAL SELECTION

The science we draw upon to explain the origins of male violence and domination is part of an incendiary political debate. The dominant explanations are largely taken for granted as 'neutral' scientific fact, but they are based on particular ideological assumptions. And even when their authors do not intend it, they serve particular ideological agendas. Such 'common sense' needs to be unpicked, in detail and with care.

In this, the place to start is with a brief account of the notion of 'fantasy families'. Prehistory has long acted as a sort of black box for gender fantasies. As we saw in our chapter on orgasms in Part One, there is a long tradition of scholars projecting their desires, anxieties and delusions about sex and families onto the past. Sometimes the prehistoric family is idyllic, peaceful and egalitarian. People chant a lot, they are close to the land, shamans cure disease, and everyone worships a higher power. Other fantasy families are brutal and competitive. They are dominated by cavemen with clubs obsessed with having sex with as many women as possible to pass on their genes.

What all these fantasy families have in common is that the people who write about them are unconcerned with evidence. Not that they do not look for evidence—they do. But they start out by knowing how things would have been, and then grab at isolated facts, however fanciful, to justify their position. And we are dealing with very powerful fantasies.

The important word in this is 'the', not 'family'. But in the same way we want to escape from universalising stereotypes of 'women' and 'men', we also need to beware of universalising 'the' family. This is actually easy to avoid. There are many kinds of family in class society, and many ways of structuring intimate relationships and nurture. Yet even more insidious than the notion of 'the family' is an ethnocentric assumption that all class societies resembled capitalism, when in fact capitalism is only one kind of class society, and recent in history.

'*The* family' and 'family values' are key ideas in the present dominant ideology in Europe and the Americas, and they are trotted out all the time. For instance, the late right-wing philosopher Roger Scruton claimed not long ago that the EU, immigrants, same-sex marriage, and even wind turbines, threaten Englishness and hard-won privileges and freedoms: 'Conservatives believe, with Burke, that the family is the core institution whereby societies reproduce themselves and pass moral knowledge to the young.'[1]

Scruton's jump from the random list of things he hates to his essentialist belief in *the* family is bizarre, extreme and ugly. Yet even those who would utterly disagree with Scruton can be seduced by the habit of universalising *the* family. Feminists who would blame the family for the situation of 'women' and gender inequality can also become trapped in circularity. Then, instead of offering a critical analysis of *the* family, they may inadvertently reproduce elements of the dominant ideology instead.

Most commonly, people talk about *the* family as if it resembles their family. This is understandable. Yet consider the range of things individuals in different countries have said to one or the other of us:

> When a teenage boy has troubles at school with other boys, he always confides in his mother. After all, his mother is always a boy's best friend. That's why men put their mothers before their wives.
>
> He should put me first ahead of his mother. I'm his wife.
>
> A man always loves his father more than anyone else.
>
> The good thing about being married to two brothers at the same time is that just when you're getting bored with the older brother, suddenly you have an energetic eighteen-year-old in your bed.
>
> A study of happy families in Dallas found that both the children and the parents agreed that in their families the parents loved their children, but the love between the parents was stronger.
>
> The English people are dreadful. They put their parents into old people's homes.

> Of course your mother has to go into a home. You have done so much for her, and you can't look after her full time.
>
> We tie Granny into a chair in the kitchen. It's the best we can do, and she likes having the grandchildren play at her feet.

All of these people were living in families in capitalist societies and all of them were talking about sentiments they considered completely normal.

Equally, sexual arrangements in class societies are not uniform. Sometimes men marry only one woman, sometimes two or more. More rarely, as in Tibet and the Marquesas, some women traditionally marry two or more men. Sometimes people try for a stable heterosexual relationship but don't formally marry. Elsewhere women and men are monogamous, or monogamish, or serially monogamous or just cheat a lot. And since the legalisation of same-sex marriage, the notion of a 'family' has perforce changed and now includes queer couples, IVF treatment and same-sex adoption of children.

We also have assumptions about how we use the word 'family' to mean 'household'. Households grow and change through time. As with differences in marriage practices, often rich people have one kind of family and one kind of household, middle-class people others, and working people yet others, though of course the differences shade from one to the other. Some people assume that a nuclear family of two parents and their children is best. Others may prize large joint households. Some people assume that one of the daughters should live with the elderly parents, others say that the son should bring the parents to live with him. The differences between us are manifold, even before we begin to look at how some people take in lodgers, and hire cleaners, au pairs, nannies, and jobbing gardeners.

But still, again and again we hear that the nuclear family was the normal form of household throughout human history. This was not the case. If it were, one might expect, for example, the English language to have a word for such an arrangement. There is no such word. Instead, we have to use the awkward two-word phrase 'nuclear family', which first appears in English only in the 1920s.

# WHY MEN?

*Darwin's Fantasies*

Charles Darwin's *On the Origin of Species by Means of Natural Selection* was published in 1859. It has had an immense impact on our understanding of the natural world. Twelve years later he published *The Descent of Man, and Selection in Relation to Sex*. But there was a problem. *The Origin of Species* was a masterpiece. *The Descent of Man* was seriously flawed because of Darwin's fantasies of human prehistory. Those fantasies were sexist, elitist, racist and imperialist.[2]

Of course, the fact that ideas are sexist, elitist, racist or imperialist is not what makes them wrong. Rather it is that often such ideas hide reality. In this case Darwin's biases got in the way of the science. And many of the nineteenth-century social philosophers whose thinking forms the backbone of our understanding of society today followed Darwin's lead.

Some readers may find it surprising that we write about Darwin in these terms. After all, we have relied on a Darwinian approach to evolution in previous chapters. And Darwinian ideas don't only 'belong' to one side of the political spectrum; thinkers who share ideas with our own have claimed him too. In the late nineteenth century, Marx, Engels and many other socialists admired Darwin immensely. And in the US today, liberals and left-wingers feel compelled to defend Darwin and evolution against the attacks of creationists. So for a long time, many people have passed on by Darwin's work without calling attention to the ugly bits. One result, however, has been a good deal of confusion on the left and among progressives about human prehistory. Another has been a failure to notice that the conservative ideas of evolutionary psychology descend in a straight line from the conservative ideas of Darwin.

To understand Darwin, we need to start with who he was. He was born in 1809, white, English and a man from a wealthy family. His wife Emma was a Wedgwood, the richest of the capitalist families in the pottery industry. Darwin spent much of his life as a Church of England minister, but with quite minimal duties. Most of his income came from the ownership of stocks and agricultural land.

Darwin was not in any way an aristocrat. Rather, he had the politics and world view of the new capitalist class. He was a pro-business liberal in politics, economics and theology. Influenced by Unitarians and Quakers, he was sexually repressed and strongly anti-slavery. Darwin believed that Britain should be run by men like him, and that the British Empire was the highest form of human progress to date.

Darwin was also a genius at natural history, what we would now call biology. As a young man, he spent several years as the naturalist on HMS *Beagle*, voyaging in both the Atlantic and Pacific. Everywhere the ship sailed, Darwin went ashore and was exquisitely observant and assiduous in collecting plant and animal specimens. He knew that geologists were demonstrating that the world was far older than the Bible implied. Other scientists and naturalists were digging up fossils of a far wider variety of animals and plants than were currently alive. The evidence was pointing to some kind of evolution. As he sailed the world, Darwin considered what kind that might be.

He came home with an answer. By 1842, he had worked out the details in a manuscript of over 200 pages. But he did not publish. He feared his ideas would destroy the authority of the Bible and lead to social upheaval. In the summer of 1842, at the height of the Chartist revolt, Darwin was living on Gower Street in central London. According to his biographers, Adrian Desmond and James Moore:

> In mid-August the country was paralyzed by a general strike... Half a million workers were out, fighting wage cuts and demanding the vote—what the Attorney General damned as the 'most formidable conspiracy ever.' ... The Cabinet went into emergency session and put the troops on alert... For three days, from 14–16 August, battalions of Guards and Royal Horse Artillery marched up through central London to the new Euston Station to put down the riots in Manchester. The troops were trailed by jeering crowds. The commotion was terrible as they passed Darwin's road, with screams of 'Remember, you are brothers,' and 'Don't go and slaughter your fellow countrymen.' By the time the battalions reached Gower Street the demonstrators were hemming them in and the soldiers had fixed bayonets. The Darwins were also hemmed in, with gangs everywhere. The streets were frightening, even with a huge police presence. Each day the situation worsened. On the 16th the station (only a few hundred yards from the house) was actually blocked, and the troops repeatedly charged the crowds to clear a way in.[3]

In this situation, the ideas in Darwin's unpublished manuscript on evolution were explosive. Many of the more extreme radicals were also atheists, opposed to both church and king, and devoted to 'transmutationist' ideas.

Transmutationism came from the ideas of Jean-Baptiste Lamarck. Today Lamarck is remembered as backward because he propounded the theory of 'the inheritance of acquired characteristics'. This theory held that individual plants and animals adapted to their environment during their lifetime, and those changes in their leaves and bodies were passed down to their offspring. Overwhelmingly, this is not the case. You get the genes your parent was born with, not the bodies they develop in later life.

But in 1842, two other things were important about Lamarck. First, he had done his work as part of the French Revolution. Second, his was a theory of evolution. It showed that nature changed, and that the Bible was wrong. So radical speakers could attract crowds of 3,000 working people to lectures on transmutation. And the government took this threat seriously, prosecuting and jailing transmutationist journalists.[4]

What made Darwin's ideas even more dangerous thirty years later was that he had solved the problem in Lamarck's work. The theory of inheritance of acquired characteristics did not work. Instead, Darwin said, there was natural variation in any species of plant or animal. The animal with a variation more suited to the environment was more likely to survive, and to have offspring that might also survive. In this way the species changed and adapted to its environment over time. Darwin did not know about genes—genetics came later. But already his theory did explain the data in a way Lamarck's did not.

By publishing, Darwin would be giving aid and comfort to the enemies of his class. He would also be punished, possibly by prosecution, but more likely by social and professional ostracism. He stayed quiet for the next fourteen years. For almost every day of those years he suffered from stomach pains and vomiting which made it hard to work more than four hours a day. The illness may have been undiagnosed malady, or the way he punished himself for his silence.

Darwin's world changed during his years of silence. The death of his daughter, Anne, destroyed his faith in God. The rule of his class in England, which had seemed so precarious in 1842, was rock solid by 1858. No one in Britain any longer expected revolution. Meanwhile, evolutionary ideas were steadily gaining ground among established scientists. Then the socialist surveyor and naturalist Alfred Wallace sent a long letter to Darwin, laying out almost the same theory of natural selection. Darwin was crushed to learn that he had been forestalled. But Darwin's friends arranged swift joint publication of Wallace's paper and one by Darwin. The next year, 1859, Darwin published his master work, *On the Origin of Species by Means of Natural Selection*.

Darwin's ideas caused consternation among the bishops of the Church of England. But over the next twenty years, his ideas did not just become acceptable, they became a defence of the status quo, a capitalist elite of white men who ruled Britain and the British Empire, over people of colour and all women.

The key turning point in this ideological progression was Darwin's publication of *The Descent of Man, and Selection in Relation to Sex*, in 1871. When Darwin published *The Origin of Species* twelve years earlier, he carefully said nothing whatsoever about the descent of humans from apes. He felt the subject was still too explosive. But the implication was obvious. One had only to look at the skulls or faces of chimpanzees or gorillas. Darwin's enemies seized upon this point. So did his defenders, Thomas Huxley foremost among them.

When Darwin published *The Descent of Man* it was an affront to the Bible. It was also an affront to social hierarchies everywhere. It said, clearly, through more than a hundred examples, that we are all animals. Moreover, Darwin intervened in an important contemporary argument about whether all humanity was one species, or several. He said humanity was one. This again was a powerful gain for those who favoured equality.

But he also made his theory safe for empire, for capitalism and patriarchy. An imperial theory of evolution was already beginning to dominate late nineteenth-century thinking, most markedly in the work of Herbert Spencer, John Ferguson McLennan, and Darwin's cousin, Francis Galton. In this theory, humanity evolved through three stages: savages, barbarians and civilised people. In *The Descent of Man*, Darwin reproduced these arguments, and provided them with the authority of his prodigious learning and genius. Here is Darwin on the extermination of barbarian races:

## WHY MEN?

> Extinction follows chiefly from the competition of tribe with tribe, and race with race... When one of two adjoining tribes becomes more numerous and powerful than the other, the contest is soon settled by war, slaughter, cannibalism, slavery and absorption. Even when a weaker tribe is not thus abruptly swept away, if it at once begins to decrease, it generally goes on decreasing until it is extinct.
>
> When civilised nations come into contact with barbarians the struggle is short, except where a deadly climate gives its aid to the native race... New diseases and vices are highly destructive, and it appears that in every nation a new disease causes much death, until those who are most susceptible to its destructive influence are gradually weeded out; and so it may be with the evil effect from spirituous liquors, as well as with the unconquerable strong taste shewn for them by so many savages. It further appears, mysterious as is the fact that the first meeting of distinct and separated people generates disease.[5]

Note the weeding metaphor. This passage is making genocide seem natural. Darwin continues:

> At some future period, not very distant as measured by centuries, the civilised races of man will almost certainly exterminate and replace throughout the world the savage races. At the same time the anthropomorphous apes ... will no doubt be exterminated. The break will then be rendered wider, for it will intervene between man in a more civilised state, as we may hope, than the Caucasian, and some ape as low as a baboon, instead of as present between the negro or Australian and the gorilla.[6]

Darwin was thinking of Aboriginal Australians. In his theory, the superiority of imperial powers is linked to the superiority of the upper classes in Britain and Europe and other 'white' countries:

> In all civilised countries man accumulates property and bequeaths it to his children. So that the children in the same country do not by any means start fair in the race for success. But this is far from an unmixed evil; for without the accumulation of capital the arts could not progress; and it is chiefly through their power that the civilised races have extended, and are now everywhere extending their range, so as to take the place of the lower races.[7]

# DARWIN, RACISM AND SEXUAL SELECTION

This ideology of class and empire was linked, you may not be surprised to hear, with a particular fantasy about women and the bourgeois family. Stephanie Coontz, writing of the United States in 1900, makes the point vividly:

> For every nineteenth century middle-class family that protected its wife and child within the family circle, then there was an Irish or a German [immigrant] girl scrubbing floors in that middle-class home, a Welsh boy mining coal to keep the home-baked goodies warm, a black girl doing the family laundry, a black mother and child picking cotton to be made into clothes for the family, and a Jewish or Italian daughter in a sweatshop making 'ladies' dresses or artificial flowers for the family to purchase.[8]

The class splitting also required comparable splitting about female sexuality. Women of the upper classes, like Darwin's dear wife Emma, were without sexual desire. So were all women, naturally. Except for savages:

> The greatest intemperance with savages is no reproach. Their utter licentiousness, not to mention unnatural crimes, is something astounding. As soon, however, as marriage, whether polygamous or monogamous, becomes common, jealousy will lead to the inculcation of female virtue; and this being honoured will spread to the unmarried females. How slowly it spreads to the male sex we see at the present day.[9]

Men were always more desirous of sex than women, and less able to contain their lust. Notice too Darwin's comments on 'unnatural crimes', code for homosexuality.

Darwin's sexism is also closely linked to his belief that men naturally compete, in the ways that upper-class men did compete in his time:

> Man is the rival of other men; he delights in competition, and this leads to ambition which passes too easily into selfishness. These latter qualities seem to be his natural and unfortunate birthright. It is generally admitted that with woman the powers of intuition, of rapid perception, and perhaps of imitation, are more strongly marked than in man; but some, at least, of these faculties are

323

characteristic of the lower races, and therefore of a past and lower state of civilisation.

The chief distinction in the intellectual powers of the two sexes is shewn by man's attaining to a higher eminence, in whatever he takes up, than can woman—whether requiring deep thought, reason, or imagination, or merely the use of the senses and hands.[10]

This is mostly common or garden sexism. But Darwin added an important new, supposedly scientific, twist. The full title of the book is *The Descent of Man, and Selection in Relation to Sex*. The second part of the title is as important as the first. *The Origin of Species* had all been about one mechanism of evolution, natural selection by survival. As he wrote *Descent*, Darwin was thinking about a second mechanism, 'sexual selection'. Darwin saw this new mechanism working in two main ways: one is female choice, the other is competition between men for mates.

Darwin also came to think that sexual selection was more important in human evolution than natural selection by survival. In *Descent*, Darwin wrote that among animal species sexual selection much more commonly affected the evolution of the male, because males were competing to attract females. This may be the case for many species. But at first sight it seems unlikely for people. As we have seen, the bodies of males and females are quite similar in size, shape and function.

Sexual selection, Darwin said, affected mainly 'secondary sexual characteristics' which develop at puberty, like facial hair and genitals in males, and breasts and genitals in females, more than ovaries and testes (the 'primary' characteristics). But the importance of these bits paled into insignificance beside the development of tools, big brains, hunting, religion, art, music and complex societies. For Darwin, all these features and qualities associated with humanity were traits gendered male. Darwin believed that although men and women inherit intelligence equally from both parents, all important human advances were made by men. This meant that clever, inventive men were selected for their intelligence. There was no specific selection for intelligent women, because it really didn't matter whether women were stupid or not. But intelligent fathers passed their genes down to both their sons and daughters.

# DARWIN, RACISM AND SEXUAL SELECTION

Darwin said that intelligence among men developed because they were competing for females. The man who was more intelligent, more socially aware, better armed and better at getting meat, would thereby be able to mate with more females. As male humans changed under the pressure of sexual selection, their female children also inherited at least some of their skills and prowess, thus allowing the species to grow more intelligent as a whole.

Thus, Darwin ties together gender, race, class and empire. The richer men with leisure in the more civilised countries develop the culture and knowledge that allow their race to conquer or exterminate other races. And these richer men develop their superior characteristics through competition with each other for female mates.

However, two intellectual problems haunted Darwin as he worked on his theory of human evolution. One was his certainty of the stronger sexual desires of women among the lower orders in Britain and the lower orders in the world. This 'knowledge' flowed from the way that Victorian ideology split 'good wives' from 'fallen women' and 'whores' in terms of personal weakness and moral turpitude and along class and racial lines.

The other intellectual problem was that Darwin also knew that in Britain the lower orders, among whom Darwin included the Irish, had more children than the upper orders. That meant they ought to be judged the winners in the battle for survival. As Darwin put it, the Celts are increasing faster than the Saxons.

Darwin had several ways of trying to lay these ghosts. In part, he put his trust in venereal disease, and hoped that 'profligate' (by which he means promiscuous) women and men will die in larger numbers. But he was also open to the arguments of his cousin, Francis Galton, for eugenics—that is, controlled breeding. Darwin writes:

> With savages, the weak in body or mind are soon eliminated; and those that survive commonly exhibit a vigorous state of health. We civilised men, on the other hand, do our utmost to check the process of elimination; we build asylums for the imbecile, the maimed and the sick; we institute poor-laws; and our medical men exert their utmost skill to save the life of every one to the last moment. ... Thus the weaker members of civilised societies propagate their

kind. No one who has attended to the breeding of domestic animals will doubt that this must be highly injurious to the race of man. It is surprising how soon a want of care, or care wrongly directed, leads to the degeneration of a domestic race... but excepting in the case of man himself, hardly any one is so ignorant as to allow his worst animals to breed.[11]

Our reading of the rationale for this classism and ableism is that Darwin knew he was juggling with dynamite. He was arguing that all races are basically the same. They belong to the same species and are equally human. And he was arguing that humans are animals. Darwin paid very little attention to ethnological examples from 'savage' and 'barbarian' peoples, though he had travelled and lived among indigenous people all over the world. He was not fundamentally interested in recent human evolution. But he was all too aware that egalitarian and dangerous conclusions could easily be drawn from his arguments. So he was protecting himself by stating his allegiance to the prevailing ideas of the dominant class about women, workers and inferior races. And he praised highly men like Herbert Spencer and Francis Galton, who were developing a detailed sociological and anthropological justification of colonial rule.

Darwin was covering his back, but he also believed what he wrote. These were the standard prejudices of men of his class, and he shared them. The unusual thing was his obsession with female desire. He came back to it chapter after chapter, often indirectly by discussing birds and butterflies. This father of ten children wanted desperately to remove the spectre of female sexual desire from the story of human evolution.

Darwin's protective colouring worked. When Darwin died, the atheist and debunker of the Bible was buried in Westminster Abbey, the resting place for the great men of England. The idea of evolution that might once have threatened all hierarchies had become an idea that justified patriarchy, empire and war.

*Roughgarden's Rainbow*

Darwin's idea of natural selection by survival was an enormous scientific breakthrough. It has been the foundation of biology ever since, and it is the approach we have used in our discussion of human evolution. No question, it's sound. The idea of sexual selection, however, soon fell out of favour in mainstream biology. The historian Cynthia Eller argues convincingly that when Eleanor Marx and the left took up Darwin's idea of sexual selection in the late nineteenth century (see Chapter 19), that association with radicals made it politically dangerous for biologists to support.[12]

But as we shall see in Chapter 19, by the 1970s feminism was considered less toxic and male chauvinism more so, and at that time evolutionary biologists resurrected the idea with a vengeance. Luckily, the biologist Joan Roughgarden has recently provided a fierce critique of the concept of sexual selection. Her work provides a serendipitous example of synergy between personal politics and scientific investigation. Roughgarden was raised as a man and then transitioned. Mustering the courage to do so gave her the courage to look at the field of biology anew. So did her long participation in the highly political gay world of San Francisco.

Roughgarden also had a couple of other things going for her. By the time she transitioned she was already a professor specialising in evolution at Stanford, an elite university, with a respected textbook already published. She had her own lab, replete with graduate students wanting to work with her. And she had done extensive work with barnacles and small Caribbean lizards, species that show a great deal of gender diversity.[13]

Her first book on animal sexuality, *Evolution's Rainbow: Diversity, Gender, and Sexuality in Nature and People,* is more personal and an easier read. Her second, *The Genial Gene: Deconstructing Darwinian Selfishness*, written in close collaboration with her students, is a more formal intellectual tour de force. In both books Roughgarden makes a powerful argument for getting rid of the idea of sexual selection entirely. By looking systematically at nature as if trans people were the norm, she sees all sorts of things that were hidden in plain sight.

Roughgarden does not disagree with the idea of female choice. As we have seen, the idea of female choice has illuminated the study of baboons, bonobos, langurs and many other species. Rather, Roughgarden disagrees with Darwin about why females are making those choices. Darwin, and those who work on sexual selection now, see females choosing to mate with the male with the highest quality genetic material they can find. They tend to identify 'high quality genetic material' with social dominance. They do this without thinking about it. For Darwin, though, it was also important that high quality males looked more attractive.

The other half of Darwin's theory of sexual selection emphasised male competition to mate. Roughgarden argues that mating success is the wrong thing to measure. What makes a difference, she says, is the ability to pass on genes to offspring who live to adulthood. And that, in many species, requires cooperation. Sometimes it requires cooperation between male and female, and sometimes by a whole group. In such species, there is *social selection*. The animal that is best able to cooperate will be the one with more descendants.

Roughgarden also has a very useful approach to monogamy. Among those species of fish where a parent cares for the offspring, more often than not it's the male who does the job. Among birds, more than 90% of species are monogamous, and the pair raise the young together.

There is also a strange thing about bird monogamy. In many species of birds, often one or more of the eggs in the nest is a result of the mother having sex with a neighbouring male, not her nest mate. Roughgarden makes a useful distinction between 'economic monogamy' and 'sexual monogamy'. Economic monogamy means two birds share a nest and raise the young together. Sexual monogamy means sex only with the nest partner. They are not the same thing. Scientists can now do genetic tests on offspring to determine who the parents are:

> A review in 2002 by Griffith and colleagues cited over 150 studies of avian parentage... The authors concluded that the average frequency of extra-pair offspring among economically monogamous bird species was 11.1% of offspring and 18.7% of broods. They also concluded that genetic monogamy [0% extra-pair paternity] had been found in less than 25% of the economically monogamous bird species studied.[14]

In other words, almost a fifth of nests had an egg with outsider (extra-pair) paternity, and three quarters of species had at least some eggs with parentage outside the nest couple raising them. Current-day followers of Darwin's model of male sexual competition have trouble making theoretical sense of these numbers. These scientists, Roughgarden says,

> Employ a dime-store novel's vocabulary to trivialize and pathologize any departures from the sexual-selection norm. In the primary peer-reviewed literature, males are described as being "cuckolded," females as "unfaithful" or "promiscuous," offspring as "legitimate" or "illegitimate," males who do not hold territory as "floaters" or "sneakers" (code for "sneaky fuckers") all of whom are "sexual parasites," small males as "gigolos," feminine males as "female mimics" or even as "transvestite serpents" or "she-males" (a pornographic reference), and so forth. The cesspool of adjectives invented ostensibly as descriptions of animal behaviour makes locker-room banter seem genteel. This vocabulary poisons any aspiration to scientific objectivity.[15]

Roughgarden is right. It's not just that biologists sometimes use this language. It's that they usually do.

But Roughgarden is not only reproving these scientists for their language. Nor is she pointing out that a large proportion of these scientists or their spouses have at some point in their lives had 'extra-pair sex', so who are they to use such words? She is saying something else—that the language they are using blinds them to understanding. Among other things, it blinds them to the mathematical reality that for every time one female bird has extra-pair sex that leads to conception, one male bird also has extra-pair sex that leads to conception. This sex is not something that is being done to males or by females. It is common enough that it must be useful to natural selection. In some way, it is part of good parenting.

Roughgarden has three interesting explanations for why wider sex might be a good strategy for reproduction. One is don't put all your eggs in one basket. Any one nest is always at risk from predators or cold. Distributing your offspring a bit makes sense as a strategy.

Her second explanation is more original. In a species where the eggs are distributed, birds have strong reason not to attack the nests of other birds. Indeed, they have reason to band together to defend all their nests from predators. Think about seabirds, nesting in tens of thousands, their nests right next to each other, ganging up to fight off skuas.

329

## WHY MEN?

Her third explanation is that sex tends to reinforce affection. She suggests that animals who must cooperate to survive may benefit from sharing pleasure together. This can work for any group of animals. Roughgarden also argues that this is an evolutionary basis for homosexuality. As she says:

> In over 300 species of vertebrates, same-sex sexuality has been documented in the primary peer-reviewed literature as a natural component of the social system. Examples include species of reptiles like whiptail lizards; birds like the pukeko of New Zealand and the European oystercatcher; and mammals like giraffes, elephants, dolphins, whales, sheep, monkeys, and bonobos...

> According to sexual selection, homosexuality is an inadvertent mistake, a deception, or a deleterious trait maintained through peculiar inheritance. Homosexuality occurs when, for example, a small snake sneaks into the territory of a large male, allows him to tire by acquiescing to homosexual copulation, and then mates with the females in his harem. Or homosexuality is a disease caused by genes that decrease fitness in one sex, but increase fitness in the other sex (sexually antagonistic pleiotropy). According to social selection [on the other hand], homosexuality is natural and adaptive for all participants and both sexes. Homosexuality along with mutual grooming, preening, sleeping, tongue rubbing, and interlocking vocalizations allows animals to work together as a team—to coordinate actions and tactilely to sense one another's welfare.[16]

These ideas are helpful in understanding human society. They particularly illuminate two things. One is that over a very broad range of societies most people enter sexual relationships where they work together to raise children. But sex outside those relationships is common as well. Some human societies have some polygamy as well, either ritually sanctioned as a man's marriage to several women, or just lived as another relationship. A few societies, but not many, have formal polyandry, where one woman has more than one husband. But in many parts of the world women often have steady relationships with more than one person.

Second, Roughgarden is not suggesting that some people or giraffes are naturally gay. Rather, she is saying that same-sex relationships are part of the natural potential in both species. That way of doing things is open to all giraffes and humans but acted on situationally.

Saying that same-sex behaviour and extra-pair sex are 'adaptive and natural' does not mean that all such relationships and events are mellow. Nor does it mean that they all help people adapt. It only means that in a particular species such behaviour, on average, over the long haul, helps survival more than it hinders survival. And that is probably as much as we can ask of sex or love in any form.

Roughgarden is also interesting on fatherhood. In effect she argues that in evolutionary terms paternal care for offspring came first—before the evolution of mammals. Mammals replaced egg laying with longer gestations, live births and mother's milk. This adaptation has considerable advantages for mammalian offspring, because their mother is a nest which she carries with her wherever she goes. But the adaptation focused childcare on females. Roughgarden suggests that males with nothing else to do pursued a path of having sex with many females.

In our account of human evolution we described how changes in childcare and shared orgasms, marking us out from other primates, have restored to the human male the emotional possibilities of fatherhood and equal, cooperative parenting that have always been enjoyed by birds. It is not an accident that when we want to lose ourselves in the transcendent possibilities of masculinity at its best, we watch films about emperor penguins in Antarctica.

This seems sense to us.

18

ENGELS, GRAEBER AND RADICAL CONFUSIONS

By the time Darwin died, two compromises had been effectively agreed in elite circles in Britain. Darwin's ideas offered incontrovertible proof that the Bible could not be true. In public debate Thomas Huxley made mincemeat of the Bishop of Oxford. So the unspoken deal was that scientists would not criticise the Bible, and religious people would not criticise science. This deal held for more than a century. Only recently has it—to a certain extent—broken down in the United States. There two minorities—right-wing creationists and militant atheists—have entered the fray. But even in the US the compromise largely holds. Some schools teach creationism and some evolution, but what is disallowed is debate between the two positions. Certainly students would learn a great deal about the scientific method from such a debate, but the politics would be explosive, and that cannot be permitted.

The second compromise left the door open for the doctrine of Social Darwinism developed by Herbert Spencer, the nineteenth-century sociologist and conservative. Spencer followed Darwin's *Origin of Species*, but argued more explicitly that the ruling classes and dominant races of each epoch were the winners in the fight for what Spencer called 'the survival of the fittest'.

Then several of Spencer's contemporaries, including the English anthropologist E.B. Tylor and the American ethnologist Lewis Henry Morgan, developed Spencer's idea of the survival of the fittest into a theory of stages of human evolution. These stages went from the most primitive to the highest stage, represented by upper-class white men in cities. The argument was that societies went through the same stages everywhere in the world, and as technology

## WHY MEN?

and productivity developed, so too did systems of kinship and marriage and religious belief, morality and civilisation. It was an anthropology fitted to the new empires that now ruled many different people around the world.[1]

More surprising, however, is the way these ideas have been taken up by those who opposed their elitist/conservative/imperialist politics. Working-class radicals in Britain had long embraced evolution with their support of Lamarck's ideas. These transmutationists welcomed Darwin's ideas and gloried in Darwin and Huxley's victories in public debates over the Bishop of Oxford and the Duke of Argyll. Radicals like Karl Marx and Friedrich Engels also saw Darwin's triumph as a victory for materialism and atheism.

Marx and Engels also began reading around in the work of other thinkers about prehistory. In the process, they adopted much of the racism of those authors. This was to have unfortunate consequences for Marxist approaches to prehistory for generations. In 1884, more than thirty years after the publication of *The Communist Manifesto*, Engels brought out a short book, *The Origin of the Family, Private Property and the State*. He wrote the book because he wanted to develop a theory that linked Marxism to the liberation of women and explained the roots of sexism with the coming of class society. For almost a century *The Origin of the Family* was the most influential Marxist or socialist book that feminists could turn to.[2]

Since its publication, the notion of 'the family' has been a stalking horse for conservative ideas. One reason for the perennial confusion is that few can imagine that this book, authored late in Engels' life, is so different from his earlier radical writing.

Unfortunately, the book is deeply flawed. It's not just the racism, sexism and homophobia, none of which are to be found in any of Engels' other books. It is also the method. Engels set out to explain the oppression of women in terms of the physical and sexual differences between men and women. He argued that the origins of gendered inequality derived from the institution of the family. In one way or another, many progressives, and socialist and Marxist feminists, followed this same tautological reasoning. For them, production is gendered masculine, men are productive and economic relations explain class. On the other hand, reproduction is gendered female, women reproduce and nurture the working population, and family relations explain the sexist divide. We have sought to avoid such circularity by starting from the physical similarities of men and women and making class central to our analysis.

But it is not easy to ignore the impact of *The Origin of the Family*, and it is an awful book. Sometimes what you forget to do reveals a good deal about who you are. When we first began work on the long article that would eventually morph into this book, Nancy said, 'One of us has to reread Engels.'

'You do it,' Jonathan said.

'You do it,' Nancy said. 'You're always going on about how great he is.'

(Jonathan writes:) So I read it. But I struggled to finish it. I was a professionally trained anthropologist and historian. The anthropology and history in the book were bad. Worse, there was sexism and homophobia all over the place. I was embarrassed, for myself, and ashamed as a Marxist. I was mortified that, speaking from a high place, I had corrected Nancy's dismissal of Engels. I remembered, as I tried to read the book, that I had tried to read it three or four times before. I had forgotten this, as Dr Freud would say. Finally, I finished it, underlining over a hundred illogical or offensive passages.

*Engels and Morgan*

Engels wrote the book in a hurry, when he was burdened with an immense amount of work editing Marx's unpublished work. What started Engels on the book was his discovery of the notes Marx made when reading Lewis Henry Morgan's *Ancient Society*, first published in 1877.

Morgan was a lawyer and Republican politician in upstate New York. As we saw in the chapter on Cahokia, Morgan was also an ethnologist who did field research with local Iroquois. Morgan's last book, *Ancient Society*, was an evolutionary analysis of the stages of human history, from savagery through barbarism to modern times.[3]

Marx's notes on Morgan were extensive, and largely summarised the book. Engels read them and was gripped. Both he and Marx had been deeply influenced by Darwin. Here, Engels thought, was a Darwinian approach to the evolution of the oppression of women. So Engels, in a hurry, published these notes as if they were Marx's own thoughts on the subject.[4]

However, there was something radical about the way Lewis Henry Morgan developed these evolutionary ideas. He argued that humanity, before agriculture, had been egalitarian and shared their goods. At the same time, they had shared women and had not lived in families. Then came agriculture, class society and families.

For Engels, this was dynamite. His hatred for sexual repression and the rules that had kept him from marrying Mary Burns—a working-class woman and the love of his life—could be linked to his hatred for class society. But Engels made a mistake in just accepting the framework of a racist anthropology. And he made a mistake in just copying Morgan's notes. It's one of the reasons his book is riddled with passages that are silly, or bigoted, or both. Here is one example, about ancient Greece:

> The Athenian family became ... the accepted model for domestic relations ... to an increasing extent among the Greeks of the mainland and colonies... But in spite of locks and guards, Greek women found plenty of opportunity for deceiving their husbands. The men, who would have been ashamed to show any love for their wives, amused themselves by all sorts of love affairs with *hetairai*; but this degradation of the women was avenged on the men and degraded them also, till they fell into the abominable practice of pederasty ... and degraded alike their gods and themselves with the myth of Ganymede.[5]

This passage is bigoted because of its homophobia. *Hetairai* were a sort of courtesan in Athens who sold sex, but only to a few clients. The myth of Ganymede, found in Homer, tells how Zeus took a beautiful boy named Ganymede as his cup bearer and lover. Ganymede, from the story, seems to be a teenager, and love between adult men and teenage boys was indeed more than tolerated in ancient Greece, as in many other societies.

The passage we've quoted is also silly because Engels is saying there was a special kind of Athenian family. But this was not what was special about Athens.

But note something else, equally important but perhaps less obvious. What Engels is saying about the dominance of the Athenian family is nonsense. However, Engels had a good classical education, and he would have known this. The problem with his book is not just the gendered and racialised stereotypes, it's the sloppy history.

Here's another quote, about race. Engels is arguing that pastoralists with herds of animals became racially superior:

> The plentiful supply of milk and meat and especially the beneficial effect of these food on the growth of children account perhaps for the superior development of the Aryan and Semitic races. It is a fact that the Pueblo Indians of New Mexico, who are reduced to an almost entirely vegetarian diet, have a smaller brain than the Indians at the lower stage of barbarism, who eat more meat and fish.[6]

Notice that there is no evidence mentioned for the superior development of the Aryan and Semitic races. These things are known and assumed.

Here is another quote where the racism and homophobia are combined. These are two extracts from a section where Engels is explaining why Germanic monogamy was superior to other forms of monogamy:

> But the greatest progress in the development of individual marriage certainly came with the entry of Germans into history... Thus, here again an entirely new influence came to power in the world with the Germans. The new monogamy, which now developed from the mingling of peoples amid the ruins of the Roman world, clothed the supremacy of men in milder forms and gave women a position which, outwardly at any rate, was much more free and respected than it had ever been in classical antiquity. Only now were the conditions realized in which through monogamy—within it, parallel to it, or in opposition to it, as the case might be—the greatest moral advance we owe to it could be achieved: modern individual sex-love, which had hitherto been unknown to the entire world...

> [But] in the course of their migrations the Germans had morally much deteriorated, particularly during their southeasterly wanderings among the nomads of the Black Sea steppes, from whom they acquired, not only equestrian skill, but also gross, unnatural vices, as Ammianus expressly states of the Taifalians and Procopius of the Herulians.[7]

It is unclear what kind of vice Ammianus accused the Taifalians of. Some scholars say that Procopius accused the Herulians of sex with animals, while others argue more convincingly that he was referring to 'warrior-based male homosexuality'.[8]

## WHY MEN?

In reading these speculations, one is reminded of a question Jonathan's mischievous father, Terry Neale, used to ask: 'We know what they did in Sodom. But what did they do in Gomorrah?'

When the answer to this question is finally discovered, we hope to be spry enough to try it.

In any case, Engels would have been aware that his readers would have assumed the gross, unnatural vice was sex between men. But perhaps the more disturbing detail is that the Germans were all right until they were corrupted by the people of the East.

It could be argued, fairly, that we are taking some of Engels' comments out of context, and that much of his discussion is more nuanced. True enough. But there are dozens of such passages. Some might argue that Engels was simply a man of his time. This is a common argument in many other cases, and almost always unjustified. Priyamvada Gopal puts it well:

> One of the most dangerous pieces of 'common sense' floating around is that critiques of racism, imperialism or sexism in the past are 'anachronistic'. It's based on the rather facile idea that Everyone in the Past Thought Exactly the Same Way and The Poor Dears Were Backward Compared to Us so we should not say anything now. It's usually a way to shut people up about empire, war, racism etc by pretending they are embarrassing themselves by missing out on deep historical nuance. Here's a tiny little newsflash. No, everyone in Victorian Britain, to take just one instance, was not uniformly racist. Nor were they uniformly behind the empire. Nor did gender roles go unquestioned. So please, before offering a piece of punditry denouncing other people for 'anachronism', do a tiny bit of research. Or if you can't be arsed, imagine how fatuous it would be if future historians thought in exactly the same way based on dominant ideologies. What's that?—we have sharp ideological faultiness? Oh, well, guess what—so did they.[9]

All of which applies to Engels. His sentiments may have been common among imperialists and racists, but such comments were rare among socialists or sexual radicals. Nothing of the kind, for example, is to be found in Oscar Wilde's 'The Soul of Man Under Socialism', written seven years after *Origin of the Family*. Such comments are very rare in the published work of Karl Marx, who did not publish his notes on Morgan. There is often something overpowering about fantasies of prehistory.[10]

In their private lives Marx and Engels were also markedly non-racist by the standards of their time and place. Jews and Irish, in 1867, were not then regarded as white in Britain. Of the two people Engels loved the most, Karl Marx was Jewish and Mary Burns was Irish.

It was a blended family: Laura, Marx's second daughter, married the socialist Paul Lafargue, a man of mixed race who would have been counted as black in the United States. The Marx family welcomed him. Marx himself was Jewish 'by race', although his father had converted to Christianity. Engels, and the Marx children, called him 'The Moor' because his skin was so dark.

Of the Irish, one incident speaks volumes. In 1867 a party of men from the Irish Republican Brotherhood attacked a police van carrying two of their leaders, Thomas Kelly and Timothy Deasy. The Brotherhood men killed a policeman in the attack, and three of them were hung for that murder, the last public execution in Britain. A fond Marx family tradition remembered that Lizzie Burns, Mary's sister and Engels' companion, had used Engels' home as a safe house for Kelly and Deasy, who were never recaptured.[11]

Still, it was not surprising that most Marxists and feminists turned away from Engels after women's liberation and gay liberation hit the fan in the early 1970s. It was still possible to cite him approvingly, but no one seriously defended the details, or even mentioned them.

But there was also a larger problem with *The Origin of the Family*, beyond its offensive assumptions and ideas about people considered 'lesser': Engels' basic theoretical argument. He had argued that property was key. The invention of property, he said, was essential to class society. And inheritance was the reason for what he called, in an admirable phrase, the 'world historical defeat of the female sex'. Property-owning men had to control the sexual lives of their wives and daughters in order to ensure their property was passed down without question.

One flaw in this theory is that it required humans not to have had any sort of family before class society. To fill in this hole, Engels followed Morgan in imagining a stage of 'primitive communism', when every adult had sex with every other adult. This was a common fantasy among male scholars, particularly Victorian clergymen.

In part, it was produced by reading reports about people with far more sexual freedom, and the scholars found it hard to imagine how that would work without a sexual free-for-all. But the idea of the communist family also allowed *the* family to begin with class society. We now know that there were all sorts of families before class, but not that sort.

The second flaw was that Engels' theory was an explanation of the reason for sexism among the propertied. Engels and Marx both thought that peasants, because they had claims to land, had been deeply influenced by property sexism. Both Engels and Marx assumed that 'the family' would disappear among workers under capitalism in the not-too-distant future, because they had no property. This did not happen. Look around you. The fact that it did not indicates something wrong with the theory.

All of that said, we think, Morgan and Engels were right about one big thing: gendered inequality began with class society. But Engels' explanation of how that worked did not hold water.

*Anti-Racist Anthropology: How We Move With, but Beyond, Engels*

It has been said so often that it has become a cliché, that anthropology developed as the handmaiden of colonialism. But it's not true. Or, rather, it was true of the anthropology of Tylor, Morgan and, unfortunately, Engels. But between 1908 and 1922 the mainstream of anthropology changed decisively. The central mission of anthropology became to rubbish the central ideology of colonialism—racism.

In the United States the charge was led by Franz Boas and his students. Boas was a socialist and committed his life to fighting racism. Bronislaw Malinowski was a more moderate radical, but his life's work was demonstrating that the colonised natives were as intelligent and emotionally complex as anyone else. From the 1920s on, anthropology was associated with sexual radicalism, primarily through the work of Malinowski and of Boas's student, Margaret Mead. Boas, Malinowski, Mead and their colleagues rejected the idea of stages of evolution, which they felt were irretrievably contaminated by racism.

Just as important, anthropologists simultaneously developed the method of fieldwork, spending at least a year with the group they studied, (ideally) learning the language, and participating in the round of native social life. And they listened to what the natives said and how they explained the world. As this method was extended to non-colonised countries, it remained a method of studying society from the bottom up, prioritising the point of view of ordinary people and how they saw themselves and the society in which they lived. Both the method and the politics of the discipline were against the prevailing hierarchy.

Anthropologists were not, by and large, open enemies of colonialism. Those among them who were, like the former Communist organisers Hortense Powdermaker and Meyer Fortes, or the Indian National Congress activist Verrier Elwin, were often denied permission to do fieldwork. At the other end of the spectrum, a few anthropologists did what was then called 'applied anthropology' and would now be called 'development work'. Some missionaries were also anthropologists. But most anthropologists looked down on both development workers and missionaries as agents of colonial authority.

Since the 1970s anti-racism has also ceased to be the raison d'être of anthropology. On the one hand, being against racism has become an accepted part of all liberal thought, so anthropology does not stand out. On the other hand, the old ideas of white superiority have been repackaged in the language of modernisation, development, secularism, cosmopolitanism, good governance, empowering women, and opposing terrorism. But in one important way the method makes the discipline radical—we are still studying up from below and listening to the words and explanations of the oppressed.

Anthropologists opposed to colonialism and racism discarded with contempt the idea of stages of development. This was an important step forward. But with that, there are three aspects of Marx and Engels' method we badly want to hang onto. The first is it focuses on the development of the productive forces over time. Empires rise and fall. Ruling classes build states, and ruled classes overthrow them. Resistance by the oppressed can delay the march of progress for centuries. But over the long haul, over timescales of many centuries, the technological development of productive forces has moved in one direction. The main reason is weapons. The ruling class that can extract a larger surplus can build larger armies with better weapons.

# WHY MEN?

In art, or music or dance, one era is not superior to another. But when it comes to killing, the Nazi concentration camps, the Dresden firestorm and the atom bombs at Hiroshima and Nagasaki represent enormous 'progress' compared to bows and arrows.

These improvements in violence are in part a matter of technology. In part they are a result of economic wealth. And in part they are a result of the ability to organise the delivery of death in complex social ways. Over the long term, those states that can kill the most efficiently, the fastest, and on the largest scale, become dominant powers. The death states dominate more and more of the world, until now they rule all of us.

The second idea we want to hang onto is the idea that the quest for surplus, and for weapons, drives the development of technology. These technological changes change the way people work, and therefore the ways society is organised. Class struggle is always with us, and changes in work and technology change those class struggles. But those struggles are not simply continual re-enactments of an endless cycle. Those class struggles change the society, and the system of classes.

Finally, we want to hang onto Marx and Engels' idea about the origins and future of humanity. The evidence is now clear. We did begin equal. And the development of capitalism has provided us with a new kind of class society. Working-class people are the first oppressed class to be concentrated in great cities, in large workplaces, educated and literate, aware of the whole world. In these new circumstances lies the possibility of returning to a world of equals. Only a possibility, of course. The evidence for pessimism, and for despair, is very strong, and all around us. But the possibility is there.

The reality of an egalitarian past and the possibility of an egalitarian future, however, do not require us to believe in morally charged stages of social evolution.

## The Dawn of Everything

Before we move on from the radical apologists for inequality, there is one more rationalisation of it that we need to address, and it comes from an unexpected corner. Any radical history of the origins of our species has also to pay attention to David Graeber and David Wengrow's recent book, *The Dawn of Everything: A New History of Humanity*. Their book is energetic, committed, kaleidoscopic, but also deeply flawed.

Their book presents us with a problem, because it is also in several key respects the opposite of this book. We have written at length about the book elsewhere. Here, it is enough to summarise briefly some of the issues that such projects—theirs and ours—pose, and how it is possible to arrive at very different conclusions.[12]

In the final paragraph of their book, Graeber and Wengrow set out clearly where they stand. They write:

> When, for example, a study that is rigorous in every other respect begins from the unexamined assumption that there is some 'original' form of human society; that its nature was fundamentally good or evil; that a time before inequality and political awareness existed; that something happened to change all this; that 'civilization' and 'complexity' always come at the price of human freedoms; that participatory democracy is natural in small groups but cannot possibly scale up to anything like a city or a nation state.
>
> We know, now, that we are in the presence of myths.[13]

So here our myth-busters, Graeber and Wengrow, are saying the opposite of the journey we have travelled over the first three parts of this book. They say that there was no original form of human society; no time before inequality and political awareness; that nothing happened to change things; that civilisation and complexity do not limit human freedom; and that participatory democracy can be practised as part of cities and states.

Such categorical statements, stated so boldly, make their claims to have written a new human history attractive. But there are two stumbling blocks. First, the very arguments they make are at odds with their own political project. Second, the evidence does not fit what they are trying to do.

Two of the key questions of our age are: how do we have a social justice revolution in our present world? And what can we learn from the history of our species that will help us go beyond this impasse?

These questions have exercised serious thinkers and activists throughout history. And now in the face of global warming, we need compelling answers urgently. These are questions Graeber and Wengrow also ask and this is surely why the book has caught people's attention.

There is, however, a third question most of us ask: how did human society become so grossly unequal?

Surprisingly, Graeber and Wengrow are not interested in this question. They say so explicitly: their first chapter is entitled 'Farewell to Humanity's Childhood: Or, why this is not a book about the origins of inequality'.[14]

One of the central arguments of their book is that inequality, hierarchy and violence have always been possible ways of organising any human society. There was no time, they say, before inequality. And although they use the words 'equality' and 'egalitarian' a good deal, they claim that equality is an empty concern, a fairy story, and to speak of an 'egalitarian society' is to say nothing.

There is an odd spin to all this.

Graeber and Wengrow ignore the new remarkable scholarship that describes the adaptation, or ecological niche, our primate ancestors and early humans found for themselves by becoming equal. This leaves Graeber and Wengrow either indifferent to or in disagreement with the classic anarchist and Marxist view that because humans had once been 'good' and equal, there was hope we could be so again. It is a curious place for them to fetch up. However, it is important to leave this debate behind. It is not about whether early humans were innately good or evil, but about what the science suggests actually happened.

The point being that Graeber and Wengrow are trying to fend off the argument that once inequality appeared as a result of farming, urban life and economic complexity, there was—there is—no hope of changing the world. Graeber and Wengrow resist this argument about farming, and clearly hope change is possible. And it becomes clear their enemy is not inequality, it is the state.

The question they ask is: how did we come to be dominated by authoritarian, bureaucratic, centralised states? And though inequalities of colonialism, slavery, classism, racism and sexism crop up throughout the book, these are not their central concern.

The political argument Graeber and Wengrow make is that people—from the beginning of time—have always been able to choose between domination and freedom. For them, people can choose to escape what they call the 'small-scale' stuckness of state control and become 'free people'.

They show little interest in either the environmental or technical limits on forms of social organisation. Indeed, they associate ecological and environmental thinking with Marxism, and therefore tyranny. For them, in short, people make history in circumstances of their own choosing. The payoff of this free-wheeling anarchist position is that it allows them to argue that, with political will, we can have a revolution and a society run by popular assemblies working through consensus.

All of which sounds excellent, and liberatory. We are not objecting to their anarchist politics, but to their cavalier use of the evidence and to the fact that their argument is deeply contradictory and conservative.

They say almost nothing about the vast literature on human evolution, aside from brief sideswipes at Hrdy and Boehm. They are not interested in the literature, because they wish to argue that inequality has always been part of the human condition and reading that literature would destabilise their position. They argue that hunting and gathering societies too were unequal, by relying heavily on the exceptions, of peoples relying on great marine surpluses, such as the Kwakiutl of the Pacific coast of North America, while paying little attention to the contrary examples. It's worth unpacking briefly just one instance of this poor use of sources.

Graeber and Wengrow describe the Calusa of Florida as 'a non-agricultural people'.[15] In one sense, these too were fisherfolk with ruling chiefs, warriors, class inequality, slavery, expensive war canoes and a reliance on fishing for sea mammals, alligators and large fish. But as Graeber and Wengrow acknowledge, the Calusa fisherfolk were the dominant group in a much larger polity. And as it happens, all the other groups were farmers, and they paid tribute to the Calusa rulers of large amounts of food, gold and enslaved European and African captives. That food enabled the Calusa elite, and 300 full-time warriors, to live without working. This was an agricultural class society.[16]

They are also generally uninterested in gender. Because they assume that inequality has always been with us, they assume that

# WHY MEN?

inequality between women and men is also innate. They are also uninterested in class, or class struggle.

These may seem harsh judgements. Indeed, we were astonished to find that *The Dawn of Everything* is really quite a conservative book. It is authority Graeber and Wengrow hate, not exploitation. This priority prevents them from acknowledging that authority has not just prevailed during the course of human history, but has been continually manufactured, through the invention of 'natural' differences and the violent enforcement of hierarchy.

In the face of this long and ever-shifting elite project, inequality has not been so easy to reject. We have seen in Part Three the high price paid by those offering resistance. And, if the project is not recognised and discussed, then there is no recognition or discussion of the different human ways of organising that came before it, ways for which we do have scientific evidence as we saw in Part One.

So we appreciate Graeber and Wengrow's wish for social justice and a better world. However, we are acutely aware of what they ignore or avoid: the scholarship and political implications of the new materials on evolution, class and gendered inequality and the material conditions of the planet and climate change. These are considerable omissions—chasms, actually—and in this respect, their book too becomes an apology for inequality.

# 19

# CHAGNON, PINKER AND WAR

In the 1970s, evolutionary psychologists returned to Darwin's idea of sexual selection. And more recent versions of Darwin's myth about human warfare also came from evolutionary psychology. More recent versions of Darwin's myth about the origins of human warfare come from evolutionary psychology. The late anthropologist Napoleon Chagnon and the psychologist Steven Pinker have been the key figures in developing this view. Each presents a fantasy family to go with their narrative of warfare. These fantasies have their roots in Darwin's work, but their differences with Darwin are just as important as his legacy. These are fantasies, not of the nineteenth century, but of our own era, and they are with us today. And as we shall see, they have had a central place in the ideological undergirding of war in the twenty-first century.

From the mid-1960s, Napoleon Chagnon did fieldwork with Yanomamo people in Venezuela. Like the Piaroa and the Pemon, the Yanomamo live along the border between Brazil and Venezuela, but in places even more isolated from the global system. They too live by slash-and-burn agriculture, although in their case bananas are their staple crop.

Chagnon started his fieldwork in 1964. In 1968 his *Yąnomamö: The Fierce People* was published by Holt, Rinehart and Winston in their series of short books designed to provide ethnographic examples for first-year anthropology courses in the United States. *The Fierce People* was by far the most successful of the dozens of case studies in the series, allegedly selling nearly a million copies.[1]

Students loved Chagnon's book. A cynic might say that it provided white Americans with the image of indigenous Americans that they had always wanted: as primitive and psychotic rebels against civilisation. But it is a cheap dig at the American college students who grew up in the 1950s watching John Wayne and the cowboy-and-Indian films of Hollywood's so-called Golden Age.

Chagnon also introduced an important intellectual argument in the book. In 1968, the counterculture in the United States, from flower power to the movement against the Vietnam War, was at its height. Chagnon begged to differ. He said that warfare was central to human prehistory, and he had a highly gendered evolutionary theory to explain why.

In *The Fierce People*, Chagnon described the Yanomamo he studied in the 1960s, saying they had very high rates of killing, and much raiding and warfare between villages. Men did the fighting, and Yanomamo men were aggressive. Men dominated women, and strong men dominated the weaker ones. There was a special ritual for men who had at least had a hand in killing someone in warfare. The men of that status, Chagnon said, were likely to marry more women and father more children than others. His data showed that men who had been involved in killing had four times as many children as other men. Four times!

Evolution, Chagnon said, encouraged warfare, male anger, male aggression, male domination, and competition between men. Like many anthropologists, Chagnon generalised from the people he studied to the human condition. He argued that the isolated Yanomamo lived much as our Stone Age ancestors had lived. His data on their customs, he said, showed that Stone Age men had also evolved to be violent, aggressive and competitive. Sexual selection moulded such men.[2]

The reader will have noticed that this bears a close resemblance to Darwin's model in *The Descent of Man*. Chagnon was of course aware of this. So were the many evolutionary psychologists who were impressed by his work. There were differences, however. Darwin's insistence on the superior races driving out and exterminating the primitive races had disappeared. So had Darwin's idea that primitive groups fought wars to win control of land. For Chagnon, the evolution of warfare could be explained by sexual competition between men to father children. For him, that was a sufficient explanation, and nothing more was needed.

There were political reasons for dropping Darwin's other ideas. By the 1960s, the explanation that civilised races naturally exterminated lesser races was no longer politically acceptable in an anthropology classroom. It was far too close to what had happened to native peoples in the United States, people had not forgotten the Holocaust and it was not all that different from the war in Vietnam.

Darwin's theory that economic conflict over land was one of the causes of human warfare was, however, acceptable in an anthropology classroom. Indeed, many anthropologists argued just that, saying that slash-and-burn farmers often fought wars for land. Harold Brookfield and Paula Brown had published a book in 1963 showing, quite convincingly, that Chimbu slash-and-burn farmers in highland New Guinea were more likely to go to war with their neighbours if they had a high population density, making an expansion of territory beneficial to the group.[3]

But for Chagnon, and for most evolutionary psychologists since, economic explanations for war have been unacceptable. On the face of it this seems strange until one remembers that an important part of the political project of evolutionary psychology is to make war natural and inevitable, and to blame the people who fight and get killed, not the people who push them into war. If men are understood to be fundamentally warlike, this discredits anti-war arguments that empires go to war to control resources and human labour.

So Napoleon Chagnon and the evolutionary psychologists who followed him quietly dropped the genocidal and economic explanations for warfare, but they kept Darwin's model of sexual selection. Saying warfare was all about competition between men and domination of women did serious political work. It combined a sexist fantasy with a fantasy of economic competition. At another level, it was an answer to wings of both the anti-Vietnam War movement and women's liberation because it was essentialist and put the blame for war and inequality on innately aggressive men. Throughout the 1970s and 1980s, evolutionary psychologists developed a routine that went: 'It is a shame that human nature is like that, and of course we don't approve of behaving like that now. That's why civilisation is such a good thing.'

Throughout the 1970s and 1980s Chagnon's book did well. It fitted with politics of neoliberalism that were being pushed so hard at the time. But then Chagnon and his acolytes ran into two major obstacles. The first was scholarly, the second political.

First, the scholarly obstacle: the anthropologist Brian Ferguson published *Yanomami Warfare*. Ferguson has devoted his life to developing an anthropology of war. His book on the Yanomamo is his masterpiece. It takes apart Chagnon's homogenising account. Ferguson noted that the Yanomamo of a particular region might go through a period of terrifying warfare, yet in other regions, or the same region at other times, people led largely peaceful lives. So Ferguson insisted that each particular outbreak of warfare required investigation. And when he looked, what he found were steel axes.[4]

We have already seen what a difference steel axes made in New Guinea. Ferguson understood they made the same difference to Yanomamo men who cut down trees for slash and burn. One man could clear five times as much land with one steel axe or machete. But first, that man had to get hold of the axe or the machete.

Until the middle of the twentieth century the Yanomamo had coped with white settler society by avoiding it. They moved further into the forest, up the rivers and into the hills. But by the middle of the twentieth century, white settlers were closing in. The Yanomamo on the edges of the forest began trading with the whites, and with their native neighbours, in any way they could to obtain goods, and above all, steel axes. When they got axes, they began to trade them to the villages further up the river. And because men were supposed to give gifts to the parents of their wives, the upriver people encouraged their daughters to marry downriver in the hope of receiving steel axes as gifts.

Ferguson found there was a time in the 1950s when the men in the area where Chagnon studied would never be apart from their steel axes. Each man had one axe if he was lucky. Every minute he was awake, he held that axe in his hand, or put it down right next to him. When he slept in the hammock, he kept the steel blade on his chest. By the time Chagnon arrived in 1964, the Yanomamo had more axes, and were not as vigilant, but axes still mattered more than any other object in their world.

Ferguson painstakingly researched every account he could find of a war or a raid among the many scattered Yanomamo communities in Venezuela and Brazil. He found many had been reported by missionaries and anthropologists. Ferguson located the people they wrote about on maps, and worked out the topography, and what was happening nearby. He found that warfare exploded when missionaries, or indeed any group of white people with steel axes, shotguns and other tools, moved into a region. Moreover, warfare radiated outward along the trade routes. The people upriver were raiding to get axes, and the people downriver were deterring anyone who tried to interfere with their control of the new trade. For a few years fighting was bitter and endemic. Then as people acquired enough steel tools, the raiding began to die down.

Ferguson's book is more than 400 pages long. It is detailed, and utterly convincing. He also established that the region Chagnon studied was racked by warfare and he found that Chagnon himself was a destabilising source of steel axes in a way that no missionary had ever been. The reason for this was that Chagnon's funding came from the geneticist James Neel, who in turn had a grant from the American nuclear research programme. 'Neel was best known for his genetic studies of survivors of the Hiroshima and Nagasaki bombings. But he was interested in indigenous populations, in part because, having never been exposed to atomic radiation, they could provide a base line for comparison.'[5] Neel also wanted to prove that village chiefs had superior genes that allowed them to dominate other men and have more children. To prove this genetically, he needed detailed information from Chagnon on genealogies and raids, but also blood samples. As a condition of the funding, Chagnon, Neel and their colleagues took blood samples from at least sixty different Yanomamo communities. And to get people to participate, Chagnon and the others offered axes as gifts to each community, gifts that created havoc along established trade routes and unleashed war.

Part of the story is actually in Chagnon's original book. *The Fierce People* tells the story of Chagnon's biggest confrontation with the most aggressive warrior in the community where he usually stayed. The man often begged Chagnon for steel. Now he was threatening Chagnon with a beating or death if he persisted in giving steel to other communities. Chagnon reports that he faced the man down.

Clearly Chagnon was culpable, but Ferguson also had another important intellectual point to make. Chagnon had written that men who had been involved in killing someone in a raid had four times as many children on average as men who had never killed. Ferguson pointed out that men who had killed were likely to be older. Everywhere in the world, older men have had more children on average than younger men. Chagnon was comparing men who had killed to all men of all ages, including men who had not yet married. Ferguson looked at the numbers again and compared men who had killed to men their own age who had not killed, and the difference in children went down from four times to twice.

Then Ferguson noted that Chagnon was only counting living men. What about the men of the same generation who had died, especially those who had died in war? They had few children. Ferguson added that small number to the number of children born to the successful killers who survived. That gave Ferguson a total for bold warriors. In these two groups combined, the average number of children born to a warrior was comparable to the average number of children born to a third group of men who went to war but were never involved in killing anyone. Hanging back from battle appeared to be a reasonable evolutionary strategy.

But, you might object, the men who were killed were probably weaklings. After all, Chagnon and others believed that evolution was favouring the strong. But as Ferguson points out, the accounts of Yanomamo society by missionaries, anthropologists and the Yanomamo activist Davi Kopenawa, all agree that revenge for a death was the most common motive admitted for warfare. And raids were targeted. People were trying to kill men who had killed others. Which, everyone agreed, meant that a fierce warrior was unlikely to survive to old age.[6]

Ferguson's takedown of Chagnon was devastating, detailed and forensic. Yet initially, it had little influence among evolutionary psychologists or on a more general public. That changed some five years later when, by 2000, the political obstacles to Chagnon's work came into play.

The underlying cause of the change was that, by the turn of the millennium, three groups of people had grown furious with Chagnon. The Yanomamo themselves were the first group. Those who knew and had worked with Chagnon hated him. They regarded him as a bully, and dangerous, and told everyone who was willing to listen that they never wanted to see that man again.[7]

The second group were the Salesian Catholic missionaries who worked among the Yanomamo and listened to their parishioners. They appealed to the authorities, and Chagnon was refused permission to do any more fieldwork in Venezuela.

Stung, Chagnon formed an alliance with Carlos Brewer and Cecilia Matos to campaign for an autonomous national park in Venezuela. Brewer was the most powerful of the large-scale gold miners in the country, and Matos was the lover of President Pérez.

The Salesian missionaries alleged that Chagnon aimed to administer the national park with all the powers of a state. The park was to be the size of Britain and would be full of Yanomamo. Meanwhile, they said, Chagnon's partners would get their hands on the gold and timber.[8]

This provoked a national outcry. In November of 1992 Hugo Chávez led an attempted coup against President Pérez. Four of the Air Force officers involved in the coup said that one of their main motivations was to get rid of Brewer, Matos and Chagnon. Several months later, 300 delegates at Venezuela's First National Congress of Amazon Indians marched through the streets chanting 'Brewer Carías and Chagnon out of Yanomami territory.' Anthropologists, scientists, ecologists and many official bodies spoke out, and there were protests in Caracas supported by the Catholic Church.

The park was cancelled. Matos and Brewer fled the country to avoid arrest for corruption, and Chagnon was thrown out of the country.[9]

The third group furious with Chagnon were Brazilian anthropologists. Among them were anthropologists infuriated by Chagnon's categorical statements about the grossly unequal treatment of women in Yanomamo, though those who sought to counter Chagnon's misogyny were mostly ignored. However, other anthropologists were not. This had to do with the situation of the Yanomamo living in Brazil. In the 1980s there was a military dictatorship in Brazil. Part of the generals' plan for developing the country was to exploit the country's rich resources, and above all, the enormous Amazon rainforest. As part of that plan, the generals encouraged gold miners to flood into Yanomamo territory.[10]

When we say gold miners, you may think of vast corporate projects, of 'extractivism'. These were not those miners. Like the

Pemon miners mentioned in Chapter 11, these were desperately poor men who panned the rivers or dug holes with their picks. They used mercury to extract the gold from the dirt, and the mercury often drove them mad and killed them young. They were wild, and violent, and often raped as well. And they brought from the towns and cities disease which had not previously reached the Yanomamo. Almost any common or garden virus or bacterium could become an epidemic in the isolated native communities.

Everyone involved, the gold miners, the Brazilian army officers, the Yanomamo and the anthropologists, knew all this. But the military government allowed the gold miners into Yanomamo territory, hoping to open it up to far wider penetration. At the same time the Brazilian government excluded journalists and anthropologists from the territory, to prevent news of killings getting out. News of one massacre, with more than a dozen dead, did reach the newspapers in 1993. The Brazilian anthropologist Alcida Ramos had lived with the Yanomamo, and now she was frantic. Ramos began organising other anthropologists, and they carried the controversy into the media.[11]

In this situation the right-wing media in Brazil carried reports on Chagnon's work to show that the Yanomamo were a fierce people who, by implication, had brought havoc upon themselves. Ramos and the others begged Chagnon to contradict this use of his work. *O Globo*, one of Brazil's leading newspapers, ran an interview with Chagnon where he repeated all his talking points about the fierce people. The Brazilian anthropologists grew more enraged.[12]

Of course, none of this proves that Chagnon was wrong. He was arguing that humanity had evolved to reward aggressive, competitive, bullying men. The fact that he was behaving like a successful bully himself did not invalidate his theory. But Ferguson's measured intellectual objections did disprove what he was saying. And there is a wider lesson here. Ferguson did not disagree with Chagnon by arguing with his methodology, his logic or his theory. Ferguson disagreed with Chagnon's mythologising by looking at all the available evidence, painstakingly, detail by detail, to make sense of it. He did not disprove Chagnon's explanation but left it behind by providing a better explanation. And the lesson was repeated several times over as a great weight of further evidence soon followed.[13]

The revisionism from the academy now combined with the public pressure converging on Chagnon's work thanks to his three groups of political opponents. Together, this turning of scholarly and public tide would see his theory lose its popularity.

The next stage of the battle began with Patrick Tierney's book *Darkness in El Dorado*, published in 2000. Tierney was a journalist. He had read Ferguson's book and talked to all Chagnon's enemies. Tierney's book focused on Chagnon's reprehensible behaviour. He told the stories about the national park, the Brazilian interview, the ugly stories of bullying, and a story of Chagnon taking a war party upriver in his speedboat to raid a sleeping enemy village. And Tierney made three even more devastating allegations. He said that the travels of Chagnon and Neel had spread a deadly measles epidemic deep into Yanomamo territory, that they knew they were doing this, and that Neel, who was a doctor, would not take time from his research to treat the victims.

These were serious accusations, and they were news. *The New Yorker* ran an excerpt, and *The New York Times* commissioned a book review. A good review in the Sunday book section of *The New York Times* was the biggest boost Tierney's (or any) book could get at that time, as most local libraries in the country would order a copy of books well reviewed there.

Fourteen years later, John Horgan, the man who wrote *The Times* review, wrote:

> I was still working on my review of *Darkness* when I received emails from five prominent scholars: Richard Dawkins, Edward Wilson, Steven Pinker, Daniel Dennett and Marc Hauser. Although each wrote separately, the emails were obviously coordinated. All had learned (none said exactly how, although I suspected via a friend of mine with whom I discussed my review) that I was reviewing *Darkness* for the *Times*. Warning that a positive review might ruin my career, the group urged me either to denounce *Darkness* or to withdraw as a reviewer.[14]

Wilson was the founder of sociobiology, the future evolutionary psychology, which viewed both competitive selfishness in humans, as well as differences between men and women, as 'natural' results of evolution. Pinker was a leading psychologist, and Dawkins had invented the selfish gene. Dennett, a cognitive scientist and philosopher, subscribed to a form of Social Darwinian fundamentalism which viewed scientific atheism as the highest form of consciousness. These were heavyweights. The fifth, Marc Hauser, a primatologist, later resigned after an internal investigation at Harvard found him 'solely responsible for eight instances of scientific misconduct'.[15]

Whether or not Horgan was right that the scholars compared notes on their letters warning him off supporting Tierney's accusations, their intervention suggests they understood the importance to evolutionary psychology of defending Chagnon. Sociobiology was then at the height of its power. This may have misled Wilson, Pinker, Dawkins and the others into assuming that the sort of power they had over other scholars' careers extended beyond the academy. But they were soon to find that the balance of power was shifting. And the implied threat to Horgan's career was a mistake. It made him angry, and as he says, he wrote a more favourable review of Tierney's book than he would otherwise have done.[16]

Here is the place to recall the story about Frans de Waal and the toilet frog. De Waal was the chimpanzee specialist who spent the 1980s and 1990s stubbornly clinging on like a toilet frog while the mainstream of biology spewed filth, until after 2000 sentiment within the discipline shifted. Where students had once calmly accepted the viciously cynical quote from Michael Ghiselin— 'Scratch an altruist and watch a hypocrite bleed'—they now found the quote repellent.

Tierney's book was published in 2000, the year de Waal's students turned. Terry Turner was a man of the left, and a respected anthropologist of Brazil. He had read galley proofs of the book and talked to Tierney and the Brazilian anthropologists. Turner wrote a formal letter to the American Anthropological Association, warning them of what was coming, and asking the AAA ethics committee to investigate Chagnon. The association of Brazilian anthropologists wrote asking the same. The executive of the AAA appointed a committee to investigate, but the anthropologists appointed to the committee were sympathetic to sociobiology and Chagnon's work. That committee duly reported that there was no case to answer.

Five years earlier that would probably have been that. But the political sensibilities among young Americans were changing fast.

The turning point was the protests of the World Trade conference in Seattle in 1999, when trade unionists and environmentalists—the

'Teamsters and Turtles'—blockaded and closed down the conference. After Seattle, activists, including anthropologists and others fighting for the rights of indigenous peoples in South America and elsewhere, joined protests in search for an alternative global future.[17]

This meant that the next year when Turner convened a panel on Chagnon's work at that winter's annual conference of the AAA, the atmosphere was electric. Graduate students, especially, were outraged. Almost 200 anthropologists, mostly graduate students, wrote to the executive to demand a balanced committee and a new investigation. The executive felt they had no choice but to comply.

The new committee investigated the allegations. They ruled that Neel and Chagnon had not spread the measles infection. The virus had already been moving up the rivers when the researchers arrived. And they said that although Neel had not devoted all his resources to treating the sick, he had treated many of them. Terry Turner, who had supported Tierney and the Brazilians, then went and read the field diaries kept by Neel, who had died in the meantime. Turner said that on the evidence of those diaries Neel had done what he could.

However, the new committee also said that all the other charges against Chagnon, including ones of fomenting warfare, transporting war parties, conspiring with gold miners and the rest, seemed true that he had done those things, and they were not things a professional anthropologist should do. Chagnon claimed that his reputation had been restored, although the committee's report was hardly a vindication. Chagnon was not destroyed, but he was wounded.

The toilet frogs were crawling out of the bowl. Still, the struggle to lay Chagnon's ideas definitively to rest, especially in public consciousness, was never going to be easy. And in this century indigenous resistance has continued and become increasingly visible. Mining, disease and the threat to the Amazonia rainforest are now regularly reported outside Latin America as international news.[18]

*Steven Pinker: Repackaging War for the Twenty-First Century*

Chagnon's great strength, and his great weakness, lay in his sexual politics. The old fantasy of aggressive, warlike men killing other men and then bedding their half-naked women still held a deep appeal for many men, successful or otherwise. And it sounded scientific. It also played into the fantasies of many successful academics, fighting the battle of ideas to win the right to sexually harass their graduate students. And, in the age of neoliberalism, it appealed more widely to professional men in an enhanced world of corporate competition.

As neoliberal economics took hold, the world of women's work was also changing, as increasing numbers became high-income professionals—academics, lawyers, executives. With women in positions of power inside corporate culture and graduate professions, sexual politics shifted. Open, combative sexism was still obvious in many quarters, but it played less well in the universities.

After 2000 Frans de Waal no longer felt like a toilet frog for defending human decency in front of biology students, in part because his students had changed. They were now far more aware of how racism and sexism worked, of the competitive environment in which they lived, and they were critical of capitalism and war.

In the midst of this political shift, Steven Pinker repackaged ideas about male aggression, violence and war from evolutionary psychology, and presented an argument that many people liked.

Pinker was a psychologist at Harvard, and already widely respected for his work on the brain and language. In 2007, Pinker gave a popular TED Talk about war, and its 'natural' place in our understanding of the world.[19]

Pinker held onto the idea from evolutionary psychology that primitive men had been by nature violent and warlike. It was the sort of evolutionary explanation Chagnon had provided, but Pinker did not emphasise the sexual politics. Instead, Pinker added another ingredient to the mix, an ingredient both old and new. He argued emphatically that humanity was becoming progressively less violent and more peaceable and prosperous. And he introduced his list—Pinker's List, as it is known—of examples from prehistory which are meant to prove that early on deadly intergroup violence was ubiquitous. And it was a part of our evolutionary history which we have left behind.

Or maybe not.

Shortly after he was elected, President Obama was nominated for the Nobel Peace Prize—for his 'extraordinary efforts to strengthen international cooperation among peoples'. And in December 2009, President Obama gave a short speech in Oslo Town Hall as he accepted the Nobel Peace Prize. He began by acknowledging that it was strange to accept a peace prize when he was 'the Commander-in-Chief of the military of a nation in the midst of two wars'. One of them, the Iraq War, was 'winding down'. 'The Afghan war', he said, was 'a conflict that America did not seek':

> Still, we are at war, and I'm responsible for the deployment of thousands of young Americans to battle in a distant land. Some will kill, and some will be killed. And so I come here with an acute sense of the costs of armed conflict—and filled with difficult questions about the relationship between war and peace, and our effort to replace one with the other.
>
> Now these questions are not new. War, in one form or another, appeared with the first man. At the dawn of history, its morality was not questioned; it was simply a fact, like drought or disease—the manner in which tribes and then civilizations sought power and settled their differences.[20]

Pinker's book *The Better Angels of Our Nature: Why Violence Has Declined*, was published in 2011, two years after Obama's speech, and the book swiftly became influential. Pinker offers a theory of war for people who dislike war but want to support some wars. He makes three basic points. One is that 'war appeared with the first man'. The second is that 'at the dawn of history', the morality of war 'was not questioned'. The third is that people like 'us'—liberals—the products of the European Enlightenment—have been doing all we can to reduce violence. Primitive people, savages, non-Europeans were and are far more violent than 'us', the 'better angels of our nature' are winning.

\* \* \*

Pinker set out to prove this by surveying a vast amount of evidence from prehistory onwards. He sought to naturalise warfare and male violence. But his problem was that for almost all of human prehistory there is simply no evidence of warfare. Moreover, the reality is that the firepower of bombs dropped from aeroplanes simply dwarfs any alternative technology, and if you measure wars in terms of numbers of people killed, the American forces were more violent than their terrorist and Islamist enemies.

Jonathan Haas and Matthew Piscitelli published an important survey in 2013. They looked at every report they could find of human remains in Europe, western Asia and the Levant from the time before 10,000 years ago (8000 BCE). That is to say, before the invention of agriculture. Haas and Piscitelli counted 2,930 'skeletal remains' in over 400 different sites. They found only five sites with evidence of violent death. In four of them there was one skeleton with a projectile point embedded in the bone. But since there was only one individual in each case, it was certainly not evidence of the systematic killing of numbers of people of another group, aka war.[21]

The point is important. We are not arguing, and nor are Haas and Piscitelli, that there was no violence among prehistoric or pre-agricultural people. The argument is about warfare—collective deadly violence against other groups. In earlier chapters, we pointed to the importance of two kinds of violence among egalitarian hunter-gatherers. One was the collective execution of bullies; the other was mothers killing their new-born children. We think both behaviours are very old. And we have little doubt that there were other individual killings long before class society.

However, Haas and Piscitelli's survey did find one site with evidence of warfare. At Jebel Sahaba, in what is now the desert in Egypt, twenty-four out of the fifty-nine people in one graveyard were buried with projectile points embedded in or close to the skeleton. The date is about 14,000 to 12,000 years ago. This may be the earliest example of deaths from warfare anywhere in the world. As Brian Ferguson has pointed out, the dating is uncertain, and these people did not necessarily die at the same time. They may have been buried over decades or centuries. So it's possible this was not warfare. But, like Ferguson, we are inclined to see it as such.[22]

The existence of the graveyard suggests a permanent settlement. Jebel Sahaba was located near a large lake in the desert, and the local people appear to have been fisherfolk. We can't help thinking again of the Chumash, the Kwakiutl and the other fishing economies with class hierarchies on the Pacific coast of North America. One guess from the archaeologists is that fighting intensified as the bed of the Nile moved and the lake dried up. But no one really knows.[23]

## CHAGNON, PINKER AND WAR

Jebel Sahaba is exceptional. Take that one example away, and we have 2,871 known skeletal remains with no evidence of war over the period from 150,000 years ago to 10,000 years ago. Even if we include Jebel Sahaba, there is no evidence of warfare anywhere in Asia, Australia, the Levant or anywhere else before 14,000 years ago.

This is not evidence that war was unknown among hunter-gatherers. It is evidence that war was rare if it existed at all. It certainly was not normal. As Richard Lee says, *Homo sapiens* lived in peace for 7,000 generations—generations are usually counted as thirty years each, which means Lee was looking back over 210,000 years.[24]

Haas and Piscitelli point out another striking feature of the archaeological record:

> Throughout Europe and large tracts of Asia all the way to Siberia, the time period from about 40,000 years ago to 25,000 years ago was all characterized by the same material cultural tradition... If you cross over into the Americas, you find a similar pattern of continent-wide material culture during the period from 13,500 to 13,000 years ago, when all peoples across the entire continent of North America were producing remarkably similar and distinct 'Clovis' projectile points. In South America all peoples were producing similar 'Fishtail' points. Everyone, across continental spaces and over long stretches of time, was making the same kinds of tools. There is a glaring lack of any kind of analogue in the [more recent/modern] ethnographic record for this kind of continental distribution of remarkably similar material culture. All of the issues of group boundaries, 'traditional enemies', different ethnicities and territoriality are simply incompatible with a model of open continent-wide social networks.[25]

The point Haas and Piscitelli are making is important. They are arguing that during periods of continental peace, technologies become homogenised because people were mobile and could safely travel, visit and trade over long distances. The examples mentioned above are from Europe and the Americas. Another striking example is the homogeneous technologies across Australia, suggesting there were long periods of peace across that continent too.

That's it, really. The evidence is in. With one very late exception in Egypt, there was almost no warfare among pre-agricultural humanity. Everyone who has looked at the evidence knows this. So Pinker ignored that evidence. And it gets worse.

In the 2007 TED Talk, Pinker showed a slide with a table of deaths in warfare. The table shows the death rate for men in warfare among nine groups: the Jivaro, the Yanomamo-Shamatari, the Mae Enga, the Dugum Dani, the Murngin, the Yanomamo-Nomowei, the Huli, the Gebusi, and the US and Europe in the twentieth century. Pinker says the table shows 'the percentage of male deaths due to warfare in a number of foraging or hunting and gathering societies'. The rates range from 15% of men dead in warfare among the Gebusi to an astonishing 60% of men's deaths among the Jivaro. By contrast, Pinker says, 0.03% of men died in warfare in America and Europe in the twentieth century, including in both World Wars. His point is that 'we' (meaning Western industrial capitalist societies) are doing much better than our ancestors did. However, his evidence is not a study of ancestral, early humans, but a comparison between present-day Western societies and present-day indigenous communities.[26]

Among the groups named in this list, in fact only the Murngin of Australia were hunter-gatherers. The others were all slash-and-burn agriculturalists mostly from New Guinea.[27] Pinker's sleight of hand here is often used by evolutionary biologists. To Pinker, these people are taken to be like prehistoric men because they are what used to be called 'primitive' peoples. That is, until recently, they were 'Stone Age' and they fought with bows and arrows, stone-tipped spears and clubs. Therefore, to Pinker they were just like hunter-gatherers. And therefore, they were hunter-gatherers. And therefore, they were like 'Early Man'.

This is the same slippage that Chagnon makes when he says that the Yanomamo he studied are a model for what our hunter-gatherer, early human ancestors were like. Yet the people Chagnon studied grew bananas as their staple crop.

Pinker's other line of argument is to look to the archaeological evidence for warfare. However, he does not look to the evidence before 12,000 years ago, for as we have seen, that will not support his case. Instead, he introduces data from more recent class societies. In *The Better Angels of Our Nature* Pinker has a list of twenty-one different sites where archaeologists have dug up the remains of people killed in war in the Neolithic period—the last seven-odd millennia of the Stone Age, after the invention of agriculture.

Brian Ferguson has taken a good long look at these twenty-one sites, from which Pinker estimates the deaths from warfare at between 15% and 25% of all adult men.

Ferguson again. He's wonderful.

'Given all the publicity for the book, it will surely be widely read', Ferguson writes as he winnows the chaff from Pinker's 'Death List' with exquisite care. He discards the three cases of double counting of reports of the same bodies and one case where there is no violent death. He says the three cases where there is only one violent death are evidence of killing, not war. The same is true of the one case where only two people were killed.[28]

Ferguson then goes through the rest of the list, case by case. He looks at Jebel Sahaba in Nubia, perhaps the earliest example of warfare we have and which we have already seen is the bloody exception. He considers two sites along the Dnieper River in what is now Ukraine dating from perhaps 8000 BCE, where there is evidence of some twenty-four violent deaths and which are 'the earliest European locations showing signs of war'.[29] One by one he takes apart the extraordinarily detailed evidence of stone weaponry and skeletal trauma. There is a site in what is now France where some twenty-five individuals, sixteen of them adults, may have died violently. The people there seem to have been complex hunter-gatherers who 'have a well-established reputation of being prone to war, in sharp contrast to nomadic hunter-gatherers'. Then Ferguson looks at burials from the Pacific coast of North America, among groups like the Chumash, with war, chiefs and slaves. He also considers the Crow Creek and Norris Farm massacres from the North American plains about 700 years ago.[30] In the chapter on Cahokia, we described something of the wars, class violence and tyrannies there at that time.

In the end, a third of Pinker's twenty-one cases Ferguson discards as irrelevant or mistaken, leaving fourteen examples 'which purportedly represent average war mortality among "prehistoric people"'. Such is Pinker's evidence that the previous 150,000-year period was far more bloody than the past fifty years in wars waged by the United States, China, the Soviet Union, Russia, France, Britain, Pakistan, India, Rwanda, South Africa and many others. And on the other side of the ledger, among peoples without agriculture, are the twenty-four bodies in a graveyard in Jebel Sahaba, and 150,000 years before that with no evidence of warfare.

As Ferguson writes of Pinker's list,

> Is this sample representative of war death rates among prehistoric populations? Hardly. It is a selective compilation of highly unusual cases, grossly distorting war's antiquity, and lethality. The elaborate caste of evolutionary and other theorizing that rises on this sample is built upon sand. Is there an alternative way of assessing the presence of war in prehistory, and evaluating whether making war is the expectable expression of evolved tendencies to kill? Yes. Is there archaeological evidence indicating war was absent in entire prehistoric regions and for millennia? Yes. The alternative and representative way to assess prehistoric war mortality is ... [by] considering whole archaeological records not selected violent cases. When that is done, with careful attention to types and vagaries of evidence, an entirely different story unfolds. War does not go forever backwards in time. It had a beginning. We are not hard-wired for war. We learn it.[31]

Almost everywhere in the archaeological digs where deaths from warfare are found after the invention of agriculture, there are earlier levels excavated where there is no evidence of warfare. Not everywhere, but almost everywhere. Then, at a certain time, there is suddenly considerable evidence of deaths in war. Ferguson asks why people began fighting wars, and he notices that two factors come up again and again: social inequality and population density. As far as we're concerned, the key is class inequality, and even that doesn't take away from our deep human disposition to equality and our determination to resist unfairness; it only makes resistance harder.

# ENVOI

During the time we've spent working towards this book, we've been doing other things as well. We spent four years looking after Jonathan's mother and then Nancy's stepfather in their old age. We also spent a great deal of time playing with and looking after our six grandchildren. And because we are political people, we've done a lot of climate activism as well.

Inevitably, our daily lives have influenced our writing. That is clear enough in our discussions of the importance of shared childcare and of love. And as we worked on this book, we could not avoid thinking about the links between human evolution and climate politics.

Our personal lives and our political ones come together in concern for our children and grandchildren. Much of our rage and fear about climate flows from our love for them. One fear is that they will die young. But even more we fear what they will have to see and to do in order to survive runaway climate change. And what they, and our species, will become.

Climate change is one reason our method in this book has been materialist. Indeed, we have been relentlessly, rigorously materialist and ecological. The whole book is, as you will have noticed, structured around the idea of adaptation. We began with the first great adaptation, how we became human by becoming equal.

By adaptation we mean the complex of a specific niche for a species in a wider ecology. That complex includes work, food, raising offspring, sex, gender and social relations. All of those things are material realities essential to survival. Love too is a material force in the world, and without it we die.

Then we moved on to the second great adaptation, the invention of class society. This was the consequence of a decisive change in the human ecological niche: the invention of agriculture and the domestication of animals.

# WHY MEN?

This was not an adaptation by all humanity at once. It was an adaptation, in many different times and places, by groups of people who banded together to gain control of more than their fair share of the food. But this adaptation, like the first one, led to changes for everyone involved in work, food, raising offspring, sex, gender and the social worlds in which people lived.

Now we face climate change. Once again, we will have to adapt to a fundamental change in our ecological place in the world. For the last two decades we have all waited for the market and the leaders of the world to begin that adaptation. During those twenty years the amount of greenhouse gases in the atmosphere has grown steadily. It has become clear that it will take a massive global movement to put into power governments who will do what has to be done.

Greta Thunberg summed it up in two tweets from the United Nations climate talks in Scotland in 2021. The first tweet was addressed to the leaders of the world, and said, 'Blah, blah, blah. Fuck you.'

The second tweet was addressed to the rest of us. She said, 'Uproot the system.'

That's the task ahead of us. It will be a great work of caring for each other and for all living things. It will also be a class struggle to change the priorities of human society. We may fail. And to become the people who can make that happen, we will have to change our whole adaptation. In trying to do that, we can take comfort and strength from the knowledge that the first great adaptation created a human nature that was egalitarian, sharing and kind. But we also need to remember that involved a constant collective effort to overturn the bullies.

The second great adaptation warns us that the needs of the majority will not necessarily triumph. But the long history of class society also teaches us that the bullies have met constant resistance, because a love of fairness and equality is also part of human nature.

# NOTE ON METHODS

In closing, we need to say a bit more about questions of method in studying gender, and to connect the ideas, events and expert findings discussed in the book.

Our approach to such very large questions has helped us to think clearly about what is happening and why, and about the 'what and why' of the history of ideas explaining human suffering, from the theories of biologists, archaeologists and anthropologists to the writing and reading of history. Our hope is that this approach will help readers to see themselves and the world around them within the arc of human history, and to fight for its future.

In the early 1970s Nancy was a passionate member of the London Women's Anthropology Group. The group met informally and looked for ways to apply the new ideas of women's liberation to their work.

They quickly learned to look at any anthropological study and ask: what are the women doing? As they began to answer that question, they suddenly understood far more about kinship and politics and religion and all the other things that had seemed to be just men's business.[1]

Many other women did the same, and that produced the new field of the anthropology of women. But there was a second lesson to be learned.

In 1994 Nancy and Andrea Cornwall edited *Dislocating Masculinity*, a comparative anthropology of men. The central argument of this book was that if you wanted to understand what the women were doing, look at the men. And vice versa. Masculinity and femininity are two halves of the same whole. Neither makes sense nor can be understood without the other.[2]

This was part of a wider movement to stop talking about women's studies and start talking about gender—about people, all together,

NOTE ON METHODS

women and men, queer people and everyone else as well. Looking at sameness and solidarity made sense to us then as it does now.

Then there were several surprising twists in our story. First, both of us, expatriate Americans who had lived in the UK most of our adult lives, found ourselves at the turn of the millennium unexpectedly teaching American undergraduates—most of them, as it turned out, young people from very wealthy families. As old hippies, we were, quite frankly, deeply shocked by sharp divisions between women and men, the misogyny, homophobia and abuse we learned about from the young people and the new colleagues who became our friends. We had expected a generation more liberal and mellow than ourselves, but what we found was anything but. So we began thinking about changes in the relation between gender and class, and the politics of the previous three decades. That was the start.

Soon we were following the accusations of abuse in the Catholic Church and—good anthropologists that we are—we began to look for ideas to help us explain what was going on more generally. So we began to look afresh not just at the politics of the previous few decades, or at a history of capitalism, but at the relation between male dominance and class societies from the outset. It soon became clear that from the very beginning of class societies, there was a strong association between male dominance and gender inequality and that they changed in tandem at culturally and historically specific moments. This suggested that we should look to class to explain why gendered inequality became the norm in class societies. But this still left us with the enormous question—why men? And you know the rest.

In this book we have extended the method to look at both class and gender together and take this further to consider the evolutionary background to ideas and habits of equality and inequality. What we have found is that, if every time you look at class, you ask: how is this gendered? suddenly you understand much more about class and class struggle.

And vice versa—if, every time you look at gender, you ask: what's happening to class relations and the class struggle? suddenly you understand much more about gender and sexual politics and how and why these things change.

## NOTE ON METHODS

We have found this method immensely productive theoretically, and in understanding our lives and our world. We hope you will find it equally useful.

*Sexual Violence*

As we worked on this book, we found a fourth way to extend the method. Every time you think about class, ask: what keeps the inequality in place? Where is the violence? Every time you think about gender, ask again: what keeps the sexism in place? Where is the violence?

Every time you think about class and class struggle, ask: where is the sexual violence? And every time you think about sexual violence, look for class enforcers and the violence of class.

That method led us to a new way of thinking. In the early 1970s Marxism had an important part to play in the women's movement and in women's studies in the academy. Traditional Marxist approaches to gender started from various places—from value theory, from women's domestic labour, rules of inheritance, stages of evolution, social reproduction or equal pay. All of these topics are important and deserve attention. But something about such starting points left sexual violence somehow peripheral. In these traditional approaches, rape is bad, but it is neither important nor central.

We cannot help thinking that this has excused generations of feminists from openly confronting the gender-based violence and harassment that has been rife in liberation, as well as conservative, politics. Perhaps more important, a large proportion of Marxist and socialist feminists work in universities, where such abuse is routine, and routinely covered up.

Knowing this reminded us of another rule of method in social science. It is always productive to look for the negative examples, things that didn't happen as much as those that did, and to pay attention to public secrets and consider the great effort everyone makes to avoid talking about, or even thinking about, those public secrets. Then ask: why? How does keeping this particular secret, say, protect the status quo, the powerful and the established relations in society?

369

Sexual violence is just such a public secret, and it is one that most often remains hidden in plain sight.

*Solidarity*

There is a political corollary to these points about method. Conflicts over gender and conflicts over class are aspects of a single struggle. On one level, almost everyone knows this. In what was once called the left, many of us feel an instinctive solidarity with others. You yourself may be a Brahmin teacher in India, a feminist social worker in Argentina or a nursing shop steward in Nigeria. But you feel that solidarity when you hear about a young Dalit woman raped by upper-caste men in an Indian village, about a Black American suffocating with a cop's knee on his neck, about garment workers striking against the dictatorship in Myanmar, or about Alan Kurdi, a 2-year-old refugee drowned in the Aegean.

That feeling of solidarity can be expressed in many ways. In some movements everyone speaks of the others as sister and brother. The labour unions in the United States have an old saying: an injury to one is an injury to all. And there is an older way of saying something similar: there but for the grace of God go I.

Behind these feelings is an understanding that such suffering is also racialised, classed and gendered suffering. And that they are all part of one struggle for equality of every kind. And behind that, for many of us, is a bedrock lifelong commitment to equality.

Our enemies, the owners and enforcers of inequality, know all about these connections too. Sometimes they know about them analytically and consciously. More often, the connections are intimate, intuitive and visceral. This is most obvious with the leaders of the new global far right, Putin, Trump, Modi, Bolsonaro, Duterte and all the rest. Language is powerful, but it is never stand-alone, but always ripe with culture and politics. In speeches, and in action, they move seamlessly from racist support for police violence to encouragement of male violence and of hatred for Muslims, black people, queer people and immigrants. It is not an accident that 'rape' is used, in many times and places, as a metaphor for what the ruling classes do to the exploited, and for what humanity has in recent centuries done to the environment and all living things.

# NOTE ON METHODS

As we wrote this book, we took great heart from the democratic uprisings in many parts of the world, from Black Lives Matter and Me Too to the climate movements like Fridays for Future, XR and Just Stop Oil. Those movements are changing the world. In what lies ahead, the struggles over gender and class and climate must move together, or we will be all lost together. We have to hope that the transforming power of love can save the world.

# NOTES

INTRODUCTION

1. E.O. Wilson 1975.
2. Hrdy 1981, viii–ix.
3. de Waal 2013, 39.
4. Ibid., 43.
5. Hunt 2020, 233–8.
6. For a wonderful, and scientifically rigorous demolition of the idea of pink and blue brains, see Jordan-Young 2010.

1. DOMINATION AND COMPETITION AMONG GIBBONS, GORILLAS, BABOONS …

1. There is also 'cryptic female choice', where processes inside the vagina and womb of the female may accept some sperm and reject others, unbeknownst to mission control. This sort of choice is certainly less common as a means of selection, and there are problems with the way the idea has been used in studies of human evolution.
2. Lappan and Whittaker 2009.
3. Barelli et al. 2008.
4. Harcourt and Stewart 2007 is a brilliant introduction to gorillas.
5. For gorilla infanticide, see ibid., 202–24; Fossey 1984; Robbins et al. 2013. For possible evolutionary advantages of male care for infant gorillas, see Rosenbaum et al. 2018.
6. Strum 1987; Sapolsky 2001; Cheney and Seyfarth 2007.

2. … CHIMPANZEES AND BONOBOS

1. For chimpanzees, start with Goodall 1986 and 1990; and Hunt 2020; then Nishida 2011; Nakamura et al. 2015, 71–140 and 372–518; Boesch 2009; Boesch et al. 2019; and Stanford 2018.
2. Hashimoto and Furuichi 2015.

3. Goodall 1990, 83–4 and 88–9.
4. Wrangham and Peterson 1997.
5. For his work on human warfare, see R.B. Ferguson 2013a, 2013b and 2015; and for chimpanzees R.B. Ferguson 2011; Horgan 2014a and 2014b. In response, see Stanford 2018, 66–90.
6. M. Wilson et al. 2014.
7. For bonobos start with Kano 1992; de Waal 1997; Stanford 1998; Furuichi 2009, 2011 and 2019; Furuichi and Thompson 2008, 1–150; Furuichi et al. 2012; Hashimoto and Furuichi 2015.
8. Stanford 1998.
9. de Waal 1988, 1996, 2005 and 2019.
10. de Waal 1982.
11. Strum 1987.
12. de Waal 2011.
13. Cheng et al. 2022; Moscovice et al. 2022; Samuni, Langergraber and Surbeck 2022.
14. Takayoshi Kano, comment in Stanford 1998, 410–11.
15. Hunt 2020, 499.

### 3. HUMANS BECAME EQUAL BY SHARING MEAT

1. Hewlett 1991. The literature on the effects of farming societies and states on hunters is large. Much of it shows the influence of Eric Wolf 1992. Start with Leacock 1954; Turnbull 1965; Morris 1982; Gordon 1992; Lee 1992; Elizabeth Thomas 2006.
2. Gardner 2000, 1–2.
3. Cormier 2003.
4. The literature on contemporary hunter-gatherers is now rich and vast. Our generalisations draw on a wide range of useful ethnographies. Some of the best are Hill and Hurtado 1996, from South America; Endicott and Endicott 2008, from Asia; Briggs 1974 and 1998, from North America; Lee 1979, Shostak 1981, Turnbull 1965, and Elizabeth Thomas 2006, from Africa; and Kaberry 1939, from Australia.
5. See Pickering 2013. Elizabeth Thomas 2006 is also useful.
6. Hill and Hurtado 1996; Howell 2010.
7. Howell 2010.
8. For central places, see Pickering 2013; Stiner and Kuhn 2019.
9. Stiner 1994; Pääbo 2014; Sykes 2020.
10. Kuhn and Stiner 2006; Nielsen et al. 2017.
11. Kuhn and Stiner 2006.
12. M. Jones 2007; Wrangham 1999 and 2009.
13. Goodall 1990, 83–4 and 88–9; Barbara Fruth, comment in Stanford, 1998.

## 4. HUMANS BECAME EQUAL BY SHARING CHILDCARE

1. Hrdy 1981.
2. Hrdy 1977.
3. Williams et al. 2008; Wrangham, Wilson and Muller 2006.
4. Hrdy 1977, Location 4174.
5. Cheney and Seyfarth 2007, 57.
6. Smuts 1985, 3–4.
7. Alberts 2019.
8. The best statement of this argument is Hrdy 2009.
9. Howell 2010; Hawkes, O'Connell and Blurton-Jones 1989.
10. Sterelny 2012.
11. See, for example, Shostak 1981; Scheper-Hughes 1993; Oliver 2002, 161.
12. Rees 2009.

## 5. HUMANS BECAME EQUAL BY SHARING ORGASMS

1. Dixson 2012.
2. Cormier and Jones 2015.
3. There is remarkably little research on the evolutionary importance of changes in the anatomy of the vagina and the clitoris. We are shocked, we tell you, shocked.
4. Cooke 2022, 59–70.
5. For a sympathetic survey, see Puts, Dawood and Welling 2012.
6. Lloyd 2005; Milan et al. 2006. There is a curious twist to the by-product story. The by-product argument was originally proposed by the anthropologist Donald Symons, and then championed by the eminent palaeontologist Stephen J. Gould. Gould's support was important because Symons was known to be sexist and Gould made the theory respectable for feminists and the left. See Symons 1979; Gould 1987.
7. Tuttle 2014, Location 9179; Savini, Boesch and Reichard 2009; Goodall 1990, 83–4 and 88–9.
8. Yamagiwa 1987.
9. Bagemihl 1999; Roughgarden 2004 and 2009.
10. Puts, Dawood and Welling 2012; Lloyd 2005; Kinsey, Pomeroy and Martin 1998 (1948); Kinsey et al. 1998 (1953); Hite 1976.
11. The key work was Koedt 1970. See also Ardener 1987 on Judy Chicago.
12. Malinowski 1929; Mead 1928. And see Lily King's 2014 roman-à-clef *Euphoria* for a fascinating portrait of Mead, Reo Fortune and Gregory Bateson doing fieldwork in New Guinea.
13. Malinowski 1929, 284–6.

14. Freeman 1990; Shankman 2009.
15. D. Marshall 1971; Suggs 1971; Dabhoiwala 2012; Laqueur 1990.
16. There is an extensive literature on female genital mutilation, also called female circumcision or cutting. Start with Hodzíc 2016; then Boddy 1989.
17. Rival 2002; Rival, Slater and Miller 1998; Elwin 1991 (1947).

6. HUMANS BECAME EQUAL BY OVERTHROWING THE DOMINANCE OF BULLIES

1. Boehm 1999 and 2012. Wrangham 2019 picks up Boehm's idea in interesting ways but stays within the evolutionary psychology paradigm.
2. de Waal 2009.
3. Boehm 2012, Location 1491. See also Stibbard-Hawkes 2020.
4. Wiessner 2005.
5. Lee 1979, 243–9.
6. Ibid., 246.
7. Briggs 1974.
8. Kaberry 1939; Hewlett 1991; Endicott and Endicott 2008; Briggs 1998; Morris 1982, 144–53.
9. Briggs 1974; Balikci 1989 (1970), 173–93.
10. For example, R. Tapper and N. Tapper 1986.
11. Peterson 1993; Wiessner 2005.
12. Peterson 1993.
13. Spencer and Gillen 2014 (1899).
14. Turnbull 1965.
15. Elizabeth Thomas 2006, 76; Morris 1982, 165.
16. Gardner 1991.
17. M. Jones 2007.
18. Tomlinson 2015; Mithen 2008; Sacks 2007; Levitin 2008.
19. Dunbar 2014.
20. P. Jones 2022, 31–51.
21. Less convincingly, Christopher Boehm 2021 argues that hunter egalitarianism has been in place for at least 60,000 years, and that this was enough time for collective executions of dominant males to select against psychopathic personalities. But we don't find the idea of psychopathic personality persuasive. Some highly effective, brutal rulers are clearly not psychopaths.
22. Nielsen et al. 2017.

7. AGRICULTURE, PREDATORY ELITES AND CLASS

1. Start with Flannery and Marcus 2012. Then see Scott 2009 and 2017; Mann 2005; M. Jones 2007.

2. Algaze 2008; Scott 2017.
3. Flannery and Marcus 2012.
4. Ibid. See also the chapters in Yoffee 2019, particularly Yoffee and Seri 2019 on Mesopotamia. And see the magnificent global survey of the many cases of collapse and overthrow in the ancient civilisations of Asia, Europe and the Americas in Scheidel 2018, 255–88.
5. M. Jones 2007.
6. Banaji 2010.
7. Graeber 2011, 13–14.
8. Hassett 2017, 35–56.
9. Middleton and Tait 1958; Evans-Pritchard 1987 (1940) and 1990 (1951); Ingold 1980.
10. Marx 2006; Lattimore 1988 (1940); Barfield 1992; N. Tapper 1991; R. Tapper 1979, 1983, 1997 and 2020.
11. Algaze 2008, Location 1093.
12. For a sophisticated analysis of what can be known about the different forms of dependent labour, see Reid 2014. See also Seri 2013; R. Wright 1998c.
13. Seri 2012.
14. Gilgamesh 1972.
15. The quotes that follow from the Myth of Atrahasis are taken from Foster 2005, 229–326.
16. For Inanna, see Leick 1994, 55–110 and 157–72.
17. Ibid., 157.
18. Yoffee and Seri 2019.

## 8. NATURALISING INEQUALITY

1. Collier 1986, 101. For a series of case studies exploring this proposition, see Cornwall, Karioris and Lindisfarne 2017.
2. Žižek 2009. And see Scheper-Hughes and Bourgois 2004, an excellent anthology.
3. Scott 1987 and 1990.
4. As it does in everyday struggles, and in writing anthropology! See Lindisfarne 2008.
5. Ann Ferguson 2000, 22–3, makes this point particularly well in her book *Bad Boys*.
6. 'Pass notes—No 4,489—Sad beige parenting', *The Guardian*, 2022, November 23, G2, 3.
7. See Strathern 1988, ix, 14–15 and 68; Cornwall and Lindisfarne 2017 (1994), 11–47; Lindisfarne and Neale 2017.
8. Klein 2014. See also Klein 2007; J. Neale 2021.

9. For a now classic discussion of the relation between cultural styles and class, see Bourdieu 1984.
10. On systems of classification, start with Douglas 1960; Leach 1976; Tambiah 1968; Lakoff and Johnson 2003 (1980).
11. Early on feminist anthropologists were lost in the contrasting labels that divided 'men' and 'women'. But an important breakthrough came with MacCormack and Strathern's 1980 critique of the pernicious nature/culture divide. By the 1990s, the binary contrast between 'hegemonic' versus 'subordinate' men had a central place in Men's and Queer Studies. (See Carrigan, Connell and Lee 1985 and R.W. Connell 1987 for an introduction to this idea.) See Cornwall 2017 for a useful summary of this progression, and Cornwall and Lindisfarne 2017 (1994) for an early cross-cultural anthropology of comparative masculinities. More recently, the idea of intersectionality has overtaken discussion of the gender binaries. But moving to the idea that all forms of discrimination are connected (which of course they are) can make it difficult to understand causality, and how and why ideas of meaningful difference change.
12. Lindisfarne and Neale 2018; Tlhabi 2012; Abdulali 2018; Gay 2018.
13. Schultz 2010.
14. Sanders 1991, 81, and see 86 and 88.
15. Karkazis 2008.
16. Plant 1988; Marhoefer 2015.
17. C. White 2003; Stokes 2010; Hedenstierna-Jonson et al. 2017.
18. On Hijras, see Nanda 1990; Reddy 2010. On *xanith*, see Wikan 1978, and the correspondence between Shepherd, Feuerstein and al-Marzooq 1978.
19. Jean-Paul Sartre, in an introduction to Fanon 2001 (1961), 15.
20. Ifeka-Moller 1975; Lindisfarne and Neale 2016.
21. There is an enormous anthropological literature on ritual. Perhaps start with V. Turner 1969; Tambiah 1968; Bloch 1989; Anonymous 2019.
22. Marriott 1966; Le Roy Ladurie 1980; Elias 1991; Scott 1990; Tucci 2001; Ehrenreich 2007. And see S. Smith 2002, who describes the sheer exuberance of transgression at a feminist festival in Michigan, and the tension and confusions transgressions create.

9. WHY MEN?

1. Cormier and Jones 2015, 45–112.
2. Graeber 2011; Scott 2009 and 2017; Graeber and Wengrow 2021; Lindisfarne and Neale 2021.
3. As for feminist critiques, a good place to start is Marina Warner's essay, 'The Bed of Odysseus', in which she examines the gendered nuances, contradictions and duplicity in Odysseus's story (1985, 88–104).

4. Lindsey 2019; Black 2015; Lindisfarne 2000.
5. Lindisfarne and Neale 2015c; and for India, Chakravarti 2016; Butalia and Murthy 2018; Dubey 2018.
6. Waldman 2018.
7. Ibid. As with other Me Too stories, Miriam Toews' 2018 book *Women Talking* and Sarah Polley's 2022 film of the book are about women struggling against the unrelenting, and unpunished, sexual abuse of women and children in a Mennonite colony in Bolivia between 2005 and 2009.
8. See Danczuk and Baker 2014; Lindisfarne and Neale 2015a; O'Toole 2021.
9. Lindisfarne and Neale 2022a.
10. Traister 2018, 3.
11. Niezen 2013; O'Toole 2021.
12. Lindisfarne and Neale 2018, 2019 and 2022a; Kantor and Twohey 2019; Farrow 2019; Edwards 2020; J. Brown 2021.
13. McCall 1994; Bourgeois 2002; Lindisfarne and Neale 2015b.
14. Bonnycastle 2013.
15. Garcia 2010; Case and Deaton 2020.
16. Cynthia Eller (2011, 20) in her brilliant feminist book on *Myths of Matriarchy* says that almost all classicists agree that there were no actual Amazons.
17. Rediker 1997; Hedenstierna-Jonson et al. 2017; Darden, Henshaw and Szekely 2019.
18. Redfern 2011.
19. Leacock 1981, 20 and 22.
20. Kipling 1890. In his detailed history of the Battle of Maiwand, while Malalai is not mentioned, Mohamad Ali does note that in the contemporary sources, 'An elderly lady, Bibi Hawa ... opened the negotiations of behalf of Ayub Khan with the British, who were by then besieged in the citadel of Kandahar' (1970, 51).
21. Enloe 1990 and 2000.
22. Alexievich 2007, x.

10. SALMON, PIGS AND RITUALS: ARE WE WRONG?

1. Moss 2000; Fitzhugh 2020.
2. Arnold 2007; Gamble 2011; Flannery and Marcus 2012, 67–71.
3. Lambert 1997; Gamble 2011, 249–74; Kennett et al. 2013.
4. Walter 2006.
5. Moss 1993, 641.
6. Hayden 2022, Location 1096.
7. R.B. Ferguson 1984; Ames 2001 and 2003; Angelbeck and Grier 2012; Flannery and Marcus 2012, 71–86.

8. Davies 2020; Jeffery and Mirazón Lahr 2020.
9. Godelier 1986.
10. Golson et al. 2017; Denham 2018.
11. For particularly good early ethnographies, see Read 1980 (1965); Rappaport 2000 (1968); Strathern 1972; Josephides 1980; R. Kelly 1993; Schieffelin 2005.
12. For warfare and land pressure, see Brookfield and Brown 1963; Meggitt 1977.
13. Salisbury 1962.
14. Thus, Boas wrote about the decorative arts of the north Pacfic coast. It was also Malinowski's project in *Argonauts of the Western Pacific* (1922), *Crime and Custom in Savage Society* (1926) and *The Sexual Life of Savages* (1929), but Malinowski's other interest in popularising anthropology and ethnographic fieldwork, these book titles and others did no favours to the Trobrianders. Evans-Pritchard did in fact make exquisite sense of *Witchcraft, Oracles and Magic among the Azande* (1937), though his scholarly account is also belied by the exoticising title.
15. Jolly 1992, 4.
16. Strathern 1988, ix.
17. Ibid., 325 and 336. See also Strathern 1972.
18. Josephides 1991, 148.
19. Strathern 1988, 4.
20. Herdt 1989, 1994 and 2005.
21. Josephides 1980.
22. D. Bell 2003 (1983).
23. Arthur Ashwin, *From South Australia to Port Darwin with Sheep and Horses in 1870–71* (ms. Copy, Canberra, Australian Institute of Aboriginal Studies, 1927), 14, quoted in D. Bell 2003 (1983), 64.
24. D. Bell 2003 (1983), 65. She is quoting M.C. Hartwig 1965, 411—*The Progress of White Settlement in the Alice Springs District and its effects upon the Aboriginal inhabitants 1860–1894*, University of Adelaide PhD Thesis.
25. *Colonial Frontier Massacres*. See also Bottoms 2013; Owen 2016.
26. *Colonial Frontier Massacres*: 'New evidence reveals Aboriginal massacres committed on an extensive scale', Newcastle University Newsroom, 16 March 2022.
27. For the price paid in suffering after conquest, see P. Wilson 1982; McKnight 2002; Austin-Broos 2009; Hinkson 2021.
28. Austin-Broos 1999, 210, quoting John Mulvaney, Howard Morphy and Alison Petch, eds, 1997, *My Dear Spencer: The letters of F. J. Gillen to Baldwin Spencer*, Melbourne: Hyland House, 270.
29. Meggitt 1962.
30. Gray 2007.

31. W. Warner 1957 (1937), 467.
32. Sharp 1952; W. Warner 1957 (1937).
33. Kaberry 1939. And see Toussaint 1999.
34. Auty 2023; entries for 'Mowla Bluff—West Kimberley', 'Auvergne Station', 'Bedford Downs (1)—East Kimberley', 'Sturt Creek—East Kimberley', 'Bedford Downs (2)—East Kimberley', 'Sturt Creek', 'Forrest River (Oombulgurri)—East Kimberley' in *Colonial Frontier Massacres*. See also Owen 2016.
35. Auty 2023. Auty names 23 dead. *Colonial Frontier Massacres*, working from earlier information, estimated 11 dead. For Hay and sexual violence, see Auty 2023, 17, 27, 71 and 185–99.
36. Auty 2023. Auty writes with insight about public secrecy: 'Unravelling the events at Forrest River is hard going. A lot of effort went into creating a chaotic narrative that would be incredibly difficult to untangle. Truth-telling in the face of persistent dissembling and concealment will probably always be this complicated… Deconstructing the events of 1926 is impossible without disentangling the other fictions which have settled around not only O'Leary's time in the Kimberley but also his previous and subsequent incongruously secret and shouted history (2023, 14 and 20).
37. Kaberry 1939, 277.
38. Radcliffe-Brown 1913 and 1930–1; Lévi-Strauss 1969 (1949); Fox 2014 (1967).
39. Hiatt 2014.
40. See Toussaint 1999; London Women's Anthropology Group 1973; Lindisfarne-Tapper forthcoming 2023.
41. Leacock 1981, 144, quoting Kaberry 1939, 25–6, 142–3 and 181.
42. Goodale 1971; Hart, Pilling and Goodale 1988. Eric Venbrux 1995 also did fieldwork in the 1980s; his book is wonderful, and is a remarkable detailed account of what can happen to a bully in an egalitarian community.
43. Hart, Pilling and Goodale 1988, 89.
44. Ibid., 58–9.
45. Gammage 2012; R. Davis 2020.
46. Pascoe 2018 (2014); R. Davis 2020.
47. We are simplifying a complex controversy here, and it can be read in other ways. To sort your way through it, go to Gerritsen 2008; Gammage 2012; Pascoe 2018 (2014); Sutton and Walshe 2021; Keen 2021; Porr and Vivian-Williams 2021; Sparrow 2021, 31–46.
48. Clements 2014; Bottoms 2013; Owen 2016.
49. Ward 2016; Scrimgeour 2020.

## 11. EQUALITY AMONG REBELS IN THE MOUNTAINS AND FORESTS

1. Among other examples we might have chosen we recommend Errington and Gewertz 1987 and 1989; Lepowsky 1993.
2. Du 2002, 4–5.
3. Scott 2009, building on Leach 1954.
4. Scott 2009, 289–92.
5. Du 2002, 194; Lepowsky 1993; Hewlett 1991.
6. Rival 2002 and 2016; Rival, Slater and Miller 1988.
7. Rival 2002, 50.
8. Ibid., 58–9.
9. Ibid., 55.
10. Ibid., 57.
11. Rival, Slater and Miller 1998, 306–7.
12. Rival 2016, 198–202.
13. Overing's key paper on gender is Overing 1986. Her monograph is Overing Kaplan 1975. And see Overing 1989a, 1989b, 1996 and 2003.
14. Overing 1986, 143–4.
15. David Thomas 1982, 21.
16. David Thomas 1982. See also David Thomas 1973; de Armellada 1964; Kingsbury 1999; Whitehead 2002.
17. David Thomas 1982, 92.
18. de Armellada 1964; David Thomas 1982, 187–226.
19. Angosto-Ferrandez 2015; Foro Penal 2019; Mosonyi 2020.

## 12. WHO WILL DIE WITH HIM?

1. Kehoe 2007, 246.
2. Schultz 2010.
3. Trigger 2003, 81–9, 151, 158–61, 475–91, 509–30 and 628–31.
4. Mbembe 2003; Arnold and Wicker 2001; Laqueur 2015.
5. 'Ancient Mesopotamia, 6000–1500BC', Exhibit No. 56, in the Raymond and Beverly Sackler Wing. The Queen's Grave and The Great Death Pit are from the Royal Cemetery of Ur (PG 1237, about 2500 BC). Note from December 2020.
6. This quote and the next two are from Leonard Woolley, 1952, *Ur of the Chaldees*, Harmondsworth: Penguin, 46–50, quoted in Leick, 2002, 114–15.
7. In a distant musical echo of the women's deaths at Ur, the tomb of the Marquis Yi of Zeng was discovered intact in central China in 1977. Among the wealth of grave goods were many musical instruments including a great set of bronze bells and the remains of many dead women musicians. The bells, which date from around 433 BC, are particularly

celebrated, while the women's deaths are barely noted in reports, leaving us with another series of confusions between the evident sexisms of the past and those of our own era. See Blum 2020; Vankeerberghen 2013; and also Sala 2017; Wolin 2022.
8. R. Wright 1998b, 79.
9. Ibn Fadlan 2012, Location 1283. Our thanks to Amanda Padoan for reminding us of Ibn Fadlan's account which Bruce Chatwin popularised in his 1989 book of essays *What Am I Doing Here?* And we owe a very great deal to our friend Nick Evans for, among much else, his help on this chapter (and see Evans 2018).
10. Ibn Fadlan 2012, Location 1294.
11. Ibid., Location 1306.
12. Ibid., Location 1330.
13. Chatwin 1989, 177.
14. T. Taylor 2002, 99–100.
15. Ibn Fadlan 2012, Location 1330.
16. Ibid., Location 1342.
17. Price 2010, 134–6; Price 2019.
18. This and the following quotes are from Price 2010, 136.
19. Price 2010, 151.

## 13. CAHOKIA: FREEDOM AND EQUALITY AFTER 'COLLAPSE'

1. On misogyny, start with Leighton 2020 and Kehoe 2022, and examples throughout this chapter.
2. Stuart 1972.
3. Lopinot 1997; Fritz 2019.
4. Pauketat 2009, 4; Alt 2018, 19.
5. Pauketat 2009, 21; J.L. Harrison 2021.
6. Alt 2018, Locations 1717 and 1794.
7. The same good geography and dendritic river system lay behind the success of the city of St. Louis after the Europeans arrived. See Hyde 2011; Johnson 2013 and 2020.
8. Pauketat 2009, 140–1.
9. Zych 2015.
10. Pauketat 2009, 70 and 64.
11. Iseminger 2010, 68–74. See also Young and Fowler 2000, 123–53.
12. Iseminger 2010, 74–5.
13. Ibid., 74.
14. Ibid.
15. Ibid.
16. Ibid., 75.

17. G. Wilson 2015, 101.
18. Iseminger 2010, 77–8.
19. Ibid., 78. See Young and Fowler 2000, 135; Alt 2015, 27.
20. Iseminger 2010, 82–3.
21. Yoffee 2005; Lekson 2010, 444–5; M. Smith 2012; Hermans 2021.
22. M. Smith and F. Berdan 2003, 6, 10–11.
23. Mann 2005, 120–1.
24. Julian Thomas 1992; R. Wright 1998b, 4, 9–10. And see Thomas's 1992 review of Gero and Conkey's edited volume *Engendering Archaeology: Women and Prehistory* for more on the feminist turn in archaeology.
25. Bright 2008; Kehoe 2022, 114; Eller 2000 and 2011.
26. Kehoe 2022, 114–15 and 131–3.
27. Slater, Hedman and Emerson 2014.
28. Ambrose, Buikstra and Krueger 2003, 217 and 223.
29. Pauketat 2009, 112.
30. Alt 2015, 27.
31. Padoan 2016, 4–5. See also Padoan 2017.
32. Padoan 2016, 15.
33. Iseminger 2010, 78. See also Young and Fowler 2000, 149–50.
34. Iseminger 2010, 78.
35. Ibid., 79.
36. Ibid., 82.
37. Pompeani et al. 2021. And see McAnany and Yoffee 2010 for a scholarly demolition of Diamond's 2005 polemic *Collapse*. On the popular, but mistaken, cliché, 'Mayan collapse', see McAnany and Gallareta Negron 2010. For a detailed history of Pueblo society in the southwest of the United States, see Wilcox 2009 and 2010. Diamond's notions of ecocide are a latter-day version of the disparaging histories of Native North Americans and Mesoamericans that have been around since the time of Columbus. Lekson 2018, 139–41 has a more benign take on Diamond and the collapse of states, and we, of course, do agree with Lekson that states rise and fall, and that collapse happens for multiple reasons. Elbein 2021 is a testament to the perennial interest in the subject.
38. Alt 2018, 82–5 and 5–14. And see Kosiba 2019.
39. Baltus and Wilson 2019.
40. Emerson, quoted in Bey 2016; J. Kelly 1997, 166.
41. Steadman 2008; VanDerwarker and Wilson 2016.
42. G. Wilson 2015, 99–104; Pauketat and Alt 2015b, 10. Though it seems that some of the former Cahokian elite were able to establish outposts and mini-estates for themselves, and certainly smaller Cahokia-like centres were later established in the south and southeast.

43. The Oneota are among the likely ancestors of the tribespeople who speak Siouan languages, including groups known today as the Omaha, Osage, Quipaw, Iowa and Kaw. Many other groups, such as the Cherokee, Choctaw, Chickasaw, who were also culturally distinct and egalitarian, coalesced.
44. Ethridge and Shuck-Hall 2009, Location 298.
45. Utley 1993, 86.
46. Kehoe 2022, 132.
47. Lang 1998. And see Roscoe 1991 and 1998.
48. Lang 1998, ix.
49. Ibid., 35.
50. Ibid., 95.
51. For possible Osage antecedents seen from an Osage point of view, see Burns 2004, 3–87; Rollings 1992, 627–95. For possible Omaha and Chickasaw antecedents, see Rausch 2015; Kaufman 2019. See also Kehoe 2007; and compare Pauketat and Emerson 1997b, 24–5.
52. Mathews 1932, 26–7 and 67–95; Burns 2004; Wolferman 1997, 11–22.
53. Wolferman 1997, 11–13; Rollings 1992, 18–21.
54. Catlin 1989, 301.
55. Rollings 1992, 38.
56. Wolferman 1997, 12; Rollings 1992, 22–32 and 45–66.
57. Burns 2004, 40–1.
58. Mathews 1932, 26–7; Burns 2004, 212; Wolferman 1997, 11–33.
59. Lang 1998, 61–3 and 88.
60. Ethridge and Shuck-Hall 2009, Location 298; Milne 2015.
61. On this further history, Hyde (2011) is the place to start. See also R. White 1991.
62. Waldo continues, 'I should know something about Indians, for I have been connected with them for more than fifty years. By them I have been rescued from death, and I have rescued them. I have been found exhausted and starving and have been hospitably entertained by them. I have fallen sick amongst the wildest tribe in America, so wild that they went utterly naked. I once remained among such a tribe for thirty days or more, much of the time unconscious: they would bring me cold water and wild berries, and try to cheer me up, and when I recovered, they assembled to bid me farewell, and seemed to be much pained at parting with me. By force of circumstances, I have entered hostile bands, and although their bows were spring and their arrows set, no arrow pierced me. I might write pages of hospitalities and kindnesses received at the hands of the Indians. ... The early mountaineers, who knew more of Indian character than any other class of men, were never unnecessarily cruel to them ... this is a subject which always arouses my indignation.'

William Waldo, *Narrative*, written in Sutherland Springs, Texas, January 1880 to Silas Bent of St. Louis, from the private papers of Sandy McLean, with our great thanks. A copy of this correspondence, *Recollections of a Septuagenarian*, can also be found in the Missouri History Museum Library and Research Center, St. Louis, Missouri.

63. Hyde 2011, 316–17.
64. Ibid.; Mathews 1932, 126–7.
65. Wolferman 1997, 107.
66. Grann 2017.
67. Appadurai 1981.
68. Solnit 2017.
69. Cummings 2015, 43–8.
70. Mooney 1996 (1896), 19.
71. Kehoe 1989; Mooney 1996 (1896); Ostler 2004.
72. Cecco 2022.
73. Rafferty and Peacock 2008, 2.
74. T. King 2012.
75. Táíwò 2022, 21.
76. Kennedy 1975; Mann 2011; R. White 1991.
77. Lekson 2010, 444–5 and 2018; Harris 2001 (1968).
78. Among White's students were anthropologists whose stories we pick up in Part Four. Some like Napoleon Chagnon remained, unreconstructed, within the evolutionary fold. Others such as Marshall Sahlins started out as an evolutionist. However, as Sahlins quipped, 'he evolved'. And there were yet others, including Eric Wolf, who left White to follow the anthropologist Franz Boas, with whom White, throughout his life, waged a vicious intellectual battle. Sahlins proved himself a remarkable ethnographer of Polynesia and later an outstanding theoretician, until his last years, when he returned to a concern with evolution in a confused set of arguments in tandem with David Graeber (Graeber and Sahlins 2017).
79. See, for instance, Evan Connell's (1984) *Son of the Morning Star*, a magnificent book to complement classics such as Vine Deloria Jr's (1969) *Custer Died for Your Sins* and Dee Brown's (1987 [1970]) *Bury My Heart at Wounded Knee*; and Celine-Marie Pascale's 2021 account of the lives of the Lakota people of the Standing Rock Nation.
80. Emerson and McElrath 2017.
81. Kehoe 2022, 33, 50 and 129. See also Kehoe 1998, 115–49.
82. Pauketat 2009, 55.
83. Bright 2008; J.T. Thomas 2019.
84. Kehoe 2022, 50, 129.
85. Alt 2018, 17.

86. Colwell 2017.
87. Kehoe 2022, 142.
88. Moss 2011, Introduction.

## 14. THE COURAGE AND CLOTHING OF JOAN OF ARC

1. Miles 2020.
2. Green 2014, 131.
3. Ibid., 132.
4. Sumption 2015, 512.
5. Ibid., 498–546; Hutchison 2017.
6. Bois 1984. His book is, among other things, part of a long Marxist scholarly war about the transition from feudalism to capitalism. We do not command the literature well enough to take a firm view on these disputes. But the key point for the story of Joan is the scale of conflict between lord and peasant, and here Bois seems a reliable guide.
7. Hinton 1977; Aiton 2007; Green 2014.
8. Thomas Basin, *Histoire de Charles VII*, quoted in Bois 1984.
9. Our account of Joan's life relies most on Warner 2013 (1981). L. Taylor 2009 and Castor 2014 are also very useful.
10. M. Warner 2013 (1981), 39–42; N.A.R. Wright 1983.
11. Castor 2014, 90.
12. M. Warner 2000 (1976).
13. Castor 2014, 165; Grigat and Carrier 2007.
14. M. Warner 2013 (1981), 143, quoting W.P. Barrett 1931, *The Trial of Jeanne d'Arc*, London, 152–4.
15. Ibid.
16. Feinberg 1996.
17. Bois 1984, 330.
18. Castor 2014, 185–6.
19. Pérnoud 1966, 219–20.
20. Beaune 1994.
21. *A Parisian Journal, 1405–1449*, trans. Janet Shirley, Oxford: Clarendon, 263–4, quoted in Crane 2002, Chapter 3.

## 15. MUTINY AND LOVE IN A TIME OF REVOLUTION

1. For ships and seafarers, see J. Neale 1985 and 1990; Rediker 1987; Linebaugh and Rediker 2000.
2. Thompson 1968; Wells 1983; J. Neale 1985 and 1990.
3. The best account of the London Corresponding Society is still Thompson 1968, 19–206.

4. The estimates of numbers are from Thompson 1968, 157–9.
5. Wells 1983.
6. For the mutinies of 1797, see Dugan 1965; Gill 1913; Coats and MacDougall 2011; Easton 2019 and 2020; Frykman 2020.
7. The story of what happened that night is taken from the transcript of the Court Martial of John Benson and Philip Francis on 30 June in ADM 1/5339. The ages, birth places and ranks of each person are taken from the muster books for the *St George* for May and June 1797 in ADM 36/12520.
8. LeJacq 2016, 410–13 and 461–5.
9. Ibid. Burg 2007.
10. LeJacq 2015, 2016 and 2021; Burg 2007; Gilbert 1976 and 1978.
11. LeJacq 2021 is good on this.
12. The transcript is in ADM 1/3339.
13. See J. Neale 1990, passim, but also 409–62 for an exploration of how and why court martials became more unfair after 2008.
14. The following is based on Anson 2011 (1913); Davidson 2006.
15. The main source for the events of that evening and the next day is the court martial of Anderson, McCann, Hayes and Fitzgerald on 7 and 8 July 1797 in ADM 1/3340.
16. It is also possible that he was English or Irish, and said he was from New York to protect himself. Both Anderson and McCann had also deserted the Navy and been recaptured, but not punished, because Peard, like all captains, had constant need of good sailors. See his letter at the start of the trial in ADM 1/3340.
17. These are exact numbers, not round numbers, and are taken from the ship's muster book for May and June 1797 in ADM 36/12520.
18. J. Marshall 1832, 23. The account that follows is also based on Laughton 1890; James 1902 (1827).
19. J. Marshall 1832.
20. J. Neale 1990.
21. Anson 2011 (1913), Chapter 10.
22. J. Marshall 1832, 24.
23. Dugan 1965, 382.

## 16. THE GENDERING OF TORTURE AT ABU GHRAIB

1. Brownmiller 1975; A. Davis 2019 (1981).
2. Anonymous 2011. On the number of Germans raped, Antony Beevor 2007 is a reliable and careful historian, and he estimates the numbers at well over a million. For Russians in Afghanistan, see Alexievich 2017. And see her remarkable book (2007) about women who fought in the Red Army during WWII.

3. Roberts 2012.
4. Ibid., 195–254.
5. We have no reliable sources on the extent of rape by American soldiers during the Korean War. See Weaver 2010.
6. RAND 2014, 10. This estimate comes from a careful study by the RAND corporation, a centre right think tank with close links to the American government and State Department. They would not have been inclined to exaggerate. On recent abuse in the US military, start with Rosenthal and Korb 2013; Penn 2014; see the brave first-person accounts at the website mydutytospeak.com, and the moving photos in Calvert 2014.
7. Spivak 1988; Riley 2013 speaks of it as 'transnational sexism'. There is a vast literature on saving Afghan women. See Gregory 2011; Lindisfarne 2002 and 2008; Abu-Lughod 2002 and 2015; Mamdani 2005; Lindisfarne and Neale 2015a and 2015c; Wimpelmann 2017.
8. Caldwell 2012. Gourevitch and Morris 2008 is also useful.
9. Caldwell 2012, 111. The email was presented in evidence at her court martial.
10. Lindisfarne and Neale 2015b.
11. E. Wright 2004.
12. Khalili 2012.
13. Caldwell 2012, 67 and 127.
14. Ibid., 65.
15. Gourevitch and Morris 2008, 115.
16. Caldwell 2012, 175.
17. Gourevitch and Morris 2008, 198.
18. Caldwell 2012, 200–1.
19. Gourevitch and Morris 2008, 180.
20. Caldwell 2012, 175.
21. Ibid., 99. See also 96–9 and 128–30.
22. Ibid., 176.

17. DARWIN, RACISM AND SEXUAL SELECTION

1. Scruton 2013. For an earlier, more mainstream take on economics and family values, see Folbre 2001.
2. Darwin 1859 and 1871. Desmond and Moore 1991 is the best biography. Richards 2017 is brilliant on sexual selection.
3. Desmond and Moore 1991, 297.
4. Desmond 1987.
5. Darwin 1871, 238–9.
6. Ibid., 200.
7. Ibid., 169.
8. Coontz 1992, 11–12.

9. Darwin 1871, 96.
10. Ibid., 324.
11. Ibid., 167.
12. Eller 2011, Kindle Chapter 5.
13. Roughgarden 2004 and 2009.
14. Roughgarden 2009, 211.
15. Ibid., 30 and 210–11.
16. Ibid., 28 and 244–5.

## 18. ENGELS, GRAEBER AND RADICAL CONFUSIONS

1. For example, Tylor 1871; Morgan 1877.
2. Engels 1884.
3. Morgan 1877.
4. Vogel 2014.
5. Engels 1884, Chapter 2.
6. Ibid., Chapter 1.
7. Ibid., Chapter 2.
8. O'Donovan n.d.
9. Priyamvada Gopal, from a post on social media, with her permission. See also Gopal 2019.
10. Wilde 1891; Harris 2001 (1968); Lekson 2018.
11. Gabriel 2011, 360–1.
12. Lindisfarne and Neale 2021; Scheidel 2022.
13. Graeber and Wengrow 2021, 525–6.
14. Ibid., 1.
15. Ibid., 150–3.
16. Santos-Granero 2010; Hann 1991.

## 19. CHAGNON, PINKER AND WAR

1. Chagnon 1968, 1992, 1994 and 2013.
2. R.B. Ferguson 1995 and 2015; Tierney 2000; Good 1991; Ramos 1995; Borofsky et al. 2005; T. Turner 2001; Fry 2013a; Corry 2013.
3. Brookfield and Brown 1963.
4. R.B. Ferguson 1995.
5. Eakin 2013.
6. Kopenawa and Elliott 2013.
7. Tierney 2000, 181–6 and 231–42; Good 1991; Ramos 1995.
8. Tierney 2000, 149–57 and 181–214; Borofsky et al. 2005, 207 and 310–12.
9. Tierney 2000, 193–4 and 197–8.

10. Ramos 1995.
11. Ibid.; Lêda Leitão Martins, in Borofsky 2005, 135–40 and 189–95.
12. Tierney 2000, 160 and notes 17 and 18 on page 356.
13. Chagnon's books and articles were re-examined. Two lengthy books criticising Chagnon appeared, and a book edited by Robert Borofsky brought together six anthropologists. Terence Turner, who made a substantial contribution to Barofsky's work, felt that he did not really do justice to the debate there and published a 72-page occasional paper going into the evidence in much more detail. See Tierney 2000; Borofsky et al. 2005; T. Turner 2001.
14. Horgan 2013. This was the Sunday book section of *The New York Times*. Most local libraries in the country order a copy of books well reviewed there.
15. Wade 2010.
16. Horgan 2013.
17. J. Neale 2002; Lindisfarne 2004 and 2010.
18. See, for example, Watts 2023.
19. Pinker 2007.
20. From the US government website.
21. Haas and Piscitelli 2013.
22. R.B. Ferguson 2013a, 116–17.
23. Haas and Piscitelli 2013.
24. Lee 2014, 222.
25. Haas and Piscitelli 2013, 183.
26. Pinker 2007. The table is taken from Keeley 2010.
27. Ryan and Jethá 2010, 183–5.
28. R.B. Ferguson 2013a, 115–16.
29. Ibid., 118.
30. Ibid., 119 and 121–5.
31. Ibid., 126.

NOTE ON METHODS

1. Lindisfarne-Tapper forthcoming 2023; London Women's Anthropology Group 1973.
2. Cornwall and Lindisfarne 2017b (1994).

# BIBLIOGRAPHY

Abdulali, Sohaila, 2018. *What We Talk about When We Talk about Rape*. New York: The New Press.

Abu-Lughod, Lila, 2002. 'Do Muslim Women Need Saving? Anthropological Reflections on Cultural Relativism and Its Others'. *American Anthropologist* 104(3): 783–90.

———, 2015. *Do Muslim Women Need Saving?* Cambridge: Harvard University Press.

Aiton, Douglas, 2007. *'Shame on him who allows them to live': The Jacquerie of 1358*. PhD Thesis, University of Glasgow.

Alberts, Susan, 2019. 'Social influences on survival and reproduction: Insights from a long-term study of wild baboons'. *Journal of Animal Ecology* 88(1): 47–66.

Alexievich, Svetlana, 2007. *The Unwomanly Face of War*. Trans. Richard Pevear and Larissa Volokhonsky. London: Penguin.

———, 2017. *Boys in Zinc*. Trans. Andrew Bromfield. London: Penguin.

Algaze, Guillermo, 2008. *Ancient Mesopotamia at the Dawn of Civilization: The Evolution of an Urban Landscape*. Chicago: University of Chicago Press.

Ali, Mohammed, 1970. *The Victor of Maiwand*. Kabul.

Alt, Susan, 2015. 'Human Sacrifice at Cahokia'. In Pauketat and Alt, 2015a, 27.

———, 2018. *Cahokia's Complexities: Ceremonies and Politics of the First Mississippian Farmers*. Tuscaloosa: University of Alabama Press.

Ambrose, Stanley, Jane Buikstra and Harold Krueger, 2003. 'Status and gender differences in diet at Mound 72, Cahokia, revealed by isotopic analysis of bone'. *Journal of Anthropological Archaeology* 22: 217–26.

Ames, Kenneth, 2001. 'Slaves, chiefs and labour on the northern Northwest Coast'. *World Archaeology* 33: 1–17.

———, 2003. 'The Northwest Coast'. *Evolutionary Anthropology* 12: 19–33.

Angelbeck, Bill and Colin Grier, 2012. 'Anarchism and the Archaeology of Anarchic Societies: Resistance to Centralization in the Coast Salish Region of the Pacific Northwest Coast'. *Current Anthropology* 53(5): 547–87.

Angosto-Ferrandez, Luis Fernando, 2015. *Venezuela Reframed*. London: Zed.

Anonymous, 2011. *A Woman in Berlin*. London: Virago.

Anonymous, 2019. 'Special Issue: Ritual as Process'. *Anthropology Today*, Part 1 35(3): 1–27 and Part 2 35(5): 1–23.

Anson, Captain W.V., 2011 (1913). *The Life of John Jervis—Admiral Lord St Vincent*. Pickle Partners.

Appadurai, Arjun, 1981. 'The Past as a Scarce Resource'. *Man: New Series* 16(2): 201–19.

Ardener, Shirley, 1987. 'A Note on Gender Iconography: The Vagina'. In Pat Caplan, ed., *The Cultural Construction of Sexuality*. London: Tavistock, 113–42.

Armbruster, Heidi and Anna Laerke, eds, 2008, *Taking Sides: Ethics, Politics, and Fieldwork in Anthropology*. New York: Berghahn.

# BIBLIOGRAPHY

Arnold, Bettina and Nancy Wicker, eds, 2001. *Gender and the Archaeology of Death*. Lanham: AltaMira.

Arnold, Jeanne, 2007. 'Credit Where Credit Is Due: The History of the Chumash Oceangoing Plank Canoe'. *American Antiquity* 72(2): 196–209.

Austin-Broos, Diane, 1999, 'Bringing Spencer and Gillen Home'. *Oceania* 69(3): 209–16.

———, 2009. *Arrernte Present, Arrernte Past: Invasion, Violence and Imagination in Indigenous Central Australia*. Chicago: Chicago University Press.

———, 2011. *A Different Inequality: The Politics of Debate about Remote Aboriginal Australia*. Sydney: Allen and Unwin.

Auty, Kate, 2023. *O'Leary of the Underworld: The Untold Story of the Forrest River Massacre*. Melbourne: La Trobe University Press.

Bagemihl, Bruce, 1999. *Biological Exuberance: Animal Homosexuality and Natural Diversity*. London: Profile.

Balikci, Asen, 1989 (1970). *The Netsilik Eskimo*. Long Grove IL: Waveland.

Baltus, Melissa R. and Gregory D. Wilson, 2019. 'The Cahokian Crucible: Burning Ritual and the Emergence of Cahokian Power in the Mississippian Midwest'. *American Antiquity* 34: 1–33.

Banaji, Jairus, 2010. *Theory as History: Essays on Modes of Production and Exploitation*. Chicago: Haymarket.

Barelli, Claudia, Christophe Boesch, Michael Heistermann and Ulrich Reichard, 2008. 'Female white-handed gibbons (*Hylobates lar*) lead group movements and have priority of access to food resources'. *Behaviour* 145: 965–81.

Barfield, Thomas, 1992. *The Perilous Frontier: Nomadic Empires and China, 221 BC–AD 1757*. Hoboken: Wiley-Blackwell.

Baxi, Pratiksha, 2014. *Public Secrets of Law: Rape Trials in India*. New Delhi: Oxford University Press.

Beaune, Collette, 1994. 'Le rumeur dans le Journal de Bourgeois de Paris'. In *Le circulation des nouvelles au moyen âge*. Rome: École Française de Rome, 191–202.

Beevor, Antony, 2007. *Berlin: The Downfall 1945*. London: Penguin.

Bell, Diane, 2003 (1983). *Daughters of the Dreaming*. Second edition, North Geelong: Spinifex.

Bell, Steve, 2009. Cartoon in *The Guardian*, 19 Feb.

Bey, Lee, 2016. 'Lost cities #8: Mystery of Cahokia—Why did North America's largest city vanish?' *The Guardian*, 17 Aug.

Bird-David, Nurit, 2019. 'Where have all the kin gone? On hunter-gatherers' sharing, kinship and scale'. In Lavi and Friesem, 2019, 15–24.

Black, Ian, 2015. 'Syrian army photographer describes torture and murder in Assad's prisons'. *The Guardian*, 1 Oct.

Bloch, Maurice, 1989. 'Symbol, song and dance as features of articulation: Is religion an extreme form of traditional authority?' In Bloch, *Ritual, History and Power: Selected Papers in Anthropology*. London: Athlone, 19–45.

Blum, Mary, 2020. *Coffin Soul Portals of the Female Xunren in Tombs of Marquis Yi of Zeng*. MA Thesis, University of Wisconsin-Milwaukee.

Boddy, Janice, 1989. *Wombs and Alien Spirits: Men, Women and the Zar Cult in Northern Sudan*. Madison: University of Wisconsin Press.

Boehm, Christopher, 1999. *Hierarchy in the Forest: The Evolution of Egalitarian Behaviour*. Cambridge: Harvard University Press.

# BIBLIOGRAPHY

———, 2012. *Moral Origins: The Evolution of Virtue, Altruism and Shame*. New York: Basic.

Boesch, Christophe, 2009. *The Real Chimpanzee: Sex Strategies in the Forest*. Cambridge: Cambridge University Press.

Boesch, Christophe et al., eds, 2019, *The Chimpanzees of the Taï Forest: 40 Years of Research*. Cambridge: Cambridge University Press.

Bois, Guy, 1984. *The Crisis of Feudalism and the Society in Eastern Normandy c. 1300–1550*. Cambridge: Cambridge University Press.

Bonnycastle, Kevin Denys, 2013. *Stranger Rape: Rapists, Masculinity and Penal Governance*. Toronto: University of Toronto Press.

Borofsky, Robert et al., 2005. *Yanomami: The Fierce Controversy and What We Can Learn from It*. Berkeley: University of California Press.

Bottoms, Timothy, 2013. *Conspiracy of Silence: Queensland's frontier Killing Times*. Sydney: Allen and Unwin.

Bourdieu, Pierre, 1984. *Distinction: A Social Critique of the Judgement of Taste*. London: Routledge.

Bourgeois, Philippe, 2002. *In Search of Respect: Selling Crack in El Barrio*. Cambridge: Cambridge University Press.

Briggs, Jean, 1974. *Never in Anger: Portrait of an Eskimo Family*. Second edition, Cambridge: Harvard University Press.

———, 1998. *Inuit Morality Play: The Emotional Education of a Three-Year-Old*. New Haven: Yale University Press.

Bright, Susie, 2008. 'From Tight Sweaters to the Pentagon Papers'. Susiebrightblogs.com. No longer available.

Brookfield, Harold and Paula Brown, 1963. *Struggle for Land: Agriculture and Group Territories among the Chimbu of the New Guinea Highlands*. Oxford: Oxford University Press.

Brown, Dee, 1987 (1970). *Bury My Heart at Wounded Knee*. New York: Vintage.

Brown, Julie K., 2021. *Perversion of Justice: The Jeffrey Epstein Story*. London: HarperCollins.

Brownmiller, Susan, 1975. *Against Our Will: Men, Women and Rape*. New York: Simon and Schuster.

Bruhns, Karen Olsen, 2006. 'Gender Archaeology in Native North America'. In Nelson, 2006, 219–58.

Burg, B.R. 2007. *Boys at Sea: Sodomy, Indecency and Court Martials in Nelson's Navy*. London: Palgrave Macmillan.

Burns, Louis, 2004. *A History of the Osage People*. Tuscaloosa: University of Alabama Press.

Butalia, Urvashi and Laxmi Murthy, eds, 2018. *Breaching the Citadel*. New Delhis: Zubaan.

Caldwell, Ryan Ashley, 2012. *Fallgirls: Gender and the Framing of Torture at Abu Ghraib*. New York: Routledge.

Calvert, Mary, 2014. 'Photos: Women Who Risked Everything to Expose Sexual Assault in the Military'. *Mother Jones*, 8 Sept.

Carrigan, Tim, R.W. Connell and John Lee, 1985. 'Towards a New Sociology of Masculinity'. *Theory and Society* 14(5): 557–604.

Case, Anne and Angus Deaton, 2020. *Deaths of Despair and the Future of Capitalism*. Princeton: Princeton University Press.

Castor, Helen, 2014. *Joan of Arc: A History*. London: Faber and Faber.

Catlin, George, 1989. *North American Indians*. New York: Penguin.

Cecco, Leyland, 2022. 'Pope apologizes for "evil" of Canada's church schools'. *The Guardian*, 16 July.

# BIBLIOGRAPHY

Chagnon, Napoleon, 1968. *Yąnomamö: The Fierce People*. First edn. Holt, Rinehart and Winston.
———, 1992. *Yanomamö: The Days of Eden*. New York: Harcourt Brace.
———, 1994. *Studying the Yąnomamö*. New York: Holt, Rinehart and Winston.
———, 2013. *Noble Savages: My Life among Two Dangerous Tribes: The Yanomamö and the Anthropologists*. New York: Simon and Schuster.
Chakravarti, Uma, ed., 2016. *Fault Lines of History*. New Delhi: Zubaan.
Chatwin, Bruce, 1989. *What Am I Doing Here?* London: Picador.
Cheney, Dorothy and Robert Seyfarth, 2007. *Baboon Metaphysics: The Evolution of a Social Mind*. Chicago: University of Chicago Press.
Cheng, Laveda et al, 2022. 'Love thy Neighbour: Behavioural and endocrine correlates of male strategies during intergroup encounters in bonobos'. *Animal Behaviour* 187: 319–30.
Cheung, Christina et al., 2017. 'Diets, social roles, and geographical origins of sacrificial victims at the royal cemetery, Yinxu, Shang China: New evidence from stable carbon, nitrogen, and sulphur isotope analysis'. *Journal of Anthropological Archaeology* 48: 28–45.
Clements, Nicholas, 2014. *The Black War: Fear, Sex and Resistance in Tasmania*. Brisbane: University of Queensland Press.
Clinger, Janet, 2005. *Our Elders: Six Bay Area Life Stories*. Xlibris.
Coats, Ann Veronica and Philip MacDougall, eds, 2011. *The Naval Mutinies of 1797: Unity and Perseverance*. Woodbridge: Boydell.
Collier, Jane, 1986. 'From Mary to Modern Woman: The Material Basis of Marianismo and its Transformation in a Spanish Village'. *American Ethnologist* 13(1): 100–7.
*Colonial Frontier Massacres in Central and Eastern Australia, 1788–1930*. Online site, University of Newcastle, Australia. Last accessed 20 March 2023.
Colwell, Chip, 2017. *Plundered Skulls and Stolen Spirits: Inside the Fight to Reclaim Native America's Culture*. Chicago: Chicago University Press.
Connell, Evan, 1984. *Son of the Morning Star*. New York: Harper.
Connell, R.W., 1987. *Gender and Power: Society, the Person and Sexual Politics*. London: Allen and Unwin.
Cooke, Lucy, 2022. *Bitch: A Revolutionary Guide to Sex, Evolution and the Female Animal*. New York: Doubleday.
Coontz, Stephanie, 1992. *The Way We Never Were: American Families and the Nostalgia Trip*. New York: Basic.
Cormier, Loretta, 2003. *Kinship with Monkeys: The Guajá Foragers of Eastern Amazonia*. New York: Columbia University Press.
Cormier, Loretta and Sharyn Jones, 2015. *The Domesticated Penis: How Womanhood Has Shaped Manhood*. Tuscaloosa: University of Alabama Press.
Cornwall, Andrea, 2017. 'Introduction'. In Cornwall, Karioris and Lindisfarne, 2017, 1–28.
Cornwall, Andrea and Nancy Lindisfarne, 2017 (1994). 'Dislocating Masculinity—Gender, Power and Anthropology'. In Andrea Cornwall and Nancy Lindisfarne, eds, *Dislocating Masculinity: Comparative Ethnographies*. London: Routledge, 11–47.
Cornwall, Andrea, Frank Karioris and Nancy Lindisfarne, eds, 2017. *Masculinity Under Neoliberalism*. London: Zed.
Corry, Stephen, 2013. 'The Emperor's New Suit in the Garden of Eden, and Other Wild Guesses or, Why Can't Napoleon Chagnon Prove Anything?' *Truthout*, 21 Sept.

# BIBLIOGRAPHY

Crane, Susan, 2002, *The Performance of Self: Ritual, Clothing and Identity during the Hundred Years War*. Philadelphia: University of Pennsylvania Press.

Cummings, Marisa Miakoⁿda, 2015. 'An Umⁿohoⁿ Perspective'. In Pauketat and Alt, 2015a, 43–8.

Dabhoiwala, Faramerz, 2012. *The Origins of Sex: A History of the First Sexual Revolution*. Oxford: Oxford University Press.

Danczuk, Simon and Matthew Baker, 2014. *Smile for the Camera: The Double Life of Cyril Smith*. London: Biteback.

Darden, Jessica Trisko, Alexis Henshaw and Ora Szekely, 2019. *Insurgent Women: Female Combatants in Civil Wars*. Washington: Georgetown University Press.

Darmangeat, Christophe, 2020a. 'Surplus, storage and the emergence of wealth: pits and pitfalls'. In Moreau, 2020, 59–70.

———, 2020b. *Justice and Warfare in Aboriginal Australia*. Langham MD: Lexington.

Darwin, Charles, 1859. *On the Origin of Species*.

———, 1871. *The Descent of Man and Selection in Relation to Sex*.

Davidson, James D.G., 2006. *Admiral Lord St Vincent: Saint or Tyrant*. Barnsley: Pen and Sword Maritime.

Davies, William, 2020. 'Responses of Upper Palaeolithic humans to spatio-temporal variations in resources: inequality, storage and mobility'. In Moreau, 2020, 131–66.

Davis, Angela, 2019 (1981). *Women, Race and Class*. London: Penguin.

Davis, Richard, 2020, 'Black Agriculture, White Anger: Arguments over Aboriginal Land Use in Bruce Pascoe's *Dark Emu*', *Borderlands* 1(1): 57–70.

de Armellada, Cesareo 1964. *Tauron Panton: Cuentos y legendas de los indios pemon*. Caracas: Ediciones del Ministerio de Educacion.

de Waal, Frans, 1982. *Chimpanzee Politics: Power and Sex Among Apes*. Baltimore: Johns Hopkins University Press.

———, 1988. *Peacemaking among Primates*. Cambridge: Harvard University Press.

———, 1996. *Good Natured: The Origins of Right and Wrong in Humans and Other Animals*. Cambridge: Harvard University Press.

———, 1997. *Bonobo: The Forgotten Ape*. Berkeley: University of California Press.

———, 2005. *Our Inner Ape: The Best and Worst of Human Nature*. London: Granta.

———, 2009. *The Age of Empathy: Nature's Lessons for a Kinder Society*. Toronto: McClelland and Stewart.

———, 2011. 'Alpha females I have known'. *Huffington Post*, 17 Nov.

———, 2019. *Mama's Last Hug*. London: Granta.

———, 2022. *Different: What Apes Can Teach Us about Gender*. London: Granta.

Deloria, Vine, Jr, 1969. *Custer Died for Your Sins: An Indian Manifesto*. Norman: University of Oklahoma Press.

Denham, Tim, 2018. *Tracing Early Agriculture in the Highlands of New Guinea: Plot, Mound and Ditch*. London: Routledge.

Desmond, Adrian, 1987. 'Artisan Resistance and Evolution in Britain, 1819–1848'. *Osiris* 3: 77–110.

Desmond, Adrian and James Moore, 1991. *Darwin*. London: Michael Joseph.

Diamond, Jared, 2005. *Collapse: How Societies Choose to Fail or Survive*. London: Allen Lane.

Dixson, Alan, 2012. *Primate Sexuality: Comparative Studies of the Prosimians, Monkeys, Apes, and Humans*. Oxford: Oxford University Press.

# BIBLIOGRAPHY

Douglas, Mary, 1960. *Purity and Danger*. London: Routledge.

Du, Shanshan, 2002. *'Chopsticks Only Work in Pairs': Gender Unity and Gender Equality among the Lahu of Southwest China*. New York: Columbia University Press.

Dubey, Priyanka, 2018. *No Nation for Women*. New Delhi: Simon and Schuster.

Dugan, James. 1965. *The Great Mutiny*. London: Andre Deutsch.

Dunbar, Robin, 2014. *Human Evolution*. London: Penguin.

Eakin, Emily, 2013. 'How Napoleon Chagnon Became Our Most Controversial Anthropologist'. *New York Times*, 13 Feb.

Easton, Callum, 2019. 'Counter-Theatre during the 1797 Fleet Mutinies'. *International Review of Social History* 64: 389–414.

———, 2020. *A Social and Economic History of the 1797 Fleet Mutinies at Spithead and the Nore*. PhD Thesis, University of Cambridge.

Edwards, Bradley, 2020. *Relentless Pursuit: My Fight for the Victims of Jeffrey Epstein*. London: Simon and Schuster.

Ehrenreich, Barbara, 2007. *Dancing in the Streets: A History of Collective Joy*. London: Granta.

Elbein, Asher, 2021. 'What Doomed a Sprawling City Near St. Louis 1,000 Years Ago?' *New York Times*, 24 April.

Elias, Norbert, 1991. *The Symbol Theory*. New York: Sage.

Eller, Cynthia. 2000. *The Myth of Matriarchal Prehistory*. Boston: Beacon.

———, 2011. *Gentlemen and Amazons: The Myth of Matriarchal Prehistory*. Berkeley: University of California Press.

Elwin, Verrier, 1991 (1947). *The Muria and Their Ghotul*. Oxford: Oxford University Press.

Emerson, Thomas, 1997a. 'Reflections from the Countryside on Cahokian Hegemony'. In Pauketat and Emerson, 1997a, 167–89.

———, 1997b. *Cahokia and the Archaeology of Power*. Tuscaloosa: University of Alabama Press.

———, 2015. 'The Earth Goddess Cult at Cahokia'. In Pauketat and Alt, 2015a, 54–60.

Emerson, Thomas, Kristin Hedman, Eve Hargrave, Dawn Cobb and Andrew Thompson, 2016. 'Paradigms Lost: Reconfiguring Cahokia's Mound 72 Beaded Burial'. *American Antiquity* 81(3): 405–25.

Emerson, Thomas and Dale McElrath, 2017. 'Excavating Communities: Lewis R. Binford and the Interpretation of the Archaeological Record in Illinois'. *Midcontinental Journal of Archaeology* 42(3):244–65.

Endicott, Kirk and Karen Endicott, 2008. *The Headman Was a Woman: The Gender Egalitarian Batek of Malaysia*. Long Grove IL: Waveland.

Engels, Friedrich, 1884. *The Origin of the Family, Private Property and the State*. Marxist Internet Archive.

Enloe, Cynthia, 1990. *Bananas, Beaches and Bases: Making Feminist Sense of International Relations*. Berkeley: University of California Press.

———, 2000. *Manoeuvres: The International Politics of Militarizing Women's Lives*. Berkeley: University of California Press.

Errington, Frederick and Deborah Gewertz, 1987. 'The Remarriage of Yebiwali: A Study of Dominance and False Consciousness in a Non-Western Society'. In Marilyn Strathern, ed., *Dealing with Inequality: Analysing Gender Relations in Melanesia and Beyond*. Cambridge: Cambridge University Press, 63–88.

# BIBLIOGRAPHY

———, 1989. *Cultural Alternatives and a Feminist Anthropology: An Analysis of Culturally Constructed Gender Interest in Papua New Guinea*. Cambridge: Cambridge University Press.

Ethridge, Robbie and Sheri Shuck-Hall, eds, 2009. *Mapping the Mississippian Shatter Zone: The Colonial Indian Slave Trade and Regional Instability in the American South*. Lincoln: University of Nebraska Press.

Evans, Nicholas, 2018. 'The Hidden Centre: Ibn Fadlan and the Khazars'. In J. Shepard and L. Treadwell, eds, *Muslims on the Volga in the Viking Age: Diplomacy and the World of Ibn Fadlan*. London: I.B. Tauris.

Evans-Pritchard, E.E., 1937. *Witchcraft, Orcles and Magic among the Azande*. Oxford: Clarendon.

———, 1987 (1940). *The Nuer*. Oxford: Oxford University Press.

———, 1990 (1951). *Kinship and Marriage among the Nuer*. Oxford: Oxford University Press.

Fanon, Franz, 2001 (1961). *The Wretched of the Earth*. London: Penguin.

Farrow, Ronan, 2019. *Catch and Kill: Lies, Spies, and a Conspiracy to Protect Predators*. London: Fleet.

Feinberg, Leslie, 1996. *Transgender Warriors*. Boston: Beacon.

Ferguson, Ann, 2000. *Bad Boys: Public Schools in the Making of Black Masculinity*. Ann Arbor: University of Michigan Press.

Ferguson, R. Brian, 1984. 'A Reexamination of the Causes of Northwest Coast Warfare'. In R. Brian Ferguson, ed., *Warfare, Culture and Environment*. Orlando: Academics Press, 267–328.

———, 1995. *Yanomami Warfare: A Political History*. Santa Fe: School of American Research Press.

———, 2011, 'Born to Live: Challenging Killer Myths'. In Robert W. Sussman and C. Robert Cloninger, eds, *Origins of Altruism and Cooperation*, Developments in Primatology: Progress and Prospects 36, New York: Springer, 249–70.

———, 2013a. 'Pinker's List—Exaggerating Prehistoric War Mortality'. In Fry, 2013b, 112–31.

———, 2013b. 'The Prehistory of War and Peace in Europe and the Near East'. In Fry, 2013b, 191–240.

———, 2015. 'History, explanation, and war among the Yanomami: A response to Chagnon's *Noble Savages*'. *Anthropological Theory* 15(4): 377–406.

Ferguson, R. Brian and Neil Whitehead, eds, 2000. *War in a Tribal Zone: Expanding States and Indigenous Warfare*. Woodbridge: James Currey.

Fitzhugh, Ben, 2020. 'Reciprocity and asymmetry in social networks: dependency and hierarchy in a North Pacific comparative perspective'. In Moreau, 2020, 233–54.

Flannery, Kent and Joyce Marcus, 2012. *The Creation of Inequality*. Cambridge: Harvard University Press.

Folbre, Nancy, 2001. *The Invisible Heart: Economics and Family Values*. New York: The New Press.

Foro Penal, 2019. *Reporte Especial sobra la Represión Politíca Ejocida de Habitantes de las Communidades Indígenas*. Caracas.

Fossey, Diane, 1984. 'Infanticide in mountain gorillas (*Gorilla gorilla beringei*) with comparative notes on chimpanzees'. In G. Hausfater and Sarah Hrdy, eds, *Infanticide: Comparative and evolutionary perspectives*. New York: Aldine.

Foster, Benjamin R., 2005. *Before the Muses: An Anthology of Akkadian Literature*. Bethesda MD: CDL.

Fox, Robin, 2014 (1967). *Kinship and Marriage: An Anthropological Perspective*. Cambridge: Cambridge University Press.

# BIBLIOGRAPHY

Freeman, Derek, 1990. *Margaret Mead and Samoa: The Making and Unmaking of an Anthropological Myth*. Cambridge: Harvard University Press.

Fritz, Gayle, 2019. *Feeding Cahokia: Early Agriculture in the North American Heartland*. Tuscaloosa: University of Alabama Press.

Fry, Douglas P., 2013a. 'Dangerous Tribes'. *European Journal of Sociology* 54: 531–6.

———, ed., 2013b. *War, Peace and Human Nature: The Convergence of Evolutionary and Cultural Views*. Oxford: Oxford University Press.

Fry, Douglas P., Charles A. Keith and Patrik Söderberg, 2020. 'Social complexity, inequality and war before farming: congruence of comparative forager and archaeological data'. In Moreau, 2020, 303–20.

Furuichi, Takeshi, 2009. 'Factors underlying party size differences between chimpanzees and bonobos: a review and hypotheses for future study'. *Primates* 50: 177–209.

———, 2011. 'Female Contributions to the Peaceful Nature of Bonobo Society'. *Evolutionary Anthropology* 20(9): 131–42.

———, 2019. *Bonobo and Chimpanzee: The Lessons of Social Coexistence*. Trans. Reiko Matsuda Goodwin. Singapore: Springer Nature.

Furuichi, Takeshi and Jo Thompson, 2008. *The Bonobos: Behavior, Ecology, and Conservation*. New York: Springer.

Furuichi, Takeshi et al., 2012. 'Long-Studies on Wild Bonobos at Wamba, Luo Scientific Reserve, D.R. Congo: Towards an Understanding of Female Life History in a Male-Philopatric Species'. In Peter Kappeler and David Watts, eds, *Long-Term Field Studies of Primates*. Berlin: Springer.

Frykman, Niklas, 2020. *The Bloody Flag: Mutiny in the Age of Atlantic Revolution*. Berkeley: University of California Press.

Gabriel, Mary, 2011. *Love and Capital*. New York: Little, Brown.

Gamble, Lynn, 2011. *The Chumash World at European Contact: Power, Trade, and Feasting among Complex Hunter-Gatherers*. Berkeley: University of California Press.

Gammage, Bill, 2012. *The Biggest Estate on Earth: How Aborigines Made Australia*. Sydney: Allen and Unwin.

Garcia, Angela, 2010. *The Pastoral Clinic: Addiction and Dispossession along the Rio Grande*. Berkeley: University of California Press.

Gardner, Peter, 1991. 'Foragers' Pursuit of Individual Autonomy'. *Current Anthropology* 32(5): 543–72.

———, 2000. *Bicultural Versatility as a Frontier Adaptation among Paliyan Foragers of South India*. London: Edwin Mellen.

Gay, Roxane, ed., 2018. *Not That Bad: Dispatches from Rape Culture*.

Gerritsen, Rupert, 2008. *Australia and the Origins of Agriculture*. Oxford: British Archaeological Reports

Ghazi, Algosaibi, 1983. *Lyrics from Arabia*. London: Three Continents.

Gilbert, Arthur N., 1976, 'Buggery and the British Navy, 1700–1861', *Journal of Social History*, 10(1): 72–98.

———, 1978, 'Sodomy and the Law in Eighteenth- and early Nineteenth-century Britain', *Societas*, 8(3): 98–113.

Gilgamesh, 1972. *The Epic of Gilgamesh*. Trans. and ed. N.K. Sanders. London: Penguin.

Gill, Conrad, 1913. *The Naval Mutinies of 1797*. Manchester: Manchester University Press.

# BIBLIOGRAPHY

Glasco, Jeffrey, 2001. *'We are a Neglected Set': Masculinity, Mutiny and Revolution in the Royal Navy of 1797*. PhD Thesis, University of Arizona.

———, 2004. 'The Seaman Feels Him-self a Man'. *International Labor and Working-Class History* 66(Fall): 40–56.

Godelier, Maurice, 1986. *The Making of Great Men: Male Domination and Power among the New Guinea Baruya*. Cambridge: Cambridge University Press.

Golson, Jack, Tim Denham, Philip Hughes, Pamela Swadling and John Muke, 2017. *Ten Thousand Years of Cultivation at Kuk Swamp in the Highlands of Papua New Guinea*. Canberra: ANU Press.

Good, Kenneth, 1991. *Into the Heart: One Man's Pursuit of Love and Knowledge among the Yanomama*. New York: Simon and Schuster.

Goodale, Jane C., 1971. *Tiwi Lives*. Seattle: University of Washington Press.

Goodall, Jane, 1986. *The Chimpanzees of Gombe: Patterns of Behaviour*. Cambridge: Harvard University Press.

———, 1990. *Through a Window: 30 Years with the Chimpanzees of Gombe*. London: Weidenfeld and Nicolson.

Gopal, Priyamvada, 2019. *Insurgent Empire: Anti-Colonial and British Dissent*. London: Verso.

Gordon, Robert, 1992. *The Bushman Myth: The Making of a Namibian Underclass*. Boulder: Westview.

Gould, Stephen J., 1987. 'Freudian Slip'. *Natural History* 87(2): 14–21.

Gourevitch, Philip and Errol Morris, 2008. *Standard Operating Procedure*. London: Picador.

Graeber, David, 2011. *Debt: The First 5,000 Years*. New York: Melville.

Graeber, David and Marshall Sahlins, 2017. *On Kings*. London: HAU.

Graeber, David and David Wengrow, 2021. *The Dawn of Everything*. London: Allen Lane.

Grann, David 2017. *Killers of the Flower Moon: Oil, Money, Murder and the Birth of the FBI*. New York: Simon and Schuster.

Gray, Geoffrey, 2007. *A Cautious Silence: The Politics of Australian Anthropology*. Canberra: Aboriginal Studies Press.

Green, David, 2014. *The Hundred Years War: A People's History*. New Haven: Yale University Press.

Gregory, Thomas, 2011, *Rescuing the Women of Afghanistan: Gender, Agency and the Politics of Intelligibility*. PhD Thesis, University of Manchester.

Grigat, Daniel and Gregory Carrier, 2007. 'Gender Transgression as Heresy: The Trial of Joan of Arc'. *Past Imperfect* 13: 188–207.

Haas, Jonathan and Matthew Piscitelli, 2013. 'The Prehistory of Warfare: Misled by Ethnography'. In Fry, 2013b, 168–90.

Hann, John, 1991. *Missions to the Calusa*. Gainesville: University Press of Florida.

Harcourt, Alexander and Kelly Stewart, 2007. *Gorilla Society: Conflict, Compromise, and Cooperation Between the Sexes*. Chicago: Chicago University Press.

Harris, Marvin, 2001 (1968). *The Rise of Anthropological Theory*. Lanham: AltaMira.

Harrison, Jessica Lou, 2021. *An Ancient DNA Perspective on Mound 72 Cahokia*. PhD Thesis in Anthropology, Indiana University.

Harrison, Peter, 2018. 'The Enlightenment of Steven Pinker'. *ABC Religion and Ethics*, 23 Feb.

Hart, C.W.M., Arnold Pilling and Jane C. Goodale, 1988. *The Tiwi of North Australia*. New York: Holt, Rinehart and Winston.

Hashimoto, Chie and Takeshi Furuichi, 2015. 'Sex Differences in Ranging and Association

# BIBLIOGRAPHY

Patterns in Chimpanzees in Comparison with Bonobos'. In Takeshi Furuichi, Juichi Yamagiwa and Filippo Aureli, eds, *Dispersing Primate Females: Life History and Social Strategies in Male-Philopatric Species*. Tokyo: Springer.

Hassett, Brenna, 2017. *Built on Bones: 15,000 Years of Urban Life and Death*. London: Bloomsbury.

Hawkes, K., J.F. O'Connell and N.G. Blurton-Jones, 1989. 'Hardworking Hadza Grandmothers'. In V. Standen and R. Foley, eds, *Comparative Socioecology: The Behavioural Ecology of Humans and Other Mammals*. Oxford: Basil Blackwell.

Hayden, Brian, 2022. 'Transegalitarian Societies of the American Northwest Plateau: Social Dynamics and Cultural/Technological Changes'. In Orlando Cerasuolo, ed., *The Archaeology of Inequality: Tracing the Archaeology of Inequality*. Albany: SUNY Press.

Hedenstierna-Jonson, Charlotte et al., 2017. 'A female Viking warrior confirmed by genomics'. *American Journal of Biological Anthropology* 164(4): 853–60.

Herdt, Gilbert, 1989. *Sambia Sexual Culture: Essays from the Field*. Chicago: Chicago University Press.

———, 1994. *Guardians of the Flute: Idioms of Masculinity*. Chicago: Chicago University Press.

———, 2005. *The Sambia: Ritual, Sexuality and Change in Papua New Guinea*. Second edition, New York: Cengage.

Hermans, Erik, 2021. 'Between the Makurians and the Maya: Reflections on Early Medieval Globalism'. *The Medieval Globe* 7(2): 1–14.

Hewlett, Barry, 1991. *Intimate Fathers: The Nature and Context of Aka Pygmy Paternal Infant Care*. Ann Arbor: University of Michigan Press.

Hewlett, Barry et al., 2019. 'Intimate living: sharing space among Aka and other hunter-gatherers'. In Lavi and Friesem, 2019, 39–56.

Hiatt, L.R., 2014. *Arguments about Aborigines: Australia and the Evolution of Social Anthropology*. Cambridge: Cambridge University Press.

Hill, Kim and A. Magdalena Hurtado, 1996. *Ache Life History: The Ecology and Demography of a Foraging People*. New York: Aldine de Gruyter.

Hinkson, Melinda, 2021. *See How We Roll: Enduring Exile between Desert and Urban Australia*. Durham: Duke University Press.

Hinton, Rodney, 1977. *Bond Men Made Free*. London: Routledge.

Hite, Shere, 1976. *The Hite Report: A Nationwide Study of Female Sexuality*. New York: Collier Macmillan.

Hodges, Glenn, 2011. 'Cahokia: America's Forgotten City'. *National Geographic*, Jan.

Hodzić, Saida, 2016. *The Twilight of Cutting: African Activism and Life after NGOs*. Berkeley: University of California Press.

hooks, bell, 2000. *Where We Stand: Class Matters*. London: Routledge.

Horgan, John, 2013. 'The Weird Irony at the Heart of the Napoleon Chagnon Affair'. *Scientific American Blog*, 18 Feb.

———, 2014a. 'Anthropologist Brian Ferguson Challenges Claims that Chimp Violence is Adaptive'. *Scientific American Blog*, 18 Sept.

Horgan, John, 2014b. 'Anthropologist Finds Flaws in Claim that Chimp Raids are "Adaptive"'. *Scientific American Blog*, 25 Nov.

# BIBLIOGRAPHY

Howell, Nancy, 2010. *Life Histories of the Dobe !Kung: Food, Fatness and Well-being over the Life-span.* Berkeley: University of California Press.

Hrdy, Sarah Blaffer, 1977. *The Langurs of Abu: Female Strategies of Reproduction.* Cambridge: Harvard University Press.

———, 1981. *The Woman that Never Evolved.* Cambridge: Harvard University Press.

———, 2009. *Mothers and Others: The Evolutionary Origins of Mutual Understanding.* Cambridge: Harvard University Press.

Hunt, Kevin D., 2020. *Chimpanzee: Lessons from our Sister Species.* Cambridge: Cambridge University Press.

Hutchison, Emily, 2017, 'Knowing One's Place: Space, Violence and Legitimacy in Early Fifteenth-century Paris'. *The Medieval History Journal* 20(1): 38–88.

Hyde, Anne, 2011. *Empires, Nations and Families: A New History of the North American West 1800–1860.* Lincoln: University of Nebraska Press.

Ibn Fadlan, 2012. *Ibn Fadlan and the Land of Darkness: Arab Travellers in the Far North.* Trans. Paul Lunde and Caroline Stone. London: Penguin.

Ifeka-Moller, Caroline, 1975. 'Female Militancy and Colonial Revolt: The Women's War of 1929, Eastern Nigeria'. In Shirley Ardener, ed., *Perceiving Women.* London: Malaby, 127–57.

Ingold, Tim, 1980. *Hunters, Pastoralists and Ranchers: Reindeer Economies and their Transformations.* Cambridge: Cambridge University Press.

Irving, Terry, 2020. *The Fatal Lure of Politics: The Life and Thought of Vere Gordon Childe.* Melbourne: Monash University Publishing.

Iseminger, William R., 2010. *Cahokia Mounds: America's First City.* Charleston: History Press.

James, William, 1902 (1827), *The Naval History of Great Britain.* Volume 2, London: Macmillan.

Jeffery, Joe L. and Marta Mirazón Lahr, 2020. 'Exploring fisher-forager complexity in an African context'. In Moreau, 2020, 255–78.

Jennings, Justin, 2016. *Killing Civilization: A Reassessment of Early Urbanism and its Consequences.* Albuquerque: University of New Mexico Press.

Johnson, Walter, 2013. *River of Dark Dreams: Slavery and Empire in the Cotton Kingdom.* Cambridge: Harvard University Press.

———, 2020. *The Broken Heart of America: St. Louis and the Violent History of the United States.* New York: Basic.

Jolly, Margaret, 1992. 'Partible Persons and Multiple Authors'. *Pacific Studies* 15(1): 137–49.

Jones, Martin, 2007. *Feast: Why Humans Share Food.* Oxford: Oxford University Press.

Jones, Paul Anthony, 2022. *Why Is This a Question?* London: Elliott and Thompson.

Jordan-Young, Rebecca, 2010. *Brainstorm: The Flaws in the Science of Sex Differences.* Cambridge: Harvard University Press.

Josephides, Lisette, 1980. *The Production of Inequality: Gender and Exchange among the Kewa.* London: Tavistock.

———, 1991. 'Metaphors, Metathemes, and the Construction of Sociality: A critique of the New Melanesian Ethnography'. *Man* (N.S.) 26(1): 145–61.

Kaberry, Phyllis, 1939. *Aboriginal Woman, Sacred and Profane.* London: Routledge.

Kandiyoti, Deniz, 1988. 'Bargaining with Patriarchy'. *Gender and Society* 2(3): 274–90.

# BIBLIOGRAPHY

Kano, Takayoshi, 1992. *The Last Ape: Pygmy Chimpanzee Behaviour and Ecology*. Palo Alto: Stanford University Press.

Kantor, Jodi and Megan Twohey, 2019. *She Said*. London: Bloomsbury.

Karkazis, Katrina, 2008. *Fixing Sex: Intersex, Medical Authority, and Lived Experience*. Durham: Duke University Press.

Kaufman, David, 2019. *Clues to Lower Mississippi Valley Histories: Language, Archaeology and Ethnography*. Lincoln: University of Nebraska Press.

Keeley, Lawrence, 2010. *War Before Civilization: The Myth of the Peaceful Savage*. Oxford: Oxford University Press.

Keen, Ian, 2021. 'Foragers or Farmers: Dark Emu and the Controversy over Australian Agriculture'. *Anthropological Forum* 31: 106–28.

Kehoe, Alice Beck, 1989. *The Ghost Dance: Ethnohistory and Revitalization*. New York: Holt, Rinehart and Winston.

———, 1998. *The Land of Prehistory: A Critical History of American Archaeology*. London: Routledge.

———, 2007. 'Osage Texts and Cahokia Data'. In F. Kent Reilly III and James F. Garber, eds, *Ancient Objects and Sacred Realms*. Austin: University of Texas Press, 246–61.

———, 2022. *Girl Archaeologist: Sisterhood in a Sexist Profession*. Lincoln: University of Nebraska Press.

Kelly, John E., 1997. 'Stirling-Phase Sociopolitical Activity at East St. Louis and Cahokia'. In Pauketat and Emerson, 1997, 141–66.

Kelly, Raymond, 1993. *Constructing Inequality: The Fabrication of a Hierarchy of Virtue among the Etoro*. Ann Arbor: University of Michigan Press.

Kennedy, Ludovic, 1975. *Nelson and His Captains*. London: Collins.

Kennett, Douglas, Patricia Lambert, John Johnson and Brendan Culleton, 2013. 'Sociopolitical Effects of Bow and Arrow Technology in Prehistoric Coastal California'. *Evolutionary Anthropology* 22: 124–32.

Khalili, Laleh, 2012. *Time in the Shadows: Confinement in Counter-Insurgencies*. Palo Alto: Stanford University Press.

King, Charles, 2020. *Gods of the Upper Air*. New York: Anchor.

King, Lily, 2014. *Euphoria*. London: Picador.

King, Thomas, 2012. *The Inconvenient Indian*. Minneapolis: The University of Minnesota Press.

Kingsbury, Nancy, 1999. *Increasing Pressure on Decreasing Resources: A Case Study of Pemón Amerindian Shifting Cultivation in the Gran Sabana, Venezuela*. PhD Thesis, York University, Toronto.

Kinsey, Alfred, Wardell Pomeroy and Clyde Martin, 1998 (1948). *Sexual Behavior in the Human Male*. Bloomington: Indiana University Press.

Kinsey, Alfred, Wardell Pomeroy, Clyde Martin and Paul Gebhard, 1998 (1953). *Sexual Behavior in the Human Female*. Bloomington: Indiana University Press.

Kipling, Rudyard, 1890. 'The Young British Soldier'.

Klein, Naomi. 2007. *The Shock Doctrine: The Rise of Disaster Capitalism*. London: Penguin.

———, 2014. *This Changes Everything: Capitalism vs. the Climate*. London: Penguin.

Koedt, Anne, 1970. *The Myth of the Vaginal Orgasm*. Boston: New England Free Press.

Kopenawa, Davi and Nicholas Elliott, 2013. *The Falling Sky*. Cambridge: Harvard University Press.

# BIBLIOGRAPHY

Kosiba, Steve, 2019. 'New Digs: Networks, Assemblages and the Dissolution of Binary Categories in Anthropological Archaeology'. *American Anthropologist* 21(2): 447–63.

Kuhn, Stephen and Mary Stiner, 2006. 'What's a Mother to Do: The Division of Labor among Neanderthals and Modern Humans in Eurasia'. *Current Anthropology* 47(6): 953–80.

———, 2019. 'Hearth and Home in the Middle Pleistocene'. *Journal of Anthropological Research* 75(3): 305–27.

Lakoff, George and Mark Johnson, 2003 (1980). *Metaphors We Live By*. Chicago: Chicago University Press.

Lambert, Patricia M., 1997. 'Patterns of Violence in Prehistoric Hunter-Gatherer Societies of Coastal Southern California'. In Debra Martin and David Frayer, eds, *Troubled Times: Violence and Warfare in the Past*. London: Gordon and Breach, 77–109.

Lang, Sabine, 1998. *Men as Women, Women as Men: Changing Gender in Native American Cultures*. Austin: University of Texas Press.

Lappan, Susan and Danielle Whittaker, eds, 2009. *The Gibbons: New Perspectives on Small Ape Socioecology and Population Biology*. New York: Springer.

Laqueur, Thomas, 1990. *Making Sex: Body and Gender from the Greeks to Freud*. Cambridge: Harvard University Press.

———, 2015. *The Work of the Dead: A Cultural History of Moral Remains*. Princeton: Princeton University Press.

Lattimore, Owen, 1988 (1940). *Inner Asian Frontiers of China*. Oxford: Oxford University Press.

Laughton, John Know, 1890, 'Peard, Shuldham'. *Dictionary of National Biography*, 1885–1890, Volume 44.

Lavi, Noa and David E. Friesem, eds, 2019. *Towards a Broader View of Hunter-Gatherer Sharing*. Cambridge: McDonald Institute for Archaeological Research.

Laville, Sandra, 2014. 'Call for prosecution to answer for trial of alleged rape victim who killed herself'. *The Guardian*, 6 Nov.

Le Roy Ladurie, Emmanuel, 1980. *Carnival in Romans: People's Uprising at Romans, 1579–80*. London: Penguin.

Leach, E.R., 1954. *Political Systems of Highland Burma*. London: LSE Monographs in Social Anthropology.

———, 1976. *Culture and Communication: The logic by which Symbols Are Connected*. Cambridge: Cambridge University Press.

Leacock, Eleanor, 1954. *The Montagnais 'Hunting Territory' and the Fur Trade*. American Anthropologist Memoir 78.

———, 1981. *Myths of Male Dominance*. New York: Monthly Review.

Lee, Richard, 1979. *The Dobe !Kung: Men, Women and Work in a Foraging Society*. Cambridge: Harvard University Press.

———, 1992. 'Art, science, or politics? The crisis in hunter-gatherer studies'. *American Anthropologist* 94(1): 31–54.

———, 2014. 'Hunter-gatherers on the best-seller list: Steven Pinker and the "Bellicose School's" treatment of forager violence'. *Journal of Aggression, Conflict and Peace Research* 6(4): 216–28.

# BIBLIOGRAPHY

Leick, Gwendolyn, 1994. *Sex and Eroticism in Mesopotamian Literature*. London: Routledge.

———, 2002. *Mesopotamia: The Invention of the City*. London: Penguin.

Leighton, Mary, 2020. 'Myths of Meritocracy, Friendship and Fun Work: Class and Gender in North American Academic Communities'. *American Anthropologist* 122(3): 444–58.

LeJacq, Seth Stein, 2015. 'Buggery's Travels: Royal Navy sodomy on ship and shore in the long eighteenth century'. *Journal for Maritime Research* 17(2): 103–16.

———, 2016. *Run Afoul: Sodomy, Masculinity, and the Body in the Georgian Royal Navy*. PhD Thesis, Johns Hopkins University.

———, 2021. 'Escaping court martial for sodomy: prosecution and its alternatives in the Royal Navy, 1690–1840. *The International Journal of Maritime History* 33(1): 16–26.

Lekson, Stephen, 2010. 'Historiography and Archaeological Theory at Bigger Scales'. In Margaret Nelson and Colleen Strawhacker, eds, *Movement, Connectivity and Landscape Change in the Ancient Southwest*. Boulder: University of Colorado Press, 443–52.

———, 2018. *A Study of Southwestern Archaeology*. Salt Lake City: University of Utah Press.

Lepowsky, Maria, 1993. *Fruit of the Motherland: Gender in an Egalitarian Society*. New York: Columbia University Press.

Lévi-Strauss, Claude, 1969 (1949). *The Elementary Structures of Kinship*. London: Eyre and Spottiswoode.

Levitin, Daniel, 2008. *This Is Your Brain on Music: Understanding a Human Obsession*. London: Penguin.

Lindisfarne, Nancy, 1997. 'Questions of Gender and the Ethnography of Afghanistan'. In J. Hainard and R. Kaehr, eds, *Dire les autres: réflexions et pratiques ethnologiques*. Lausanne: Editions Payot, 61–73.

———, 2000. *Dancing in Damascus: Stories*. Albany: SUNY Press.

———, 2002. 'Gendering the Afghan War'. *Eclipse: The Anti-War Review* 4: 2–3.

———, 2004. 'Another World is Possible'. *Anthropology Today* 1–3.

———, 2008. 'Starting from Below: Fieldwork, Gender and Imperialism Now'. In Armbruster and Laerke, 2008, 23–44.

———, 2010. 'Cochabamba and Climate Anthropology'. *Anthropology Today*, 1–3.

Lindisfarne-Tapper, Nancy, forthcoming 2023. 'When the Anthropology of Women was Revolutionary—A Memoir'. In Emine Onaran Incirlioğlu and Gabriel Rasuly-Paleczek, eds, 'Commemorating Paul Stirling 25 Years After He Passed Away'. *Austrian Studies in Social Anthropology*, 1.

Lindisfarne, Nancy and Jonathan Neale, 2015a. 'Sexual Violence and Class Inequality'. *Anne Bonny Pirate*.

———, 2015b. 'Gang Abuse in Oxford'. *Anne Bonny Pirate*.

———, 2015c. 'Oil Empires and Resistance in Afghanistan, Iraq and Syria'. *Anne Bonny Pirate*.

———, 2016. 'Strike against Rape at South African University'. *Anne Bonny Pirate*.

———, 2017. 'Masculinities and the lived experience of neoliberalism'. In Cornwall, Karioris and Lindisfarne, 2017, 29–50.

———, 2018. 'Blasey Ford, Kavanaugh and seven useful insights about sexual violence'. *Anne Bonny Pirate*.

# BIBLIOGRAPHY

———, 2019. '#MeToo and the Class Struggle at Work'. *Anne Bonny Pirate*.

———, 2021. 'All Things Being Equal'. *Anne Bonny Pirate*.

———, 2022a. 'Harvard, Sexual Politics, Class and Resistance'. *Anne Bonny Pirate*.

———, 2022b. 'Putin, Modi and Trump: Ukraine and Right-wing Populism'. *Anne Bonny Pirate*.

Lindsey, Ursula, 2019. 'Lessons of Defeat: Testimonies of the Arab Left'. *The Point*, 14 Jan.

Linebaugh, Peter, 1991. *The London Hanged: Crime and Civil Society in the Eighteenth Century*. London: Verso.

Linebaugh, Peter and Marcus Rediker, 2000. *The Many Headed Hydra: Sailors, Slaves, Commoners and the Hidden History of the Revolutionary Atlantic*. London: Verso.

Lizot, Jacques, 1994. 'On Warfare: An Answer to N.A. Chagnon'. *American Ethnologist* 21: 845–62.

Lloyd, Elisabeth, 2005. *The Case of the Female Orgasm: Bias in the Science of Evolution*. Cambridge: Harvard University Press.

Loewen, James, 1996. *Lies My Teacher Taught Me: Everything Your American History Textbook Got Wrong*. Second edition, New York: Simon and Schuster.

London Women's Anthropology Group, 1973. *London Women's Anthropology Workshop*. London.

Lopinot, Neal, 1997. 'Cahokian Food Production Reconsidered'. In Pauketat and Emerson, 1997, 52–68.

MacCormack, Carol and Marilyn Strathern, eds, 1980. *Nature, Culture and Gender*. Cambridge: Cambridge University Press.

Malinowski, Bronislaw, 1922. *Argonauts of the Western Pacific*. London: Routledge.

———, 1926. *Crime and Custom in Savage Society*. New York: Harcourt Brace.

———, 1929. *The Sexual Life of Savages in North-Western Melanesia*. London: Routledge.

Mamdani, Mahmood, 2005. *Good Muslim, Bad Muslim: America, the Cold War, and the Roots of Terror*. New York: Pantheon.

Mann, Charles, 2005. *1491: The Americas Before Columbus*. London: Granta.

———, 2011. *1493: Uncovering the New World Columbus Created*. London: Granta.

Marhoefer, Laurie, 2015. *Sex and the Weimar Republic: German Homosexual Emancipation and the Rise of the Nazis*. Toronto: University of Toronto Press.

Marriott, McKim, 1966. 'The Feast of Love'. In M. Singer, ed., *Krishna: Myths, Rites and Attitudes*. Honolulu: East-West Center.

Marshall, Donald, 1971. 'Sexual Behaviour on Mangaia'. In Donald Marshall and Robert Suggs, eds, *Human Sexual Behavior: Variations in the Ethnographic Spectrum*. New York: Basic.

Marshall, John, 1832. *Royal Naval Biography*. Volume 3, Part ii.

Marx, Emmanuel, 2006. 'The Political Economy of Middle Eastern and North African Pastoral Nomads'. In Dawn Chatty, ed., *Nomadic Societies in the Middle East and North Africa: Entering the 21$^{st}$ Century*. Leiden: Brill.

Mathews, John Joseph, 1932. *Wah 'Kon-Tah: The Osage and the White Man's Road*. Norman: University of Oklahoma Press.

Matoesian, Gregory, 2001. *Law and the Language of Identity: Discourse in the William Kennedy Smith Rape Trial*. New York: Oxford University Press.

Mbembe, Achille, 2003. 'Necropolitics'. *Public Culture* 15(1): 11–40.

# BIBLIOGRAPHY

McAnany, Patricia and Tomas Gallareta Negron, 2010. 'Bellicose Rulers and Climatological Peril? Retrofitting Twenty-First Century Woes on Eighth-Century Maya Society'. In McAnany and Yoffee, 2010, 142–75.

McAnany Patricia and Norman Yoffee, eds, 2010. *Questioning Collapse: Human Resilience, Ecological Vulnerability, and the Aftermath of Empire*. Cambridge: Cambridge University Press.

McCall, Nathan, 1994. *Makes Me Wanna Holler: A Young Black Man in America*. New York: Vintage.

McGuire, Randall, 2006. 'Marx, Childe and Trigger'. In Ron Williamson, ed., *The Archaeology of Bruce Trigger: Theoretical Empiricism*. Montreal: McGill University Press, 61–79.

McKnight, David, 2002. *From Hunting to Drinking*. London: Routledge.

———, 2005. *Of Marriage, Violence and Sorcery: The Quest for Power in Northern Queensland*. London: Routledge.

Meggitt, Mervyn, 1962. *Desert People*. Sydney: Angus and Robertson.

———, 1977. *Blood Is Their Argument: Warfare Among the Mae Enga Tribesmen of the New Guinea Highlands*. Palo Alto: Mayfield.

Mead, Margaret, 1928. *Coming of Age in Samoa*. New York: Morrow.

Middleton, John and David Tait, eds, 1958. *Tribes without Rulers: Studies in African Segmentary Systems*. London: Routledge.

Milan, Erika Lorraine, Gillian Brown, Stefan Linquist, Steve Fuller and Elisabeth Lloyd, 2006. 'Review Symposium: Sometimes an Orgasm is Just an Orgasm'. *Metascience* 15: 391–435.

Miles, Laura, 2020. *Transgender Resistance: Socialism and the Fight for Trans Liberation*. Bookmarks.

Milne, George Edward, 2015. *Natchez Country: Indians, Colonists, and the Landscapes of Race in French Louisiana*. Athens: University of Georgia Press.

Mithen, Steven, 2008. *The Singing Neanderthals: The Origins of Music, Language, Mind and Body*. Cambridge: Harvard University Press.

Monbiot, George, 2018. 'Contrary to Reason'. *The Guardian*, 7 Mar.

Mooney, James, 1996 (1896). *The Ghost Dance Religion and the Sioux Outbreak of 1890*. North Dighton MA: JG Press.

Moreau, Luc, ed., 2020. *Social Inequality before Farming: Multidisciplinary Approaches to the Study of Social Organization in Prehistoric and Ethnographic Hunter-Gatherer-Fisher Societies*. Cambridge: McDonald Institute for Archaeological Research.

Morgan, Lewis Henry, 1887. *Ancient Society*.

Morris, Brian, 1982. *Forest Traders: A Socio-Economic Study of the Hill Pandaram*. London: Athlone.

Moscovice, Liza et al., 2022. 'Dominance or Tolerance: Causes and consequences of a period of increased intercommunity encounters among bonobos (*Pan paniscus*) at LuiKotale'. *International Journal of Primatology* 43: 434–59.

Mosonyi, Esteban Emilio, 2011. *Northwest Coast: Archaeology as Deep History*. Cambridge: SAA Press.

———, 2020. *El puebla indígena Pemón, víctima propiciatora de especulaciones geopolíticas*. Caracas: Provea.

Moss, Madonna, 1993. 'Shellfish, Gender, and Status on the Northwest Coast: Reconciling Archaeological, Ethnographic, and Ethnohistorical Records on the Tlingit'. *American Anthropologist* 95(3): 631–52.

# BIBLIOGRAPHY

Nakamura, Michio, Kazuhiko Hosaka, Noriko Itoh and Koichiro Zamma, eds, 2015. *Mahale Chimpanzees: 50 Years of Research*. Cambridge: Cambridge University Press.

Nanda, Serena, 1990. *Neither Man nor Woman: The Hijras of India*. London: Wadsworth.

Narayan, Darshana, 2022. 'The Dangerous Populist Science of Yuval Noah Harari'. *Current Affairs*, 6 July.

Neale, Caroline, 1985. *Writing Independent History: African Historiography 1960–1980*. Westport CN: Greenwood.

Neale, Jonathan, 1985. *The Cutlass and the Lash: Mutiny and Discipline in Nelson's Navy*. London: Pluto.

———, 1990. *Forecastle and Quarterdeck: protest, discipline and mutiny in the Royal Navy, 1793–1814*. PhD Thesis, University of Warwick.

———, 2002, *You Are G8—We Are 6 Billion*. London: Fusion.

———, 2021. *Fight the Fire: Green New Deals and Global Climate Jobs*. The Ecologist.

Nielsen, Rasmus et al., 2017. 'Tracing the peopling of the world through genomics'. *Nature* 541: 302–10.

Niezen, Ronald, 2013. *Truth and Indignation: Canada's Truth and Reconciliation Commission on Indian Residential Schools*. Toronto: University of Press.

Nishida, Toshisada, 2011. *Chimpanzees of the Lakeshore*. Cambridge: Cambridge University Press.

O'Donovan, Connell, n.d. 'Pirates, Marauders and Homos, oh my! Homosexuality among the Ancient Heruli'. ConnellOdonovan.com

Oliver, Douglas, 2002. *Polynesia in Early Historic Times*. Honolulu: Bess.

Ostler, Jeffrey, 2004. *The Plains Sioux and U.S. Colonialism from Lewis and Clark to Wounded Knee*. Cambridge: Cambridge University Press.

O'Toole, Fintan, 2021. *We Don't Know Ourselves: A Personal History of Ireland Since 1958*. London: Head of Zeus.

Overing, Joanna, 1986. 'Men Control Women? The "Catch 22" in the Analysis of Gender'. *International Journal of Moral and Social Studies* 1(2): 135–56.

———, 1989a. 'Personal Autonomy and the Domestication of the Self in Piaroa Society'. In G. Jahoda and I.M. Lewis, eds, *Acquiring Culture: Cross Cultural Studies in Child Development*. London: Croom Helm, 169–92.

———, 1989b. 'Styles of Manhood: An Amazonian contrast in tranquillity and violence'. In Signe Howell and Roy Willis, eds, *Societies at Peace: Anthropological Perspectives*. London: Routledge.

———, 1996. 'Who is the Mightiest of Them All? Jaguar and Conquistador in Piaroa Images of Alterity and Identity'. In A. James Arnold, ed., *Monsters, Tricksters and Sacred Cows: Animal Tales and American Identities*. Charlottesville: University of Virginia Press, 50–79.

———, 2003. 'In Praise of the Everyday: Trust and the Art of Social Living in an Amazonian Community'. *Ethnos* 68(3): 1–22.

Overing Kaplan, Joanna, 1975. *The Piaroa: A People of the Orinoco Basin*. Oxford: Clarendon Press.

Owen, Chris, 2016. *Every Mother's Son Is Guilty: Policing the Kimberley Frontier of Western Australia, 1882–1905*. Perth: University of Western Australia Publishing.

Pääbo, Svante, 2014. *Neanderthal Man: In Search of Lost Genomes*. New York: Basic.

# BIBLIOGRAPHY

Padoan, Amanda, 2016. 'Who Will Die With Him? The Challenges of Employing a Gendered Methodology in Archaeology'. Unpublished essay written for the MPhil in Gender at the University of Cambridge.

———, 2017. 'Gendering the Traces'. *International Journal of Student Research in Archaeology* 3: 68–74.

Pascale, Celine-Marie, 2021. *Living on the Edge: When Hard Times Become a Way of Life*. Cambridge: Polity.

Pascoe, Bruce, 2018 (2014). *Dark Emu: Aboriginal Australia and the Birth of Agriculture*. Second edition, Broome: Magabala.

Pauketat, Timothy, 2009. *Cahokia: Ancient America's Great City on the Mississippi*. New York: Penguin.

Pauketat, Timothy and Susan Alt, eds, 2015a. *Medieval Mississippians: The Cahokian World*. Santa Fe: School for Advanced Research Press.

Pauketat, Timothy and Susan Alt, 2015b. 'Medieval Life in America's Heartland'. In Pauketat and Alt, 2015a, 1–12.

Pauketat, Timothy and Thomas Emerson, eds, 1997a. *Cahokia: Domination and Ideology in the Mississippian World*. Lincoln: University of Nebraska Press.

Pauketat, Timothy and Thomas Emerson, 1997b. 'Introduction: Domination and Ideology in the Mississippian World'. In Pauketat and Emerson, 1997a, 1–29.

Penn, Nathaniel, 2014. 'Son, Men Don't Get Raped'. *GQ*, Sept.

Pérnoud, Regine, 1966. *Joan of Arc: By Herself and Her Witnesses*. New York: Stein and Day.

Peterson, Nicolas, 1993. 'Demand Sharing: Reciprocity and the Pressure for Generosity among Foragers'. *American Anthropologist* 95(4): 860–74.

Pickering, Travis Rayne, 2013. *Rough and Tumble: Aggression, Hunting and Human Evolution*. Berkeley: University of California Press.

Pierpoint, Claudia Roth, 2004. 'The measure of America: how a rebel anthropologist waged war on racism'. *The New Yorker*.

Pinker, Steven, 2007. 'TED Talk—A Brief History of Violence'. YouTube.

———, 2011. *The Better Angels of Our Nature: Why Violence Has Declined*. New York: Viking.

———, 2018. *Enlightenment Now: The Case for Reason, Science, Humanism and Progress*. New York: Viking.

Plant, Richard, 1988. *The Pink Triangle: The Nazi War Against Homosexuals*. New York: Holt.

Pompeani, David et al., 2021. 'Severe Little Ice Age drought in the midwestern United States during the Mississippian abandonment of Cahokia'. *Nature Scientific Report* 11:13829.

Porr, Martin and Ella Vivian-Williams, 2021. 'The Tragedy of Bruce Pascoe's Deep Emu'. *Australian Journal of Archaeology* 87(3): 300–4.

Price, Neil, 2010. 'Passing into Poetry: Viking-Age Mortuary Drama and the Origins of Norse Mythology'. *Medieval Archaeology* 54(1): 123–56.

———, 2019. *The Viking Way: Magic and Mind in Late Iron Age Scandinavia*. Oxford: Oxbow.

Puts, David A., Khytam Dawood and Lisa Welling, 2012. 'Why Women Have Orgasms: An Evolutionary Analysis'. *Archives of Sexual Behavior* 41: 1127–43.

Radcliffe-Brown, A.R., 1913. 'Three Tribes of Western Australia'. *Journal of the Royal Anthropological Institute* 43: 143–94.

# BIBLIOGRAPHY

———, 1930–1. 'The Social Organization of Australian Tribes'. *Oceania* 1: 34–63, 206–46, 322–41, 426–56.

Rafferty, Jane and Evan Peacock, eds, 2008. *Time's River*. Tuscaloosa: University of Alabama Press.

Ramirez, Janina, 2022. *Femina: A New History of the Middle Ages Through the Women Written Out of It*. London: Ebury.

Ramos, Alcida Rita, 1995. *Sanumá Memories: Yanomami Ethnography in Times of Crisis*. Ann Arbor, University of Wisconsin Press.

RAND, 2014. *Sexual Assault and Sexual Harassment in the U.S. Military: Top Line Estimates for Active-Duty Service Members from the 2014 RAND Military Workplace Study*. National Defense Research Institute.

Rappaport, Roy, 2000 (1968). *Pigs for the Ancestors: Ritual in the Ecology of a New Guinea People*. Long Grove IL: Waveland.

Rausch, Donna J., 2015. 'Being Chickasaw at Shiloh'. In Pauketat and Alt, 2015a, 11–16.

Read, Kenneth, 1980 (1965). *The High Valley*. New York: Columbia University Press.

Reddy, Gayatri, 2010. *With Respect to Sex: Negotiating Hijra Identity in South India*. Chicago: Chicago University Press.

Redfern, Rebecca C., 2011. 'A Reappraisal of the Evidence for Violence in the Late Iron Age Human Remains from Maiden Castle Hillfort, Dorset, England'. *Proceedings of the Prehistoric Society* 77: 111–38.

Rediker, Marcus. 1987. *Between the Devil and the Deep Blue Sea: Merchant Seamen, Pirates and the Anglo-American Maritime World, 1700–1750*. Cambridge: Cambridge University Press.

———, 1997. 'Liberty Beneath the Jolly Roger: The Lives of Anne Bonny and Mary Read, Pirates'. In Margaret Creighton and Lisa Norling, eds, *Iron Men, Wooden Women: Gender and Seafaring in the Atlantic World 1700–1920*. Baltimore: Johns Hopkins University Press, 1–33.

Rees, Amanda, 2009. *The Infanticide Controversy: Primatology and the Art of Field Science*. Chicago: University of Chicago Press.

Reid, John Nicolas, 2014. *Slavery in Early Mesopotamia from Late Uruk until the Fall of Babylon in the Longue Durée*. Oxford University PhD Thesis.

Richards, Evelleen, 2017. *Darwin and the Making of Sexual Selection*. Chicago: University of Chicago Press.

Riley, Robin Lee, 2013. *Depicting the Veil: Transnational Sexism and the War on Terror*. London: Zed.

Rival, Laura, 2002. *Trekking Through History: The Huaorani of Amazonian Ecuador*. New York: Columbia University Press.

———, 2016. *Huaorani Transformations in Twenty-First Century Ecuador: Treks into the Future of Time*. Tucson: University of Arizona Press.

Rival, Laura, Don Slater and Daniel Miller, 1998. 'Sex and Sociality: Comparative Ethnographies of Sexual Objectification'. *Theory, Culture, and Society* 3(15): 294–321.

Robbins, Andrew et al., 2013. 'Impact of male infanticide on the social structure of gorillas'. *PLoS One* 8(11): e78526.

Roberts, Mary Louise, 2012. *What Soldiers Do: Sex and the American GI in WWII France*. Chicago: University of Chicago Press.

Robinson, Andrew, 2015. *The Indus: Lost Civilizations*. London: Reaktion.

# BIBLIOGRAPHY

Rollings, Willard, 1992. *The Osage: An Ethnohistorical Study of Hegemony on the Prairie-Plains*. Columbia: University of Missouri Press.

Roscoe, Will, 1991. *The Zuni Man-Woman*. Santa Fe: University of New Mexico Press.

———, 1998. *Changing Ones: Third and Fourth Genders in Native North America*. New York: St Martins Griffin.

Rosenbaum, Stacey, Linda Vigilant, Christopher Kazuwa and Tara Stoinski, 2018. 'Caring for infants is associated with increased reproductive success for male gorillas'. *Nature Scientific Reports* 8, article 15223.

Rosenthal, Lindsay and Lawrence Korb, 2013. *Twice Betrayed: Bringing Justice to the U.S. Military's Sexual Assault Problem*. Center for American Progress.

Roughgarden, Joan, 2004. *Evolution's Rainbow: Diversity, Gender, and Sexuality in Nature and People*. Berkeley: University of California Press.

———, 2009. *The Genial Gene: Deconstructing Darwinian Selfishness*. Berkeley: University of California Press.

Ryan, Christopher and Cacild Jethá, 2010. *Sex at Dawn*. New York: Harper.

Sacks, Oliver, 2007. *Musicophilia: Tales of Music and the Brain*. New York: Knopf.

Sala, Ilaria Maria, 2017. 'Archaeologists have found proof that an ancient Chinese dynasty used foreign slaves'. qz.com, 22 June.

Salisbury, R.F., 1962. *From Stone to Steel: Economic Consequences of a Technological Change in New Guinea*. Wellington: Victoria University Press.

Samuni, Liran, Kevin Langergraber and Martin Surbeck, 2022. 'Characterization of *Pan* social systems reveals in-group/out-group distinction and out-group tolerance in bonobos'. *PNAS* 119(26): e2201122119.

Sanders, Paula, 1991. 'Gendering the Ungendered Body: Hermaphrodites in Medieval Islamic Law'. In Nikki Keddie and Beth Baron, eds, *Women in Middle Eastern History: Shifting Boundaries in Sex and Gender*. New Haven: Yale University Press, 74–96.

Santos-Granero, Fernando, 2010. *Vital Enemies: Slavery, Predation and the Amerindian Political Economy of Life*. Austin: University of Texas Press.

Sapolsky, Robert, 2001. *A Primate's Memoir: Love, Death and Baboons in East Africa*. New York: Vintage.

Savini, Tommaso, Christophe Boesch and Ulrich Reichard, 2009. 'Varying Ecological Quality Influences the Probability of Polyandry in White-handed Gibbons (*Hylobates lar*) in Thailand'. *Biotropica* 41(4): 503–13.

Scheidel, Walter, 2018. *The Great Leveler: Violence and the History of Inequality*. Princeton: Princeton University Press.

———, 2022. 'Resetting History's Dial: A Critique of David Graeber and David Wengrow, The Dawn of Everything: A New History of Humanity'. *Zenodo*.

Scheper-Hughes, Nancy, 1993. *Death Without Weeping: The Violence of Everyday Life in Brazil*. Berkeley: University of California Press.

Scheper-Hughes, Nancy and Philippe Bourgois, eds, 2004. *Violence in War and Peace: An Anthology*. Oxford: Blackwell.

Schieffelin, Edward, 2005. *The Sorrow of the Lonely and the Burning of the Dancers*. London: Palgrave.

# BIBLIOGRAPHY

Schultz, Celia, 2010. 'The Romans and Ritual Murder'. *Journal of the American Academy of Religion* 78(2): 1–26.

Scott, James C., 1987. *The Weapons of the Weak: Everyday Forms of Peasant Resistance*. New Haven: Yale University Press.

———, 1990. *Domination and the Arts of Resistance: Hidden Transcripts*. New Haven: Yale University Press.

———, 2009. *The Art of Not Being Governed: An Anarchist History of Upland Southeast Asia*. New Haven: Yale University Press.

———, 2017. *Against the Grain: A Deep History of the Earliest States*. New Haven: Yale University Press.

Scruton, Roger, 2013. 'Our values have been betrayed'. *The Guardian*, 11 May.

Scrimgeour, Anne, 2020. *On Red Earth Walking: The Pilbara Aboriginal Strike, 1946–1949*. Melbourne: Monash University Publishing.

Seri, Andrea, 2012. *Local Power in Old Babylonian Mesopotamia*. Sheffield: Equinox.

———, 2013. *The House of Prisoners: Slavery and State in Uruk During the Revolt Against Samsu-Iluna*. Berlin: De Gruyter.

Shankman, Paul, 2009. *The Trashing of Margaret Mead: Anatomy of an Anthropological Controversy*. Madison: University of Wisconsin Press.

Sharp, Lauriston, 1952. 'Steel Axes for Stone-Age Australians'. *Human Organization* 11(2): 17–22.

Shelach, Gideon, 1996. 'The Qiang and the Question of Human Sacrifice in the Late Shang Period'. *Asian Perspectives* 35(1): 1–26.

Shepherd, Gill, G. Feuerstein and S. al-Marzooq, 1978. 'The Omani *Xanith*'. *Man* 13(4): 663–71.

Shostak, Marjorie, 1981. *Nisa: The Life and Words of a !Kung Woman*. Cambridge: Harvard University Press.

Slater, P., K. Hedman and T. Emerson, 2014. 'Immigrants at the Mississippian Polity of Cahokia: Strontium Isotope Evidence for Population Movement'. *Journal of Archaeological Science* 44: 117–27.

Smith, Michael, ed., 2012. *The Comparative Archaeology of Complex Societies*. Cambridge: Cambridge University Press.

Smith, Michael and F.F. Berdan, eds, 2003. *The Postclassic Mesoamerican World*. Salt Lake City: University of Utah Press.

Smith, Sarah, 2002. 'A Cock of One's Own'. In Merri Lisa Johnson, ed., *Jane Sexes it Up: True Confessions of Feminist Desire*. New York: Four Walls Eight Windows.

Smuts, Barbara, 1985. *Sex and Friendship in Baboons*. New York: Aldine de Gruyter.

Solnit, Rebecca, 2017. *The Mother of All Questions*. Chicago: Haymarket.

Sparrow, Jeff, 2021. *Crimes Against Nature: Capitalism and Global Heating*. Melbourne: Scribe.

Spencer, Baldwin and F.J. Gillen, 2014 (1899). *The Native Tribes of Central Australia*. Global Grey.

Spikins, Penny, 2019. 'Sharing and inclusion: generosity, trust and response to vulnerability in the distant past'. In Lavi and Friesem, 2019, 57–70.

Spivak, Gayatri Chakravorty, 1988. 'Can the Subaltern Speak?' In Cary Nelson and Lawrence Grossberg, eds, *Marxism and the Interpretation of Culture*. Basingstoke: Macmillan, 271–313.

# BIBLIOGRAPHY

Stanford, Craig, 1998. 'The Social Behavior of Chimpanzees and Bonobos: Empirical Evidence and Shifting Assumptions'. *Current Anthropology* 39(4): 399–420.

———, 2018. *The New Chimpanzee: A Twenty-First Century Portrait of Our Closest Kin*. Cambridge: Harvard University Press.

Steadman, Dawnie Wolfe, 2008. 'Warfare Related Trauma at Orendorf, A Middle Mississippian Site in West-Central Illinois'. *American Journal of Physical Anthropology* 136: 51–64.

Sterelny, Kim, 2012. *The Evolved Apprentice: How Evolution Made Humans Unique*. Cambridge: MIT Press.

———, 2021. *The Pleistocene Social Contract: Culture and Cooperation in Human Evolution*. Oxford: Oxford University Press.

Stibbard-Hawkes, Duncan, 2020. 'Egalitarianism and democratized access to lethal weapons: a neglected approach'. In Moreau, 2020, 83–102.

Stiner, Mary C., 1994. *Honor among Thieves: A Zooarchaeological Study of Neanderthal Ecology*. Princeton: Princeton University Press.

———, 2002. 'Carnivory, Coevolution and the Geographic Spread of the Genus *Homo*'. *Journal of Archaeological Research*, 10: 1–63.

Stiner, Mary C. and Steven Kuhn, 2019. 'How Hearth and Home Made us Human'. *Journal of Anthropological Research* 75(3): 305–27.

Stokes, Martin, 2010. *The Republic of Love: Cultural Intimacy in Turkish Popular Music*. Chicago: University of Chicago Press.

Strathern, Marilyn, 1972. *Women in Between: Female Roles in a Male World: Mount Hagen, New Guinea*. London: Seminar.

———, 1988. *The Gender of the Gift*. Berkeley: University of California Press.

Strum, Shirley, 1987. *Almost Human: A Journey into the World of Baboons*. New York: Random House.

Stuart, George, 1972. 'Who Were the "Mound Builders"?' *National Geographic Magazine* 147(5): 783–801.

Suggs, Robert, 1971. 'Sex and Personality in the Marquesas: A Discussion of the Linton-Kardiner Report'. In Marshall and Suggs, 1971.

Sumption, John, 2015. *Cursed Kings: The Hundred Years War IV*. London: Faber and Faber.

Sutton, Peter and Kerry Walshe, 2001. *Farmers or Hunters: The Dark Emu Debate*. Melbourne: Melbourne University Press.

Sykes, Rebecca, 2020. *Kindred: Neanderthal Life, Love, Death and Art*. London: Bloomsbury.

Symons, Donald, 1979. *The Evolution of Human Sexuality*. Oxford: Oxford University Press.

Táíwò, Olúfẹ́mi, 2022. *Against Decolonisation: Taking African Agency Seriously*. London: Hurst.

Tambiah, S.J., 1968. 'The Magical Power of Words'. *Man* 3: 175–208.

Tapper, Nancy (Lindisfarne), 1991. *Bartered Brides: Politics, Gender and Marriage in an Afghan Tribal Society*. Cambridge: Cambridge University Press.

Tapper, Richard, 1979. *Pasture and Politics: Economies, Conflict and Ritual among Shahsevan Nomads of Northwestern Iran*. London: Academic.

———, ed., 1983. *The Conflict of Tribe and State in Iran and Afghanistan*. New York: St. Martins.

———, 1997. *Frontier Nomads of Iran: A Political and Social History of the Shahsevan*. Cambridge: Cambridge University Press.

# BIBLIOGRAPHY

Tapper, Richard and Nancy Tapper, 1986. '"Eat This, It'll Do You a Power of Good": Food and Commensality among Durrani Pashtuns'. *American Ethnologist* 13(1): 62–79.

Tapper, Richard with Nancy Lindisfarne-Tapper, 2020. *Afghan Village Voices: Stories from a Tribal Community*. London: I.B. Tauris.

Taylor, Larissa Juliet, 2009. *The Virgin Warrior: The Life and Death of Joan of Arc*. New Haven: Yale University Press.

Taylor, Timothy, 2002. *The Buried Soul: How Humans Invented Death*. London: Fourth Estate.

Thomas, David John, 1973. *Pemon Demography, Kinship and Trade*. PhD Thesis, University of Michigan.

———, 1982. *Order without Government: The Society of the Pemon Indians of Venezuela*. Urbana: University of Illinois Press.

Thomas, Elizabeth Marshall, 2006. *The Old Way: A Story of the First People*. New York: Farrar, Straus and Giroux.

Thomas, Julian, 1992. 'Gender, Politics and American Archaeology'. *Anthropology Today* 8(3): 12–13.

Thomas, J.T., 2019. 'Who's Afraid of Sally Binford: Life After Anthropology'. *Medium*, 12 Nov.

Thompson, E.P. 1968. *The Making of the English Working Class*. London: Penguin.

Tierney, Patrick, 2000. *Darkness in El Dorado: How Scientists and Journalists Devastated the Amazon*. New York: W.W. Norton.

Tlhabi, Redi, 2012. *Endings & Beginnings: A Story of Healing*. Johannesburg: Jacana.

Toews, Miriam, 2018. *Women Talking*. London: Faber and Faber.

Tolentino, Jia, 2019. *Trick Mirror: Reflections on Self-Delusion*. New York: Random House.

Tomlinson, Gary, 2015. *A Million Years of Music: The Emergence of Human Modernity*. New York: Zone.

Toussaint, Sandy, 1999. *Phyllis Kaberry and Me: Anthropology, History and Aboriginal Australia*. Melbourne: Melbourne University Press.

Traister, Rebecca, 2018. *Good and Mad: The Revolutionary Power of Women's Anger*. New York: Simon and Schuster.

Trigger, Bruce, 2003. *Understanding Early Civilizations: A Comparative Study*. Cambridge: Cambridge University Press.

Tucci, Giuseppe, 2001. *The Religions of Tibet*. London: Routledge.

Turnbull, Colin, 1965. *Wayward Servants: The Two Worlds of the African Pygmies*. London: Eyre and Spottiswood.

Turner, Terence, 2001. *The Yanomami and the Ethics of Anthropological Practice*. Occasional Paper, Cornell University Latin American Studies Program.

Turner, Victor, 1969. *The Ritual Process: Structure and Anti-Structure*. Chicago: University of Chicago Press.

Tuttle, Russell, 2014. *Apes and Human Evolution*. Cambridge: Harvard University Press.

Tylor, E.B., 1871. *Primitive Culture*. Two volumes, London: John Murray.

Utley, Robert, 1993. *The Lance and the Shield: The life and Times of Sitting Bull*. New York: Henry Holt.

VanDerwarker, Amber M. and Gregory D. Wilson, 2016. 'War, Food and Structural Violence in the Mississippian Central Illinois Valley: The Archaeology of Food and Violence'. In

# BIBLIOGRAPHY

VanDerwarker and Wilson, eds, *The Archaeology of Food and Warfare: Food Insecurity in Prehistory*. Cham: Springer, 75–105.
Vankeerberghen, Griet, 2013. '"Yellow Bird" and the Discourse on Retainer Sacrifice in China'. In Pierre Bonnechere and Renaud Gagné, eds, *Human Sacrifice: Cross-cultural Perspectives and Representations*. Liège: Presses Universitaire de Liège, 175–203.
Venbrux, Eric, 1995. *A Death in the Tiwi Islands: Conflict, Ritual and Social Life in an Australian Aboriginal Community*. Cambridge: Cambridge University Press.
Vogel, Lisa. 2014. *Marxism and the Oppression of Women*. Second edition, Chicago: Haymarket.
Wade, Nicholas, 2010. 'Harvard scientist guilty of misconduct'. *New York Times*, 20 Aug.
Waldman, Katy, 2018. 'Reading Ovid in the Age of #MeToo'. *The New Yorker*, 12 Feb.
Walter, M. Susan, 2006. 'Polygyny, Rank, and Resources in Northwest Coast Foraging Societies'. *Ethnology* 45(1): 41–57.
Ward, Charlie, 2016. *A Handful of Sand: The Gurundji Struggle, after the Walk-off*. Melbourne: Monash University Publishing.
Warner, Maria, 1985. *Monuments and Maidens: The Allegory of the Female Form*. London: Weidenfeld and Nicolson.
———, 2000 (1976). *Alone of all Her Sex: The Myth and the Cult of the Virgin Mary*. New York: Vintage.
———, 2013 (1981). *Joan of Arc: The Image of Female Heroism*. New York: Vintage.
Warner, W. Lloyd, 1957 (1937). *A Black Civilization: A Social Study of an Australian Tribe*. New York: Harper.
Watts, Jonathan, 2023. 'Investigate Bolsonaro for genocide of indigenous people—Brazilian minister'. *The Guardian*, 7 Feb.
Weaver, Gina Marie, 2010. *Ideologies of Forgetting: Rape in the Vietnam War*. Albany: SUNY Press.
Wells, Roger, 1983. *Insurrection: The British Experience, 1795–1803*. Gloucester: Alan Sutton.
White, Charles, 2003. *The Life and Times of Little Richard*. London: Omnibus.
White, Richard, 1991. *The Middle Ground: Indians, Empires and Republics in the Great Lakes Region, 1650–1815*. Cambridge: Cambridge University Press.
Whitehead, Neil, 2002. *Dark Shamans: Kanaimà and the Poetics of Violent Death*. Durham: Duke University Press.
Wiessner, Polly, 2005. 'Norm Enforcement among the Ju/'hoansi Bushmen: A Case of Strong Reciprocity?' *Human Nature* 16(2): 115–45.
Wikan, Unni, 1978. 'The Omani Xanith: A Third Gender Role?' *Man* (N.S.) 13(3): 473–5.
Wilcox, Michael, 2009. *The Pueblo Revolt and the Mythology of Conquest: An Indigenous Archaeology of Contact*. Berkeley: University of California Press.
———, 2010. 'Marketing Conquest and the Vanishing Indian: An Indigenous Response to Jared Diamond's Archaeology of the American Southwest'. In McAnany and Yoffee, 2010.
Wilde, Oscar, 1891. 'The Soul of Man Under Socialism'. Marxist Internet Archive.
Williams, J.M. et al., 2008. 'Causes of Death in the Kasekela Chimpanzees of Gombe National Park, Tanzania'. *American Journal of Primatology* 70: 766–77.
Wilson, Edward O., 1975. *Sociobiology: The New Synthesis*. Cambridge: Harvard University Press.
Wilson, Greg, 2015. 'Incinerated Villages in the North'. In Pauketat and Alt, 2015a, 99–104.

# BIBLIOGRAPHY

Wilson, Michael and 29 others, 2014. 'Lethal aggression in Pan is better explained by adaptive strategies than human impacts'. *Nature* 513: 414–17.

Wilson, Paul, 1982. *Black Death, White Hands*. Sydney: George Allen and Unwin.

Wimpelmann, Torunn, 2017. *The Pitfalls of Protection: Gender, Violence and Power in Afghanistan*. Berkeley, University of California Press.

Wolf, Eric, 1992. *Europe and the People without History*. Berkeley: University of California Press.

———, 1999. *Envisioning Power: Ideologies of Dominance and Crisis*. Berkeley: University of California Press.

Wolferman, Kristie, 1997. *The Osage in Missouri*. Columbia: University of Missouri Press.

Wolin, Daniela, 2022. 'Decapitated Heads as Elite Visual Culture in Late Shang China'. *Cambridge Archaeological Journal* 32(3): 189–204.

Woolley, Leonard, 1952. *Ur of the Chaldees*. London: Penguin.

Wrangham, Richard, 1999. 'The Raw and the Stolen: Cooking and the Ecology of Human Origins'. *Current Anthropology* 40: 567–94.

———, 2009. *Catching Fire: How Cooking Made Us Human*. London: Perseus.

———, 2019. *The Goodness Paradox: How Evolution Made Us Human*. London: Profile.

Wrangham, Richard and Dale Peterson, 1997. *Demonic Males: Apes and the Origins of Human Violence*. Bloomsbury: London.

Wrangham, Richard, Michael Wilson and Martin Muller, 2006. 'Comparative rates of violence in chimpanzees and humans'. *Primates* 47: 14–26.

Wright, Evan, 2004. *Generation Kill*. New York: Putnam.

Wright, N.A.R., 1983. '"Pillagers" and "brigands" in the hundred years war'. *Journal of Medieval History* 9(1): 15–24.

Wright, Rita, ed., 1998a. *Gender and Archaeology*. Philadelphia: University of Pennsylvania Press.

———, 1998b. 'Gendered Ways of Knowing in Archaeology'. In Wright, 1998a, 1–19.

———, 1998c. 'Technology, Gender, and Class: Worlds of Difference in Ur III Mesopotamia'. In Wright, 1998a, 79–110.

Yamagiwa, Juichi, 1987, 'Intra-and inter-group interactions of an all-male group of virunga mountain gorrillas (*Gorrilla gorilla beringei*)'. *Primates* 28: 1–30.

Yoffee, Norman, 2005, *Myths of the Archaic State: Evolution of the Earliest Cities, States, and Civilizations*. Cambridge: Cambridge University Press.

Yoffee, Norman, ed., 2019. *The Evolution of Fragility: Setting the Terms*. Cambridge: McDonald Institute for Archaeological Research.

Yoffee, Norman and Andrea Seri, 2019. 'Negotiating Fragility in Ancient Mesopotamia: Arenas of Contestation and Institutions of Resistance'. In Yoffee, 2019, 183–96.

Young, Biloine Whiting and Melvin L. Fowler, 2000. *Cahokia: The Great Native American Metropolis*. Urbana: University of Illinois Press.

Žižek, Slavoj, 2009. *Violence*. London: Profile.

Zych, Thomas, 2015. 'The Game of Chunkey'. In Pauketat and Alt, 2015a, 71–4.

# INDEX

!Kung, 48, 52, 67–8, 89–91, 93, 187, 201
ǂTomasho, !Kung healer, 90

*1491* (Mann), 240
9/11, 300, 304

Abbasid empire, 225
Abel, 113–4
abortion, 12, 69–70
adaptation, 19–21, 76–9, 84, 96, 145, 331, 367–8
   birth intervals, 63, 66, 69
   and climate change, 16, 42
   hunter-gatherers, 1, 4, 17, 47–50, 71, 98, 109, 128, 334
   primates, 24, 27, 29, 41, 46, 63
   *See also* agriculture; same sex adaptation
Abdulali, Sohaila, 140
Aboriginal Australians. *See* Australian Aboriginals
*Aboriginal Women, Sacred and Profane* (Kaberry), 184
Abu Ghraib prison, 161, 220, 297–8, 302–12
Afghanistan, 114, 116–7, 126, 160–1, 298–300, 304
   Afghan women, 298–304

Africa, human evolution in, 24, 27, 50–1, 55–9, 98, 169
*Against our Will* (Brownmiller), 297
agnotology, 256
agriculture, 167, 234–6
   Andean, 104, 114
   and class, 103–15
   grain, 104–5, 124, 195
   invention of, 2, 11, 19, 101–115, 124, 163–5, 169, 192, 196, 360, 363–4, 367
   irrigation, 105–6, 110, 112, 115–116, 119, 170, 172, 199
   Mesopotamia, 104, 115–6
   New Guinea, 104, 171–8
   *See also* slash and burn farming; tubers
Aka, 46–7, 58, 95, 199
Akkadian, 224
Alaska, 48, 167, 264
alcohol 182
Algaze, Guillermo, 116–7
alpha males, 6, 26, 32–3, 42–4, 63–5, 71–2, 87–8, 94, 98, 145
Alt, Susan, 243, 246–7, 263
Amazonia, 14, 47, 196, 202, 206–9, 211, 353–4, 363

419

# INDEX

ambush hunting. *See* hunting
American Anthropological Association (AAA), 356–7
American Indian Movement (AIM), 241
American Revolution, 260
Amsterdam, 85
anal sex, 289–90
anarchism and anarchists, 148–9, 198–9, 344–5
anatomy, 19–21
    changes in human evolution, 51, 55–6, 71–74, 84, 98
    primate, 71
    *See also* brain size; genitals
*Ancient Society* (Morgan), 261, 335
Andaman Islanders, 48
Andes, 104, 114
anthropology and anthropologists, 1, 10–11, 34–5, 47–8, 54–5, 62, 74, 80–2, 87–95, 114, 148, 163, 165, 169, 174–5, 178–9, 207–8, 211, 229, 242, 256, 335, 350–3, 386, 391
    American, 254, 257–8, 261–3, 313, 346–9
    Australian, 181–190
    Brazilian, 353–4
    British, 8
    feminist, 184, 186–90, 197–8
    French, 171
    racist and anti-racist, 182–3, 326, 333–4, 336, 340–1
    silence of, 183–5
    of women, 367–8
apes, 19, 21–4, 30, 49, 56–7, 59, 66–7, 70–5, 78, 84, 99
Appadurai, Arjun, 256

archaeology and archaeologists, 1–2, 8, 11, 15, 46, 50, 82, 88, 94, 106–8, 111, 120, 126, 147–8, 160, 163–4, 166–7, 172, 220, 222, 224, 229, 232, 234–40, 245–8, 256, 259–60, 360–2, 364, 367
    American exceptionalism, 261–2
    feminist, 241–4, 263–4, 384
    molecular, 49
    New Archaeology, 262–3
    racist and anti-racist, 261–3
    sexist, 232, 241–4, 249, 263
Arctic hunters, 46, 91, 114
Argyll, Duke of, 334
Aristotle, 137
*Ars Amatoria*, 154
art, 95
Artaud, Antonin, 242
*Art of Not Being Governed* (Scott), 198–9
Ashanti, 199
Arab, 221, 298
Arthur and his Round Table, 94
Ashwin, Arthur, 180
Assad, Hafez, 152
Assyrian beards, 120
Atrahasis, myth of worker god, 119–20
Australian Aboriginals, 11, 14, 46, 48, 55, 92–4, 164–6, 178–94
    agriculture, 192–3
    marriage, 188–92
    *See also* Australian massacres; traders and slave raiding in Australia

# INDEX

Australian Aboriginal groups
   Anmatyerre, 181–2
   Aranda or Arrente, 93
   Kaytete, 181
   Tasmanian, 48, 181
   Walbiri or Walpiri, 181, 183
   Warumungu, 180
   See also Australian Aboriginals; Australian massacres; Kimberleys; Murngin; Warrabri; Tiwl
Australian colonial massacres
   Forrest River, 185
   Kimberleys, 184–5, 381
   Lumbia, 185
   O'Leary, 381
   Queensland, 181
   silence of anthropologists, 183–5
   Tasmania, 181
axes, stone and steel, 9, 49, 111, 174–5, 177, 184, 196, 244, 262, 350–1
Aztecs, 232, 240

baboons, 7–8, 19–21, 23–7, 31–3, 40, 42, 45–6, 53, 61, 63–5, 71–3, 86, 88, 322, 327
Babylon, 117–20, 222
Bad Science, 6–7
   See also scientific method
Bagemihl, Bruce, 78
Baghdad, 225, 305, 307
bananas
   DNA similar to humans, 30
   for provisioning chimpanzees, 35, 37–38
   as staple crop, 347

Barelli, Claudia, 21–2
Basin, Thomas, 270
Basra, 115
Bastille, 269
Bathurst Island, 190
Beaune, Collette, 281
Bedford, Duke of, 275, 277–8
Bedouin, 114
Beevor, Anthony, 388
Bell, Diane, 179–82, 187, 191, 193
Benin, 222
Beowulf, 147
*Better Angels of Our Nature* (Pinker), 359, 362–3
Bhagavad-Gita, 148
Bible, 118–9, 138, 289, 319–21, 326
big men and rubbish men, 169–78
*Biological Exuberance* (Bagemihl), 78
Binford, Lewis, 262–3
Binford, Sally Rosen, 241, 263
'Birdman', 237–8, 243–4
   See also Cahokia
Bishop Wilberforce of Oxford, 333–4
binary categories, 77, 132–4, 137–40, 233, 378
*Bitch* (Cooke), 75
Black Atlantic, 284
Black Death in Eurasia, 135, 268–70
Black Lives Matter, 16, 179, 371
*Black Civilization* (Warner), 183–4
Blair, Cherie, 301
Blair, Tony, 301

# INDEX

Boehm, Christopher, 10, 87–9, 345
Bois, Guy, 269–70, 277–8, 384
Bollywood, Lollywood and Nollywood, 137
Bonnycastle, Kevin Denys, 157
Boas, Franz, 175, 340
bonobos, 8, 19–21, 29–30, 35, 39–45, 50, 57, 59, 66–7, 71–5, 84–6, 98–9, 145, 327, 330, 374
borders and walls, 21, 78, 195, 199
Borofsky, Robert, 391
Botswana, 52, 63, 90
boundaries, blurred, ambiguous and transgressed, 128–32, 140–4, 271, 277
'Bourgeois of Paris', the, 281–2
brain size, 26, 30, 57, 65, 67, 94–5, 324, 337
Brazil, 47, 69, 128, 211, 217, 347, 350–1, 353–7
breasts, 74, 139, 273, 281, 324
Briggs, Jean, 10, 90–1
Britain, 81, 126, 135–6, 141–2, 153–4, 160–1, 163, 180, 249, 255, 284–5, 291, 300–1, 319, 321–6, 334, 337–8, 341, 363
See also England; Scotland; UK
British Columbia, 167, 259
See also First Nations (Canada); Kamloops
British empire, see colonialism, British
British Museum, 81, 222–4
British Navy, see Royal Navy
Brittany, 275

bronze and Bronze Age, 111, 116
tin mines in Herat and Badakhshan, 116
Brookfield, Harold, 349
Brown, Paula, 349
Brownmiller, Susan, 297
Bryan, Kelly, 303, 308–10, 312
Buddhism, 186, 199–200
bullies and bullying, 1, 8, 29, 49, 86–91, 99, 103–5, 110–1, 126, 139, 148, 155, 173, 215, 352–5, 360, 366
comforting losers among primates, 40, 65
killing bullies, 88–9
Burgundians and Burgundy, 269–71
burials. See graves
Burma and Burmese, 199
Burns, Lizzie, 339
Burns, Louis, 253
Burns, Mary, 336, 339
Bush, George, 6, 300–1, 304, 311
Bush, Laura, 301
by-product theory, 76–7, 83–4, 375
See also nipples; orgasms

Caboche, Pierre, 269
Cabochion Revolt of 1513, 269
Cadiz, 287, 291, 295
Cahokia, 14, 221, 231–48, 256–7, 259–60, 262–5, 280, 283, 313, 335, 363, 384
Cain, 113–4
Caldwell, Ryan Ashley, 302–12
Calais, 275, 277, 281

# INDEX

Calusa, 169, 345
Canada, 38, 48, 153, 259
  *See also* First Nations
cannibals, rumours of, 202–3
canoes, 166–9, 191–2, 236, 245
capitalism, 69, 113, 124, 135–6, 148, 171, 177–8, 213, 219, 249, 255, 260, 283–5, 316–9, 321–2, 340, 342, 358, 362, 368
  *See also* class society; neoliberalism
carnivores, 24, 30, 39, 45–6, 50–5, 61
Caroni River, 211
*Case of the Female Orgasm* (Lloyd), 76–7
caste, 13, 142, 152–3, 155, 370
Catholic Church. *See* Christianity
Catlin, George, 253–6
Cauchon, 'Peter the Pig', Bishop of Beauvais, 275, 278–80
Central African Republic, 46
Chagnon, Napoleon, 15, 313, 347–57, 362, 386, 391
Charles VII of France, 271–5, 279
Chartism, 319–20
Chatwin, Bruce, 226, 383
Chavez, Hugo, 217, 353
Cheney, Dick, 304
Cheney, Sarah, 63
Children, 81, 85–6
  abuse of, 153–6
  in class societies, 110–1, 116–8, 131–2, 135–6, 150, 271–2, 316–7
  among egalitarian farmers, 200–2, 207–8, 214–8

and evolution, 15, 52–3, 58–9, 73–4, 322–3, 325–6, 339, 348–9, 352
  among hunter gatherers, 93–7, 187–9, 204–5, 249
  intersex, 140–1
  and love, 146, 331
  pink and blue, 129
  shared childcare, 1, 8, 56, 61, 65–71, 85–6, 98–9, 116–8, 331
  victims of colonialism and racism 180–3, 191, 259, 301, 305–6
Chimpanzees, 8–9, 19–20, 26, 29–45, 50, 52–3, 59, 61–3, 66–7, 69, 71–8, 86–8, 145, 159–60, 321, 356
*Chimpanzee Politics* (de Waal), 41–3
China, 14, 78, 104, 147–8, 161, 196, 198–201, 301, 363
  ancient, 104, 147, 195, 222, 256, 382–3
  Great Wall, 195
  *See also* Lahu
chivalry, 135, 267
Chumash, 166–7, 169, 260, 263
Christianity, 103–4, 110, 138, 186, 192, 199, 202, 303, 255, 258, 260, 294, 298, 339
  Capuchins, 211, 216
  Carmelites, 269
  Catholic Church, 143, 154–5, 218, 259, 353, 368
  Church of England, 318, 321
  Jesus, 126, 273, 280, 303
  Salesians, 353

423

# INDEX

Unitarians, 318–9
CIA (Central Intelligence Agency), 302, 304–5, 310
Cinderella, 131
Ciudad Bolivar, 217
class and class societies, 7, 24–5, 38, 47–8, 97, 101, 163–71, 177–9, 195, 222, 229, 232–3, 234, 240–2, 260–4, 270, 272, 272, 274, 313, 315, 322, 326, 231–5, 333–5, 345, 360, 362–5, 378
   invention of class societies, 2–3, 11–1, 15–6, 29, 49, 103–121, 124–7, 164–5, 231, 365
   See also elites; ruling class; workers; working class
class and gender, 2–3, 13–4, 83, 133–65, 179, 220, 224, 231, 248–9, 251–3, 256–7, 264, 276, 297, 313, 323–4, 326, 334–340, 346, 368–9
   See also gender inequality; sexual violence
class struggle, 14–16, 124–7, 244–8, 264, 268, 274, 277–8, 298, 342, 346, 366, 371
classless societies, 171, 176, 195–218, 269–71, 360
   See also egalitarian societies
climate change, 2, 16, 19, 50, 56, 135, 245, 322, 344–6, 365–6, 371
clitoris, 40, 54, 73–80, 83, 374–80
   See also orgasms
Clovis technology, 361

*Collapse* (Diamond), 45
Collier, June, 124
*Colonial Frontier Massacres* (Lyndall Ryan), 181
colonialism and settler colonialism, 10, 14–5, 89, 117, 197, 202–3, 249, 285, 313, 326, 340–1, 344
   American, 197, 250, 254–8, 262–4
   Australian, 171–2, 178–194, 232
   British, 180
   Chinese, 201
   Dutch, 211
   French, 249
   Portuguese, 47
   Venezuelan, 216–7
   See also Australian colonial massacres; Australian trading and slave raiding; Ghost Dance religion; Osage; shatter zones; stages theory of evolution
*Coming of Age in Samoa* (Mead), 80–1
*Communist Manifesto* (Marx and Engels), 334
competition in evolution, 1, 3, 9, 25–7, 42, 72–3, 87–8
   between females, 24
   between males, 20–1, 24, 30–9, 348–58
   over territory, 22–3
Congo River, 39
continua, 13, 58, 79, 139, 147, 152
contradiction, 2, 12, 112, 128–9,

# INDEX

131, 136, 140, 148, 154–5, 176, 263
*See also* dialectic
Cooke, Lucy, 75
cooking, 34, 54, 56–8, 68, 81, 88, 91, 94, 98, 206, 209, 213, 249, 284
*See also* fire
Cook, James, 164
Coontz, Stephanie, 323
Cormier, Loretta, 10–11, 47, 73, 77
Cornwall, Andrea, 367, 378
corveé labour, 110
*Creation of Inequality* (Flannery and Marcus), 106
*Crisis of Feudalism* (Bois), 269–70
cross-dressing, 272, 275–82
*See also* transgender; Two-spirit people
Crow Creek massacre, 247, 363
cryptic female choice, 373
Cummings, Marisa Miako<sup>n</sup>da, 257
Cusquel, Pierre, 279–80
Custer, George Armstrong, 249

Dalai Lama, 143–4
Dalit, 370
*Dancing in the Streets* (Ehrenriech), 144
Darby, Joseph, 309
dark age, 113, 150
*Dark Emu* (Pascoe), 192
*Darkness in El Dorado* (Tierney), 355–6
Darwin, Anne, 320
Darwin, Charles, 3, 10, 15, 78, 165, 313, 318–29, 333–5, 347, 349

See also Social Darwinism
Darwin, city in Australia, 190–2
Darwin, Emma, 318
Dauphin. *See* Charles VII of France
Davies, William, 169
Davis, Angela, 297
Davis, Javal, 306
Davis, Ken, 309
Dawkins, Richard, 355–6
*Dawn of Everything* (Graeber and Wengrow), 313, 342–6
debt, 109–10, 117
demand sharing, 92–3
demonic male controversy, 33–9
*Demonic Males* (Petersen and Wrangham), 34–5
Denisovans, 54–5
*Daughters of the Dreaming* (Bell), 179
Dennett, Daniel, 355–6
Desmond, Adrian, 319, 389
*Descent of Man* (Darwin), 15, 318, 321, 324, 348
*Desert People* (Meggitt), 183
de Waal, Frans, 5–6, 10, 41–3, 145, 356, 356
dialectic, 1, 112–3, 128–9, 131–2, 137, 142, 154–6, 176
*See also* contradiction; scientific method
Diamond, Jared, 1, 245, 384
Diana, Princess, 133
diet, 9, 22, 30, 45, 52–9, 85, 98, 168, 174, 233–4, 242, 337
in primates, 12, 30, 35, 39, 110
difference and 'difference', 12–4, 16, 59, 69, 77–79, 86, 89–90,

# INDEX

99, 101, 123–139, 145–7, 151, 159, 176, 189–201, 204, 206, 208, 219, 248–9, 317, 334, 346, 355, 359
digging sticks, 9, 49–50
dimorphism, sexual, 30, 71, 145, 250
*Discipline and Punish* (Foucault), 242
*Dislocating Masculinity* (Cornwall and Lindisfarne), 367
divide and rule, 13, 127–32, 139, 147, 298
dividual, 130
  *See also* partible
DNA, 2, 29–30, 32, 49, 106, 160, 245–6
*Doll's House* (Ibsen), 176
*Domestication of the Penis* (Cormier and Jones), 73
dominance hierarchies in primates, 2–3, 8, 17, 22–46, 49, 62–4, 71, 86
  *See also* bullies and bullying
Domrémy, 267, 270–1, 274
Dugan, James, 295
Dunbar, Robin, 95–6
Durkheim, Emile, 158
Du, Shanshan, 198–201

Eana. *See* Inanna
economics, economic equality and inequality, 3, 11–12, 19, 48, 93, 134–5, 155, 164–6, 170–1, 174, 176–8, 184, 187–9, 193, 214, 219, 224–5, 234, 240, 248–50, 260, 284, 318–9, 334–5, 342, 344, 349, 360, 366, 376, 381, 385
  *See also* capitalism; economic change and gender; Marxism
Ecuador, 14, 84, 196, 202, 206
egalitarian societies, 1–2, 8, 14, 17, 69, 83, 87, 89–91, 97–9, 105, 109, 113–4, 123, 160, 168, 170, 177, 187, 195–218, 231, 233, 245–57, 260, 264, 315, 326, 336, 342–5, 360, 366, 376, 381, 385
  *See also* classless societies
Egypt, ancient, 46–8, 104, 222, 233, 360–1
Ehrenreich, Barbara, 144
Eldorado, Venezuela, 217
Elkin, A. P., 183
Eller, Cynthia, 327, 379
elites, 1–3, 6–7, 11–13, 15, 26, 103–113, 116, 123–30, 135–48, 151–3, 156–7, 160–1, 170, 219, 224, 232, 235–41, 244–47, 257, 260, 264, 283, 298, 301, 321, 333, 345–6
  *See also* class and class societies; ruling class
Elizabeth I, 135
Elwin, Verrier, 84, 341
Emerson, Thomas, 246–7
emotions, overlapping, 130–1
emperor penguins, 331
empire, 112–5, 135, 161, 199, 221, 224–5, 245, 283–5, 291–2, 319, 321–6, 334, 338–9, 341, 349
enforcers and violence, 11, 95, 105, 108, 110–11, 119, 125–6, 132, 146–9, 155, 171, 191, 370

426

# INDEX

Engels, Friedrich, 10, 15, 165, 171, 261, 313, 318, 333–42
England, 11, 82–3, 267–8, 270–1, 275–82, 294–5, 316, 318, 320–1, 326
  English Civil War, 284
  *See also* Joan of Arc
Enlil, 119
Epstein, Jeffrey, 155
essentializing gender, 11, 132, 139–40, 316, 349
Euphrates river, 115–119
Europe, 83–87, 94, 135, 143–4, 195, 241, 260–1, 267–8, 283–5, 292, 299, 316, 322, 362
  ancient, 50, 54–6, 98, 106, 147, 169, 221, 225, 241, 256, 360–1
Evans-Prtichard, E. E., 175
evolution, 19–21, 78–80, 263, 347–64
  human, 1–12, 17, 29, 34, 38–9, 46, 50, 54, 61–9, 71–88, 103–4, 113–4, 149–52, 161–2, 313, 315–42, 344–5, 368–9, 373
  learning in evolution, 68, 210
  primate, 22, 25–6, 41, 44
  same-sex sex, evolutionary advantages, 330–1
  *See also* Darwin; Engels; Roughgarden; Social Darwinism
evolutionary psychology, 3–8, 21, 25–6, 68, 75–6, 80, 149, 263, 313, 318, 347–64
*Evolution's Rainbow* (Roughgarden), 75–7, 327

exchange. *See* gift exchange; marriage
exploitation, 11, 108, 113, 148–9, 170–1, 184, 193, 197, 208, 222, 243, 346
  corveé, 110
  rent, 109–10, 268
  serfdom, 11, 46, 109–10, 146, 268
  sharecropping, 109
  taxes, 109–10, 112, 115, 125, 178, 199, 269, 277
  wage labour, 10, 135–6, 175, 216, 268, 283–4, 286, 319
  *See also* debt; slavery; working class

*Fallgirls* (Caldwell), 302–12
families, 12, 57–9, 83, 97, 108–9, 111, 117, 125, 137, 148, 166–7, 177, 182, 205, 216–7, 225, 247–8, 253, 261, 265, 271, 275, 299, 323, 336, 368
  fantasy families, 315–6, 347
  nuclear families, 4, 314
  'the' family, 315–17, 334–5, 339–40
  *See also* grandparents
feasts, 94–5, 107–8, 173–7, 205–6, 246
Feinberg, Leslie, 276–7
female choice. *See* sexual selection.
feminism and feminists, 4–7, 62, 69–70, 76–83, 96, 137–8, 156, 175–6, 179, 184, 188, 198, 224, 232, 241, 243, 261,

427

# INDEX

264, 297, 301, 313, 316, 327, 334, 339, 369–370
  *See also* anthropology; archaeology; primatology
Ferguson, Anne, 377
Ferguson, R. Brian, 34–8, 350–5, 354–5, 360, 363–4
Fertile Crescent, 104
  *See also* Mesopotamia; Egypt
fire, 34, 48–9, 185, 201, 227, 281
  as destruction, 120–1, 246
  in Australia, 192–3
  in evolution, 56–8, 92, 94. 98
  *See also* cooking
First Nations (Canada), 38, 259
  Baffin Island, 90–1
  Bella Coola, 167
  Coast Salish, 167
  Haida, 167
  Kwakiutl, 167, 345, 360
  Inuit, 90–2
  Nootka, 167
  Tlingit, 167–8, 264
  Tsimshian, 167
  *See also* Kamloops Residential school; Native American groups
fisherfolk, 164, 166–8, 345, 360
Fishtail technology, 361
Flannery, Kurt, 106
food, 19–22, 24, 30–1, 37–8, 46–7, 49, 57–59, 71, 88, 226, 337, 355
  control of food, 11, 101, 103–5, 108–115, 143, 147, 149, 152, 165–9, 173, 177–8, 185, 192, 208, 345, 366

shared food, 8, 48, 51–3, 56, 91–3, 107, 187–9, 193, 204–5, 212–3
foragers. *See* hunter-gatherers
Ford, Christine Blasey, 140
Foucault, Michel, 242
Fowler, Melvin, 237–8
Fortes, Meyer, 341
France, 17, 267–282, 285, 291, 299–300, 363
  revolution of 1789, 269, 285, 291
  *See also* anthropologists; colonialism and settler colonialism
Freeman, Derek, 82
Freud, Sigmund, 85, 137, 335
friendship, 6, 24–6, 31–2, 40–2, 64–5, 84–5, 88, 91–3, 96–7, 104, 115, 151, 173–4, 177, 181, 201, 213, 218, 368
Furuichi, Takeshi, 10

Galton, Francis, 321, 325–6
Gamble, Lynn, 166
*Game of Thrones* (Martin), 113, 267
Ganymede, 336
Gardner, Peter, 47, 94
Garriga, Father Benito de la, 211
Guadeloupe, Revolution of 1794, 291
Gay, Roxane, 140
*Gender and Archaeology* (Wright), 241
Gender, 114–5, 156, 159, 219–22, 239–40, 241, 243–4
  and class society, 124–7
  definition of, 130

# INDEX

division of labour, 4, 54–59, 61, 136–7, 161, 165, 167–8, 172–3, 224, 231, 250–1, 358
economic and gendered change, 224
essentialized gender, 11–3, 86, 132, 139–40, 316, 349
exceptions to our argument, 163–194
gender equal societies, 195–218
gender equality and inequality, 3–6, 11–14, 48, 70, 77, 83, 97, 103, 133–144, 147, 149, 151, 153, 163–194, 219, 231–3, 248–52
gender and evolution, 19, 56, 78
gender marking, 15, 129–30
gender similarities and differences, 12–3, 71–2, 77–8, 86, 99
pink girls and blue boys, 13, 129
*See also* anthropology; archaeology; feminism; LGBTQ; masculinity; rape; sex; violence, sexual
*Gender of the Gift* (Strathern), 175–6
*Genial Gene* (Roughgarden), 78, 327
genitals, 13, 26, 31, 71–5, 142, 205, 281, 311, 324
*See also* clitoris; labia; nipples; orgasms; penises; testicles; vaginas; vulvas

genocide, 193, 229, 240, 257–8, 261, 264, 322
*See also* Australian colonial massacres; Ghost Dance religion; holocaust
genome
chimpanzee, 9, 39
human, 9, 39, 55
gene for making women come, 76
Germany, 141, 285, 298–300, 323
Germanic monogamy, 337–8
Ghiselin, Michael, 5–6, 356
Ghost Dance religion, 258
gibbons, 8, 21–4, 30, 46, 71–3, 78, 96, 145
gift exchange, 173–6
*See also* feasts; ritual
Gilgamesh, 118, 147
Gillen, Francis, 93, 182–3
*Girl Archaeologist* (Kehoe), 263
God and gods, 15, 29, 92–3, 119–20, 127, 137, 140, 148–9, 200, 208–9, 221, 224, 237, 336
Christian, 271–2, 274–6, 279–80, 289, 320
Godelier, Maurice, 171, 174, 177
Gomorrah, possible sexual innovations in, 338
Gonds, 84
Goodale, Jane C., 190–2
Goodall, Jane, 10, 30–5, 37–8, 145
*Good and Mad* (Traister), 155
Gopal, Priyamvada, 338

429

# INDEX

gorillas, 8, 20, 22–4, 30–1, 50, 56–7, 62, 66, 71–3, 78, 86, 145, 321
Gould, Stephen J., 375
Gourevitch, Philip, 306, 308, 311
Graeber, David, 15, 110, 149, 313, 342–6
grandparents, 66–8, 91, 200, 317, 365
    grandmother hypothesis, 68
    grandparents as midwives, 200
    menopause, 66–7
Grann, David, 256
graves, 49, 106–8, 160, 167, 204, 222–4, 228–45, 257, 259, 262
    controversy over Native American, 360–5
    See also Cahokia; funerals
Great Death Pit, 222–4
    See also Ur
Green, David, 268
Griffith, Simon, 328
grooming in primates, 26, 31, 42–4, 64, 96, 330

Haas, Jonathan, 360–1
Hadza, 48
Haida. See First Nations (Canada)
Haitian Revolution, 285, 291
Han, 199
Harari, Yuval Noah, 1
Harcourt, Alexander, 10
Hardy, Thomas, revolutionary cobbler, 285–6
Harman, Sabrina, 14, 302–12
Hart, C. W. M., 190–2
Hauser, Mark, 355–6

Harvard, 3–5, 358
Hawthorne, Nathaniel, 132
Hebrews, 104, 118–9, 258
Henry VI of England, 275
Henry VIII, 135
Herat, ancient, 116
Herdt, Gilbert, 176–7
Herulians, 337
*hetairai*, 336
Hill Pandaram, 93
Hindus and Hinduism, 142, 186, 258
Hiroshima and Nagasaki, 342, 351
Hite, Shere, 79–80
*HMS Beagle*, 319
Holden, Preston, 263
Hollywood, 126, 137, 155, 348
holocaust, 349
*Homo erectus*, 54, 83
*Homo sapiens*, 54, 98, 361
homosexuality. See LGBTQ
homophobia. See LGBTQ
Horgan, John, 355–6
Homer, 147–8, 336
horses, 4, 49–50, 54, 110–5, 135, 185, 226–7, 248–9, 252, 267, 269–74, 319
Howell, Nancy, 11, 67–8
Hrdy, Sarah Blaffer, 4–5, 10, 61–70, 98, 345
Huaoroni, 14, 84, 187, 196–7, 202–6, 210, 212
    See also Jivaro
human nature, 1–4, 7–8, 11, 14, 16, 34, 109, 137, 154, 313, 349, 366
human sacrifice, 221–9, 237–44, 289

# INDEX

Hundred Years War, 269–70
Hunt, Kevin, 9, 44
hunter gatherers, 48–59, 65–8, 107
   'complex' hunter gatherers, 13, 123
   contemporary, 10, 46–54, 66–9, 88, 94, 163–9
   *See also* egalitarian societies; First Nations (Canada)
hunting, 44–55
   ambush hunting, 1, 29, 46, 51–6, 71, 98, 145
   division of labour between men and women in hunting, 54–9
   *See also* anatomy; egalitarian societies; hunter gatherers
Huxley, Thomas, 321, 333–4
Hyde, Anne, 255

Ibn Fadlan, 225–227
Ibsen, Henryk, 176
Ice Age, Eurasian, 50–2
ideology and ideologies, 6, 11–2, 44, 95, 99–101, 114, 123–40, 145, 147, 150, 176–8, 198, 213, 242, 247, 261, 263, 283, 315–6, 321–5, 338–40, 347
Illinois, 14, 235, 239, 247
impingement, 130–1
   *See also* Strathern
Inanna, 120–1
Indigenous Australians. *See* Australian Aboriginals
inequality, invention of, 2–3, 11–13, 19, 48, 86, 99, 101, 144, 164–5, 169, 329, 346, 365–6 101
   *See also* agriculture, invention of
infanticide, 23–4, 32, 35–6, 61–5, 69–70, 75, 98
inheritance of acquired characteristics, 320, 334
   *See also* Lamarck; transmutation
Indian National Congress, 341
Inka, 322
insurrection, 119–21, 244, 246
   *See also* uprisings
intersex people, 140–2, 250
   hijras and *xanith*, 142
   medieval Muslim law, 140–1
   in ancient Rome, 47
   in United States, 141
Inuit. *See* First Nations (Canada)
Iran, 104, 114, 304
Iraq, 14, 104, 115, 126, 161, 220, 222, 297, 300–312
Ireland and Irish people, 132, 141, 154, 156, 285–7, 293, 296, 323–5, 339
Iseminger, William, 238–40, 244
Ishtar. *See* Inanna
Islam and Muslims, 110, 138, 140–1, 298, 301, 304, 360
Islamophobia, 13, 298, 301, 360, 370
Islington mass demonstrations (1795), 286
Israel, 104, 260

Japan, 34, 153, 163, 184, 192
   Kabuki, 142
   Takarazaka, 142
jealousy, 86, 137, 189–90, 213, 323

431

# INDEX

Jebel Sahaba, 360, 363–4
Jefferson, Thomas, 255, 260
Jeffery, Joe, 169
Jerusalem, 118
Jervis, John. *See* St. Vincent
Jews, 156, 222–3, 239
   not seen as white, 339
Jivaro, 362
   *See also* Huaoroni
Joan of Arc, 14, 220, 241, 267–282
Joan of Kent, 268
Jolly, Margaret, 175
Jonathan, co-author, 211, 218, 335, 338, 365
Jones, Martin, 11, 94
Jones, Sharyn, 11, 73, 77
Jordan-Young, Rebecca, 373
Josephides, Lisette, 177

Kaberry, Phyllis, 184–9, 191, 193
Kachin, 199
Kalahari, 69, 89
Kamloops Indian Residential School, 259
Karkazis, Katrina, 141
Kavanayen, Venezuela, 216–7
Kehoe, Alice, 220, 241–2, 249, 263–4
Kenya, 64–5
Kerala, 93
Khalifa, Mustafa, 152
*Killers of the Flower Moon* (Grann), 256
Kilometre 88, 217
King, Thomas, 260
Kinsey, Alfred, 79–80

Khmer, 199
Kipling, Rudyard, 161
'Kiss with a Fist', 128
Klein, Naomi, 135
Kopenanwa, Davi, 352
Kuhn, Steven, 55–6
Kuk Swamp, 171–2
Kurdi, Alan, 370

labelling, 130, 132–3, 136–42, 150, 307
   *See also* binary categories; unmarked categories; marking difference; marking gender
labia, 73, 77
   *See also* genitals
Ladvenu, Martin, 279–80
*Lady Chatterley's Lover* (Lawrence), 153
Lafargue, Paul, 339
Lahu, 14, 196–201
Lamarck, Jean-Baptiste, 320, 334
Lambert, Patricia, 167
landowners, 109, 111, 125, 153, 268, 284–5
land rights, landlords and ownership, 11, 91, 105–12, 117, 124–5, 134–36, 146, 148, 151, 153, 160, 170, 172–85, 192–4, 196–7, 207, 217, 245, 255, 259–61, 267–8, 284–5, 318, 340, 348–50
   *See also* colonialism and settler colonialism; lords
Lang, Sabine, 250–4
language in evolution, 94–5
langurs, 62, 69, 77, 327

# INDEX

Lascaux cave art, 83
Last Common Ancestor (LCA), 38–9
Leacock, Eleanor, 189
Lebanon, 104
Lee, Richard, 10, 67–8, 89–91, 361
LeJaqc, Seth Stein, 288
Lekson, Stephen, 261–2
'Lethal aggression in *Pan*', 35–8
Levi-Strauss, Claude, 137
LGBTQ people, 140–2, 310
   'buggery' and 'sodomy' in the Royal Navy, 220, 283, 286, 288–90
   homophobia and persecution, 132–4, 141–2, 144, 287–90, 298, 310, 334–8
   and love, 296, 329–30
   in popular culture, 141–2
   same sex-sex in animals, 20–1, 40, 75, 78, 84, 327, 329–331
   solidarity with, 292–4
   *See also* cross-dressing; queer; transgender; Two-spirit people
Lhasa, 143–4
Libya, 304
Lindisfarne, Nancy. *See* Nancy, co-author
Little Old Men of the Osage, 253
   *See also* Osage
Little Richard, 142
Lloyd, Elizabeth, 76–80, 83
*Local Power in Old Babylon* (Seri), 117
London Corresponding Society, 285–6

London Women's Anthropology Group, 367
lords, 11, 14, 108–9, 111–3, 119, 149, 268–82, 284
   *See also* land rights
Louisiana Purchase, 260
love, 1, 11–12, 42, 68–70, 85, 96–7, 109, 128–32, 136–9, 145–6, 151, 153–4, 160, 201, 204, 226, 259, 267, 289, 294–5, 301–2, 309, 316, 331, 335–7, 339, 365–6, 371
   lovers and love-making, 14–5, 82, 85, 96–7, 118, 129, 132, 139, 146, 153, 201, 208–9, 294, 302, 336, 353
lynching in the United States, 153, 297, 299
   *See also* massacres; Australian colonial massacres

macaques, 75
Maduro, Nicolas, 217
Magdalene Laundries, 132
Mahabharata, 148
Maiden Castle hill fort, 160
Maiwand, battle of, 160–1, 379
Malinowski, Bronislaw, 80–2, 165, 175, 340
Manchester, 319
Mann, Charles, 240–1
Marcus, Joyce, 106–8
marking difference, 12, 128, 130, 139, 141, 151
   *See also* labelling
Marquesas, 82, 317
marriage, 13, 48, 103–4, 131–3, 136–7, 168, 173, 178–9,

433

# INDEX

186–92, 200–2, 205–6, 251, 253–4, 316–7, 323, 330, 334
  *See also* polygamy; weddings
Marriott, McKim, 130
Martin, George R. R., 267
Marx, Eleanor, 327
Marx, Emmanuel, 114
Marx, Karl, 318, 334–5, 338–9
Marx, Laura, 339
Marxism and Marxists, 15, 48, 96–7, 148–9, 171, 177, 263, 304, 334–335, 339–45, 369
Mary, mother of Jesus, 273
masculinities, 6, 120, 124, 134, 141–2, 161, 171, 177, 204, 227–9, 243–4, 252–3, 282, 297, 331, 334–5, 367–8, 378
massacres
  of Pemon, 217
  United States, 258–9, 263
  *See also* Australian colonial massacres
matriarchy, myths of, 241, 379
Maxwell, Ghislaine, 155
Maya, 196, 222, 232, 236, 240, 384
Mbuti, 93
McCarthyism, 263
McLennan, John Ferguson, 321
Mead, Margaret, 80–2, 250, 375
meat. *See* hunting; food
Meggitt, M. J., 183
Melbourne, University of, 182
Melville Island, 190
*Men as Women, Women as Men* (Lang), 250
men's studies, 378
menopause, 66–7

*See also* grandparents
menstruation, 210, 251
  by men, 209–10
  danger of menstrual blood, 198, 208
Mesoamerica, ancient, 104, 106, 169, 235–6, 240, 384
Mesopotamia, 106, 110, 115–21, 138, 222–3, 237, 256
  *See also* myths
*Metamorphoses* (Ovid), 154
Mexico, 104, 222, 233, 235, 248–9, 261–2
  Gulf of Mexico, 236–7
military rape, 152, 297–300
  *See also* violence and gender; violence, sexual
Minakshi temple, 47
mining
  ancient Herat and Badakhshan, 116
  on Pemon land, 217
  on Yanomamo land, 353–4, 357
Mirazon Lahr, Marta, 169
Mississippi, 153, 297
Mississippi River, 233, 235, 260
Mississippian culture, 248
  *See also* Cahokia
Missouri, 248, 252
Missouri River, 235, 247, 255
Modi, Narendra, 142, 370
monogamy, 8, 76, 78, 85, 103–4, 317, 323
  in birds, 328–9
  Germanic, 337
Montenegro, 87
Moore, James, 319

# INDEX

Moreau, Luc, 169
Morgan, Lewis Henry, 10, 261–3, 313, 333–6, 338–40
Moss, Madonna, 168, 264
movement, freedom of, 91–4
Murngin, 183–4, 262
Musa, Baba, 126
music and dance, 15, 95–6, 123
Mutinies of 1797, 283–296
    *Hermione*, 286
    Spithead and the Channel Fleet, 286
    Thames Estuary and the Nore, 286
Mutiny on *HMS St George*, 292–6
    Anderson, John, 292–5
    Benson, John, 287–90 292, 294–6
    Fitzgerald, James, 293–5
    Francis, Philip, 287–90
    Frazer, John, 290
    Hayes, John, 293–5
    McCann, Michael, 292–5
    Pearce, Capt. Shuldham, 292–4
    Playford, Thomas, 287
    Tippet, John, 287–8
    *See also* St. Vincent
Myanmar, 199, 370
mydutytospeak.com, 389
myths, 137, 145, 147, 149, 186–194, 203, 256
    Mesopotamian, 118–20
    Pemon, 215–6
    Piaroa, 208–10
    *See also* myth of matriarchy
Nancy, co-author, 211, 217–8, 235, 365–6

National Guard, Venezuela, 217
Native American culture and history, 11, 114
    *See also* Cahokia; Ghost Dance religion; Native American groups; Two-spirit people
Native American groups
    Apache, 197, 262
    Blackfoot, 249
    Cherokee, 114, 385
    Chickasaw, 385
    Choctaw, 385
    Iowa, 385
    Iroquois, 160, 199, 261, 335
    Kaw, 385
    Omaha, 385
    Oneota, 248, 385
    Osage, 252–6, 385
    Patwin, 167
    Pomo, 167
    Pueblo, 262, 337, 384
    Quipaw, 385
    Sioux, 197, 249, 262
    *See also* Cahokia; Calusa; Chumash; Ghost Dance religion; Two-spirit people; Native American plains people
Naturalizing inequality, difference and gender, 114, 123–44
natural selection, 5, 20, 313, 318–24, 326, 329
*Nature*, 35
*Nature's Rainbow* (Roughgarden), 78
Neale, Jonathan. *See* Jonathan, co-author
Neale, Terry, 338

# INDEX

Neanderthals, 54–6
Neel, James, 351, 355, 357
neoliberalism, 3, 6, 304, 349–50, 358
  *See also* capitalism
neolithic, 362
Netherlands, 41
  Dutch revolution and empire, 284–5
  *See also* colonialism; Australia, traders and slave raiding
*Never in Anger* (Briggs), 90
New Guinea groups
  Baruya, 171, 177
  Chimbu, 349
  Dugum Dani, 362
  Gebusi, 362
  Huli, 362
  Mae Enga, 362
  Sambia, 176–7
  Trobrianders, 80–3, 165, 380
  Vanatinai Islanders, 199
  Waghi, 171
  *See also* New Guinea highlands society; Papua New Guinea
New Guinea highlands society, 163–4, 169–78, 195–6, 349
  *See also* New Guinea groups; Papua New Guinea
*New York Times*, 355–6, 391
Nilotic people, 114
nipples, male, as byproducts, 76–7
Nishida, Toshi, 30, 34, 38
Nobel Peace Prize, 358–9
Nollywood, 137
Normandy, 269–70, 299–300
Norris Farm, 247, 363

Norse sagas, 147
North American exceptionalism, 232, 263
North American plains people, 114, 197, 231, 248–60, 263
Northern Territory of Australia, 179
North Pacific fishing societies, 13, 123, 163–4, 167–9

Obama, Barack, 358–9
oil wars, 134, 300
O'Keeffe, Georgia, 156
Olmec, 236
*Order without Government* (Thomas), 211–17
orgasms, 1, 71–86, 99, 129, 131, 156, 315, 331
*Origin of the Family* (Engels), 15, 261, 334–40
*Origin of Species* (Darwin), 15, 318, 321, 324, 383
Orinoco, 207, 211, 217
Orleans, siege of, 272–4
Osage. *See* Native American groups
Other Government Agencies (OGA), 305
overthrowing rulers, 14, 87–94, 104–9, 112–3, 245, 341, 377
  *See also* bullies; insurrections; mutinies; resistance
Ovid, 153–4

Padoan, Amanda, 243–4, 383
paleo-fantasy, 4, 21, 66, 88, 313, 315, 318–25, 338–40, 347, 349, 357–8

436

# INDEX

Palestine, 104, 161
Palestinian hanging position, 310–11
Paliyan, 47
*Pan*, genus, 29
Papua New Guinea, 13–14, 80, 164, 170–1
 *See also* New Guinea highlands society; New Guinea groups
Paris, 152, 171, 269, 274–5, 281–2, 291
partible people, 130–1
 *See also* dividual; Strathern
pastoralists, 337
 Australian ranchers, 180–1, 185
 herders, 103–6, 113–5
patriarchy. *See* sexism
Pauketat, Timothy, 234, 242–3, 247, 263
peasants, 14, 110–2, 125, 133, 160, 235, 241, 244
peasant revolts, 161, 235, 241, 267–74, 277–8
 England in 1381, 268
 Jacquerie in 1358, 269
 Lahu, 199
 Normandy in 1436, 270
Pemon, 14, 196–7, 206, 210–8, 347, 353–4
Penelope, 160
penises, 32, 40, 53–4, 71–3, 77, 79, 139, 208–9, 216, 229, 290, 308
Persian Gulf, 115, 142
Peterson, Dale, 34
Peterson, Nicholas, 92
Piaroa, 14, 196–7, 202, 206–13, 216, 347

Pierre, Isambart de la, 280
pigs, 49, 165, 169, 172–8
Pinker, Stephen, 1, 15, 313, 347, 355–64
pirates, women
 Bonny, Anne, 160
 Ching Shih, 160
 O'Malley, Grace, 160
 Read, Mary, 160
Piscitelli, Matthew, 360–1
polygamy, polyandry and polygyny, 167, 251, 254 317, 330
Powdermaker, Hortense, 341
predators. *See* carnivores
Price, Neil, 228–9
primates, 1–8, 19–21
 *See also* bonobos; chimpanzees; gibbons; gorillas; langurs
primate research sites
 Amboseli, 65
 Arnhem Zoo, 41–2
 Gombe, 23, 30, 33–5, 37–8, 62, 78, 87, 159–60
 Kibale, 34
 Mahale, 30, 34–5, 37, 47–8
 San Diego Zoo, 42
 Virunga Volcano, 78
 Yerkes Primate Research Centre, 42–3
primatology, 1–8, 10–11, 31, 61–2, 68, 75–6, 84, 87, 356
 feminist, 62
'primitive', 10, 15, 38–9, 165, 175, 197, 233, 260, 333–4, 339–40, 347–8, 358–9, 362
 *See also* stages theory of evolution; racism
Procopius, 337

# INDEX

*Production of Inequality* (Josephides), 177
Protector of Aboriginies, 182–3
prostitution. *See* sex work
provisioning, 35, 37–8
Prynn, Hester, 132
Psalm 137, 118–9
'psychopathic', 376
*pucelle* (maid), 272–4
Puabi, Queen, 222–3, 232
Puts, David, 79
Pygmies, *See* Aka; Mbuti
Pyramid of the Sun, 233
Python, Monty, 138

Quakers, 318–9
Qeensland, 181
queer, 12, 129–30, 133, 138–42, 152, 250, 296, 317, 367–8, 370

racism, 10, 12–5, 54–5, 128, 131–4, 138, 142, 153, 156, 165, 175, 179, 182–3, 185, 192–3, 231–2, 240–1, 246, 257–8, 261–3, 297–8, 301, 313, 318, 334, 336–44, 358, 370
Radcliffe-Brown, A. R., 165
Ramos, Alcida, 354
RAND Corporation, 389
rape. *See* violence, sexual
ration bowls, 120–1
rebels and rebellions, 14, 112, 161, 199, 207, 268–70, 283, 347–8
   *See also* peasant revolts; resistance

Redfern, Rebecca, 160
religion, 96–7, 123, 126–7, 139, 143, 186, 199, 242, 241–2, 246, 253, 280, 298, 333–4, 367
   *See also* Buddhists; Christianity; Ghost Dance religion; Hindus; Islam; rituals
reproduction, not only explanation of sex, 78
reproductive strategies, 77–8
resistance, 1, 11, 13–7, 94, 101, 113, 125–7, 132, 136–143, 147, 151, 159–61, 170, 193–4, 197, 219, 241, 244–8, 257, 270, 274, 277, 283, 305–6, 308, 341, 346, 357, 364, 366
   *See also* bullies; insurrection; mutinies; overthrowing rulers; peasant revolts
Revolt of the lesser gods, 119–20
Rheims, 274
Rhodes University, 143
Riley, Robin, 301
rituals, 14, 68, 81, 92, 95–6, 107, 120, 123, 131–2, 140–1, 174, 177–9, 182, 185–7, 193–4, 204, 214, 219–29, 233, 237–54, 274, 285, 295, 309, 348, 378
   ritual homosexuality, 177
   rituals of reversal, 143–4
   *See also* graves; weddings
Rival, Laura, 11, 84, 202–6
Roberts, Mary Louise, 299–300
Rome, ancient, 47
Roughgarden, Joan, 15, 78, 326–31

# INDEX

Royal Horse Artillery, 319
Royal Navy, 14, 220, 283–96
   attitudes to male-male sex, 287–290, 292–4
ruling class, 12–3, 108–11, 116–7, 124–30, 133–5, 139, 152, 160, 199, 219, 235, 245, 264, 333, 341, 344, 370, 372
   *See also* elites; overthrowing rulers
runaways from class society, 106, 112–3, 146
Russia, 161, 163, 225, 301, 363
Rwanda, 229, 363
Ryan, Lyndall, 181

sacrifice. *See* human sacrifice
Saddam Hussein, 305
sago, 104, 172
Sahlins, Marshall, 11
Sakhalin Island, 163
sailing ships, as complex machines, 283–4
sailors, 285–6
Salesian missionaries. *See* Christianity
salmon, 38, 123, 167–9
Sambia. *See* New Guinea groups
Samoa, 80–3
St. Louis, Missouri, 233
St. Vincent, Admiral Lord, 290–6
San Francisco, 78, 327
San people, 48
   *See also* !Kung
Santa Barbara Channel, 166
Sartre, Jean-Paul, 142
Satan, 275, 289
Saudi Arabia, 304

savannah and human evolution, 24, 50–1, 65, 74, 212–3
*Scarlet Letter* (Hawthorne), 132
Schultz, Celia, 140
scientific method, 5–6, 9–10, 35–6, 38–9, 77–80, 132–3, 219–20, 329, 354, 367–71
Scott, James C., 149, 198–9, 207
Scruton, Roger, 316
Seattle protests at WTO (1999), 356–7
secondary sexual characteristics, 13, 74, 324
sectarian and religious inequality, 13, 128, 131–2, 153
sensual bonding, 99, 204–5
serfdom, 11, 46–7, 109–10, 146, 268
   *See also* slavery
Seri, Andrea, 117
sex, 3–4, 11–3, 97, 120, 139, 141–4, 149, 152–4, 156, 215–6, 228–31, 251, 272–3, 280–1, 297–9
   in evolution, 54–5, 58, 66, 71–86, 88, 94, 98–99, 103–4, 315–331
   among primates, 8, 20–2, 25–6, 29–34, 38–41, 43–4, 62, 71–5, 84
   same-sex sex among animals. *See* LGBTQ
   in United States, 83
   *See also* LGBTQ; violence, sexual
sexism, 3–4, 11–15, 50, 124, 127–36, 139–41, 161, 171, 175–9, 182, 185–6, 189–90,

# INDEX

198, 232, 241–2, 263, 265, 298, 301, 313–318, 323–5, 328–9, 334–40, 349, 357–8
*Sexual Assault and Sexual Harassment in the U. S. Military* (RAND), 300
sexual imagery, 84–5, 145–6, 156
*Sexual Life of Savages* (Malinowski), 80–1, 380
sexualisation, 85, 130
    of dominance and violence, 85, 130
    of everything in human evolution, 85, 130
sexual selection, 15, 20, 62, 71–4, 78, 318, 321–31, 347–9
sex work, 131, 152, 154, 156, 192–3, 286, 299
    *See also* whore stigma
Seyfarth, Robert, 63
Shakespeare, 136–7
shamans, 208–10, 214–5, 251, 315
Shan, 199
Shankman, Paul, 82
sharing food. *See* food
Sharp, Lauriston, 184
shatter zones, 184, 249, 252–6
sheep, 116–7, 180, 288, 330
Shonka Sabe (Black Dog), 255–6
siamangs, 21
sire hypothesis, 76
Sioux, 197, 249, 262
Sitting Bull, 249
slash-and-burn agriculture, 13–4, 103–4, 123–4, 163–5 169–78,

195–202, 207, 211–2, 347–50, 362
slavery, 11, 14–5, 46–7, 105, 109–12, 116–21, 123, 125, 128, 146–50, 152, 155, 163, 167–8, 191, 224–229, 234, 239, 244, 255, 258, 260, 283–5, 291, 319, 344–5, 363
    *See also* Australia, traders and slave raiding
Smuts, Barbara, 64–5
social construction, 6
Social Darwinism, 103–4, 113–4, 232, 333–4, 355–6
    *See also* stages theory of evolution
*Social Inequality before Farming* (Moreau), 169
social intelligence in primates, 24–7, 33, 57, 94
sociobiology, 3–7, 355–6
    *See also* evolutionary psychology
*Sociobiology* (Wilson), 3
sociology and sociologists, 7, 157–8, 302, 306, 326, 333
Sodom, 289
'sodomy'. *See* LGBTQ
Solnit, Rebecca, 256
Soprano, Tony, 156
sorcery, 204, 210, 214–5, 272, 279
    *See also* shamans
*Soul of Man under Socialism* (Wilde), 338
South Africa, 128, 143, 363
South Dakota, 247, 258
Southeast Asia, uplands of, 46, 198–9, 206–7

440

# INDEX

Soviet Red Army, 143, 161, 298, 300
Spencer, Baldwin, 93, 182–3
Spencer, Herbert, 261, 321, 326, 333
Spivak, Gayatri, 301
stages theory of evolution, 38–9, 103–4, 110, 112–4, 261–2, 321–2, 333–5, 340–2, 369
*See also* Social Darwinism
Stanford, 7, 327
states, 14–5, 103–5, 108–9, 111, 115–6, 125–6, 142–3, 148–51, 156–7, 161, 170–1, 178, 181, 195–9, 201, 206–7. 222, 224–5, 231–6, 240–2, 245–7, 257, 259–264, 284, 334, 341–5, 353, 374
Stiner, Mary, 11, 55–6
stone age technology, 50, 116, 348, 362
*See also* axes
Sterelny, Kim, 68
Stewart, Kelly, 10
storage, 49, 51, 105–6, 165–8, 171–2, 193, 234–5
*Stranger Rape* (Bonnycastle), 157
Strathern, Marilyn, 130–1, 175–6
strikes, 285–6, 319
Strum, Shirley, 10, 42
Sturluson, Snorri, 148
submission, 2, 63, 86–8, 99, 145–6
Suggs, Robert, 82
suicide, 158, 201
*Suicide* (Durkheim), 158
Sumer, 137–8, 222–3

Sumption, John, 269
Surinam, 211
surplus, 11, 38, 103–5, 109–116, 146, 163–7, 170–5, 193, 199, 224, 234, 341–2, 345
survival of the fittest. *See* natural selection
Sydney, University of, 183
Syria, 104, 152, 302
sweet potatoes. *See* tubers
Symons, Donald, 375

Tahiti, 85
Takamura, Patsy, 310–1
Takarazuka, 142
Tamil, 47
Tanzania, 30, 48, 62, 87
Tasmania, 48, 181
taxes, 109–10, 112, 115, 125, 178, 199, 269, 277–8
Taylor, Timothy, 226
temples, 47, 107–10, 116–7, 120–1, 222, 248
Teotihuacan, 233
testicles, 8–9, 42, 71–3
*See also* genitals
territoriality in primates, 20–3, 30–4, 37–8, 42–4, 49, 78
textiles, 108, 116–7, 224
*See also* wool; woollen textiles
Thai (ethnic group) and Thailand, 22, 78
theatre of cruelty, 219, 242, 280–2, 288–90
*See also* torture
Thomas, David John, 211–6
Thomas, Elizabeth Marshall, 11
Thunberg, Greta, 366

# INDEX

Tibet, 143–4, 317
Tierney, Patrick, 355–7
Tierra del Fuego, 48
Tigris river, 115, 117, 119
Till, Emmett, 153, 297
Tiwi, 190–2
Tlhabi, Redi, 140
toilet frog, Australian, 1, 5, 356–7
Tokuyama, Nahoka, 44
Toltec, 236
torture, 127, 152–3, 158–60, 219, 220, 278–9, 297–8, 302–12
Tower of London, 268, 285–6
trade and traders, 46–7, 106–8, 114, 163, 168, 178, 197, 203, 232, 236, 248, 254–5, 257, 284, 340, 351, 361
   Chumash, 166–7
   Highland New Guinea, 173–5
   Mesopotamia, 116–120, 224
   *See also* Vikings
Traders and slave raiding in Australia
   Dutch slave raiders, 191
   Malay traders, 184
   Japanese traders, 184, 192
   Portuguese slave raiders, 191
   White traders, 184
Traister, Rebecca, 155
transgender, 12, 78, 120–1, 130, 140–2, 208, 251, 276–7
   *See also* gender; Joan of Arc; LGBTQ; Two-spirit people
*Transgender Warriors* (Feinberg), 276
transmutation, 320, 334

trauma, 73–4, 193–4, 363
tribbing, 40, 75
Trigger, Bruce, 222
*Trashing of Margaret Mead* (Shankman), 82
Trump, Donald, 370
Trump, Melania, 131
Tuareg, 114
tubers, 29, 50–3, 57, 98, 104–5, 169–75, 178
Turkey, 104, 141–2
Turner, Terence, 356–7
Turnbull, Colin, 93
Two-spirit people, 250–2
   *See also* LGBTQ; queer; transgender
Tyler, Wat, 268
Tylor, E. B., 261, 333, 340

*Understanding Early Civilizations* (Trigger), 222
Unitarians. *See* Christianity
United Irishmen, 286
U S army, 161, 258, 299–300, 302–312
United Kingdom (UK), 134–5
United States, 69–70, 79–83, 128, 134–6, 156, 169, 183, 197, 235, 249, 257–64, 301–2, 323, 333, 339–40, 347–9, 363, 370
   *See also* US army
universalising discourses, 126–7
Ur, 222–4, 232, 234
Uruk, 115–21

vaginas, 40, 66, 72–4, 77–80, 83, 272

# INDEX

Venbrux, Eric, 381
Venezuela, 14–5, 196–8, 211, 217, 347, 350, 353
Victorian, 15, 325, 338–9
Vietnamese (ethnic group), 199
Vietnam War, 34, 161, 300, 348–9
Vikings, 14, 160, 220–1, 225–9, 239, 260, 280
violence and gender, 1, 11–2, 14–5, 19, 85, 91, 97, 108, 111, 132, 134, 140, 163–5, 174, 176–80, 207, 223, 232, 237–41, 243, 247–8, 255–7, 262–4, 280, 301, 342, 344, 358–64, 370
   among primates, 32, 34–38, 41–42
   by subordinate men, 156–7
   cults of male violence, 2–3, 101, 147–9
   'domestic' abuse, 12, 149–151, 182, 185, 193
   female, 159–61, 170–1, 379, 388
   male, 124–7, 145–7, 195, 197, 219, 225–9, 251, 304, 313, 315
   why men? 145–162
violence, sexual, 12, 130–2, 307–8, 369–70
   Catholic Church 154–5, 259, 368
   MeToo, 16, 153–5, 179, 371, 379
   military rape, 299–302
   rape 131, 136, 140, 146, 152–9, 184–5, 193–4, 225, 228, 271, 273, 279–80, 288–9, 297–301, 309, 354, 369–70, 388
   *See also* pirates, women; war and warfare
Volga River, 220–1, 225

Waghi, 171–2
Wagner, Richard, 137
Waldman, Katy, 153–4
Waldo, William, 255, 385–6
war and warfare, 1, 6, 15, 38, 81, 104, 111–4, 117, 119–20, 126–7, 134–6, 141, 147–9, 152–3, 158–61, 164–8, 180–1, 197, 201–4, 206, 211, 218, 232, 247, 249, 251–5, 258, 262, 267–71, 276–8, 283–6, 291–2, 298–302, 313, 322, 326, 338, 345, 347–64
   in chimpanzees, 29, 33–8, 44
Warner, Marina, 378
Warner, W. Lloyd, 183–4, 191
Warrabri, 179–80
Wayne, John, 348
weapons, 51–4, 56, 67, 88, 93–4, 108, 111–3, 145–7, 161, 203–4, 223, 226–7, 246–7, 270–8, 341–2, 363
weaving sheds, 116–121
weddings, 110, 132, 143, 168
Wedgwood family, 318
Weinstein, Harvey, 155
Wengrow, David, 115, 313, 342–6
Westminster Abbey, 326
*What Soldiers Do* (Roberts), 299
Whigs, 291

443

# INDEX

White, Leslie, 262
white people, 10–11, 13, 15, 81, 90, 128, 133, 138, 153, 158, 180–6, 190–1, 193, 202–3, 253, 255, 260, 264, 297–301, 318, 321–2, 333, 339, 341, 347–51
'Who Will Die With Him' (Padoan), 243–4
whore stigma, 272–3, 325
 *See also* sex work
Wiessner, Polly, 89
Wilcox, Michael, 384
Wilde, Oscar, 141, 338
Wilson, Edward O., 3, 355–6
Wilson, M. L,. 37
Wisdom, Matthew, 308
witchcraft, 225, 272, 380
 *See also* sorcery
*Witchcraft, Oracles and Magic among the Azande* (Evans-Pritchard), 380
Wolferman, Kristie, 253
Wooley, Leonard, 222–4, 232
women. *See* gender; feminism; LGBTQ; queer; transgender; Two-spirit people
women's liberation, 62, 69, 80, 136, 143, 150, 175, 339, 349, 367
 *See also* feminism
women-men and men-women. *See* Two-spirit people
Women's Revolt, Nigeria, 142
women's rituals and knowledge in Australia, 186–7, 193
Woodburn, James, 11, 149
woolen textiles, 116–8, 224
workers, 119, 125, 131, 155, 224, 235–6, 272, 283–6, 319, 326, 340, 370
working class, 4, 110, 133–5, 138, 143–4, 155–8, 284–6, 320, 334–6, 342
World Trade Center, 300
World Trade Organization (WTO), 356–7
Wounded Knee, 258
Wrangham, Richard, 34–7
Wright, Evan, 304
Wright, Rita, 224, 241

*xanith* in Oman, 142, 378

Yale, 7
Yamagiwa, Juichi, 78
Yanomamo, 15, 196, 347–357
*Yanomamo: The Fierce People* (Chagnon), 347–8, 351
*Yanomami Warfare* (Ferguson), 350
Yi of Zeng, tomb of, 382–3
Yoruba, 222

Zion, 118
zipper problem, 76, 84
Žižek, 125–6